ADOLESCENT DEVELOPMENT

AND THE LIFE TASKS

ADOLESCENT DEVELOPMENT

Guy J. Manaster

University of Texas at Austin

AND THE LIFE TASKS

87

Allyn and Bacon, Inc.

Boston · London · Sydney · Toronto

Illustrations by Michael Crawford

Library of Congress Cataloging in Publication Data

Manaster, Guy J
  Adolescent development and the life tasks.

  Bibliography: p.
  Includes index.
  1. Adolescent psychology. I. Title.
BF724.M27   155.5   76-43349
ISBN 0-205-05547-8

To my parents
who did so well for me
and
to my children
in the hope I can do as well

Contents

Preface

Many books in the field of adolescent psychology are encyclopedic—something this book endeavors to avoid. The references here were selected as representative of the work in the field, but as the literature is becoming so massive, even a selected bibliography becomes large.

Although the title of this book should convey in a very general way what it is about, I thought of calling it "Adolescent Development and the Life Tasks" *or* "A Group of Essays Trying to Put Together What Is Thought about Adolescence to Help Make Understandable What Is Known about All Normal Adolescents of Different Backgrounds." I have integrated the central areas in which adolescence is seen as different—as a separate stage—and then related these areas to each other and to research on the behavior, attitudes, and personality of adolescents. Some of this integration is speculative, but I would prefer to consider it theoretical. Maddi (1968) states that a theory should be important, operational, parsimonious, stimulating, usable, and empirically valid. At this point I hope only that the perspectives herein are some of the above.

The book has an unusual format in that an integrating chapter (Chapter 8) is set in the middle. The first seven chapters present the definition of adolescence and, you might say, the pure psychological research and theory on the distinctiveness of adolescence in terms of biological, cognitive, moral, sex-role, personality, and emotional development. They also include the more global theories of adolescence. In the eighth chapter the reader will gain a broad picture of adolescents today—a kind of "gestalt" that will put the facts and ideas of the first chapters together. In the last six chapters the understanding already garnered will be applied to research knowledge about the adolescent in the primary areas of his life, in his basic life tasks: love and sex, work and school, friends and community, self, and the meanings of life—religion.

The book is divided into two main parts, first, what is going on in the body and mind of adolescents, i.e., what is peculiar or particular to adolescence, and, second, how this is seen and how manifested in adolescents' behavior in pursuit of their life tasks.

Tavormina (1974) reviewed two recent adolescent texts, commenting:

> . . . With the recent surge of research and theoretical interest in adolescence, it is becoming increasingly difficult to survey the area in any systematic fashion. In fact, the constantly changing nature of adolescents themselves suggests that what was "contemporary" . . . in 1973 may be just history in 1974. [p. 404]

The first half of this book presents the facts and ideas about adolescents that are presumably unchanging—the developmental aspects. The second half presents and analyzes contemporary adolescent behavior and attitudes as a function of the developmental aspects and the social influences of this time in history.

This book is strictly about adolescence and adolescents. Many areas in psychology and development could be included at length (such as methodological or social issues and creativity) and usually *are* part of books about adolescents. I prefer to stick to the topic of adolescence per se. General, social, and developmental points are included only as they bear directly on adolescence.

Adolescence continues for some persons in America into their twenties, whereas for others it terminates in their mid-teens. Although adolescents of all ages will be mentioned, this book puts its greatest emphasis on high-school-age youth. Post–high-school adolescents include both college and noncollege youth, but unfortunately, little research or knowledge exists about the latter. To infer from post–high-school youth to high-school youth, in areas where little high-school-age literature exists, discriminations will be made. But the paucity of knowledge about noncollege youth makes these discriminations and inferences tentative.

Dr. Rudolf Dreikurs, in discussing the applicability of "the significance of the observer" phenomenon found in research in theoretical physics, concluded, "All research findings reflect the subjective bias of the researcher" (1966, p. 5). I believe this also pertains to analysis of previous research literature, development of theory, and social science observations.

On the other hand, Adler stated, "As soon as a scientific system is offered to the world, it appeals to individuals, both laymen and scientists, with a trend of mind similar to that of the author of the system and provides them with a scientific foundation for an attitude towards life which they had achieved previously" (Ansbacher and Ansbacher, 1956, p. 197).

This book represents my knowledge and biases on this topic; I could write it no other way. You will accept or reject what I have said to the degree it agrees with your biases and, of course, as it is understandable and factually correct. Whether you accept or reject the theses I present, I hope they assist you in understanding and dealing with adolescents and that they provoke thinking and research on more types of adolescents in more places.

The staff of the Department of Educational Psychology at the University of Texas at Austin, Steve Haunschild, Hope Whitehall, and Doris Sauls have provided all the support one could hope for on a project of this type. Many students and colleagues have shared their ideas with me on points of mutual interest: Thomas A. DiNardo, David J. Ernsberger, S. Thomas Friedman, Robert J. Havighurst, Rachel Hertz-Lazarowitz, Marc R. King, Robert F. Peck, Charles Douglas Saddler, and Richard Sinclair. I have tried to show them my appreciation and this is another attempt. My wife, Jane, has done a little bit of everything on this project. There would be no book without her assistance, support, editing, encouragement, suggestions, and hope.

To the Reader and Instructor

In writing this book I have relied heavily on my experience teaching courses in adolescent development. The book is intended to present information and those few conclusions that can be drawn at this time in the history of adolescent developmental psychology. *But* I present a large number of hypothetical statements, possible meanings to the data, and theories in the text. Not everyone will agree with these hypotheses, but some should provoke thought and future research. I hope the reader will consider and discuss the hypotheses in this book. For the instructor, I know that many of these positions can elicit argument and discussion. I see the book as one that can be learned from, and, equally important, one that can be taught from.

Guy J. Manaster

PART I
Development

Adolescence–
Definitions and Demands

CHAPTER 1

This book is about adolescents: those persons described as being at the stage, age, attitude, aptitude, size, shape, or place of adolescence. Through history adolescence has been variously defined and adolescents have been variously described. But the adolescents described by Aristotle and Socrates over 2,000 years ago sound a lot like some groups of adolescents today!

G. Stanley Hall (1916) presented two volumes that signified the beginning of a new scientific field—adolescent psychology. Hall described adolescence as a period of "storm and stress," a description that is still used and still applicable. According to Hall, adolescence begins at puberty, around age 12 or 13, and ends when full adult status has been attained, by age 22 to 25. Hall defines the beginning of adolescence by a physiological change and the end by psychosocial change.

Since Hall's initial efforts, a multitude of definitions of adolescence have been presented. Dorothy Rogers traces the term adolescence to its Latin root, *adolescere*, which means "to grow into maturity." She defines adolescence as "a process rather than a period, a process of achieving the attitudes and beliefs needed for effective participation in society" (1972b, p. 9). In fact, Rogers points out that definitions of adolescence fall into categories: adolescence as a period of physical development, as an age span, as a discrete developmental stage, as a sociocultural phenomenon, and as a way of life or a state of mind.

The definitions presented below cover a broad range of behavioral-science views of adolescence, including those of sociologists, educators, and (primarily) psychologists. Because human development can only be understood through full knowledge in the behavioral and social sciences, all available perspectives will be used here.

3

WHAT IS ADOLESCENCE?

A selective review of definitions of adolescence may help us reach the answers to the question, "What is adolescence, really?"—assuming there really is an answer to that question.

Few, if any, definitions of adolescence rely solely on physical change, although many definitions begin with a physical base and then expand to more general concepts. A case in point is by Anderson, who says that adolescence "is divided into an early and late period, extends from puberty to the attainment of full height and weight and the cessation of growth. It is the period in which the person moves out of the home circle and becomes physically and mentally independent" (1949, p. 64). Strang says that adolescence "is usually described as the developmental stage beginning with puberty—the period when sexual maturing occurs and the attaining of the emotional, social, and other aspects of adult maturity. This does not mean at the end of this period all the adolescent growth trends are complete. Adolescence simply marks a peak in human growth and change; it does not complete growth nor preclude further change" (1957, p. 180).

Ambron presents a good catchall definition: "Adolescence is the bridge between childhood and adulthood. It is a time of rapid development: of growing to sexual maturity, discovering one's real self, defining personal values, and finding one's vocational and social directions. It is also a time of testing: of pushing against one's capabilities and the limitations as posed by adults" (1975, p. 393).

As Ambron pushes the limits of the psychological definition, calling adolescence a "time of testing," Erikson similarly notes that "Adolescence is a period of rapid change—physical, physiological, psychological, and social; a time when all sameness and continuities relied on earlier are more or less questioned again" (1963, p. 261). Erikson thus raises both the social- and cognitive-change aspects of adolescence. As does Piaget: "The adolescent, unlike the child, is an individual who thinks beyond the present and forms theories about everything, delighting especially in considerations of that which is not" (Piaget, 1947, p. 148); and, adolescence is "the age of great ideals and the beginning of theories, as well as the time of simple present adaptation to reality" (Piaget and Inhelder, 1969, p. 130).

In this tradition, Elkind describes early adolescence, "roughly the years from 12 to 16," as

> ... an *allegro* of rapid growth that transforms the child into an adult. It is the period in which the young person attains adult stature and appearance. By the time the adolescent is 16, he has attained sexual maturity, in the physical sense, at any rate, and is capable of procreation. Finally, during the years from 12 to 16, the adolescent develops formal or abstract thinking abilities that permit him to

engage in scientific and philosophical thinking, to plan realistically for the future, and to understand the historical past (1971, p. 93).

Both the general and the more cognitive definitions of adolescence presented illustrate the extent, maybe the extreme, development that is thought to describe and define adolescents. From the perspective of adolescence as an age span, a review of over 100 definitions found the earliest age for onset of adolescence as age 8 and the latest age for the end of adolescence to be around age 25. A more typical and conservative estimate is given by Kennedy: "Adolescence: the transitional years between puberty and adulthood in human development; usually covers the teens" (1975, p. 489).

To the extent that we are able to identify the beginning of adolescence by physical change, it is relatively easy to associate ages. However, since there is no physical event marking the end of adolescence, the legal demarcation of the beginning of adulthood has been used to signify the end of adolescence. Hurlock first described adolescence as "the years extended from the time the child becomes sexually mature, about age 13 and 14 for boys, to legal maturity, at 21 years of age" (1964, p. 28). Later, she said, "As it is used today, the term adolescence has a broader meaning and includes mental, emotional, and social as well as physical maturity. Legally, in the United States, the individual is mature at age 18" (1975, p. 173). Considering all the developmental changes implied in the general definitions of adolescence, it is hard to conclude that the signing of a bill lowering the age of maturity should suddenly decrease the time during which the changes occur.

However, "one can view adolescence as a change in group belongingness. The individual has been considered by himself and by others as a child. Now he does not wish to be treated as such" (Seidman, 1953, p. 33). And one might further view the legal change to adulthood as a further change in group belongingness. At the beginning of adolescence the age at which the new adolescent and others consider him an adolescent varies and, so, too, there is great variance in when the individual and others view the legal adult as a real adult.

The idea of adolescence and then adulthood as socially defined is illustrated by Hollingshead, who calls the adolescent years a period in life "when the society in which he functions ceases to regard him . . . as a child and does not accord him full adult status, roles and functions" (1949, pp. 6–7). Also, Landis (1945) states that "viewed from a sociological perspective, adolescence comprises that period in life when the individual is in the process of transfer from the dependent, irresponsible age of childhood to the self-reliant, responsible age of adulthood. The maturing child seeks new freedom, and in finding it, becomes accountable to society" (p. 23).

A definition by Schulz fits both the distinct stage and sociocultural-phenomenon categories of definitions: adolescence is "a normative crisis when the young adult is permitted to experiment with various adult roles without having to pay the consequences of full public responsibility" (1972, p. 323).

Following are two definitions that fit the distinct-stage category, but are general, nevertheless. In the first, Ausubel says, "Adolescence is a distinctive stage in personality development precipitated by significant changes in the bio-social status of the child" (1954, p. xiii) . . . which "not only includes the physical phenomena of pubescence, but also all of the behavioral, emotional, social and personality changes occurring during this developmental period" (1954, p. 73). In the second, Eisenberg (1969) states, "Adolescence may be defined as a critical period of human development manifested at the biological, psychological, and social levels of interaction, of variable onset and duration, but marking the end of childhood and setting the foundation for maturity" (p. 21).

A distinct-stage definition by Blos recognizes "adolescence as the terminal stage of the fourth phase of psycho-sexual development, the genital phase, which had been interrupted by the latency period . . ." (1962, p. 1). "The term adolescence is used to denote the psychological processes of adaptation to the condition of pubescence" (1962, p. 2) . . . "the sum total of all attempts at adjustment to the stage of puberty" (1962, p. 11). This psychoanalytic interpretation of adolescence is particularly interesting in that there are no upper-age bounds on the distinct stage. In a sense, this definition accommodates the behavior, often called adolescent, if not childish, of the 30, 40, or 50-year-old who divorces and appears less responsible and possibly promiscuous, who "plays around."

UNIVERSALITY OF ADOLESCENCE

When a definition relies on physical development, i.e., puberty, as the onset or indicator of adolescence, a universality is implied—everyone goes through it. When a definition relies on or includes theoretically related psychological correlates or manifestations of physical change, universality may be implied by the theory but elaborate empirical testing is necessary for validation. When a definition refers to age span and/or sociocultural phenomena, universality is not implied, since the meanings of the age period and/or sociocultural phenomena are particular to, and vary among, societies and cultures. When definitions are general and, therefore, include physical, psychological, age, and sociocultural phenomena, they may have universal applicability to the degree that they limit or eliminate the concept of adolescence in particular cultures.

Kiell agrees with Benedict (1934) that "adolescence is a physiological state 'as definitely characterized by domestic explosions and rebellion, as typhoid is marked by fever'" (Kiell, 1964, p. 12). Bloch and Niederhoffer indicate the universality of adolescence, saying that a period of striving for adult status occurs in all cultures, producing similar experiences and reactions. Just how intense and vehement the expression of the adolescent experience is in each culture depends on factors such as "the general societal attitudes toward adolescence, the duration of the adolescent period itself, and the degree with which the society tends to facilitate patterns, ceremonials, rites, and rituals, and socially support emotional and intellectual preparation" (1958, p. 17). But Bloch and Niederhoffer go on to say that if a society does not provide for the transition to adulthood the adolescent group itself will generate forms of behavior and rituals to serve the same function.

It is easy to see that in our society there has been little support (emotional, intellectual, and ceremonial) in the long period of adolescence to lessen the intensity of the adolescent experience. However, among some subgroups, particularly religious denominations, ceremonies and structures have been developed which give adolescents a secure status and a set of responsibilities which appear adultlike.

Often the adolescents who participate in the activities of their religion seem different, or "straight," to their nonactive peers. Their peers, not having a subgroup support system, are at the mercy of the general societal attitudes. They are the ones who delve into the behaviors and rituals of adolescence that are developed by the adolescent group itself. As part of no other group, and with questions of where they belong, they do what their peers do.

Clothes have long been a key to a feeling of belonging for adolescents. If you wear the "in," currently appropriate, clothes you feel that you "fit in," or at least there is a chance you might be able to get in. It is a painful experience for an adolescent who does not have the kind of clothes his or her friends consider right. There is a feeling that one's costume alone separates you from the others.

With the growing concern about teenage alcoholism, the function of drinking as both a behavior and a ritual which separates the adolescent from childhood and makes him or her appear part of an adultlike group should be mentioned. The Friday night, or after-football, beer blast is an exciting gathering which gives the adolescent a feeling of having come of age. Although not sanctioned by society, it is frequently seen by parents as something the kids have to do in their transition to adulthood.

Bloch and Niederhoffer seem to be saying that if the society does not consider adolescence important, major, or lengthy, and clearly demarcates the entrance into adulthood of emotionally and intellectually prepared children, the intensity of the adolescent experience may be greatly lessened; but the experience will occur.

Instances of No Adolescence

There are examples in the anthropological or cross-cultural literature of societies in which there is either no adolescent period or no "turbulent" adolescent period. An often used example by Mead (1935) of the Arapesh society in New Guinea shows an initiation rite at age 13 for boys; they are prepared for the initiation, do not become upset or ashamed or self-conscious, and proceed directly into adulthood. Their adult status and puberty coincide and there is no adolescent period present in this society.

In a case study of the Cheyenne Indians, Hoebel points out that "Cheyenne youth have little reason to be rebels-without-cause. They slip early into manhood, knowing their contributions are immediately wanted, valued, and ostentatiously rewarded" (1960, p. 93). He attributes this to the basic postulates underlying Cheyenne culture, which are dominant in controlling Cheyenne behavior: "children (excluding infants) have the same qualities as adults; they lack only experience. . . . Children should, on their level, engage in adult activities. . . . Children become adults as soon as they are physically able to perform adult roles" (1960, p. 99).

Sieg takes this notion into account when she suggests "that the stage of adolescence is not a stage necessary to human development, but is merely a cultural phenomenon—necessary, perhaps, to our culture, but not present in all cultures" (1971, p. 337). She then defines adolescence as "the period of development in human beings that begins when the individual feels that adult privileges are due him which are not being accorded him, and that ends when the full power and social status of the adult are accorded to the individual by his society" (1971, p. 338).

COMPREHENSIVE DEFINITION

It is pretty hard in the social and behavioral sciences to reach agreement and establish consensus on almost any point. But there *is* concurrence that in America today there is a period of time during which young people are adolescents. The onset of adolescence for an individual will begin with puberty (except in cases of precocious puberty—under age 7). In addition, for some individuals, the onset of adolescence may occur prior to puberty—if a change in group belongingness is forced by the immediate environment and the greater society. That is, a girl, for example, who has not reached puberty but who attends a junior high school or a senior high school where the majority of students are pubescent or postpubescent may (1) think of herself as adolescent—part of the adolescent group; (2) be thought of by her peers, teachers, and parents as adolescent; (3) begin to take on the attitudes and behaviors she thinks appropriate to this stage; and (4) begin to think about and plan for the future. Taking on the clothes, fads, and fashions may be an indicator of the process of identifying with the adolescent group for prepubescent girls. An intriguing indicator of the pressure to belong and to conform and the child-adolescent's wish to belong is the optimistic use of a bra, before it is necessary—sometimes referred to as a "training bra."

Boys in the same position, prepubescent and not as physically mature as their peers, may also take on the attitudes and style they feel is appropriate to being (or pretending to be) adolescent. These boys not only may try to look like older, more mature adolescents through dress and hair style, but also may attempt to "prove" that they are adolescent, worthy participant members of the adolescent group. Proving oneself may, and unfortunately, sometimes does, lead the young adolescent boy to reckless, irresponsible, and/or unlawful behavior. Moreover, the less mature boy may be "used" by the more mature adolescents he emulates and with whom he aspires to associate. "The guys told me to say that to her, . . . or break that window, . . . or get a car," etc., is the kind of quote that teachers, principals, and juvenile officers frequently hear from these boys.

The onset of adolescence, then, in an inclusive definition, (1) is based on a physical change, i.e., puberty; (2) may be facilitated by social factors, i.e., change in group belongingness that is self-perceived or desired; or (3) is defined by age and related social situations, i.e., when you're in the eighth grade and 13, you're considered an adolescent.

The adolescent period extends from its onset until the individual reaches adult maturity; until he or she is accorded the full power, social status, and responsibilities of the adult; and until he or she becomes physically, mentally, emotionally, socially, and legally independent from the perspective of adult maturity. If we consider adult maturity at a minimal or threshold level, a level which permits an individual to think, feel, behave, and be accepted as an adult, we recognize and allow by our definition considerable and continuous growth, development, and maturing in adulthood.

The age span implicit in these delimitings of the onset and end of adolescence is fairly variable. Essentially, we can say that adolescence in the United States at this time in history usually begins at or after the age of 10 but not later than age 13, and ends by age 18 for some and by the early to mid-20's by almost all.

During the period of adolescence, then, the individual is in the process, through learning and testing himself and society, of achieving the attitudes, beliefs, and skills needed to be an adult, and, hopefully, an effective participant in society. In the next section of this chapter, the attitudes, beliefs, and skills that need to be learned, the tasks of adolescence, will be presented and discussed.

But what about the terms that have been used in the definitions and descriptions of adolescence, such as "storm and stress," "peak in human growth and change," "a time when all is questioned again," "the age of great ideals," "a normative crisis," "a critical period"? Are these terms applicable to adolescence as a stage? Are they applicable to all adolescents? A major purpose of this book is to investigate the process of adolescence and the generalizability of these terms to all adolescents.

The Difficulties with Generalizing about Older Adolescents

The period of adolescence that ends with leaving high school will be investigated in this book. In general, reaching legal adulthood at the age of 18 coincides with the finishing of high school. However, there are qualitative differences in the social situation of adolescents after high school which are so dramatic and extensive that consideration of a single group called adolescents after that point is probably not valid or valuable.

Most adolescents proceed through late high school or finish high school. There are similarities among virtually all adolescents to this point in their lives—they attend school, they live at home as members of a family, and the primary financial support for them comes from their parents. On leaving high school, however, a greater diversity of lifestyles is available to the late adolescent. Some continue to live at home and start to work; some marry and move away; some stay home, work, and attend college; some go away to university, living at home during vacations; some go into the armed services, etc., etc.

Some adolescents, on finishing high school, by virtue of their age and adult legal status as well as occupational and marital status, consider themselves to be and are considered adults. Other adolescents, on finishing high school, look ahead to a long period as official students in college and graduate school, or a long period as students of themselves and life. They may not wish to and may not take on many of the responsibilities of adulthood, and thus may not be granted the power and status of adulthood.

Many of the late adolescents, or young adults, in this later group exhibit the themes and transformations that characterize a stage called "youth" by Keniston (1975). Some of the themes Keniston proposes as crucial to defining youth as a stage of life have been used earlier in definitions of adolescence—themes such as tension between self and society, alternating feelings of isolation and idealism, youth-specific identities and youthful countercultures. Are these themes issues of personal import for adolescents through high school? Are the themes and the terms used earlier to describe adolescents when referring to those who have left high school more applicable to those following certain paths? Might the aspects of environment and background which influence the future an adolescent sees for himself, and the planning taken with that future in mind, affect the quality of adolescence for him? These questions will be investigated in this attempt to understand adolescence through high school.

DEMANDS OF ADOLESCENCE

In the most general sense, two demands are made on the individual during the period of adolescence. First, from the vantage of developmental psychology, although of equal or less importance to the individual, the individual must make the transition from child to adult; he or she must come out at the end of the adolescent period prepared to be an adult. Second, and more important on a day-to-day basis for adolescents, he or she must "make it" as an adolescent—make it through adolescence.

This dilemma presents itself to college students frequently enough when they consider the "hurdles" of college and the rewards for completion of these hurdles. You have to put up with the requirements and the basics in order to get into the courses and programs you feel you need to end up doing what you want. You have to delay gratification, in the psychological sense, weighing and balancing immediate gratification with future gratification. And you must analyze the present presses and meanings of your behavior in terms of the long-term, future presses.

The adolescent through high school must also make these kinds of evaluations. The younger adolescent does not have experience in planning and thinking for the future. Therefore the dual demands to be an adolescent (with the many meanings this has for self, parents, teachers, and peers) and to become an adult are problematic.

An example of this kind of dilemma has to do with sex and the ability to establish satisfactory sexual relationships. With the history of a double standard, and its continued existence to some extent, many adolescents are unsure of how far to go sexually. If they adhere to a standard dictated or suggested by their parents or their church and associate with peers of like mind, the problem will be lessened and they will only have to restrain their natural impulses (which can be problem enough!) But if their friends have different standards from their parents, the problem will be greater. And today, for the majority of adolescents who are bombarded with contradictory approaches by parents, friends, peers, church, and media, the problem *is* great. An answer to the present adolescent situation may be to do what everyone is doing (if you can figure that out). An answer to the future problem is to do what you "should." If these answers cohere, the immediate tension is less. If your view of you in the future is clear, the answer may also be clear and the tension involved minimal. But the press to come to grips with questions of this sort is the general demand of adolescence.

In order to deal with the present and future nature of the demands of adolescence, two conceptions of these demands will be merged throughout the book. The *developmental tasks*—those demands placed on persons in one stage to foster satisfaction at the next stage—and the *life tasks*—those areas of life which demand attention and effective coping at all times—will be looked at together in order to understand the process of adolescence.

Life Tasks and Developmental Tasks

" 'For the sake of clarity' Adler divided all the problems of life into three parts: 'problems of behavior towards others, problems of occupation, and problems of love'" (Ansbacher and Ansbacher, 1964, p. 429).[1] These three major problems have been termed the life tasks. "Work, society, and sex, Adler and subsequent Adlerians wrote, comprise the three life tasks with which each person must cope and attempt to find solutions" (Dreikurs and Mosak, 1966, p. 18). Put another way, "The human community sets three tasks for every individual. They are: work, which means contributing to the welfare of others, friendship, which embraces social relationships with comrades and relatives, and love, which is the most intimate union" (Dreikurs, 1953, pp. 4–5).

Neufield (1955) suggested "Four 'S' Problems—Subsistence, Society, Sex and Self," and Dreikurs and Mosak (1967) agreed that Adler implied a fourth life task, "getting along with oneself." Moreover, Mosak and Dreikurs (1967), through an analysis of Adler's writings, justified a fifth life task, the existential task, which defines "the need to adjust to the problems beyond the mere existence on this earth and to find meaning to our lives, to realize the significance of human existence through transcendental and spiritual involvement" (Dreikurs and Mosak, 1966, p. 22).

The views of Alfred Adler and his followers will often be referred to in this text. In order to understand human beings one needs a framework, and the Adlerian framework is very useful in attempting to understand adolescents. The most concise statement of the Adlerian position is presented in the General Information section of the *Journal of Individual Psychology*, published by the American Society of Adlerian Psychology. The *Journal* endeavors to continue the tradition of Alfred Adler's Individual Psychology and:

> is devoted to a holistic, phenomenological, teleological, field-theoretical, and socially oriented approach. . . . This approach is based on the assumption of the uniqueness, self-consistency, activity, and creativity of the human individual (style of life); an open dynamic system of motivation (striving for a subjectively conceived goal of success); and an innate potentiality for social living (social interest).

The reader will see the direct and indirect emphasis of this position as the adolescent is viewed as a total, complete individual (holistic), whose own feelings

---

1. Two volumes by Heinz and Rowena Ansbacher (1956, 1964) are the most complete, in-depth treatises and references on the psychology of Alfred Adler. Many of the references from Adler in the rest of this book will be taken from one or the other of the Ansbachers' books. Some of the quotations have only been translated into English in the Ansbachers' texts, but I have relied on them heavily to impress the reader, who wants to look further into Adlerian psychology, with the value and ease with which these books may be used for that purpose.

and perspectives (phenomenological) influence his or her own personal goals (tele-ological) within his or her own environment (field-theoretical) as he lives as a member of society, as he must (socially oriented approach).

Taking a holistic approach, which fits best the Adlerian view, we must grant the interrelatedness of the tasks, as does Adler:

> These (five) problems are never found apart; they all throw crosslights on the others; and indeed, we can say that they are all aspects of the same situation and the same problem—the necessity for a human being to preserve life and to further life in the environment in which he finds himself (Adler, 1932, p. 241).

All the problems of life can be included within the five life-task headings: love and sex, work and school, friends and community (society), self, and the meaning of life (the existential task). The tasks have different importance to different indi-viduals through their lives. But from early adolescence to death all their problems and all their efforts are inevitably related to these life tasks.

These tasks give us a framework for looking at the manner in which one copes with the environment—from the internal environment (self), to the most external environment (the self and the universe). The value of the life-task approach rests in allowing us to maintain a holistic view of people while categorizing the goals of their efforts within five distinct but related tasks.

Havighurst's (1972) developmental tasks may be looked at as providing the specific tasks that must be learned at each age stage in order to successfully cope with the life tasks. Havighurst presents the developmental tasks appropriate at each stage, describes the nature of the task, and its biological, psychological, and cultural basis. The biological, psychological, and cognitive-developmental bases for the common difficulties attributed to adolescents will be delineated, with their cultural basis, in the first part of this book. The second part of the book will be an attempt to apply these bases to understanding the life tasks in adolescence. Havighurst's developmental tasks of adolescence will be subsumed within the life tasks.

A developmental task is defined as

> a task which arises at or about a certain period in the life of the individual, success-ful achievement of which leads to his happiness and to success with later tasks, while failure leads to unhappiness in the individual, disapproval by the society, and difficulty with later tasks (Havighurst, 1952, p. 2).

Adolescent development presents a number of biological, cognitive, and psychological challenges for adolescents. Society presents all adolescents with many situational challenges. The developmental and situational challenges combine in the problems of the life tasks for adolescents.

Table 1. *Developmental Tasks and the Life Tasks with Which They Are Associated.*

Developmental Tasks	Life Tasks
1. Achieving new and more mature relations with agemates of both sexes	Friends and Community (Love and Sex)
2. Achieving a masculine or feminine social role	Self (Friends and Community); Love and Sex
3. Accepting one's physique and using the body effectively	Self, Love and Sex
4. Achieving emotional independence of parents and other adults	Self, Friends and Community (Love and Sex)
5. Preparing for marriage and family life	Love and Sex
6. Preparing for an economic career	Work and School, Self
7. Acquiring a set of values and an ethical system as a guide to behavior—developing an ideology	Existential (Friends and Community)
8. Desiring and achieving socially responsible behavior	Friends and Community, Work and School, Existential

Havighurst's developmental tasks are more specific than the life tasks. The life tasks "feel" more current and immediate to the adolescent. Table 1 illustrates the relationships between the developmental tasks of adolescence and the life tasks. In a holistic approach such as Adler's, the life tasks are related and overlapping. So, too, the developmental tasks are interrelated. The discussion below will speak to the major associations between the developmental tasks and the life tasks.

Developmental Task 1. Achieving new and more mature relations with agemates of both sexes. Life Task. Friends and Community (Love and Sex). Interacting with peers as equals, rather than as one of a group established from without, and unequal at that, is a new development at adolescence. Society expects, and certainly middle-class parents press for, social development and social success. Of the different expectations accorded by social class, the more formal, organized groups are presented to the middle-class adolescent. Nonetheless, through opportunities for friendship more through choice than convenience, and group belongingness in small to large, formal and informal groups, the adolescent develops in the life task of friends and community. The nature of each adolescent's social success during adolescence is felt keenly at the time. Success in the long term with this developmental task may influence mate selection, occupational choice, and the quality of social life the adolescent has when an adult.

Developmental Task 2. Achieving a masculine or feminine social role. Life Task Self (Friends and Community), Love and Sex. The all-pervasive and rigid sex roles of the past are clearly changing. The development of a viable conception of oneself as a man or a woman will be more difficult during this transitional period. When there was no choice to be made, the vast majority of people recognized no problem. During this period of change each adolescent will have to develop for himself or herself a workable notion of sex role, which must be workable in inter-action with the roles adopted by others. Within the framework of the life-task self, a significant portion of this issue rests. But, too, the nature of love and sex relation-ships, friendships and community roles, and occupational choice will be influenced by one's decisions and effectiveness in this developmental task.

Developmental Task 3. Accepting one's physique and using the body effectively. Life Task Self, Love and Sex. The physical changes at adolescence demand of each adolescent a reevaluation, a rethinking, of one's physique and one's stature relative to one's peers. The changes that occur are not necessarily for the better for each adolescent. They may not see themselves in relation to their peers as ranking as high in strength or beauty. They may have developed a sense of themselves including a sense of their body which does not fit with their new body. Regardless of how they feel they are, within the limits of physical fitness and beauty aids, they are stuck with their new bodies, their new physiques. Prior self-conceptions may interfere with acceptance of one's new physical appearance and it is primarily within the life-task self that the adjustment must be made. Rejecting one's body and not learning how to use it effectively may prohibit, or severely limit, the adolescent's ability to be close physically to another person, which obviously may inhibit development and satis-faction in the life task of love and sex.

Developmental Task 4. Achieving emotional independence of parents and other adults. Life Task Self, Friends and Community (Love and Sex). Ambivalence marks both parental and adolescent attitudes toward this developmental task. Parents want their children to feel affection for them while becoming independent adults, and their adolescent children want the same for themselves. At the same time, the parents are only too aware of the difficulties and pitfalls that confront the developing adolescent. They do not feel confident that their adolescent can success-fully make it without parental help. The adolescent is confused and does not know the pitfalls but is equally unsure if he or she can make it alone.

At best there is give-and-take in the process of gaining and giving independence. At worst there is rebellion and rejection. Within the self the battle over independence with continued affection for the parents goes on. The more active life-task areas for working out this developmental task are with friends and love objects. In cases of excessive or continuing childish dependence the work and school tasks are affected. Does the adolescent achieve for himself or for his parents? Does he choose his career for himself or for his parents?

Developmental Task 5. Preparing for marriage and family life. Life Task Love and Sex. The interdependence of the developmental tasks is illustrated in discussing this one. Preparing for marriage and family life involves education in the meaning and operation of marriage and long-term relationships, but assumes for success both the achievement of satisfactory relations with persons of the opposite sex and emotional independence of parents. The learnings that are a part of this developmental task and the bulk of the love and sex life task in adolescence are particularly difficult for the adolescent who has not made progress in the two assumed developmental tasks. Whatever one's definition of marriage, and whatever marriage in its evolution may become, the need for a close relationship with another will maintain itself. Adolescence is the period in which the initial attempts and learnings to do this are practiced and experienced.

Developmental Task 6. Preparing for an economic career. Life Task Work and School, Self. The two goals of this task according to Havighurst involve organizing and planning so that one can enter a career, and feeling that one can do so. In school, adolescents are in the process of developing their sense of what they can do well and determining what they want to do. For adolescents in high school, although many of them do work for money, school achievement itself is their work. The habits, attitudes, and successes in school form a basis for their progress into the adult working world. To take a job at any level demands preparation and the feeling that the choice was made on the basis of one's own wishes and perception of abilities.

Developmental Task 7. Acquiring a set of values and an ethical system as a guide to behavior—developing an ideology. Life Task Existential (Friends and Community). The seeds of the values and ethical system that one will eventually adopt are presented through all the influences that act on individuals in a society. Parents' values, peer and community values, and the values and ethical system of one's church are most readily available to the developing person. The conclusions one makes about his or her own values include a strong element of self. That is, whether one accepts an existing system intact (as in believing and living by the absolute tenets of an organized religion), or develops a unique, composite system, in the end the choice is one's own. This developmental task for most adolescents may be seen in their coping with the existential life task and religion. When they develop their own creed, or when their developing values are, say, more similar to their friends' and less similar to their parents', the potential grows for conflict in the other life-task areas. If, and as, adolescents experiment and fluctuate with ideologies, they run into conflicts between their behavior and the expectations of others in all life tasks.

Developmental Task 8. Desiring and achieving socially responsible behavior. Life Task Friends and Community, Work and School, Existential. The goals of this developmental task include the development of a social ideology which allows the adolescent, when an adult, to be a responsible participant in his or her community and country. To be a responsible adult, and a responsible citizen, demands that one "take account of the values of society in one's personal behavior" (Havighurst, 1972, p. 75). Where in the life tasks does "desiring and achieving socially responsible behavior" come in? Everywhere! This means that, as an adolescent, one learns, tries, and experiments with what he or she thinks and feels to be the "right," "good," and "responsible" way to behave for the self, loved ones, friends, and, if you will, for God and for country.

Summary

The developmental tasks of adolescence are clear descriptions of abilities and viewpoints that the adolescent must have to move successfully into adulthood. They are described in such a way that students of adolescence and those who are working or will work with adolescents can understand them. The life tasks are not as neat. They are, in a sense, the "where you live" descriptors. This merging of the developmental tasks and the life tasks is intended to reinforce the value of the developmental tasks by allowing us to see adolescent development where the adolescent lives it and feels it.

One note of a clinical nature—an adolescent, or for that matter a person of any age, may encounter difficulty in one life task, or in one developmental task within a life task. This difficulty may cause the individual concern and anguish. Yet the problem may be confined to the one life task, and may therefore be a problem for counseling with an educational or instructional emphasis. If the difficulty in one life task affects performance in another, or is mirrored by difficulties in other life tasks, the problem may be more personal and demand more intensive counseling or psychotherapy.

Physiological Development

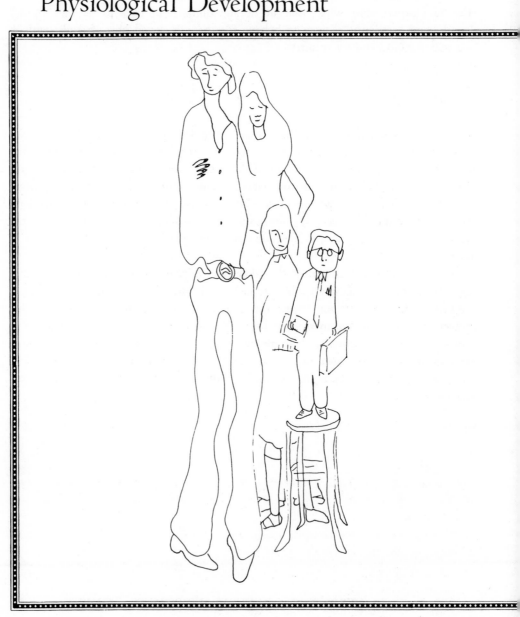

CHAPTER 2

A number of excellent treatises on physiological development in adolescence elaborate on the biological changes and the courses of these changes from puberty through adolescence. The intention herein is to present the relevant facts on the order and ages of physiological changes for boys and girls and the meaning of these changes to the adolescent. The assumption made throughout this book is that all behavior is social, in that all personal-physical events are of relevance to individuals in their social nature, i.e., as they see themselves and as they act in relation to the groups and individuals with which they identify and with which they have significant contact.

This chapter will describe the physiological changes that take place in adolescence for boys and girls, the order of the changes, and the ages of the changes. The ages and order of the physiological changes will then be considered as they psychologically and socially affect those adolescents who are early and late in coming to them. The second major portion of the chapter will deal with the trend over time, called the secular trend, for adolescents to mature earlier. Lastly, the "generation gap" will be looked at from the perspective of the secular trend.

PHYSIOLOGICAL CHANGES

The physiological changes at adolescence that carry social significance, for the adolescent and for those who see and deal with him, are most easily categorized as those having to do with the growth spurt in height, weight, and muscle, and those changes having to do with sexual development, both the primary and secondary sexual characteristics.

19

Adolescent Growth Spurt

After the extraordinary initial growth spurt from birth to 2, growth in height is very constant over the remaining 18 or so years with the exception of a second growth spurt, called the adolescent growth spurt, which occurs in early adolescence (Krogman, 1943; Watson and Lowrey, 1951; Tanner, 1961). The velocity of height gain per year, showing clearly the adolescent growth spurt for girls and boys, is given in Figure 1.

The growth spurt for girls occurs approximately two years earlier than the growth spurt for boys. In the data in Figure 1, first published in 1939, the spurt for boys occurred on the average between 13 and 15.5 years of age. On average the peak velocity, the highest rate of height gain, for boys is about 10 cm. a year, while the average peak velocity is somewhat less for girls.

Prior to the growth spurt there is little difference in height between girls and boys (about a 2 percent difference), whereas after the growth spurt the difference in height between boys and girls is about 8 percent (Tanner, 1964).

In terms of height, then, the adolescent growth spurt, because it comes later and is of greater intensity in males, has the effect of producing males taller than

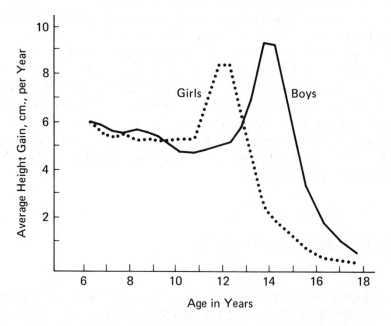

Figure 1. *Adolescent Increment Growth Curves in Height for Boys and Girls Who Reached Puberty at the Average Times. (Reprinted by permission from J. M. Tanner,* Growth at Adolescence, *2nd edition. Oxford: Blackwell Scientific Publications, Ltd., 1962.)*

females. With individual differences and differences in timing and intensity, it may be said that almost all parts of the body participate in the growth spurt such that the adolescent at the end of the growth spurt has the size, shape, and strength characteristics of an adult male or female.

Development of Primary and Secondary Sex Characteristics

Figures 2 and 3 show the sequence of events in physical development in adolescence including the height spurt and the primary and some secondary sex characteristics for boys and girls. Primary sex characteristics refer to sex organs, whereas secondary characteristics refer to developments such as axillary hair, voice change, and the other physical features which distinguish men and women.

"There is general agreement among endocrinologists that the events of the adolescent growth spurt take place under hormonal control" (Committee on Adolescence, 1968, p. 105). The rapid development of the reproductive system and the

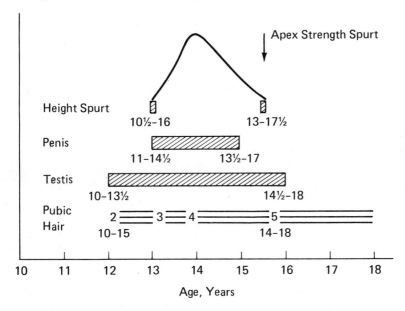

Figure 2. *Diagram of Sequence of Events at Adolescence in Boys. An Average Boy Is Represented; the Range of Ages within Which Each Event Charted May Begin and End Is Given by the Figures Placed Directly Below Its Start and Finish. (Reprinted by permission from J. M. Tanner,* Growth at Adolescence, *2nd edition. Oxford: Blackwell Scientific Publications, Ltd., 1962.)*

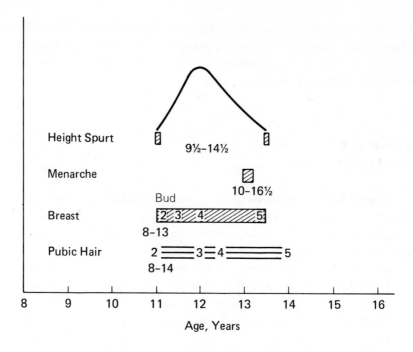

Figure 3. *Diagram of Sequence of Events at Adolescence in Girls. An Average Girl Is Represented; the Range of Ages within Which Some of the Events May Occur Is Given by the Figures Placed Directly Below Them. (Reprinted by permission from J. M. Tanner, Growth at Adolescence, 2nd Edition. Oxford: Blackwell Scientific Publications, Ltd., 1962.)*

secondary sex characteristics are related physiologically and thereby chronologically to the spurt in height and muscle at adolescence. This is obvious in Figures 1 and 2.

As these diagrams indicate, the age range that is normal for the onset and termination of the physiological developments is great. However, the sequence of events occurs within approximately the same amount of time for each individual. That is, for boys, looking at Figure 2, a boy who begins his growth spurt early, at 10½, will complete it when he is around 13. His penis growth will also occur at the early ages of the scale, beginning, say, at 11, and ending at 13½. Although there are individual differences in the rate of maturation, growing through this sequence, it is normal for these events to hang together. It would be unusual indeed for a girl to begin her breast development early, at age 8 or 9, and her height spurt early, at age 9½ or 10, but not reach menarche (have her first period) until later, say 15½ or 16. Even though the order of these developments may differ slightly from individual to individual, may be completed within somewhat longer or shorter periods of time, and may begin over a fairly long age range, the sequence normally is a cohesive, clear growth period for the individual adolescent.

The sequence of physical changes in development for boys and girls is outlined in Table 2. This sequence is not invariant but is most usual. The usual time for these developments to occur is indicated in the table. It is worth noting that, in general, children who begin to mature earlier, that is, who enter pubescence earlier, move through the sequence of development at a faster rate than those who begin to mature later.

In conjunction with the growth spurt and related development at puberty, there is growth in strength, speed, stamina, and coordination. The increase in these abilities is overall greater and continues to grow longer in American boys than American girls. There is a very strong social element in athletics in America, both in the sex-appropriate sports and activities and in the need to excel. The growth potential is there for boys more than for girls but it is there for both sexes, although there appears to be no physiological reason for greater awkwardness in adolescence for either sex.

Sex differences in performance are considerable during adolescence. The slopes of the performance curves are steep for boys, while those for girls are rather flat. In all performance tasks, except throwing, the average performances of girls fall within one standard deviation of the boys' means during early adolescence. From 14 years of age on, the average performance of girls is consistently outside the limits encompassed by one standard deviation below the boys' mean performance. . . . It is interesting to note that recent cross-sectional studies, using physical fitness tests

Table 2. *Usual Sequence of Physical Changes in Development. (Adapted from Committee on Adolescence, 1968, p. 108.)*

Girls	Boys
Full growth	Beginning growth of testes
Initial enlargement of breasts	Straight, pigmented pubic hair
Kinky pubic hair	Beginning penis enlargement
Menstruation	Early voice changes
	First ejaculations
	Kinky pubic hair
	Age of maximum growth
	Axillary hair
	Marked voice changes
	Development of beard

incorporating similar skill items, indicate a slight, but continued improvement in the running and jumping performance of girls through 17 years of age. This would seem to emphasize the importance of cultural factors in determining the motor performance of adolescent girls (Malina, 1974, p. 128).

Early and Late Maturing

In this section a number of studies comparing adolescents who matured very early with adolescents who matured quite late will be presented. They will be cited to show the importance of these events to young people. But these studies compare adolescents at the extremes, albeit normal extremes, of the sequence. Within the normal age range of physiological development there are great differences both within and between the sexes, but there is a normative standard:

> . . . in normal individuals, chronological age, physique age, and psychosocial age coincide. For example, a boy 13 years of age looks and behaves like a 13 year old. His physical maturation and psychosocial behavior are appropriate for his chrono-logic age (Money and Clopper, 1974, p. 175).

A few weeks or months between when signs of maturation begin in one child and when they begin in the child's friends can be a time of considerable worry and concern—whether one is earlier or later than the friends.

For boys it is possible within the normal time of development that a boy or boys in a class may have finished their growth spurt, have fully developed reproductive organs, have deep voices and be shaving, while other boys in the class have not begun or are just beginning the sequence of adolescent physical development. For girls the same variance generally applies. Some girls will be almost their adult height, fully able to reproduce, with full breast development while other girls in their class are only beginning or have not begun the process of puberty.

The divergence in levels of physical maturity within each sex group is even greater among adolescents regardless of sex, that is, as a single group. Comparing Figures 2 and 3 one can see that many girls have begun to mature, are growing more quickly, have begun to menstruate and develop breasts before any boys of their same age, in their school class, are in pubescence. At the other end of this developmental sequence almost all, if not all, girls in a class, of an age cohort, will have completed their growth spurt and be almost fully developed in primary and secondary sex characteristics whereas a number of boys in the class will only be entering the sequence of pubertal developments.

It seems important to note that after very early childhood at no time before adolescence is there the divergence in physical development among agemates as there is at adolescence. The differences between children of the same age have been only slight differences in developmental level and primarily individual differences due to other factors. Adolescents have to cope with the varied times and rates of physical maturation within their group. And interestingly enough, after adolescence, with wider age ranges comprising peer or social groups, i.e., twenties, thirties, middle aged, there is no period, until old age, where there is again such great variance in physical development within social or peer groupings.

Psychosocial Effects of Early and Late Maturation

Studies relating early and late maturation to personality development, attitudes, and behavior treat boys and girls separately. Jones studied the personality and adjustment of early and late-maturing boys, including one study in which the boys were tested again in adulthood (Jones and Bayley, 1950; Jones, 1957; Mussen and Jones, 1957; Mussen and Jones, 1958; Jones, 1965). Overall, early-maturing boys showed a number of advantages over late-maturing boys, including higher ratings from peers and adults on variables such as physical attractiveness, greater athletic prowess and heterosexual status, more self-confidence, and independence. Late maturers were seen as less attractive but were rated as higher in sociability, social initiative, and eagerness. The hypothesis "that the late-maturers' emphasis on social activity and their social initiative and participation are largely of an attention-getting, compensatory nature" was supported by Mussen and Jones (1958, p. 451). In the follow-up study in adulthood, Jones (1965) found that the early maturers continued to be socially successful in adulthood as they had been in adolescence. The late maturers in adulthood could not be said to be unsuccessful but appeared to have compensated and were described as insightful, exploring, independent, and impulsive. Frisk et al. detailed a number of ways in which "delayed development constituted a problem for both girls and boys, but particularly for the latter" (1966, p. 139), as in poor physical performance, sex-role doubts, and feelings of failure.

Although they had not expected to find the same pattern for girls as for boys, Jones and Mussen did, and they concluded "that late-maturing adolescents of both sexes are characterized by less adequate self-concepts, slightly poorer parent-child relationships, and some tendency for stronger dependency needs" (1958, p. 500). Jones and Mussen had predicted that early-maturing girls would have more negative self-feelings and interpersonal attitudes. In a study to determine "for girls whether level of physical maturity is a determinant in prestige during adolescence," Faust found that "for girls precocious physical development tends to be a detriment in prestige status during sixth grade, while it tends to become a decided asset during the three succeeding years" (1960, p. 182). Frisk et al. found in a group of adolescents with "psychic problems" particularly high proportions of early-maturing girls and concluded that, among the girls, "early maturation often led to a crisis in connection with the development to womanhood" (1966, p. 137).

A study by Weatherley (1964) relating physical maturity and personality for early, late, and average maturers showed the same differences for early and late-maturing boys as in the earlier cited studies, with the average maturers more similar to the early-maturing boys. For girls the same pattern existed but not as clearly.

What can we make of these findings? First, the studies cited are on white American youth in general. When Mussen and Bouterline-Young (1964) investigated this issue among Italian-American boys they did not find the same pattern of differences between early and late maturers, suggesting that body build may be of greater importance to American youth in general. It follows therefore that there would be social value and related personal gain to earlier maturers in the white American culture. This certainly is the case for early-maturing males but this is not as clear for early-maturing females. The converse should also hold true; that is, late maturers would suffer socially and personally because they would be valued less. This seems to hold more for late-maturing boys than for girls.

The diagram in Figure 4 should be borne in mind in interpreting these data, as well as a simple social fact: basically everyone wants to belong. The earliest maturing girls and the latest maturing boys are clearly, for a period of time, odd—they are different from their friends. The difference is generally positive for early maturers in that they are admired and valued, even if envied.

The difference generally has negative social value for later maturers. Looking at Figure 4 in light of these observations and the studies cited, it can be seen that early-maturing girls who gain points by being more "adult" physically also lose points by being different from peers and having to be the first to learn the burdens and hazards of adult sexuality. Early-maturing boys gain much socially and personally from their early maturation and do not stand out from the total group because some girls have already begun to mature. In the same way, the late-maturing

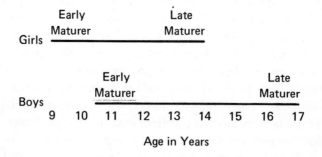

Figure 4. *Age Relationships among Early and Late-Maturing Girls and Boys.*

girl, although behind her female agemates in physical development, is still ahead of the late-maturing boys. The late-maturing girl suffers and bears some scars because of the social effects of her late maturation but not as severely as the late-maturing boy who is also the odd-man-out.

Teachers, parents, and even researchers (Jones and Mussen, 1958) find early-maturing adolescents more appealing to work with. One expects more from an adolescent who looks more adult than from an adolescent who still looks like a child. Peers seem to expect, from early-maturing adolescents, more than their speed and strength superiority warrants. Peers also assume that new areas of knowledge and expertise have been opened to the early maturer, and show them some deference. As an adolescent, the author had two friends, both very bright and both good athletes. One was an early maturer (it seemed by far the earliest in our class), whereas the other was average. The average-age maturer showed great respect and deference to the early maturer, who accepted it as the "big man" he was. Interestingly, that deference is still shown today, when they are equal partners in business, and equally bald.

Boys and girls, whether early, on time, or late in maturing, are interested in the way they look and the way they compare to their peers. If they are different or some aspect of their appearance is not valued, they will be aware of it and concerned to some degree. Frazier and Lisonbee (1950) found 61 percent of the boys and 72 percent of the girls in their tenth-grade sample desired change in their physical selves. They wanted change and were concerned with such things as their proportions, complexion, weight, hair, height, strength, features, etc.

Adults continue to have difficulties coping with and adjusting to changes in their physical selves, as in balding, menopause, and so on. However, adolescence is the first time when an individual has to deal with great and dramatic changes in the body and the only time when one has to compare oneself with others in the same position.

THE SECULAR TREND

As parents and teachers shake their heads and wonder why kids are doing things younger than they used to (dating, smoking, rebelling), they are witness to the effects of a phenomenon known as the "secular trend." Put most succinctly by the principle author on the subject, Tanner,

> During the last hundred years there has been a very striking tendency for the time of adolescence to become earlier, and for the whole process of growth to speed up.

Thus, children born in the 1930's, for example, were considerably larger at all ages than those born in the 1900's. The change seems chiefly or entirely to be one of body size rather than of proportion or build (1961, p. 113).

Utilizing data on (1) heights and weights of children at each age, (2) longitudinal growth curves with emphasis on the peak of the growth curve, and (3) age at menarche, first menstrual period, in girls, collected by a great variety of researchers over a 300-year period, Tanner (1965) came to a number of conclusions about the extent of the secular trend.

Data for height and weight extend, for Scandinavia, back to the 1880's and other European and American data back to the early 1900's. The combined data show an increase in height of from 2 to 3 cm. each decade from the 1900's to the present for 10 to 14-year-olds. For weight, Scottish data on 11-year-olds show an increase of about five pounds from 1932 to 1948, despite the Depression and World War II (Scottish Council for Research in Education, 1953). Referring to British, Scandinavian, and North American data, Tanner (1961) concluded that between 1880 and 1950 average increases of about 1 lb. and ½ in. per decade were found for ages 5 to 7; 4 lbs. and 1 in. per decade for adolescence; and about ½ in. per decade increases were found for adults.

Although there is some increase in height and weight of adults, the differences between height and weight of children of the same age over the last hundred years are due primarily to the fact that children are reaching maturity at progressively earlier ages. Fifty years ago, full height in men was reached at about age 26 whereas today it is reached at about 19. From the Norwegian data it appears that the growth spurt has shifted from about age 17 a century ago to age 14 at present. All the data from Europe and America are in good agreement, showing that menarche has been getting earlier for the last 100 years at a rate of as much as three and four months per decade. The differences in age of menarche between generations are illustrated in a recent study by Damon et al. (1969) which showed the mean age for menarche for mothers in the sample of American whites as 14.38 and the mean age of their daughters as 12.88.

There are a number of reasons cited for the decrease in age of the growth spurt and menarche. The two most substantial reasons are nutrition and what is often referred to as "hybrid vigor"—marrying and breeding from outside the traditional breeding group (as has occurred increasingly with greater migration nationally and internationally). Controversy continues as to which cause is more important.

Both the nutrition and breeding factors may be reflected in the fact that considerable variation in height and weight occurs with occupational class, overcrowding, and size of family. In the Scottish data, for example, average height decreased with the increase in family size, at a rate of 0.27 inches for each addition to the family. The corresponding decrease in weight was 0.65 pounds. Size also varied by social class, "the sons of the professional and employer parents being about 3 inches taller and 8 pounds heavier than the sons of unskilled manual laborers; the girls, similarly, about 2½ inches taller and 6 pounds heavier" (Scottish Council for Research in Education, 1953, p. 87). The secular trend, however, overshadows social class differences, i.e., even with the current differences between classes, the lower-class children of today are taller than the upper-class children of the last century.

Although not frequently articulated, followers of the secular trend have asked and worried about its lower age limit. "Obviously, such a trend could not continue indefinitely, or little girl babies would someday become sexually mature in the cradle." And evidence suggests "that the downward trend has now stopped. Some scientists suggest that the average age of 12½ (where the downward curve has leveled off) may represent the 'physiological limit' for early onset of the menses" (Jennings, 1975, p. 179).

Implications of the Secular Trend

As clearly as can be determined, the physical changes at adolescence are timeless. They have for centuries occurred in the same pattern for all growing humans and there have been no recent evolutionary changes. It may be said that, with the exception of timing, kids today are physically passing through puberty as did you and your peers.

In relating the secular trend to other changes in adolescents today it is important to mention that societal changes affect adolescents at least as much as they do adults. Whether adolescents are more amazed and cynical about the state of the world than adults, whether the adolescent generation came to this position before adults, or whether adolescents are just more vocal, are issues which may be distantly related to earlier maturity. The effect of the times on adolescents will be examined later in this book. A number of other possible social significances for adolescents and young adults emanate from the secular-trend phenomena.

If the generation gap is larger today than in the past, or at least the recent past, there is no doubt that technology, and the state of the world, are having an effect. But the secular trend may also be responsible. Consider the following conjectures: (1) changes in the sexual mores, early dating and marriage, and unwed teenage mothers, would not have been considered, nor feasible, when puberty occurred at a later age; (2) if cognitive development follows a trend similar to height and weight, then changes in the schools, particularly curriculum, may have been and still may be demanded by these developmental changes; (3) the expectations society has for staying in school seem less than realistic when fully mature (physically) youth are made to sit in schools designed (physically and organizationally) for children; (4) the legal age of majority, laws regarding censorship and availability of birth control devices, etc., have and will be affected by the secular trend. Society and culture are based on tradition and law. Many traditions and laws established over the last 200 years may have to be revised as they pertain to an age group which is notably more mature than when the laws and traditions began. The generation gap is partly a reaction to the need for these changes.

Petroni (1972) points to the exaggeration of the generation-gap concept in general usage, saying "The under-thirty and over-thirty are almost automatically presumed to occupy polar positions on most issues" (p. 221). This discussion has attempted to show that the generation gap is a natural function of a changing world and the changing developmental rate of youth. Moreover, the gap is seen as a natural difference of opinion which may be greater or lesser, depending on a host of personal and subcultural variables; but a massive polarization between youth and their elders is not implied.

The generation gap is least intellectualized and most emotional when brought home, when parent and adolescent meet without understanding. There are a variety of reasons for the problems between parents and adolescents which will be discussed at various times throughout this book. Here the issue is how the parent-adolescent relations are affected by the secular trend.

We can posit that, on the average, parents are over 25 years older than their children, accounting for younger and older parents as well as numbers of children. In attempting to relate to another person we all try to refer to our own experience. Our empathy for and understanding of others is in part built on our ability to infer from our feelings about situations to the feelings of others about situations seen as similar to ours. Parents refer to their own adolescent experiences when trying to understand the experiences and feelings of their own adolescent. As trite as this may seem, with the rate of change in the world and particularly America in the last 50 years, the values and the goals to which an adolescent was exposed 25 years ago were vastly different from those his child is being exposed to today. This is all to say that the attitudes of parents differ from the attitudes of their adolescents to the degree that adult attitudes differ from adolescent attitudes at any one time. But parent-adolescent attitudes differ, also, as adolescent attitudes and values today differ from those of adolescents approximately 25 years ago.

The secular-trend data also show that there is considerable difference in age of maturation over the course of a 25-year generation. The data from Damon et al. (1969) is pertinent here, showing a 1.4 year age difference between the average age of menarche of mother and daughter. As attitudes, interests, and behaviors are related to developmental age, i.e., a girl past menarche is different from a girl before menarche, the question of parental understanding and empathy for an adolescent who is much more developed than the parent was at the same age arises. If the mother draws parallels between herself and her daughter in light of menarche, the child's developmental age instead of the child's chronological age, their generation gap should not be as great. In fact, mothers of today's adolescents developed at an age closer to the age their sons are maturing than the age their daughters are maturing. In this regard, pointing to the differences in ages of maturation between the contemporary parent and contemporary adolescent generation, the father is the furthest out of line. His son is probably maturing (using the four-month-per-decade decrease in age of menarche as a general rule of thumb) approximately ten months earlier than he did. But his daughter will be maturing approximately three years earlier than he did (the two-year average difference in age of maturation between the sexes plus the effect of the secular trend over 25 years). Put in this way, the difficulties parents, notably fathers, have in empathizing with the changes in their adolescents may become clearer. This may be especially hard for a father who had no sisters. As an oldest son with a younger brother, the author must confess a sense of incredulity as he lives with his well-developed, early-maturing twelve-year-old daughter.

CONCLUSION

The major effects of physiological change in adolescence discussed in this chapter may have important consequences for individual adolescents and for society. However, the usual, normal changes that occur in the body of the adolescent probably provoke the greatest amount of anxiety, concern, and consideration among the greatest number of adolescents.

> The changes in size, build and composition from pre-adolescence to adolescence result in an altered bodily configuration. The developing adolescent must adjust to his or her "new" body. The manner in which an adolescent boy or girl comes to terms with his or her altered morphology has significant behavioral correlates. The adolescent's body image is, to a large extent, revised, especially in terms of appearance, limits of strength, and coordination (Malina, 1974, p. 128).

From various perspectives, effects of, and adjustment to, the adolescent's "new" body will be examined throughout this book. But for everyone, the first part of us others see is our body, our physical appearance. At adolescence, when we put so much of ourselves into question, adolescents may stress that portion of themselves which they, and others, can concretely notice as well as what they think others see which isn't there. This seems the case for 15-year-old Josh, the hero of *There Must be a Pony*:

> I got this gigantic complex people were only talking about the way I looked because they couldn't come up with anything else to say about me. Like how bright I was,

or what a smashing sense of humor I had, or about my personality. Mainly, I guess you couldn't tell if I was smart or funny or even HAD a personality—because I couldn't communicate with people I felt because I couldn't do anything brilliant, people could only comment about me like they would about a piece of French pastry or something (Kirkwood, 1960, p. 18).

A recent "guide to puberty" recognizes the worry and embarrassment associated with physiological changes at puberty and through adolescence. The adolescent is advised not to be ashamed or afraid because the changes are normal. They are told to remember "that you're not the only one who has ever gone through this difficult time. It happened to your parents. It happened to your heroes . . . they all came through it pretty well. So will you" (Mayle, 1975, p. 5).

Cognitive Development

MCRAWFORD

CHAPTER 3

In this chapter, cognitive development in adolescence will be defined and described within the context of the theory originated by Piaget. Piaget's cognitive development will be compared and contrasted to measured intelligence. Research will then be cited bearing on the age of onset and attainment of formal operations, the final stage of cognitive development in adolescence according to Piaget, and relationships with other developmental and cultural phenomena. Cognitive development in adolescence, as it is manifest affectively, will be presented with particular reference to Elkind's ideas. The chapter will end with a point of view, hopefully applicable to the following chapters, which questions the usual conclusions about cognitive development in adolescence.

PIAGET'S THEORY OF COGNITIVE DEVELOPMENT

In stage theories, such as Piaget's, there are a series of stages or levels, identifiably different, through which individuals pass in a specific, invariant order. The stages in Piaget's theory represent an ordered set of differences in the way people think. Infants, young children, and grade-school children proceed through different thinking modes, different stages. The final childhood stage of cognitive development is the concrete-operations stage, toward which all normal children are presumed to move.

In order to understand cognitive development in adolescence, one must understand the final stage of cognitive development, the formal-operations stage, the level to which adolescents presumably move, as well as concrete operations, the stage from which they move. The following describes and compares, in brief, the concrete and formal-operational levels of thought.

Concrete and Formal Operations

In concrete operations the child is concerned with, or focuses on, relations between objects which the child classifies, categorizes, and orders. In formal operations the adolescent or adult has the ability to think about the possible as well as the real. Instead of having to deal with things as they "are," with hypotheses about how things are, the formal-operational person may deal with how things "might be," with hypotheses about how they might be. This allows the person with Formal Operations to consider relations between relations, to work with proportions, correlations, and probability. "The term formal is used because a person at this level of thinking possesses the ability to consider the possible and, therefore, is able to reason about the form of an argument apart from its content" (Peel, 1960, p. 115).

The most salient characteristic of formal operations, differentiating it from concrete operations, is that thought becomes oriented toward possibility and separated from reality. That is, thought is no longer dependent on concrete content. Thought becomes abstract in that it can proceed in the absence of the data of reality. All differences between concrete and formal operations can be seen as reducible to "the subordination of reality to possibility" (Inhelder and Piaget, 1958, p. 255).

A second characteristic of formal operations in adolescence is the use of the hypothetico-deductive method. Inhelder and Piaget illustrate this:

> The most distinctive property of formal thought is this reversal of direction between reality and possibility; instead of deriving a rudimentary type of theory from the empirical data as is done in concrete inferences, formal thought begins with a theoretical synthesis implying that certain relations are necessary and thus proceeds in the opposite direction. Hence, conclusions are rigorously deduced from premises whose truth status is regarded only as hypothetical at first; only later are they empirically verified. This type of thinking proceeds from what is possible to what is real (1958, p. 251).

The formal-operational child initiates his thought processes with a set of hypotheses which are successively confirmed or denied as the empirical data of reality dictate. However, the formal-operational person can proceed in the absence of any empirical data, "can consider hypotheses which may or may not be true, and consider what would follow if they were true" (Hunt, 1961, p. 230).

The third characteristic is that formal operations are second-order operations because they are operations performed on the results of first-order operations, concrete operations. The person with formal operations has the "ability verbally to manipulate relationships between ideas ('second-order relations') in the absence of recently prior or concurrently available concrete-empirical props" (Ausubel and Ausubel, 1966, p. 405). Lovell (1971) agrees that the best characterization of formal operations is as second-order operations. The logic available through the use of the characteristics of formal operations is termed propositional logic.

In sum the three characteristics differentiating formal operations from concrete operations are: reality becomes subordinate to possibility, the hypothetico-deductive method, and propositional logic based on second-order operations.

Abstraction

Another approach to the changes in cognition and approaches to reasoning which occur during adolescence focuses on the increasing abstractness of adolescent thought. A short description of this approach, although it is not completely equivalent to Piaget's, may help in understanding these phenomena. Hayakawa (1964) presented the term "abstraction ladder" to describe the changes, from a linguistic point of view, which take place in the process of learning through adolescence to adulthood. He posited that a consciousness of abstracting is indicative of adulthood.

A sentence-preference test has been devised by Peel (1975) to look at the changes that occur in adolescence in preference for and use of abstraction. He makes a "distinction between two aspects of forming a concept, by which extending the array of exemplars might be called generalizing, and formulating the rule for including instances would require an act of abstracting" (p. 177). A generalized but concrete definition might be "An island is a feature of the earth's surface," whereas "The island is a geographical notion," although particular, is an abstract concept.

Each item in Peel's test contains four sentences with the same key word, and the subject is asked to check the sentence that he prefers as most significant for him. The sentences are keyed as abstraction (A), generalization (G), and membership (M). Membership may be likened to categorization, a concrete operation. The fourth sentence in each item is not relevant to our discussion here. Examples of test items follow:

A The city is an administrative concept going back to Roman times.
M Liverpool is a city.
G A city is a unit of local government.

G Playing is a universal activity among higher animals.
A Playing is frequently discussed in studies of children.
M Playing is tennis and football.

M Mars is a planet.
A The planet is an astronomical class.
G A planet is a heavenly body.

As Figure 5 shows, Peel found an increase in generalizing and an even more marked increase in abstracting during the adolescent years 12 to 16. The preference

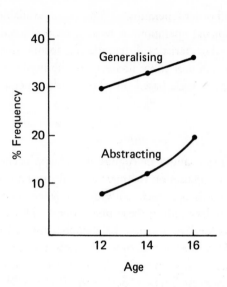

Figure 5. *Age Trends in the Tendencies to Abstract and Generalise. (Reprinted by permission from E. A. Peel, "Predilection for generalising and abstracting,"* British Journal of Educational Psychology, *1975 [45], 177–188.)*

for and use of *M*, membership, decreased during these years. Of particular note in interpreting these results is that with age in adolescence not only does the ability to abstract increase but the preference to abstract, the preference for abstraction, increases. In the coming chapters, as correlates of cognitive development are discussed, it will be well to remember that at least some adolescents, as they grow older, wish to, and prefer to, deal with concepts abstractly. The wish to venture into the world of abstraction appears to be a part of moving into formal operations.

Other Factors in Cognitive Development

The reader of this book may have to rely on memory in order to get the feeling of what it was like to begin to move into the formal-operations stage. The three characteristics which differentiate formal operations from concrete operations have in common a base to thought, a base to thinking about issues or a particular issue, which is ephemeral, nebulous, prospective, intangible. That may be overdoing it a bit, but it means that in formal-operational thought the individual is dealing from possibilities, hypotheses, propositions. The concrete, clear, tangible basis for thinking about an issue is still available and used, as in the concrete-operations stage. However, as formal operations develops, the adolescent finds that new perspectives open as thought operates from the base of possibilities, hypotheses, and propositions. This may be immensely exciting, but may also be somewhat frightening. It sometimes has the feeling of whole new worlds opening, and, as with all adventures, new cognitive adventures have their pitfalls.

Ginsburg and Opper (1969) point to four influences or factors in cognitive development: (1) maturation of the nervous system, (2) active personal physical experiences, (3) environmental effects (including culture, language, and education), and (4) equilibration. In the succeeding pages, studies and conclusions as to the importance of these factors on understanding adolescent cognitive development will be presented.

Theoretically, in order for these influences to have an effect on the growing and changing intellect, an organizing concept is necessary. The experiences one has, the reality one experiences, internal or external, are perceived and ingested as they fit the manner in which one thinks at that moment (the process Piaget calls assimilation). Either in order to assimilate reality or on assimilating new realities and experiences, one's cognitive structure, the way one thinks, may have to, or will, change. This process Piaget calls accommodation. Very simply, when information, or an experience, is not understood and is rejected or forgotten, there is no assimilation or accommodation and cognitive structure remains as it was. However, the usual process of ingesting experiences demands a continuous effort to balance what one experiences so it is known and understood. This total process, the organizing concept in Piaget's theory of cognitive development, is called "equilibration." "Equilibration is defined as compensation for an external disturbance" (Muuss, 1968, p. 153). Piaget defines intelligence as a "form of equilibration . . . toward which all cognitive functions lead" (Piaget, 1962, p. 120). This process, which has an important motivation function, is crucial in understanding adolescents.

VALIDITY OF PIAGET'S STAGES

Although for Ausubel and Ausubel (1966), existence of the "two particular stages," concrete and formal, was not substantiated, they termed "irrelevant" the various arguments which disputed the legitimacy of Piaget's stages of intellectual development. The "irrelevant" criticisms included the facts that: the transition between stages is not abrupt but occurs gradually, age variability in transition exists between and within cultures, children fluctuate in the level of cognitive functioning they manifest over time, children may move to formal operations in some subject-matter fields and subfields while not having yet done so in others, and environmental factors influence the rate of cognitive development.

The above arguments, although irrelevant to the issue of the validity of Piaget's stages, are very relevant to the issues of intelligence, age, cultural and individual differences in cognitive development. Although there are very difficult problems of measurement, Piaget's formulations, particularly as they apply in general and to formal operations, have been validated (Gallagher, 1973; Elkind, 1963; Wallach, 1963). Lovell, after extensive research, concluded that "The main stages in the development of logical thinking proposed by Inhelder and Piaget have been confirmed" (1961, p. 149).

RELATIONS BETWEEN FORMAL OPERATIONS AND OTHER ASPECTS OF DEVELOPMENT

Relation between Formal Operations and Measured Intelligence

By intelligence we simply mean a measurement construct designating level of ability in performing a graded series of tasks implicating the component aspects of cognitive functioning at any given stage of intellectual development (Ausubel and Ausubel, 1966, pp. 411–412).[1]

This definition of measured intelligence points to a basic characteristic in the construction of intelligence tests—that the tasks be appropriate to the general age-stage group for whom they are designed. Question tasks at an abstract, formal-operational level are either not presented to, or not answered appropriately by, persons who have not reached this stage. Formal-operational tasks are more prevalent and successfully passed in tests designed for persons approaching and in the formal-operations stage. To the extent that the intelligence tests given to preadolescents and adolescents implicate "the component aspects of cognitive functioning at" the formal operations "stage of intellectual development," a relationship should be found between intelligence-test scores and level of cognitive operations at adolescence.

Several studies of cognitive development have included IQ as a variable. Case and Collinson (1962) and Lovell and Shields (1967) found a positive relationship between IQ (or mental age) and incidence of formal operations. A review by Lovell lends support to the contention that there is a positive relationship between IQ and attainment of formal operations: "The available data again confirm that it is not

1. David P. Ausubel and Pearl Ausubel, "Cognitive Development in Adolescence," *Review of Educational Research*, Vol. 36, No. 4, 1966. Copyright 1966, American Educational Research Association, Washington, D.C.

until 13 or 14 in ordinary pupils and 11 to 12 in the very able, that formal thought is possible" (1968, p. 17). Studies comparing groups of children varying in intelligence levels support the same contention (Jackson, 1965; Stephens and McLaughlin, 1971). Dudek, Lester, Goldberg, and Dyer (1969) found significant correlations between the Wechsler Intelligence Scale for Children (WISC) and several of Piaget's measures, concluding that although the purposes and theory underlying the construction of the two measures of intelligence, Piaget's and the WISC, are different, they are highly correlated and seem to be sampling, or tapping, the same cognitive processes to the degree that they are correlated.

A study by Yudin (1970), designed expressly to investigate the relation between IQ and formal operations, is very persuasive. Yudin studied three age groups of white lower-middle-class boys. Each age group was divided into three subgroups on the basis of IQ scores. High-IQ subjects reached formal operations earlier than middle and low-IQ subjects, between whom there were no differences. Additionally, middle or average-IQ subjects progressed to formal operations between ages 12 and 14 whereas low-IQ subjects did not accomplish this until 14 to 16. Yudin summarized the results of the study, noting that age and intelligence interact in the development of formal operations. Significant gains are made by average-intelligence adolescents from ages 12 to 14, by low-intelligence adolescents from ages 14 to 16, but those of superior intelligence show "almost linear development" of formal operations.

Relation between IQ and age, maturation, size, and social class. For many reasons, such as statistical, test construction, test administration inconsistencies, and intraindividual variations, some change in IQ scores from testing at one age to another is usual and expected. Nonetheless, highly significant correlations of about .60 between IQ scores in childhood and adolescence, and correlations of about .80 between IQ scores in adolescence and adulthood are found (Bradway and Thompson, 1962).

> The greatest changes in IQ occur among those who score in the average range between 90 and 110, but even though there is an absolute change in score, the chances are that the person will remain in the average category. Put differently, if we think of IQ standing in terms of gross categories such as above average, average and below average, rather than in terms of absolute scores, then the IQ does remain relatively stable from childhood through adolescence (Elkind, 1968, pp. 136–137).

The dispute over the relative power of heredity and environment in determining or affecting intelligence continues unabated. Heredity, as it relates to size, maturation, and environment, as evidenced in social class and cultural differences, will be looked at in relation to measured intelligence, but always keeping in mind that the greatest differences in measured intelligence are individual. In the following section this same view will be used with cognitive development to formal operations.

There is ample evidence for the following conclusions, which it must be remembered refer to group differences (thus allowing for overlap between groups and individual exceptions). "Children who are physically advanced for their age do in fact score higher in mental ability tests than those who are less mature, but of the same chronological age" (Tanner, 1961, p. 44). This difference, though small, is consistent at all ages studied and is presumed, but not known, to disappear in adulthood. "One consequence of the relation of test scores to physical maturity is that large children, who on average are more advanced, score higher than small children of the same age" (Tanner, 1961, p. 46). This difference, too, is thought to diminish but not necessarily vanish in adulthood.

Terman et al.'s (1925) findings in the Genetic Study of Genius, which started with over 1,500 young people with very high IQ's averaging about 150, emphasized these points. The children in the study were "nonrepresentative physically as well as intellectually" (Herrnstein, 1971, p. 52). Overall they tended to be bigger in height and weight, stronger, and more mature sexually earlier than average. They were also nonrepresentative of the general population by ethnic group and social class, with a large percentage of professionals' children.

"Children from different socioeconomic levels differ in average body size at all ages, the upper groups being always larger" (Tanner, 1961, p. 109). "The correlation between IQ and social class is undeniable, substantial, and worth noting. A cautious conclusion, based on a survey of the scientific literature, is that the upper class scores about thirty IQ points above the lower class" (Herrnstein, 1971, p. 50). Without disputing the issue of relative importance of heredity and environment in causing these findings, it is clear that age at maturation, and size, are related to intelligence in adolescence, in the same way that social class is related to the physical and mental measures.

In the chapters to come the case will be presented that group differences in attitudes, behaviors, and the whole emotional world of adolescence may be analyzed with these relationships in mind. The tremendous variance in size, age of maturation, and particularly intelligence within groups, notably socioeconomic groups, must be remembered. The Scottish Council concluded, "The difference between the groups is not that the 'upper' social classes contribute more intelligent children to the total population; it is that a higher percentage of their children are intelligent" (Scottish Council for Research in Education, 1953, p. 45). Put another way,

Only about 10 percent of our people meet the criteria for the upper and upper-middle classes, while about 65 percent are in the working class and below, . . . But only 50 percent of the people have subnormal (below 100) IQ's. And so, there must be at least 15 percent of our population in the bottom classes with supranormal (above 100) IQ's (Herrnstein, 1971, p. 50).

Relation between Attainment of Formal Operations
and Age, Social Class, and Culture

Piaget originally hypothesized that the onset of formal operations occurred at approximately age 11 or 12, reaching equilibrium, and stabilizing around the age of 14 or 15 (Inhelder and Piaget, 1958). Subsequent research has shown the situation to be more complicated with such variables as intelligence level, socioeconomic status, cultural background, and amount of schooling, affecting age of attainment of formal operations (cf. reviews by Ginsburg, 1972; Lovell, 1971).

Goodnow (1962) administered several tasks and a reasoning test to European and Chinese middle and lower-class adolescents, showing minor differences on some tasks but major differences on the test of reasoning, a test requiring formal-operations ability. Middle-class subjects performed better than lower-class subjects regardless of ethnicity.

Feldman and Markwalder (1971) studied black, white, and Chinese children of various ages and social-class levels. They found that blacks made more concrete-operational responses and fewer formal-operational responses than whites or Chinese. They attributed this to disparities in the ages at which formal operations are attained across the groups. Vernon (1965) found English children performed at higher levels on various tasks than West Indian children, but he did not have social class controlled.

Greenfield (1968) studied rural and urban, schooled and unschooled children of the Wolof tribe in Senegal. She found that performance on concept-formation problems was dependent on schooling. Unschooled rural and urban children failed to improve performance after the age of eight or nine. In contrast, the "Wolof schoolchildren . . . did not differ essentially from Western children in this respect" (Greenfield, 1968, p. 7).

Stephens, Piaget, and Inhelder (1966) in a longitudinal study are finding that higher mental ages are necessary in order to achieve formal operations in some task areas. A number of other studies have shown variability not only in the age at which formal operations is attained, but also in the areas of experience for which formal thought is available (Case and Collinson, 1962; Lovell, 1971; Lovell and Butterworth, 1966).

Additional findings further complicate a complicated situation. Huttenlocher (1964) investigated the development of formal reasoning in concept-formation problems. His results showed essentially no improvement in formal thought processes after the seventh grade, i.e., no development in cognitive operations as a function of age after 13 or 14.

Higgins-Trenk and Gaite (1971) provide evidence indicating that many adolescents may not attain the stage of formal operations until the late teens or early twenties, if at all. These researchers administered one task and three situational problems varying on a closeness-to-self dimension to four groups of adolescents drawn from grades 7 through 12. The results showed a developmental trend toward more formal-operational responses from younger to older subjects. However, even in the oldest group (mean age 17.7 years), "over 50% of the [subjects] were not responding at the level of formal operational thought" (Higgins-Trenk and Gaite, 1971, p. 202). These striking results prompted the authors to call for a revision in current thinking about formal operations in adolescence. Whereas it is commonly held that soon after pubescence the normal adolescent attains formal operations, Higgins-Trenk and Gaite suggest that the normal adolescent will reach formal operations in the late teens or early twenties, if at all. The importance of findings of this nature are recognized by Piaget (1972b) who recently called for research on the development of formal thought between the ages of 15 and 20.

This call is beginning to be answered. A recent study by Arlin (1975) suggests that a fifth stage in cognitive development may occur, either after formal operations or as a second part of formal operations. Arlin renamed the formal-operations stage the "problem-solving" stage. The new fifth stage was named the "problem-finding" stage, saying "processes characteristic of this new stage would include creative thought vis-à-vis 'discovered problems,' the formulation of generic problems, the raising of general questions from ill-defined problems, and the slow, cognitive growth represented in the development of significant scientific thought" (p. 603). Although Arlin acknowledges that this first study was exploratory and must be cautiously interpreted, the findings are encouraging. It appears that this stage makes good sense and follows the demands of stages that the first is necessary but not sufficient for the next. With problem-solving ability one could (though not necessarily) develop a problem-finding ability. This differentiation probably further narrows the numbers of persons at the highest stage (known).

The studies cited in this section show that cognitive development in adolescence is influenced by maturation of the nervous system (age differences in formal-operations attainment), personal and environmental experiences and effects (as in class, educational, and subcultural differences), yet is not universally equal. Not all adolescents reach formal operations, or reach it to the same level—across all tasks. The idea clearly is that for a variety of reasons and influences, differences exist between individuals and groups in measured intelligence as well as attainment of formal operations, cognitive development.

Some years ago a student in my adolescent course, who was a sixth-grade teacher in a suburban school, came up after class with a perplexing problem. She felt that maybe it had something to do with cognitive-developmental changes at the onset of adolescence. She had recently given an essay exam to her class and found that many of the students who she thought were her best students had not done at all well, whereas some of her poorer students had done exceptionally well. The exams she had given before were all short-answer or multiple-choice tests. We both wondered whether she had not changed the nature of the exam from a test of concrete operations to a test of formal operations. We also wondered whether we could see any differences among her "changelings."

I must confess that our analysis of this problem was not rigidly scientific. However, we first looked at the essay exam. She had asked questions of a "What if" and "How might" nature. She had in effect asked for development of hypotheses and propositions. And our impression was that the children who had done better on this exam were more mature physically, taller, and, through inspection of school records, were found to be more frequently of professional parents. I cannot cite significant correlations, or say we proved anything. However, I would suggest that teachers try to become sensitive to the changing nature of the thought processes of at least some of their pupils during these years, and recognize the factors which may be influencing individual differences in these changes.

Relation between Formal-Operational Thought and Affect

Formal thought, to the degree that it develops in any one individual, develops differentially. With age, abilities become more specialized according to practice and need. An individual may operate at the formal level in some tasks and not in others. So too, all of one's thought, not only task-specific thought, may or may not be at the formal stage. One's thoughts about oneself, others, right and wrong, family, society, and the world may be affected by the development of formal operations.

Elkind (1968, 1969) most clearly shows the social, affective, and behavioral effects of dealing with the new thoughts of formal operations. "Much of what is considered typically adolescent in the way of emotionality can only be fully understood in the context of formal-operational thought" (Elkind, 1968, p. 152). The formal-operational adolescent finds himself in many of the same (family, home, neighborhood, etc.) and many new situations (changing schools, new peers, new responsibilities, etc.). New situations open for all youth new possibilities and demands for acting, feeling, and thinking. But the formal-operational youth begins to see all aspects of life (the five life-task areas: love and sex, friends and community, work and school, self, and existential) as they have been known to be, as they *actually, really* are, and also as they might be, as they *possibly* could be.

It is these new thoughts about what the world might be that present the challenge of adolescence to the formal-operational adolescent. Responses may range from new highs about the adolescent's strengths and the beauty of the possibilities for himself or herself and the world, to deep depressions about his or her weaknesses and faults, and the impossibility of breaching the gap between what is and what might be.

Responses of one kind or another may persist for an adolescent as they are in concert with an already extant personality, or they may vary greatly as is appropriate. That is, one effect of the new thoughts on an adolescent is to give him or her a broader perspective for reinforcing his or her view of self and the world. But the new possibilities demand testing the accuracy of conclusions; equilibration is, in this case, the adolescent bringing the new possibilities into his or her system and accommodating them, i.e., compensating for an external disturbance. As Peel states that "the urge to come to intellectual terms with one's world provides the mainspring of intellectual development" (1963, p. 494), we may say coming to intellectual terms with one's world, for the adolescent developing formal operations, is also coming to personal and affective terms with oneself and one's world.

From this perspective, the degree of personal upset an adolescent encounters in coming to formal operations is a function of the ease with which his or her existent cognitive structures, as applied to the self and his or her world, as well as specific learning tasks, can accommodate the new thoughts the formal-operation stage elicits. Put another way, the new thoughts of formal operations will be more upsetting to a youth who comes to formal operations with cognitive structures, and the personality or lifestyle emanating therefrom, which are inappropriate for dealing with the reality of life and the possibilities for development.

A first effect of the personal challenge of formal operations is to force the adolescent to establish a new equilibrium accommodating his new thoughts to reestablish his personality with the new data. The assimilation and accommodation process which makes up equilibration is set off by "external disturbances" which may be thought of here as new information and new ideas. In a sense the adolescent feeds upon himself, feeds on the new ideas created by himself. Yet the changes that are disturbing to his equilibrium are accommodated to an existing self and assimilated by an existing self which in the normal adolescent promotes self-growth but does not grossly affect self-consistency. The adolescent coming into formal operations has not spent much time or effort considering the kind of person he might be, could be, or should be in light of a full range of possible selves. Much of the identity issue for adolescents is a question of establishing equilibrium between the existing self and the disturbances that the use of propositional logic aimed at oneself brings.

This produces a second behavioral effect of formal operational thought in adolescence, an "experimenting" effect. The adolescent to this point has known "concretely" what he or she is and can do, and what his or her personal world is like. With formal operations they attempt to find out what they might be and the potential of their ability, thoughts, and feelings. The "extreme" behaviors of adolescence and the wide swings in behavior and moods are examples of experimenting. Can I love so fully that death doesn't matter? Can I be totally crushed by rejections and still survive? Can I change the world, make it what I think (this week) it should be? Can I live in the world as it is? Can I perform to the applause of the world? Can I be overlooked in spite of my ability? Can I show my parents the way? Can I do what I must without them? There must be an infinity of possibilities and contradictions that a formal-operational adolescent can construe and test in the process of coming to grips with the realistic possibilities for himself and the world.

As the formal-operational adolescent considers these potentials and thinks about his own thinking and thoughts, he comes to believe that others are as preoccupied with his appearance and behavior as he is (Elkind, 1969). Elkind presents two constructions which are the result of this preoccupation, which he calls the egocentrism of adolescence. They are the "imaginary audience" and the "personal fable."

The adolescent is said to be anticipating the reactions of the persons around him as if they saw him with his eyes, seeing his strengths, weaknesses, and concerns as he does for himself. And he thinks they are as intensely interested in the minutiae of his appearance and behavior as he is. This tremendous pressure of always being on stage in front of an "imaginary audience" accounts in part for adolescent self-consciousness, overreaction to self-perceived successes and failures, and a need for privacy and seclusion, to get off stage (which, of course, everyone will notice too).

"While the adolescent fails to differentiate the concerns of his own thought from those of others, he at the same time overdifferentiates his feelings. . . . (H)e comes to regard himself, and particularly his feelings, as something special and unique" (Elkind, 1969, p. 503). The adolescent develops a "personal fable," a story he tells himself which accentuates his uniqueness, his greatness and worth, and the reactions of others to his victories, defeats, and death. In a circular way, the adolescent develops his fable out of the feeling that his thoughts and behaviors are of universal and eternal importance, and then uses the fable to reinforce this. Adolescent egocentrism is said by Elkind to decrease by age 15 or 16 when, according to Elkind and Piaget, formal operations are supposed to be better established.

The purpose of this section has been to introduce the manner in which formal-operations development affects the social and affective sides of adolescent behavior. In addition, this section has illustrated the extent to which the development of formal operations and its social and affective correlates are generalized to all adolescents. The extent of these generalizations is questioned in the next section.

SUMMARY—APPROPRIATENESS OF TERMING ADOLESCENCE THE STAGE OF FORMAL OPERATIONS

It has been shown to this point that measured intelligence is related to cognitive development as defined by Piaget and that both forms of intellectual development are related to other variables. Inhelder and Piaget acknowledged these factors in the following quotes: "The appearance of formal thought [at adolescence] . . . is a manifestation of cerebral transformation due to the maturation of the nervous system." The studies citing relationships with physical maturation and early maturation pertain here. "[But] the maturation of the nervous system can do no more than determine the totality of possibilities and impossibilities at a given stage." These words parallel statements about heritability or the genetic portion of measured intelligence. "A particular social environment remains indispensable for the realization of these possibilities," as can be seen in the social-class differences in IQ and attainment of formal operations. "It follows that their realization can be accelerated or retarded as a function of cultural and educational conditions" (Inhelder and Piaget, 1958, p. 336).

Adolescents are said to be in the stage of formal operations. The logic and data in this chapter do not allow this characterization and demand a more tentative statement. Formal operations develop during adolescence but not all adolescents attain formal operations. Of those who do, there are differences in level of attainment and patterns of abilities in which formal operations are attained. Lastly, development of formal operations may continue through, at least, young adulthood.

Many of the problems and tasks associated with adolescence are related to changes in the social situation in which adolescents find themselves. But, it is hypothesized here, other tasks and problems associated with adolescence are related to cognitive development at it occurs in adolescence. In order to pursue this hypothesis in succeeding portions of this book, a set of probabilities will be presented in light of the preceding sections, and the hypothesis will be expanded in light of these probabilities.

We will posit that higher IQ and earlier and eventually greater attainment of formal operations are related, singly or in combination, to early maturation, bigger size, higher socioeconomic status (SES), better education, and particular cultural backgrounds. Excepting many individual differences and mentioning that these are characterizations or generalizations, we might, on the other hand, posit that lower IQ plus later and little or no attainment of formal operations are related, singly or in combination, to late maturation, smaller size, less SES, poor education, and particular cultural backgrounds.

Five general types of cognitive development in adolescence, expressed in terms of timing and degree of development of formal operations, are presented in Table 3. The types are constructed from the statement of tentative conclusions earlier in this section. These types are rank ordered in terms of the theoretical probabilities that persons of these developmental types would attend college. Lastly, in Table 3 the developmental types are labeled as to whether or how the description of adolescents in the psychological research and theoretical literature apply to each type.

Two assumptions underlie the probability columns in Table 3. The college-attendance probability rank ordering is based on the known relations between IQ

Table 3. *Cognitive Developmental Types in Adolescence, Probabilities for College Attendance, and Application of General Descriptions of Adolescents.*

College Probabilities Rank Ordered	Developmental Types	Probable Applicability of General Descriptions Descriptions Should:
1	Develop Formal Operations on Time	Hold
2	Develop Some Formal Operations over Time	Hold in Part
3	Develop Formal Operations Late	Hold with Age Differences
4	Develop Some Formal Operations Late	Hold in Part with Age Differences
5	Develop No Formal Operations	Not Hold

and school achievement and social class and particular cultural backgrounds and attendance at college. As we have also presupposed positive relationships between these variables and attainment of formal operations, the rank ordering posits the same manner of relationship between formal-operation attainment and college attendance.

The column referring to the probable applicability of the general descriptions of adolescence in the literature is based on a separate premise. It is often stated that what psychologists know about people is based primarily on university under-graduates because so much psychological research is carried out with university undergraduates as subjects. This is not altogether true, nor is it altogether false. Much research has been done in high schools and junior high schools, but here too there has been a preponderance of research in schools in or near universities or in more progressive schools, schools more open to research. Very little research, com-paratively, has been done on out-of-school youth, either high-school dropouts or graduates. Cumulatively psychological research on adolescents overrepresents in-school youth, particularly in better schools, and in-college youth.

Moreover, the psychological theorists who have dealt with adolescence were prominent psychiatrists with upper-class patients or were professors in highly selec-tive institutions. They have thus experienced primarily patients and students apt to be of higher SES, IQ, and well into or having attained formal operations. In addition, their own "super" intellects may have affected their own adolescence and their views on adolescence in general.

The column labeled "probable applicability of general descriptions" is based on the premise that, in the main, the study of nonrepresentative, higher intelligence youth is descriptive of them alone and is not as applicable to other youth.

These hypotheses will be examined through analysis of the psychological theories of adolescence and research on the life tasks. At this point, a few words about each of the hypothesized cognitive-developmental types in adolescence is needed.

The "develop formal operations on time" type refers to those adolescents who are able to use formal thought in a variety of areas within the general age limits proposed by Piaget. It is presumed that they most probably are above-average intelligence, SES, and maturity and of cultural and/or familial backgrounds conducive to growth of the intellect. They will most probably attend college. The personal and social trials, travails, and tasks usually ascribed to adolescents most probably apply to them.

The "develop some formal operations over time" type does not develop formal operations as quickly or over as broad a range of areas as the previous type. They may be lower on the associated variables than the previous type. And the confusions and difficulties associated generally with adolescence will not pertain to them as intensely as the previous group.

The "develop formal operations late" type will develop formal operations but does not begin development as early as the "on time" type. This may be because of later maturation and/or deficiencies in experiences due to sociocultural factors. The qualities of adolescence will apply to them but later than for the first type. They may be thought of as late bloomers.

The "develop some formal operations late" type will experience the storms and stresses of adolescence to a lesser degree and later than the literature would predict.

The "develop no formal operations" type will have the problems of adolescence that come from changing social groups and settings. But they will not have the personal-emotional problems said to be part of adolescence which, it is said here, result from developing formal operations. They are least likely to attend a university, and least likely to be mobile, geographically or socially.

The development of formal operations in adolescence is of great importance, particularly in its relation to further education and its personal and emotional effects. The hypothesized clusters of variables related to formal-operations attainment all influence college attendance probability. But the related variables are by no means causative. Rather, here as always, it is the individual who ultimately determines a destiny such as college attendance. In attempting to understand adolescents, change and new experiences produce the "storm and stress," the "crises," of adolescence. The social, physical, and situational changes that are necessarily a part of growing up, of adolescence, produce storm, stress, and crises. The cognitive changes, as and if they occur, produce additional storms, stresses, and crises.

Moral Development

CHAPTER 4

Many common adolescent problems have to do with conceptions of right and wrong—what "should" or "should not" be done. The Watergate hearings made it clear that these problems were not unique to adolescents. In order to understand the magnitude and quality of these dilemmas for adolescents, we will look at psychological literature on the development of moral judgment and moral behavior, and look at moral development and cognitive development as they interrelate and develop differentially among the various subgroups of adolescents.

The moral-developmental theories and research of Piaget and Kohlberg which follow are based on the assumptions characteristic of cognitive-developmental theories. In speaking about social-emotional development, which includes moral development, Kohlberg presents four additional related assumptions:

(1) Affective development and functioning, and cognitive development and functioning are not distinct realms. "Affective" and "cognitive" development are parallel; . . . (2) There is a fundamental unity of personality organization and development termed the ego, or the self. . . . Social development is, in essence, the restructuring of the (a) concept of self, (b) in its relationship to concepts of other people, (c) conceived as being in a common social world with social standards. . . . (3) All of the basic processes involved in "physical" cognitions, and in stimulating developmental changes in these cognitions, are also basic to social development. In addition, however, social cognition always involves role-taking. . . . (4) The direction of social or ego development is also toward an equilibrium or reciprocity between the self's actions and those of others toward the self. . . . The social analogy to logical and physical conservations is the maintenance of an ego-identity throughout the transformation of various role relationships (1969, p. 349).[1]

These assumptions will become evident in the discussions that follow.

1. Lawrence Kohlberg, "Stage and Sequence: The Cognitive-Developmental Approach to Socialization," in David A. Goslin (ed.), *Handbook of Socialization Theory and Research.* © 1969 by Rand McNally College Publishing Company, Chicago.

53

MORAL DEVELOPMENT ACCORDING TO PIAGET

Piaget, in his studies of moral development, looked at the judgments that children made while playing games and in answering questions about stories with moral dilemmas. These strategies have continued to be used by Kohlberg and his followers, who greatly improved on the techniques and theory of Piaget, who pioneered in this area. Piaget's position is presented here both for its historical significance and because its relative simplicity may help us understand the grosser differences between the way children usually define right and wrong and the way adolescents and persons at higher cognitive levels do.

According to Piaget (1948), two sets of attitudes, or cognitive orientations, the heteronomous and the autonomous, characterize and differentiate between young children's and older persons' definitions of right and wrong and sense of justice.

The young child's egocentrism does not allow him a relativistic perspective. This, added to the confusion or inability to distinguish his subjective stance from the objective world about him, leads him to attribute moral rules with fixed eternal characteristics. Piaget calls this moral ideology "moral realism."

Older persons come to see rules as a result of group effort and cooperation. The individual is not subjugated to predetermined rules but rather has an "autonomous" relation to others and rules which he can differentiate. Piaget calls this the moral ideology of "mutual respect."

In Table 4, the attributes of sense of justice and observable aspects of definitions of right and wrong that Kohlberg extracted from Piaget's characterizations of the "moral realism" and "mutual respect" ideologies are presented.

Kohlberg differs with Piaget on the relevancy of some of these attributes to the question of form or structure of cognitions in moral judgment. He shows that the dimensions which are a matter of content rather than form do not prove through research to adhere to regular and universal age trends of development. Kohlberg concludes, "While Piaget attempted to define two stages of moral judgment (the heteronomous and the autonomous), extensive empirical study and logical analysis indicate that his moral stages have not met the criteria of stage he proposes, as his cognitive stages do" (1969, p. 375).

MORAL DEVELOPMENT
ACCORDING TO KOHLBERG

To correct the deficiencies he noted in Piaget's conceptualizations in the area of moral development, Kohlberg worked for many years to develop a more specific

Table 4. *Right and Wrong, Sense of Justice, from Moral Realism and Mutual Respect Ideologies as Developed by Piaget. (Put in tabular form and abstracted with permission from L. Kohlberg, "Moral Development and Identification," in H. W. Stevenson [ed.], Child Psychology [Chicago: National Society for the Study of Education, 1963, pp. 314–315].)*

Younger Children's Moral Realism Ideology	Older Children's Mutual Respect Ideology
1. Objective responsibility	Intentionalism
2. Rules unchangeable	Rules flexible
3. Absolutism of value (judgment universal)	Relativism—many points of view
4. Moral wrongness defined by sanctions	Moral judgments independent of sanctions
5. Duty defined as obedience to authority	Duty defined as conformity to peer expectations
6. Defines obligations ignoring reciprocity	Defines obligations in terms of rights of contract and exchange
7. Expiative justice—punishment for transgressor	Restitutive justice—restoration to the victim
8. Immanent justice—culprit will be struck down	Naturalistic causality—logic of the social order brings justice
9. Belief in collective responsibility	Belief in individual responsibility
10. Punishment by authority	Retaliative reciprocity by victim
11. Favoritism by authority in distributing goods	Impartiality, equality, distributive justice

typology which met the criteria for regular, universal stages. His phenomenal dissertation (1958) and the subsequent efforts by him and his followers have shown his success.

Kohlberg developed ten hypothetical moral dilemmas which are presented to the subject individually in a one-to-one interview situation (although they have since been given to groups in written form). As the subject responds to the probing questions of the interviewer, the full nature of the subjects' thinking about each dilemma is elicited. For example:

In Europe, a woman was near death from cancer. One drug might save her, a form of radium that a druggist in the same town had recently discovered. The druggist was charging $2,000, ten times what the drug cost him to make. The sick woman's husband, Heinz, went to everyone he knew to borrow the money, but he could only get together about half of what it cost. He told the druggist that his wife was dying and asked him to sell it cheaper or let him pay later. But the druggist said, "No." The husband got desperate and broke into the man's store to steal the drug for his wife. Should the husband have done that? Why? (Kohlberg, 1969, p. 379).

The subjects' responses are judged, and coded, according to one or more of the twenty-five aspects of moral judgment (Table 5). The ratings for each dilemma on the aspects of moral judgment combine to give an overall rating on the "Classifi-

Table 5. *Coded Aspects of Developing Moral Judgment. (Sizer, Theodore R.,* Religion and Public Education, *"Moral and Religious Education and the Public Schools" by Lawrence Kohlberg. Copyright © 1967 by Houghton Mifflin Co. Used by permission of the publisher.)*

Code	Description	Aspects
I. Value	Locus of value—modes of attributing (moral) value to acts, persons, or events. Modes of assessing value consequences in a situation.	1. Considering motives in judging action. 2. Considering consequences in judging action. 3. Subjectivity vs. objectivity of values assessed. 4. Relation of obligation to wish. 5. Identification with actor or victims in judging the action. 6. Status of actor and victim as changing the moral worth of actions.
II. Choice	Mechanisms of resolving or denying awareness of conflicts.	7. Limiting actor's responsibility for consequences by shifting responsibility onto others. 8. Reliance on discussion and compromise, mainly unrealistically. 9. Distorting situation so that conforming behavior is seen as always maximizing the interests of the actor or of others involved.
III. Sanctions and Motives	The dominant motives and sanctions for moral or deviant action.	10. Punishment or negative reactions. 11. Disruption of an interpersonal relationship. 12. A concern by actor for welfare, for positive state of the other. 13. Self-condemnation.

Table 5—*Continued*

Code	Description	Aspects
IV. Rules	The ways in which rules are conceptualized, applied, and generalized. The basis of the validity of a rule.	14. Definition of an act as deviant. (Definition of moral rules and norms.) 15. Generality and consistency of rules. 16. Waiving rules for personal relations (particularism).
V. Rights and Authority	Basis and limits of control over persons and property.	17. Non-motivational attributes ascribed to authority (knowledge, etc.). (Motivational attributes considered under III above.) 18. Extent or scope of authority's rights. Rights of liberty. 19. Rights of possession or property.
VI. Positive Justice	Reciprocity and equality.	20. Exchange and reciprocity as a motive for role conformity. 21. Reciprocity as a motive to deviate (e.g., revenge). 22. Distributive justice. Equality and impartiality. 23. Concepts of maintaining partner's expectations as a motive for conformity. Contract and trust.
VII. Punitive Justice	Standards and functions of punishment.	24. Punitive tendencies or expectations. (a) Notions of equating punishment and crime. 25. Functions or purpose of punishment.

cation of Moral Judgment into Levels and Stages of Development" (Table 6). The "aspects of moral judgments" in Table 5 refer to concepts that are crucial to moral issues, such as punishment, revenge, and rights of property, which are thought to be present in all societies. For our purposes, the levels and stages themselves are sufficiently informative and are applicable to the aspects, so we will dwell on their validity and relationships.

Kohlberg's levels and stages form a typological scheme, which describes the specific content, thereby overcoming Kohlberg's objection to Piaget's scheme. The typology is composed of three distinct levels of moral thinking within each of

Table 6. *Classification of Moral Judgment into Levels and Stages of Development. (Sizer, Theodore R., Religion and Public Education, "Moral and Religious Education and the Public Schools" by Lawrence Kohlberg. Copyright © 1967 by Houghton Mifflin Co. Used by permission of the publisher.)*

Levels	Basis of Moral Judgment	Stages of Development
I.	Moral value resides in external, quasi-physical happenings, in bad acts, or in quasi-physical needs rather than in persons and standards.	Stage 1: Obedience and punishment orientation. Egocentric deference to superior power or prestige, or a trouble-avoiding set. Objective responsibility. Stage 2: Naively egoistic orientation. Right action is that instrumentally satisfying the self's needs and occasionally others'. Awareness of relativism of value to each actor's needs and perspective. Naive egalitarianism and orientation to exchange and reciprocity.
II.	Moral value resides in performing good or right roles, in maintaining the conventional order and the expectancies of others.	Stage 3: Good-boy orientation. Orientation to approval and to pleasing and helping others. Conformity to stereotypical images of majority or natural role behavior, and judgment by intentions. Stage 4: Authority and social-order maintaining orientation. Orientation to "doing duty" and to showing respect for authority and maintaining the given social order for its own sake. Regard for earned expectations of others.
III.	Moral value resides in conformity by the self to shared or shareable standards, rights, or duties.	Stage 5: Contractual legalistic orientation. Recognition of an arbitrary element or starting point in rules or expectations for the sake of agreement. Duty defined in terms of contract, general avoidance of violation of the will or rights of others, and majority will and welfare. Stage 6: Conscience or principle orientation. Orientation not only to actually ordained social rules but to principles of choice involving appeal to logical universality and consistency. Orientation to conscience as a directing agent and to mutual respect and trust.

which are two related stages (as seen in Table 6). The levels and stages are considered as separate moral philosophies and views of the social-moral world. In general the three levels are characterized as:

1. the preconventional level, in which children define good and bad in terms of physical consequences (punishment, reward, favors),
2. the conventional level, where the emphasis is on conforming, as in the preconventional level, but also with maintaining, supporting, and justifying the social order, and
3. the postconventional level, in which the adolescent or adult develops his own autonomous, moral principles which have validity and applicability separate from his identification with other persons and groups.

These levels and stages are presumed and, as we shall see, appear to meet the criteria for a stage theory. They represent an invariant developmental sequence—a person moves forward through the stages (although not necessarily to the highest stage) without skipping a stage as he develops.

Relation of Moral Development to Other Variables

Before reviewing the levels and stages in greater detail and relating them to sociocultural factors, some general points should be made about Kohlberg's view of structure and content in moral development. Stage structure is not determined by the content of an individual's values or choices, nor does it determine those choices. The structure of moral thought reflects the basic and central theory or frame of reference through which the individual thinks and builds his thoughts. Content may reflect structure or it may not. It may do so in two ways specifically. The stage a person is at may influence the person's value hierarchy. Prediction of moral values and moral action requires that alternatives are ordered by a hierarchy related to the individual's basic structure (Kohlberg and Turiel, 1971). As an example, the highest value of stage 2 is individual need, whereas stage 4 places social order over individual need but questions whether property or human life is primary. Stage 6 unquestionably places human life as the highest value. In this way the stage a person is at (structure) influences the values he holds (content) and has available in decision making. Stage also is seen in content as the person is seen to be sensitive to aspects of situations to which persons at other stages are not yet, or no longer are, sensitive. As an example, principled subjects, at level III in Table 5, would be sensitive to issues of justice in a cheating situation while subjects at the conventional level would not be.

A difficult issue, to be discussed at greater length further on, has to do with moral behavior and age-developmental analysis (Kohlberg, 1964). A young child, an older child, or an older adult for that matter, may all resist temptation. They may all behave in a manner which appears to be equally moral. However, they may all behave in this manner for different reasons, i.e., according to their different stages. It is therefore difficult to show a consistent age by developmental-level relationship. As has been said, content may reflect structure, but behavior will not necessarily reflect stage. Moral-behavior ratings show only a low correlation to later ratings, whereas longitudinal predictability is higher for moral judgments (Kramer, 1968).

Is moral development correlated with cognitive development? From various studies, correlations from .30 to .50 have been found for 12-year-olds between group IQ scores and moral-judgment level, showing that there is a cognitive base to moral maturity. "The relation of moral judgment to intellective development is suggested by the fact that our stage definitions assume that Piagetian concrete operations are necessary for conventional (Stages 3 and 4) morality and that formal operations are necessary for principled (Stages 5 and 6) morality. . . . The Piagetian rationale just advanced, as well as other considerations, suggests that cognitive maturity is a necessary, but not a sufficient, condition for moral judgment maturity" (Kohlberg, 1969, p. 391).

If a particular cognitive-developmental level is necessary for the attainment of a particular moral-developmental level, but is not sufficient for it, then research should show that persons with that cognitive level will not necessarily have reached the moral level, but all persons at that moral level should have reached that cognitive level. This is exactly what Tomlinson-Keasey and Keasey (1974) found in a study of college women. "In no instance is there a principled moral thinker who does not evidence a substantial amount of formal operational thought" (Keasey, 1975, pp. 43–45). However, there were women at the formal-operational level who did not evidence principled moral thinking. In reviewing this literature Keasey (1975) concluded "that cognitive development facilitates moral development" (p. 54).

Kohlberg labeled the levels and stages he defined somewhat differently in his 1964 chapter than in the 1969 reference used for Table 6. For the sake of better understanding the earlier labels, follow this guide:

- Level I   Premoral (Preconventional)
     Stage 1   Punishment and obedience orientation
     Stage 2   Naive instrumental hedonism
- Level II   Morality of Conventional Role Conformity (Conventional)
     Stage 3   Good-boy morality of maintaining good relations, approval of others
     Stage 4   Authority maintaining morality
- Level III   Morality of Self-Accepted Moral Principles
     Stage 5   Morality of contract, of individual rights, and of democratically accepted law
     Stage 6   Morality of individual principles of conscience

Kohlberg and Gilligan (1971) noted the relationship between development through the cognitive stages of Piaget and development through the moral stages of Kohlberg. Although growth to a new higher cognitive stage is not enough to bring one to a new higher moral stage, it is necessary before moral maturation can occur. The earliest cognitive-development stage, which Piaget called the sensorimotor period, is typified by the symbolic, intuitive thought of the infant and does not relate to Kohlberg's six stages—but rather to an earlier "I want what I want" period. Concrete-operational thought is necessary for attainment of Level I morality. Concrete-operational thought is characterized by "inferences carried on through system of classes, relations, and quantities maintaining logically invariant properties and which refer to concrete objects" (Kohlberg and Gilligan, 1971, p. 1063). As a child (age 6–10) develops, first, the ability to form conceptions of stable categorical classes and, second, conceptions of quantitative and numerical relations of variance, he has the basic, though insufficient, cognitive abilities for the first two moral stages.

Kohlberg goes on to describe three substages of formal-operational thought. In a sense the first two substages describe more complex logical operations that are a step removed from the clear references to concrete objects of the earlier stage. But the first two substages of formal operations are not described, as the third substage is, as "true formal thought," including "construction of all possible combinations of relations, systematic isolation of variables, and deductive hypothesis-testing" (Kohlberg and Gilligan, 1971, p. 1063). The first two substages of formal operations are seen as necessary conditions for the development of the moral stages, 3 and 4, of the conventional level. "True formal operations" are necessary in order to develop postconventional moral judgments, Level III.

In sum, children at the concrete-operations cognitive or logical stage have the necessary thinking ability to make Level I moral judgments. Early adolescents, adolescents, and adults who function at the early formal-operations substages may make Level II judgments. Lastly, adolescents and adults who have developed true formal operations may also, if environmental and experiential conditions warrant, make Level III judgments. It should be noted that, whereas substages of the logical stages relate directly to specific moral stages through Level II stages, true formal operations is seen as a necessary but not sufficient condition for moral stages 5 and 6. It appears that it is not the cognitive stage, once formal operations are attained, which determines whether a person makes moral judgments from a perspective of social contract and higher law (stage 5) or a perspective of universal ethical principles individually held. Rather it must be personal differences in background and experience which allow formal-operational persons to reach either stage 5 or 6 morality.

Validity of Kohlberg's Theory

From a variety of research approaches, Kohlberg's moral stages have been shown to be valid, i.e., to adhere to the criteria for a stage theory. Longitudinal evidence (Kohlberg and Kramer, 1969; Kramer, 1968) has demonstrated a definite increase in moral-stage level with age as opposed to the inconsistency of results with moral character and moral-conduct measurements (Kohlberg, 1964). The stages show a predictable age-related patterning within individuals (Rest, Turiel, and Kohlberg, 1969). Laboratory experiments have also borne out the invariant-sequence concept applied to these stages (Turiel, 1969). And it is clear that a person at a given stage understands the next higher stage better than the succeeding stages, showing the invariant direction of development. Shown in another way, Rest (1968) found that, under normal conditions, a person will not revert to a preceding stage—in fact, he may reject the lower stage as inadequate. The consistency of an individual's judgments are indicated by the fact that, on average, 50 percent of an individual's moral judgments fit a single stage. Finally, the concept of equilibrium suggests that age should lead to increasing consolidation (equilibrium) and that the higher stages reflect more equilibrated stages (Turiel, 1969), which has in fact been proven (Turiel, 1969; Kramer, 1968).

One of the most crucial and interesting criteria for the validity of a stage theory is its universality. In order to determine the universality of a theory, attitude, behavior, or whatever, it must be studied among diverse groups. To establish beyond a shadow of a doubt the universality of a phenomenon, one would be required presumably to sample from all existent identifiable groups. Scientists are satisfied that, by sampling from groups which differ, culturally or socially in particular and known ways, conclusions as to universality may be drawn. "The point we are trying to make is simply that the type and the number of cultures chosen dictate the limits of analysis and interpretation. For the broadest predictability and inferential analysis, relationships between at least three cultures must be studied" (Manaster and Havighurst, 1972, p. 159).

Kohlberg (1969) presents evidence from studies of middle and lower-class urban boys in Taiwan, Great Britain, Mexico, Turkey, and the United States. Figure 6 shows the percentages for each stage of moral judgment for 10, 13, and 16-year-old middle-class urban boys from the U.S., Taiwan, and Mexico. The figure shows that, at age 10 in all three countries, the most prevalent stage is the lowest stage of moral development, stage 1, with decreasing percentages of each succeeding stage in order of increasing difficulty or maturity. At age 13, stage 3 statements are most prevalent in all countries, with stage 5 and 6 little used. By age 16 the order in the U.S. is stage 5 highest, then Level II stages, then Level I stages with stage 6 least frequently used. At age 16 in Taiwan and Mexico the order by level most to least frequent, is II, I, III. Although the orders are not exactly the same, particularly

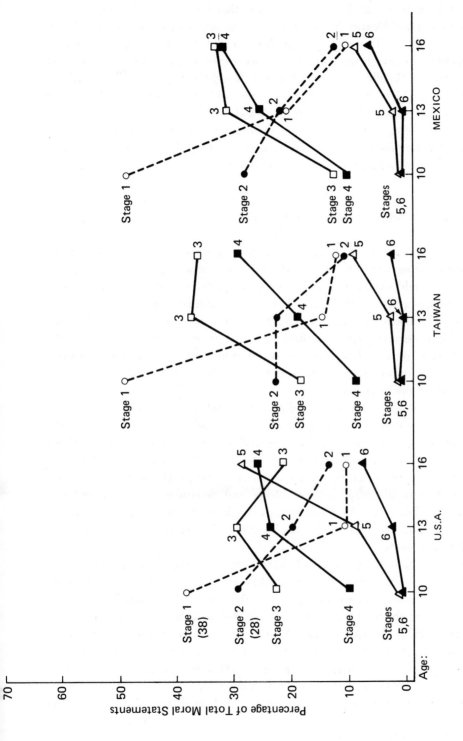

Figure 6. *Age Trends in Moral Judgment in Middle-Class Urban Boys in Three Nations. (Reprinted by permission from Lawrence Kohlberg, "Stage and sequence: The cognitive-developmental approach to socialization," in David A. Goslin [ed.], Handbook of Socialization Theory and Research, © 1969 by Rand McNally College Publishing Company, Chicago, p. 384.)*

stage 5 for 16-year-olds in the U.S., it is clear that the rates of development are slower in Taiwan and Mexico than the U.S. But the stages are evident in all cultures.

In comparing preliterate villagers in Mexico and Turkey, Kohlberg found a striking similarity between the patterns of moral development from age 10 to 16 in the two villages. "While conventional moral thought (Stages 3 and 4) increases steadily from age 10 to 16, at 16 it still has not achieved a clear ascendancy over premoral thought (Stages 1 and 2). Stages 5 and 6 are totally absent in this group. Trends for lower-class urban groups are intermediate in rate of development between those for the middle-class and the village boys" (Kohlberg, 1969, pp. 382–383). The case for the universality of the moral-judgment stages is strongly made.

Moral Judgments, Behavior, and Stage Transitions

At each stage of moral development, as at each stage of cognitive development, the individual's thinking forms an organized system of interacting parts and processes. Logically, we would expect that, at any stage, individuals would need to have an organized perspective. "Equilibrium" leads to an understanding of the developmental process as the reorganizing of thoughts as new inputs lead to disequilibrium. The need for a coherent, organized thinking process at each stage is evident in the individual's need to act. Regardless of the direction of behavior, the individual needs to feel that reasons exist for his behavior. Without an organized judgmental base, there would not be action.

However, a difficulty in the moral-developmental stages is that, as has been mentioned, the emphasis is on structure of thought and not on content. Yet the structure of thought at the various stages indicates predispositions to particular contents. That is, reliance on authority may determine the nature of a judgment— and the choice of authority may then determine action. Or at a higher stage, property or human life may take precedence and determine judgment and presumably related behavior. As Kohlberg has developed the moral-dilemma stories, responses may vary in content, but the judgmental level may be the same for quite different contents.

Nonetheless, Kohlberg's moral-judgmental measures show considerable predictive validity, whereas measures of moral attitudes and opinions have been notoriously unsuccessful as predictors of moral behavior in the past. As an example of the role of moral reasoning ability in behavior at the low end of Kohlberg's scale, Freundlich and Kohlberg (1971) showed in a sample of low-SES adolescents that 83 percent of delinquents were at the pre-conventional Level I, while only 27 percent of nondelinquent adolescents were at Level I. Krebs (1971) tested cheating behavior, using four experimental tasks, and determined moral-developmental level, using Kohlberg's stories. Subjects at the pre-conventional level cheated more (73 percent) than did subjects at the conventional level (66 percent), whereas only 20 percent of the subjects at the principled level cheated. Kohlberg (1969) found 11 percent of principled-level college students cheated, while 42 percent of the same college group who were at the conventional level cheated. In a study of the participants in the Berkeley free-speech movement sit-ins, Haan, Smith, and Block (1968) randomly sampled the university student population and found that 80 percent of the stage 6 students had sat-in, 50 percent of the stage 5 students had, and only 10 percent of the students tested who were at Level II, stages 3 and 4, had participated in the sit-ins.

While maturity of moral judgment

is only one of many predictors of action in moral conflict situations, it appears to be a quite powerful and meaningful predictor of action where it gives rise to distinctive ways of defining concrete situational rights and duties in socially ambiguous situations (Ernsberger, 1975).

The exact timing of transitions to new moral stages is no more clearly determined than the ages of transition to new cognitive-developmental stages. Inasmuch as they are related, this makes sense. It seems as if there is a parallel in the research and conclusions at this date for both cognitive and moral development. In the previous chapter it was seen that current thinking shows cognitive development continuing into adulthood and proceeding at different rates for different people. These rates were dependent on maturational, personal, and social experiences. The notions of extended cognitive development have not been researched to any degree and, as we saw, somewhat clouded the kind of definitive conclusions it would be nice to be able to make. So, too, research and thinking in the moral-development area are progressing in the same direction, and too little has been done to date to present definitive conclusions.

Although relationships between moral-judgmental level and moral behavior have been shown, until recently Kohlberg felt that adolescents regressed in moral stage during the course of transitions to new stages, and that moral development was pretty well completed in adolescence. However, he now maintains that moral development goes on into adulthood, and that, although adolescents may develop an awareness of principled moral reasoning, an actual commitment to its ethical employment does not develop until adulthood (Kohlberg, 1973). Moreover, reanalysis of moral judgments made during transitions to Level III are seen not to regress to earlier stages, but are more sophisticated forms of the same stage.

Particularly as this pertains to high-school youth, Level III thought and judgment, as previously thought, may in fact be appeals to new higher authority, "conscience" and "moral law," but not principled judgments in their fullest committed meaning. In a sense, this is progress—this is the beginning of the transformation of stage 4 thinking as new elements are assimilated, and the beginning of the transition to stage 5 thought. Turiel (1974) investigated the transition to stage 5 and found support for the hypothesis that in moving from one stage to another, an awareness of the inadequacies and contradictions of the existing stage promotes rejection of the logic of that stage and creation and construction of the new stage.

Turiel points out that the transition from stage 4 to stage 5 does not generally occur until late adolescence or young adulthood. It appears that the autonomy characteristic of post-high-school living, new experiences, and a wider set of experiences, and most notably college attendance, provide the impetus to question the stage 4 orientation and begin the transition to stage 5 (Kohlberg, 1973; Turiel, 1974).

Therefore, the judgments of high-school-age adolescents which appeared to be principled are more probably a sophisticated stage 4. Turiel studied high-school students and college undergraduates using the moral dilemma stories and found, as expected, conflict and disequilibrium in the beginnings of the transition to Level III judgments.

> The first striking feature of their judgments was the forceful denial of morality. Typically it was stated that: (a) all values are relative and arbitrary, (b) one should not judge what another person should do, (c) it is up to every individual to make his own decisions, and (d) terms like "duty," "good," "should," or "moral" have no meaning. The second striking feature was the inconsistent way in which this relativism was applied. In addition to viewing moral values as arbitrary, there was a strong commitment to moral positions on specific issues. The simultaneous denial of morality and presence of moral assertions reflects the transitional process itself (Turiel, 1974, p. 19).

The adolescents who come to this point of transition must feel the conflict. The live-and-let-live philosophy that obtains in the morning conflicts dramatically with the angry reaction to a classmate who did not do what he "should," a friend who acted "bad," or a parent who did not do his or her "duty." The conflict and inconsistency may not be as apparent to the adolescent as it is to the parent, teacher, or friend. But it can be quite surprising. In the effort of maintaining equilibrium, the adolescent will attempt to make it seem coherent and organized but may experience difficulty in making it seem so.

Not all adolescents experience this transition, as most adults develop only to the level of conventional moral judgment, stages 3 and 4. Remembering that formal operations is a necessary, but not sufficient, requirement for the attainment of Level III moral judgments, Kuhn et al. (1971) found in a study of adolescents and adults that 60 percent of their subjects over age 16 had reached formal operations but only 10 percent definitely showed principled moral thinking.

Affective, cognitive, and moral development parallel each other. In adolescence, those who are developing more, or more quickly, may experience greater conflict and tumult. In a world which itself is tumultuous, maintenance of a consistently clear moral-judgment level must facilitate a greater feeling of security. Adolescents in transition probably feel the tumult doubly, both within and without.

I sometimes wonder whether every adolescent has not been confronted by a parent asking "How are you going to act?" This section, and this chapter, have alluded to one reason why that is such a hard question for adolescents to answer.

Sex-Role Development

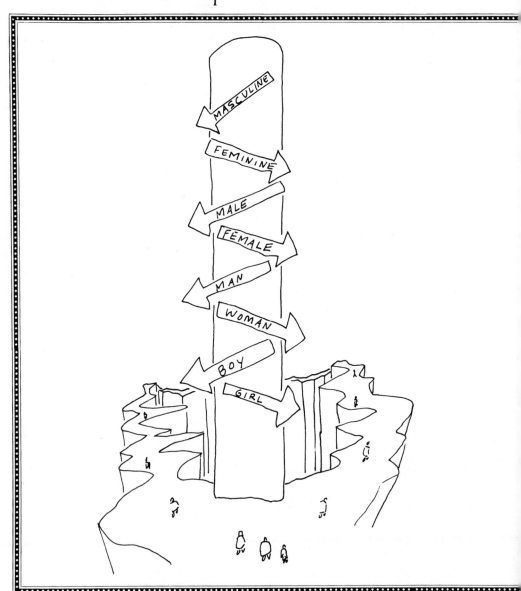

CHAPTER 5

When a child is born, the parents immediately ask two questions, "Is it healthy?" and "What is it?" (except the occasional overexcited and confused new parent such as myself who asked the nurse immediately upon the birth of our first child, "How old is it?"). The answer to the question "What is it?" is either "A girl" or "A boy." After determining the physical condition of the baby, the single most important question parents ask about their new child is its sex. With the information that "I have a daughter" or "I have a son" the new parent may begin to muse about and conjure up differentiated images of what life in the ensuing years will be like as one raises a boy or a girl. It is not unusual for the new father to begin the next day painting the baby's room pink, if he has a new daughter, or blue, if he has a new son. And the baby on coming home a few days later would not be able to discriminate nor understand why there is a walking-talking doll in her pink room, or a large professional football on the shelf in his blue room, the gift from grandma or grandpa. But these gifts are the beginning inputs in the child's socialization into an appropriate sex role, and indicate the continuing sex-role expectations.

PSYCHOLOGICAL SEX DIFFERENTIATION

Much of the current controversy over the role of women in our society, and internationally, hinges on the issue of whether and how males and females differ in the broadest psychological connotations. Toward an understanding of this issue, here we will explain, discuss, and interpret four points: (1) how the differences in the psychological nature of man and woman develop, if indeed they exist—the development of psychological sex differentiation: (2) what

69

these differences are; (3) where our society is in relation to such theories and facts, i.e., the maintenance of traditional sex-role stereotypes; and (4) how the developing adolescent deals with his or her sex-role identity in our changing times.

Three major psychological theories have been advanced to explain the process of psychological sex differentiation, that is, the developmental process whereby male children grow to be "like" older boys and adult men in the society, and female children grow to be "like" older girls and adult women in the society, in their behavior, feelings, and attitudes.

The first of the theories grew out of the Freudian and psychoanalytic theoretical traditions and emphasizes that sex differentiation occurs through a process of imitation. The idea is that children, most probably unknowingly, choose a same-sex model. The children try to emulate, to imitate, this person's behavior. This person acts as the model for the child's behavior, and the child attempts to model his or her own behavior according to his perception of the behavior of his same-sex model. Within this theory, most likely the child will choose his or her parent as the model.

Social-learning theory, with its emphasis on the occurrence and effectiveness of positive and negative reinforcement in influencing psychological sex differentiation, is the second major theory. In essence, this theory presumes that parents, other family members, and others in the society positively reinforce (by rewarding and praising boys for behaving as they think boys should) or negatively reinforce (by discouraging boys from behaving in feminine or unmanly ways and activities). In like manner the social-learning theory would see girls receiving positive reinforcement for behaving in ways that the reinforcers, parents and others, see as feminine and receiving negative reinforcement for behaving in ways that are seen as masculine. Boys or girls, whether they understand what is happening or not, would behave in the sex-appropriate manner in order to receive the reinforcement.

The third theory of psychological sex differentiation relies on a cognitive-developmental interpretation. In this theory the child comes to recognize himself as a boy or girl, sex types himself or herself, and develops a conception of, and begins to categorize, behaviors and activities as appropriate to one sex or the other. So by the age of four the boy knows he is a boy and wants to do "boy things" and the girl knows she is a girl and, in keeping with her gender identity, wants to do "girl things." (At dinner the other evening our children had a choice of chocolate or strawberry ice cream for dessert. They all chose both. But apologetically, our five-year-old daughter turned to her six-year-old brother and said, "You know, chocolate is a boy's color and pink is a girl's color." Scornfully, he looked at her and retorted, "Everyone knows that.")

The believers in each of these theories have maintained that their own theory is sufficient to explain the process of psychological sex differentiation. However, it is becoming clearer that there is considerable overlap among the theories. As an example, the controversy between the social-learning and the cognitive-developmental advocates continues unabated, yet a prime proponent of the social learning view, Mischel (1970), can point to the areas of overlap and the possibilities from drawing the viewpoints together. In effect, he says that the social-learning view can accommodate cognitive-developmental formulations about the role of cognitions and self-concepts of sex-role identity as influences on personality. However, he feels that the cognitive-developmental view places too much emphasis on these positions to the exclusion of the valuable aspects of the other position. He says, "The question is not the existence of such cognitions and self-concepts, but rather how adequately they in themselves account for complex sex-typing and socialization phenomena" (1970, p. 59).

In the opinion of this author, the value of the cognitive-developmental theory does not lie solely in how adequately cognitions and self-concepts "in themselves account for complex sex-typing and socialization phenomena." Rather, the adequacy and value of the cognitive-developmental theory lie in its explanatory power while subsuming the notions of the other two theories. "A child's conception of what is appropriate behavior for a male or female will depend both upon what he sees males and females doing and upon the approval or disapproval that these actions elicit differentially from others" (Maccoby and Jacklin, 1974, p. 2).

Both because the cognitive-developmental view can accommodate the other two theories to some degree, and because it is useful in explaining and understanding developmental change as in adolescence, we agree most closely with it and the following conclusions of Maccoby and Jacklin:

> We believe that the processes of direct reinforcement and simple imitation are clearly involved in the acquisition of sex-typed behavior, but that they are not sufficient to account for the developmental changes that occur in sex-typing. The third kind of psychological process—the one stressed by cognitive-developmental theorists such as Kohlberg—must also be involved. This third process is not easy to define, but in its simplest terms it means that a child gradually develops concepts of "masculinity" and "femininity," and when he has understood what his own sex is, he attempts to match his behavior to his conception. His ideas may be drawn only very minimally from observing his own parents. The generalizations he constructs do not represent acts of imitation, but are organizations of information distilled from a wide variety of sources, a child's sex-role concepts are limited in the same way the rest of his concepts are, by the level of cognitive skills he has developed. Therefore the child undergoes reasonably orderly age-related changes in the subtlety of his thought about sex-typing, just as he does with respect to other topics. Consequently, his actions in adopting sex-typed behavior, and in treating others according to sex-role stereotypes, also change in ways that parallel his conceptual growth (1974, pp. 365–366).[1]

1. E. E. Maccoby and C. N. Jacklin, *The Psychology of Sex Differences*. Stanford, Calif.: Stanford University Press, 1974. Used with permission of the publisher.

The sex-role development discussed to this point has all occured in childhood. The child comes to adolescence with a "sex-role identity" which "usually refers to an awareness and acceptance of one's biological gender and an awareness that there are culturally defined attitudes and behaviors which are associated with gender" (Dreyer, 1975, p. 207).

Although there are a variety of sex-role identity types, which will be discussed later in this chapter, it has been considered that, in almost all individuals by the time of adolescence, sex-role identity is so firmly embedded as to be practically immutable. Even in extreme cases such as gynecomastia (breast growth in the male) and hirsutism (abnormal body-hair growth in girls), gender identity does not come into question. The adolescent so afflicted wants medical treatment to return his or her body to normal, to the body characteristics associated with the sex with which he or she identifies. Money and Clopper (1974) point out that incongruous pubertal development, the extreme cases, do not correlate with bisexuality or homosexuality. Dating and romantic involvements follow the earlier gender-identity differentiation.

Since sex-role identity is essentially fixed prior to adolescence, the problem for adolescents is one of sex-role preference. Sex-role preference refers to the choice an individual makes to adopt a particular set, or constellation, of attitudes and behavior which are sex typed. At a time when roles in society (economic, familial, and social) were clearly defined as appropriate to one sex or the other—sex typed— the adolescent's problem was minimal, i.e., a male, with male sex-role identity, chose male sex-typed attitudes and behaviors. Today that choice is not as clear and, seemingly, will be even less clear in the future.

This implies that today's adolescents cannot rely for establishing their sex-role identity and sex-role preferences on a well-defined set of "culturally defined attitudes and behaviors which are associated with gender." Block (1973) has introduced a definition of sex-role identity that allows the individual to make sex-role preference determinations, be a mentally healthy person, and be adaptable to traditional, present, and future conceptions of sex role. Block says, "Sexual identity means, or will mean, the earning of a sense of self in which there is a recognition of gender secure enough to permit the individual to manifest human qualities our society, until now, has labeled as unmanly or unwomanly" (1973, p. 512).

In the next section of this chapter we will summarize the scientific justification for the sex differences that our society has labeled as unmanly or unwomanly, before returning in the following section to whether society still considers these differences valid.

SEX DIFFERENCES—MYTHS AND REALITY

The title to this section promises more than the section can deliver. The most current and complete review and analysis on this topic is Maccoby and Jacklin's book, *The Psychology of Sex Differences*. After an exhaustive review, in which they attempt to account for the biological, psychological, and social factors that might produce sex differences, they summarize their findings. However, they clearly admit the tenuous nature of their findings, a natural result of comparing so many studies varying greatly in samples, data-collection strategies, and theoretical assumptions. Even though the "realities" of sex differences presented by Maccoby and Jacklin may not be the final answer, their conclusions do represent the most advanced state of the art on these issues.

Maccoby and Jacklin looked at the beliefs, and possibly myths, about sex differences and categorized their findings in three ways: those beliefs about sex differences which were unfounded, those which they felt were fairly well established in the scientific literature, and those which remain open questions, either because the research literature is insufficient or because the findings themselves are ambiguous. Included in the category of unfounded beliefs are the beliefs "that girls are more 'social' than boys," . . . "that girls are more 'suggestable' than boys," . . . "that girls have lower self-esteem," . . . "that girls are better at rote learning and simple repetitive tasks, boys at tasks that require higher-level cognitive processing and the inhibition of previously learned responses," . . . "that boys are more 'analytic,'" . . . "that girls are more affected by heredity, boys by environment," . . . "that girls lack achievement motivation," . . . "that girls are auditory, boys visual" (1974, pp. 349–351).

The belief that girls have greater verbal ability than boys, boys have greater visual-spatial ability, and boys have greater mathematical ability are considered to be well founded. A fourth belief that Maccoby and Jacklin considered to be fairly well established in the social-science literature is that males are more aggressive than females. This finding is important in its own right but is particularly noteworthy in that it is the only social-personality characteristic or trait on which sufficient evidence exists to conclude that males and females differ.

For the beliefs like girls are more fearful, timid, and anxious, boys have a higher activity level, males are more competitive, males are more dominant, females are more compliant, and girls show more nurturance and maternal behavior, the evidence is either too scanty or too contradictory to justify conclusions pro or con.

You may ask yourselves, as Maccoby and Jacklin asked themselves, how these beliefs, how these stereotypes about sex differences continue to be perpetuated when the facts do not substantiate them. It appears that here, as in so many areas of our lives, we look for confirmation of our beliefs and trust only the evidence which supports them. The beliefs and stereotypes presented in this section, whether corroborated or not, along with other similar stereotypes have, in general, long been accepted. They have influenced behaviors and decisions and the course of people's lives. There is much talk of changing sex roles and "exploding the myths." How rapidly are sex roles really changing, and how is this affecting adolescents?

THE PERSISTENCE OF SEX-ROLE STEREOTYPES

The persistence of sex-role stereotypes and the lower status of women in society seem well illustrated by Aristotle, who said, "Woman may be said to be an inferior man," and the continuation of this theme through the late nineteenth century as in Tennyson's "God made the woman for the man, and for the good and increase of the world." It is only since the onset of the Industrial Revolution that questions have been raised about "the woman's place is in the home," and male dominance related to strength. Nonetheless, the mythical sex differences appear to be still with us, as the following examples will show.

Williams, Bennett, and Best (1975) studied the awareness and the expression of sex stereotypes in young children and found that over 60 percent of the kindergarten and second-grade children examined held the belief that males are more aggressive, strong, adventurous, coarse, independent, loud, dominant, and ambitious, and females are more appreciative, emotional, sophisticated, and soft hearted. They summarized their findings as follows: "(a) knowledge of sex stereotypes appeared to develop in a similar manner among both boys and girls, (b) kindergarten children show an appreciable degree of knowledge of adult sex stereotypes, (c) this knowledge increases to the second-grade level but shows no further increase during the next two years" (p. 640). This finding speaks both to the validity of the cognitive-developmental theory of sex-role differentiation, and to the persistence of sex-role stereotypes. Clearly these children have differentiated beliefs of how males and females behave to incorporate into their gender identity and for use in sex typing. Moreover, these young children believe these stereotypes today. As they develop is there any reason for their stereotypic beliefs to alter if the greater society, their parents, teachers, and the media do not show these beliefs to be incorrect?

Rosenkrantz et al. (1968) studied sex-role stereotypes and self-concepts in college students. They found those stereotypic traits which were valued for males and those which were valued for females. Examples of the stereotypic traits valued for females were talkative, tactful, gentle, aware of feelings of others, interested in own appearance, neat in habits, quiet, strong need for security, appreciative of art and literature, and expressive of tender feelings. Stereotypic traits valued for males in cluded aggressive, independent, unemotional, objective, dominant, active, competitive logical, worldly, and adventurous. Their results supported the view that, despite changes in the legal status of women and the range of behaviors permissible for men and women today, both college men and women define and agree with the historical sex-role stereotypes. Additionally, despite their saying that they believe in equality of the sexes, college men and women agree that the stereotypic characteristics and behaviors associated with masculinity are more socially desirable than those associated with femininity.

Ponzo and Strowig (1973), in a study of sex-role identity of high-school students, used an adjective checklist to ascertain the norms for behavior descriptive of, and appropriate for, teenage boys or girls. They found 65 adjectives for males and 59 for females which discriminated significantly between the sexes and which were along traditional sex-role stereotype lines.

Many years ago Adler also concerned himself with the role that the sexes occupy in our society and lamented the inequality and resulting feeling of inferiority of many women and men who felt that they were not masculine enough. In 1910 he wrote:

> The search for the sexual role usually begins in the fourth year of life and increases the child's curiosity. . . . Not knowing the significance of his sexual tools, the child seeks the difference between the sexes in dress, hair, bodily and mental traits, and in doing so, often makes mistakes. . . .
>
> To this is added the arch evil of our culture, the excessive pre-eminence of manliness. All children who have been in doubt as to their sexual role exaggerate the traits which they consider masculine, . . . (Ansbacher and Ansbacher, 1956, pp. 54–55).

Even in 1927 Adler wrote, "The advantages of being a man are, under such conditions (as exist in our society), very alluring. We must not be astonished, therefore, when we see many girls who maintain a masculine ideal either as an unfillable desire, or as a standard for judgment of their behavior; this ideal may evince itself as a pattern for action and appearance. It would seem that in our culture every woman wanted to be a man" (Adler, 1927, in Ansbacher and Ansbacher, 1956, p. 108).

Adler called this phenomenon, of women wanting to be men rather than inferior women, and men having to be man enough (to be a "real man")—the masculine protest. In line with Block's definition it will be good when some day men and women can choose their own way of behaving without the thought that certain things and ways are male or female—and that male ways are better. Unfortunately the superior-inferior evaluation of sex-typed attitudes and behaviors is still with us and provides a source of anxiety and confusion for adolescents.

Bieliauskas (1974) reported three studies of high school and college students carried out in the 1970's which did not show that the male "above" and female "below" valuation of the sexes had changed. He concluded that as long as the masculine superiority idea was maintained, the masculine protest would remain.

A hopeful note in this regard was struck by Ponzo and Strowig, who found what they termed "an emergent trend" in the sex-role identity of their high-school subjects. These subjects showed sex-role identities which blended the behaviors traditionally held and considered to be male or female. Although hopeful, Ponzo and Strowig concluded,

> In the present decade and in the decades to come it seems likely that for personal optimal development a person will require a sex-role identity that is a blending of attributes to be appropriate for only one or the other sex. Subjects' responses indicated that their sex-role identities were more in the emergent direction than the traditional, but that they viewed appropriate male and female along traditional lines. These lingering traditional stereotypes may cause conflicts among teenagers over appropriate ways to behave, and may restrict them from freely adopting emergent sex-roles that appear to be more conducive to academic success. The school should be a place in which efforts are made to change the traditional stereotypes and help people resolve sex-role conflicts (1973, p. 141).

SEX-ROLE DEVELOPMENT IN ADOLESCENCE— EFFECTS AND PROBLEMS

On the face of it, this discussion of sex-role development would indicate no functional reason for additional sex-role development to occur in adolescence. In childhood, the individual by and large has come to a conclusion about his own identity and its coherence with the stereotypes accepted by the society for his or her sex and the opposite sex. We have seen that children hold views of male and female sex roles and stereotypes that are very similar to those held by adolescents and the adult society.

However, to conclude that there is no sex-role development in adolescence, nor any reason for this development to occur, would be wrong. Most adolescents hold a firm and relatively unchanging sex-role identity.

If the sex roles, the sex-determined role standards, operative in the society were in agreement with the sex-role identity of the individual there would be no reason for change. If the sex roles in the society were functional for the society and its members there would be no reason for the adolescent to change or alter his or her sex-role identity. If the sex roles in the society were static, and thus the same for the individual in adolescence as when he learned and adopted them in childhood, there would be no reason for change. If the individual did not develop new abilities and perspectives, as in cognitive development in adolescence, there would be no reason to question and change.

However, none of these *ifs* are true for most or all adolescents. The traditional sex-determined role standards are not desirable for several reasons, which Ellis and Bentler (1973) point out. First, in keeping with Adler's position, differential esteem is accorded male roles and female roles, and the female roles are inferior. As much evidence attests, both for the group and the individual, the attribution of inferior qualities and ascription to inferior roles produces negative social and emotional outcomes. Secondly, people are not satisfied with the traditional sex-role standards. When asked what kind of person one would like to be like, males and females both reply that their "ideal person" is not the same as the sex-stereotypic traditional person. That is, they would prefer to be an amalgam of male-valued and female-valued traits rather than solely described by the traits valued for their own sex.

Finally, a significant amount of literature suggests that traditional sex-determined role standards are not only nonfunctional but perhaps dysfunctional. For example, traditional sex-determined role standards appeared to have negative consequences for personality development, marital harmony, originality in females, and in males, level of achievement motivation, and problem-solving performance. In general, writers have suggested that traditional sex-role standards produce unnecessary internal conflicts and are incompatible with both individual and societal interests (Ellis and Bentler, 1973, p. 28).

Overall, the traditional sex-role standards are undesirable because they are demeaning and restrictive. They restrict or negate the potential to develop a sex-role identity according to Block's definition. As long as individuals are concerned with whether their behavior, image, and identity is unmanly or unwomanly, they are by virtue of expending energy on that concern limiting their potential to develop and manifest purely human qualities. Unfortunately, the time and prospects for development of sexual identity according to Block's definition seem remote.

So most adolescents today come into this period with a conception of themselves as budding men or women. From Adler's time to the present, there has been support for the position that masculinity means not being feminine and femininity means not being masculine. The height or extreme of being a he-man means being "all man," not feminine at all. The height or extreme of femininity implies being truly "the little woman," helpless—"Frailty, thy name is Woman." The John Waynes, Clint Eastwoods, and Hugh Hefners "walking tall" through our high-school corridors avoid at all costs, and there are many, showing any feminine characteristics. The Shirley Temple, Olivia Newton-John—southern belles who walk next to them—

would never let on that they are capable or knowledgeable—"Why I could never do that, you're so big and strong."

These extremes of sex-role stereotypes are still prevalent, and adolescents who adhere to an extreme ideal, or have adopted a stereotypic sex-role identity, feel lesser in relation to this extreme. Moreover, the females may feel doubly put down by not being even the extreme female which is not in itself as good as the extreme male.

Persons adhering to these extreme masculine or feminine sex identities or aspiring to this level of sex typing, as well as those relatively few persons who maintain a sex-reversed identity (the masculine-female and the feminine-male) are all restricted and limited by the boundaries of masculine or feminine behavior they feel appropriate to them. The sex-role identity, described as an "emerging trend" by Ponzo and Strowig, was considered to be hopeful in that individuals of this type could express themselves behaviorally and emotionally from a fuller scope of potential behaviors, masculine and feminine.

The emergent-trend type appears to be similar to what Bem (1975) termed the "psychologically androgynous" individual. She develops the thesis that "because his or her self-definition excludes neither masculinity nor femininity the androgynous individual should be able to remain sensitive to the changing constraints of the situation and engage in whatever behavior seems most effective at the moment, regardless of its stereotype as appropriate for one sex or the other" (1975, pp. 634–635). In support of this thesis she cites studies which have shown consistently that high-femininity females exhibit high anxiety, low self-esteem, and low social acceptance; and that although high masculinity during adolescence for males relates to better psychological adjustment, in adulthood high masculinity correlates for males with high anxiety, high neuroticism, and low self-esteem. Moreover, children and adolescents of both sexes who are more highly sex typed are found to be lower overall in intelligence, spatial ability, and creativity.

Bem ran two studies, one of which was designed to elicit stereotypically masculine behavior—independence in a conformity-demanding situation, and the second of which was designed to elicit stereotypically feminine behavior—playing with a kitten when given the opportunity. The idea was simply that androgynous persons of both sexes could excel, could display the masculine independence or feminine playfulness, whereas nonandrogynous persons, highly sex-typed persons, could only excel in or display, sex-appropriate behavior. Overall, her thesis was supported by the results of the study, although the feminine females could not be said to have exhibited either the masculine independence or feminine playfulness, from which we can again infer that the feminine-female role and type is more seriously debilitating. Bem concludes that "the current set of studies . . . provides the first empirical demonstration that there exists a distinct class of people who can appropriately be termed androgynous, whose sex-role adaptability enables them to engage in situationally effective behavior without regard for its stereotype as masculine or feminine. Accordingly, it may well be . . . that the androgynous individual will someday come to define a new and more human standard of psychological health" (1975, p. 643).

There are, then, persons, described as androgynous or of the emergent trend, for whom the traditional sex-role standards are not as limiting because they can choose to behave as they wish regardless of the sex-role demands. These persons, it would seem, should be prepared to accept readily changes in sex-role standards within the society toward a more egalitarian system. That is to say, as the restrictions on males performing "feminine" behaviors and vice versa are lessened, these persons almost automatically fit in. But what of the individuals who have accepted and adopted the traditional sex-role standards?

Resistance to changing sex roles can be expected, and does exist, particularly from persons who have maintained and adopted the traditional sex roles for themselves. It is easy to see how threatening it might be for a male of the John Wayne type who finds respect for his total masculinity diminishing and women encroaching on his territory. When we consider the antagonism that has long been felt and shown toward persons with sex-reversed identities, it is possible to generalize this antagonism to greater numbers of people who show what has been considered sex-inappropriate behavior and characteristics during a time of changing sex roles. Changing sex roles in the society may provoke problems if not change for the adolescent who has entered this period with the traditionally appropriate sex-role identity.

The three considerations raised thus far in this chapter regarding the necessity for change in sex-role identity or new developments in sex-role identity are: (1) the restrictive and limiting nature of traditional sex roles, (2) the varying adaptability of existing sex-role types, masculine, feminine, and androgynous, and (3) the demands made, particularly on people with traditional sex-role identities or sex typing, in a society with changing sex roles, which may refer to problems and issues of adult development as well as adolescent development. Yet these issues may be more pressing, more immediate and critical, for adolescents because they are meeting them at a stage where they are expected to deal with them for the first time.

Physical, cognitive, and moral development, the three areas of development in adolescence discussed in the previous chapters, can be seen as relating to sex-role development and need for change in sex-role identity and preference in adolescence. With physical change and new interest in sexual matters, adolescents are forced to consider whether they are up to (within their own definition) being a man or a woman. If an adolescent develops cognitively, to the point of restructuring his or her conception of himself as a human being as well as a man or woman, change may occur. And to the degree that in adolescence one questions the morality of sex roles from the perspective of principle, as opposed to contract or conforming, one may reevaluate his acceptance of sex roles in the society and his own identity.

Block (1973) pointed out that the prevailing cultural norms, the traditional sex-role standards, make it more difficult for women to achieve "higher levels of ego functioning" (p. 526), and that, perhaps, this accounts for fewer women, in the studies reviewed, with androgynous sex-role definitions. However, for both sexes Block found some support for the hypothesis that greater maturity on Kohlberg's Moral Judgment Test is associated with more androgynous self-definition. Achievement of higher levels of ego functioning (more mature, dynamic self-definitions) tends to include elements of traditional sex-role definitions of both sexes, i.e., to be more androgynous, thereby illustrating the interrelationships among moral, sex-role, and personality development.

In the life-task chapters that follow, sex differences will be noted and discussed. However, sex differences will not be emphasized. Taking a somewhat futuristic view, and assuming that the readers of this book will be concerned with adolescents in some capacity in the future, sex differences may be considered a cultural artifact, an historical anomaly that is still with us to some degree but is in the process of change. Many adolescent boys will be concerned that they are not as manly as they "should" be. Many adolescent girls will choose occupations because they are "feminine" occupations. Many adolescents will find the sex typing of behaviors and lifestyles an issue in their decisions. But if this chapter has done nothing more, it has tried to show that, although the stereotypes still exist, they are changing; that, although children and adolescents still identify themselves by sex in the traditional ways, there are significant numbers who do not; and, lastly, there is almost no valid psychological or scientific justification for the belief in the stereotypes.

Personality Development

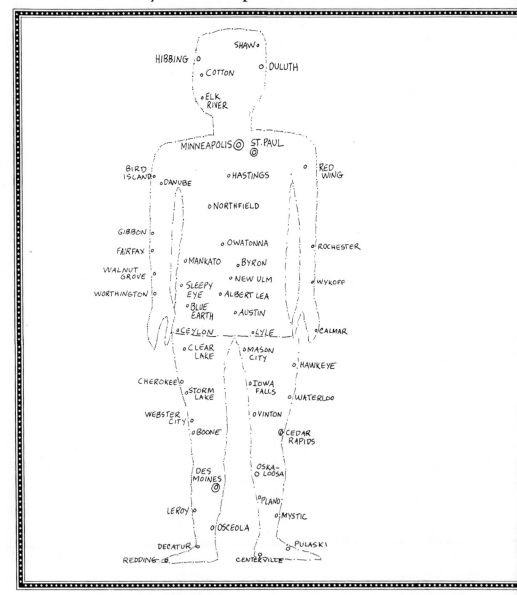

CHAPTER 6

Adolescence is characterized as a period of change. So far we have discussed developmental change in physiology, cognition, and conceptions of morality. From many perspectives, certainly that of many parents, it would appear that there is considerable personality change during adolescence. The position will be taken in this chapter, supported by both theoretical and research literature, that little or no personality change occurs in adolescence. The phenomena which look like personality change in adolescence, and the type of research which has given credence to the personality change thesis, will be examined.

DEFINITIONS OF PERSONALITY

It is probably impossible, and certainly not worthwhile, to discuss personality without defining it. "Personality" as used by psychologists does not mean degree of personableness or likeability or congeniality which is how it is more frequently used by "normals" (nonpsychologists). Within the psychological literature there are many definitions of the term, which seem to depend on the theory under study. "Personality consists concretely of a set of values or descriptive terms which are used to describe the individual being studied according to the variables or dimensions which occupy a central position within the particular theory utilized" (Hall and Lindzey, 1957, p. 9).

After examining almost fifty definitions of personality, Allport defined personality as "the dynamic organization within the individual of those psychophysical systems that determine his unique adjustment to his environment" (1937, p. 48). Allport later summarized a discussion of the structure of personality, saying,

The most comprehensive units in personality are broad intentional dispositions, future-pointed. These characteristics are unique for each person, and tend to attract, guide, inhibit the more elementary units to accord with the major intentions themselves. This proposition is valid in spite of the large amount of unordered, impulsive, and conflictful behavior in every life. Finally, these cardinal characteristics are not infinite in number but for any given life in adult years are relatively few and ascertainable (Allport, 1955, p. 92).

Maddi, an important contemporary personologist, that is, a student and specialist in personality theory and research, defines personality as

a stable set of characteristics and tendencies that determine those commonalities and differences in the psychological behavior (thoughts, feelings, actions) of people that have continuity in time and that may or may not be easily understood in terms of the social and biological pressures of the immediate situation (1968, p. 10).

Personality definitions emphasize a set, or the organization, of an individual's ways which make him appear distinctly and consistently different from others and distinctly and consistently like himself. The essence of an individual's set of characteristics or tendencies resides in the simplicity of its organization and its "continuity in time."

In a way, you recognize this when you meet someone again after a long period of time and think, "Same old Joe." You may be reacting to his superficial mannerisms, which are more peripheral to personality; but you may also be reacting to his "modus operandi," the way he copes, which you remember, or to the feeling you get from the person, which you also remember. That is, this long-lost friend will have a pattern to his behavior and will have a goal or goals in relating, to which you react. Although he will have changed in many ways, some of the attitudes he expresses or certain of his behaviors are peculiarly him, and bring back that "old feeling."

Adler's conception of lifestyle, which at times he equated with self, man's own personality, and the unity of the personality, bears a lovely resemblance to the juxtaposition of individual uniqueness and social-biological pressures in Maddi's definition.

If we look at a pine tree growing in a valley we will notice that it grows differently from one on top of a mountain. It is the same kind of a tree, a pine, but there are two distinct styles of life. Its style on top of the mountain is different from its style when growing in the valley. The style of life of a tree is the individuality of a tree expressing itself and molding itself in an environment. We recognize a style when we see it against a background of an environment different from what we expect, for then we realize that every tree has a life pattern and is not merely a mechanical reaction to the environment.

It is much the same way with human beings (Adler, 1929, in Ansbacher and Ansbacher, 1956, p. 173).[1]

PERSONALITY CONSISTENCY

It is within the stability, organization, and consistency of a person's thoughts, feelings, and actions as part of his culture and as uniquely himself, that the meaning of personality lies. It is important to note that consistency is an element in the definition of personality. In some manner the distinctive characteristics that differentiate one individual from others in the psychological and behavioral realms must be consistent over time so that the individual can psychologically and behaviorally be "himself" to himself and others. A number of theorists have discussed this.

Very simply, in the Adlerian perspective the individual comes to his own view of himself and his world and determines where he must be to be OK—getting there is his goal. This goal, called at times "fictional final goal" or "guiding self-ideal," is developed early and held with only slight alteration through life. "The goal of the mental life of man becomes its governing principle, its causa finalis. Here we have the root of the unity of the personality, the individuality" (Adler, 1923, in Ansbacher and Ansbacher, 1956, p. 94). The goal is a personal creation and therefore unique for each person, depending as it does on the "meaning he gives to life." An individual's lifestyle is not clearly evident to himself or others. It is expressed vaguely in all the ways he strives for his goal. The individual cannot articulate his goal but strives for it in any way, whether it appears consistent or inconsistent, that he can.

There are some crucial points in these positions from Adler. The individual has his own conception of his goal, which he consistently strives to reach, but in the process of striving he develops his own strategies to reach his goal. That is, his behavior is aimed toward his goal, but the observer may not recognize the consistency because he may not recognize the goal.

By the time a child is five years old his attitude to his environment is usually so fixed and mechanized that it proceeds in more or less the same direction for the rest of his life. His apperception of the external world remains the same. The child is caught in the trap of his perspectives and repeats increasingly his original

1. From *The Individual Psychology of Alfred Adler: A Systematic Presentation in Selections from His Writings,* edited and annotated by Heinz L. Ansbacher, Ph.D., and Rowena R. Ansbacher, Ph.D. © 1956 by Basic Books, Inc., Publishers, New York.

mental mechanisms and the resulting actions (Adler, 1930, in Ansbacher and Ansbacher, 1956, p. 189).[2]

Allport discussed personality unity both as striving and in relation to the self-image. Referring to the unity-through-striving doctrine, Allport cites the position that "what integrates our energies is the pursuit of some goal" (1961, p. 380). He also refers to Lecky's work, one of the long-standing references on self-consistency. Lecky defined personality "as an organization of values which are felt to be consistent with one another" (1951, p. 152).

> Behavior expresses the effort to maintain integrity and unity of the organization. . . .
> In order to be immediately assimilated, the idea formed as the result of a new experience must be felt to be consistent with the ideas already present in the system. On the other hand, ideas whose inconsistency is recognized as the personality develops must be expelled from the system (Lecky, 1945, p. 135).

Lecky's theory, stressing maintenance of the unity of the system, also seems to present a form of equilibrium and a process of assimilation and accommodation to new experience imposing on the existing personality schema.

In adolescence, with all of the changes that occur, emotional crises, instability, and reorganization appear. During this period when the adolescent may be adapting and revising his values and outlook, Lecky points out that "the need for unity is most acute" (1951, p. 159).

David Glass (1968), in a very complete review of theory and research in consistency and personality, shows the continuing viability of the concept as well as growing sophistication in its use. He says,

> One of the older doctrines in psychology holds that man cannot tolerate inconsistency among his cognitions and that he continually strives to eliminate it. The existence of inconsistency makes him uncomfortable, makes him feel something is wrong. . . . Two elements are inconsistent if, for any reason, they do not fit together. Cultural values, personal standards, or past experience may dictate that the two do not fit (Glass, 1968, pp. 788–789).

The psychology of Alfred Adler is often called *individual psychology* because it is based on the doctrine of the unity of the personality. "This name, which is so often misunderstood, is derived from the Latin word 'individium,' which literally means 'undivided,' 'indivisible'" (Dreikurs, 1953, p. 56). This discussion has illustrated by definition and theory the indivisibility, the unity, the consistency of the individual, of personality.

2. *Ibid.*

As this discussion has proceeded, I hope you have come to a conclusion and a confusion. The conclusion I hope you came to is that the individual, his personality, his self, must be a consistent whole as he sees himself. If he sees or feels inconsistent internally or about his behavior he will feel uncomfortable. To alleviate this discomfort he will act, mentally or behaviorally, to bring himself back into a self-perceived state of consistency.

As an example, a Democratic state official may find himself pulling for a Republican to win the presidential election. Although there is nothing necessarily illogical about a Democrat pulling for a particular Republican, the logic of his position has to do with the monies he expects the state to get if that Republican were president. On the other hand, he may feel uncomfortable as an honest person, he may feel inconsistent, and he will therefore have to find the reason to make his inconsistent behavior consistent for him.

Let us construct another example, using a key dissonance-reducing phrase, a phrase of a type often used by adolescents to make what they *want* to do consistent with what they think they *ought* to do. In counseling sessions the following often comes up: the young man says, in essence, "She's really a great girl. I like her. I'd like to make it with her. But I don't know whether she is that kind of girl. If she is, I'll try. If she isn't that kind of girl, or if I can't tell, I guess I shouldn't do anything. But I really like her. *I could even* love her." As the monologue continues, the young man can build his interest, dedication, and passion for the girl to the point where all his actions are justified in the name of love. Certainly the most noble and pure of youth in the heat of the moment, with love in his heart, cannot be held accountable if he oversteps some bounds. And the bounds of proper behavior for the youth may not be thought, by him, applicable if he is in love: Reason enough to be in love for an honorable young man who needs to be consistent in word and deed. "I could even love her" (if necessary).

There must be an infinite number of ways in which the objectively inconsistent and illogical can be construed by an individual as consistent and logical within his personality system. In like manner, what appears on the surface as logical and consistent may be inconsistent in the context of a person's goal. In many instances an adolescent will reject or avoid an opportunity for what would appear to be substantial personal-social recognition. His act makes no sense to someone who understands the societal reward system, how to get ahead. But it is entirely consistent and makes good sense to the adolescent whose personal goal is safety—not standing out, not being noticed, not receiving special recognition—comfortable, inconspicuous safety. As disjointed, irrelevant, and incomprehensible an individual's behavior, attitudes, and feelings may seem, we can only conclude that they are consistent within the unity of his personality.

Having expanded on the conclusion, the confusion persists. Consistency has been used in two ways: personality consistency as it exists within the individual at any one time, and consistency of the personality over time. It is more usual to refer to these two types of personality consistency as personality consistency and personality stability, respectively. In order to emphasize the position being taken here, that the same dynamic which influences consistency at one time also influences consistency (stability) over time, reference will continue to be made to "two types of personality consistency." The need for unity and consistency at any one time precludes great and continuous change over time, because changes over time demand inconsistencies and disunities at many places along the time span. Once an individual develops the schema of his self-image, world image, and personal goal (his lifestyle or personality), he will maintain it intact over time. To repeat:

> By the time a child is five years old his attitude to his environment is usually so fixed and mechanized that it proceeds in more or less the same direction for the rest of his life. His apperception of the external world remains the same (Adler, 1930, in Ansbacher and Ansbacher, 1956, p. 189).[3]

As in almost all issues in psychology there is dispute over these conclusions. Ample theory has been cited to show both the existence and the need for personality consistency at any one time and over time. Research does not exist to prove the unity of the personality at any one time—it would have to investigate the whole personality and all its parts. But there is research on aspects of personality consistency over time, and this is cited in the next section.

Research on Personality Consistency

The magnitude of difficulties in conducting and interpreting research on personality consistency over time, personality stability, is immense. There are two basic traditional approaches to doing this kind of research in which the question is the similarity or difference between ages on one or more personality variables. They are cross-sectional and longitudinal research.

In cross-sectional research, subject samples from more than one age or stage group are compared on the personality variable under investigation. If the age samples are comparable on other variables, such as sex, socioeconomic status, ethnicity, etc., the differences and direction of differences found between the age groups will be presumed to have a developmental function. That is, in interpreting the data, the investigator assumes that in specific basic aspects when the subjects in his sample were or will be the ages tested, they will be the same or very similar on these aspects. For example, if you were testing 15 and 20-year-olds using a cross-sectional design,

3. *Ibid.*

to conclude that the differences or similarities found between the age groups showed consistency or inconsistency of a developmental nature, you would have to assume that the 20-year-olds were like the 15-year-olds when they were themselves 15, and that the 15-year-olds will be like the 20-year-olds when they become 20. There are many variables (childrearing, economic situations, or world events) which might intervene to make this assumption false.

The other research strategy for looking at developmental change or continuity is the longitudinal design in which the same sample, same people, are retested at two or more ages. In this type of research it is possible to study the developmental interrelationships within the same individuals over time. Longitudinal studies are limited because they (1) are quite expensive to run, (2) obviously take a long time to conduct, (3) lose subjects from beginning to end, which interferes with the assumption of random sampling, (4) are affected by the national and world events peculiar to the time of the study, and (5) either have to give the same tests over and over or have to give different tests for age-appropriate reasons at different ages wherein test comparability is questionable (Kuhlen, 1952). Even with all the limitations, "where one is concerned with developmental processes through time, repeated testing in a longitudinal design is essential" (Holtzman et al., 1968, p. 132). Therefore this section will concentrate on longitudinal studies to explore the question of personality consistency into and from adolescence.

We will look first at some longitudinal studies in which the subjects were first tested or interviewed in childhood, or even infancy, and later reexamined in adolescence. Anderson (1960) concluded, from 5–7-year follow-up testing of all subjects who had been 4th to 12th graders in a Minnesota county, that intelligence measures were more important predictors of later adjustment than personality measures, which had little predictive validity. MacFarlane, Allen, and Honzik (1954) correlated behavior problems, such as sleep restlessness and food finickiness, with personality characteristics, such as shyness, dependency, and irritability, measured at various times between 21 months and 14 years. They found that the size of the correlations (the degree of relationship) varied greatly across ages, even between the closest ages tested.

Neilson (1948) asked judges to match personality sketches of 15 children, based on Shirley's famous observations of children until they were two years old, with independently developed sketches prepared from test and interview data taken when they were adolescents. The judges were able to match the early childhood and adolescent sketches at better-than-chance rate.

A number of studies hypothesized and found relationships between personality deviations or behavior problems in childhood and similar disturbances in adulthood (Bender, 1953; Eisenberg, 1956; Morris, 1956), despite therapeutic interventions in some instances. As in these clinical studies, which show the persistence of disturbed personality and behavior, Bandura and Walters (1963) show the persistence of antisocial childhood behavior into adolescent delinquent behavior, citing Glueck and Glueck (1950) and McCord, McCord, and Zola (1959).

Several studies indicate significant consistency between personality variables or patterns from early adolescence through to late adolescence or adulthood. Schoeppe and Havighurst (1952) reported that the degree of achievement on a number of the developmental tasks investigated were essentially determined by 13 years of age. Gardner and Moriarity (1968) pointed out that the patterning of psychological defenses at preadolescence were more fully developed than had been thought before and were similar to the patterning in a group of adults. Tuddenham (1959) was justifiably impressed with the stabilities of personality ratings he found in a 19-year follow-up study of subjects, who were then approximately 33 years old, from the adolescent growth study of the University of California's Institute of Human Development. Peck and Havighurst (1960) in the "Prairie City" study found high correlations between conscience development and emotional independence at age 10 and 16. Offer and Offer (1970) in a 7-year follow-up study of adolescent boys with average self-images found consistency in coping styles, problem areas and responses to the problems, and adherence to parental value systems.

Kagan and Moss (1962), authors of one of the most important and influential studies of this type, carried out on subjects from the Fels Research Institute's longitudinal population, came to the following conclusions, one of which was dramatic in its appearance in so many instances. A few behaviors exhibited during the 3 to 6 age period, and many of the behaviors exhibited by children from 6 to 10, predicted fairly well adult behaviors that theoretically would be related. Among the adult behaviors which were related to reasonably similar, or analogous, behaviors or behavioral tendencies in childhood were "passive withdrawal from stressful situations, dependency on family, ease-of-anger arousal, involvement in intellectual mastery, social interaction anxiety, sex-role identification, and pattern of sexual behavior" (p. 266).

The strongest influence, they found, on consistency was the appropriateness of an individual's behavior for his or her sex as defined by the culture.

> The individual's desire to mold his overt behavior in concordance with the culture's definition of sex-appropriate responses is a major determinant of the patterns of continuity and discontinuity in his development (Kagan and Moss, 1962, p. 269).

They go on to say that everyone has an idea of "the person he would like to be and the goal states he would like to command" (p. 271). The question of development of an "ideal self" is considered in the next section, whereas the personal goal has been discussed with reference to Adler earlier in this section. "It would appear that the desire to be an 'ideal male' or 'ideal female,' as defined by the individual, comprises an essential component of everyman's model" (Kagan and Moss, 1962, p. 271), and carries considerable weight in maintaining personality in a consistent pattern as the individual pursues his ideal self and personal goal.

In concluding this section, the difficulty remains in confirming the degree of personality continuity which the theorists affirm and which many of these studies indicate. Individuals may change their behaviors, attitudes, and values in many areas which are not central to their personality or lifestyle. If these behaviors, attitudes, and values are studied to test their consistency over time, because the investigator believes them central or basic, low but significant correlations may be disappointing. As Kohlberg notes: "Most theories of personality formation do not assume trait stability, however. They assume rather that personality undergoes radical transformations in development but that there is continuity in the individual's development through these transformations" (1969, p. 370).

It seems, with the enormous room for error in measurement and method, and the unique personality patterns and constellations under study, that significant relationships in group data clearly indicate the presence of extremely strong threads of personality consistency over time. Overall, the research with global personality characteristics shows a moderately high degree of consistency over time, whereas research focused on more specific traits shows little consistency. Almost by our definition of personality these should be the findings if personality is consistent at any one time and also continuously over time. We must agree with the conception of dynamic consistency as defined by Yarrow and Yarrow (1964), in which they point out that one would not expect a person at two different ages to exhibit exactly the same overt behavior and personality characteristics. Although this would produce high-level consistency data, it does not account for developmental transformations in which the new behaviors are dynamically related to earlier behavior patterns and functions. It is at this level of analysis that consistency is high.

Why Adolescent Personality Appears Inconsistent

Developmental and Social Reasons. To paraphrase, "extremism in the name of personal growth is a need, if not a right, of adolescents." The onset and growth in formal operations for many adolescents open new vistas for thought and behavior. Almost as a form of reality testing, adolescents try out their new thoughts and behaviors with friends, parents, and others to assess their reactions, as well as the adolescent's own reactions. In addition to the "reality-testing" function, the trying out of new hypotheses and potentials in thought and action can be very stimulating and just plain fun. In toto, as reality testing and an enjoyable facet of being an adolescent, this has been referred to earlier as an "experimenting" effect of the development of formal operations in adolescence.

You can ask yourself whether you felt a thrill, an excitement, when you "over-did" a behavior or emotion when you were an adolescent. Having been "crossed," or at least contradicted, by your parents, you got angry. As you stamped out of the room, during a momentary pause, you looked for some way of really showing your anger. Although it "wasn't like you," you slammed a door, kicked a wall, and threw a pillow. Or the first time you "lost in love"—which may have been when your favorite pop star married—you lay across your bed sobbing and sobbing and enjoying the tears. Maybe you remember stating and debating fiercely for a point or cause in which you believed at the time, but knew you wouldn't believe forever. It might have been when you told your doctor father you had decided to make pots, or your potter father you wanted to be a doctor. It might have been when you sat by the pool and expounded on the socialist state, or when you explained the justice and rationale of the domino theory to your anti-war friends. You may remember sitting up half the night with your best friend detailing your hopes and fears and very firmly saying what kind of person you were—it felt great to be able to lay this out clearly and definitely but you doubted much of what you were saying. Even if it wasn't like you, you knew you could try it—whatever it was. So you tried on a style, or position, or behavior, and even if it didn't fit, you enjoyed the act and the fact you could do it.

Much of the perceived inconsistency in adolescent behavior reflects the individual adolescent experimenting with the new potentialities of formal-operational development. However, as has been shown, not all adolescents develop formal operations.

There is a second major factor in the apparent inconsistency and lack of continuity in the personality of the adolescent. The adolescent starts to move from a limited area (home, immediate neighborhood, old friends) which he understands into the greater community which presents many tasks, roles, and situations which he does not understand. This will be discussed at greater length in the sections on Lewin and on the "situational element" in each of the life-task chapters. Suffice it to say, as the adolescent approaches new arenas—new schools, work experiences, new friends, dating, clubs, and organizations at school, church, in the community, and so on—he may not know how to behave. He may be unsure of what is expected of him, and how adequately he is able to perform in each of these arenas and specific situations.

As well-adjusted, competent, self-assured adults, we probably approach a new situation with some caution, attempting to gather relevant information so we know as much as possible of what to expect in the new situation. Regardless of our understanding of, and expectation for, the new situation, we enter it with some degree of confidence that we can adequately handle it. To put it another way, our behavior in all situations, whether new to us or not, has to be acceptable because we are, individually, what we are. With the sense of competence and self-assurance of normal, adjusted adults we take the position in all our undertakings that we are OK.

An adolescent embarking on and passing through the new situations and tasks that are presented to him does not know whether he is OK. He does not know whether the style he has used before will satisfy these new situations. He does not have the breadth of experience to feel confident that he can generalize style and understanding to the new tasks. Rather, he tries to find the appropriate style from modeling competent others he knows or has seen, even in movies or on television, and anticipating what he has seen them do or acting as they would in the same situation. In a concrete way, he tries on the behavior he senses as appropriate or most effective for the roles in which he finds himself.

To some extent when you observe a boy on his first date, you see him open the door as his older brother would, walk with the slouch or swagger of his entertainment or sports idol, criticize the movie with the verve of the Today Show's movie critic, and treat the waiter as his father does. His date may exude the purity of Rebecca of Sunnybrook Farm, carry herself like a Hepburn or Taylor or Raquel Welch, be as reticent and unsure as she feels, or as assertive as Bella Abzug. She may at times be like her mother, sister, friend, or idol. It is not that either of these adolescents loses himself or herself in the process. It is only that they do not know yet how they should, can, and will behave. In the process of fitting themselves into new roles they attempt to use available and preferred models to guide them until they can behave naturally and comfortably as themselves in these situations. And parents, teachers, and friends see them as inconsistent during the times the adolescent is experimenting.

It is important to remember that the choice of models and styles of coping the adolescent uses, even if transitory and unusual for him, will be in keeping with his personal goals and his personality. But it may be very difficult to determine this while observing bits of behavior rather than patterns of behavior.

We are saying here then that adolescent behavior and personality appear inconsistent when the adolescent is "experimenting" with new cognitions or new situations in order to find his attitudinal and behavioral style, i.e., that style which best fits his personality and moves him toward his personal goals.

Research-Method Reasons. In the section on research in personality consistency and continuity we have seen that longitudinal research investigating general, or broad, personality variables and patterns finds considerable continuity from childhood through adolescence into adulthood. We have also seen that there have been, for good reason, few complete and competent studies of this nature. Therefore most of the studies of consistency or change over time in adolescence have been cross-sectional. The results of these studies have reinforced the view of inconsistency and discontinuity—apparently unjustifiably so.

One research strategy, which is developing and being more widely used, speaks to this issue and controls the factors that put the findings of longitudinal and cross-sectional research at such variance. Before discussing this strategy, and in order to understand it, a few words about the meaning of "generation" are needed. In Chapter 2, generation was referred to in reference to parent and child generations. Approximately a 25-year age difference was posited between the parent and child generation. The ages of the members of the parent generation could cover a broad range, as could the ages of the members of the child generation, but the differences between their ages would remain constant. In this context a generation includes a broad age range of persons with a common attribute, i.e., parent or child, and for that matter obviously an individual may be a member of both generations.

Generation may refer also to groups with more general or presumed common attributes or attitudes which relate to their common age, whatever the range, and the commonalities in social history they hold by virtue of living at the same ages at the same points in time. There have been many recent uses of the term in this way, the prewar generation, postwar generation, the Sputnik generation, the "Now" generation, and even the "Pepsi" generation.

What is the range of age that constitutes a generation? Put another way, in research on personality and attitudes, when a difference between two age groups is found does it relate to differences emanating from differences in common social history (generational differences) or to differences resulting from maturation and additional experience (developmental differences)? What is the smallest age increment producing differences?

We would all expect, and indeed research has found, differences in many cognitive, behavioral, and attitudinal variables between 20-year-olds and 60-year-olds. Clearly some of these differences are generational, unless you believe that the 20-year-olds will not differ from the 60-year-olds when they become 60. So, too, some of these differences are developmental, unless you believe that the 20-year-olds will be the same at 60 as they are at 20. This is clear and understandable when we speak of 20-year-olds and 60-year-olds. But do these same types of differences exist between, say, 12 and 14-year-olds or 15 and 18-year-olds, and if so to what degree? This question prompted the previous question: what is the range of age that constitutes a generation?

In the course the author has taught on adolescent development the last few years, on a number of occasions a student has made a point about today's adolescents through reference to a younger sibling. The point has always been that the younger sibling and friends were different from the student or more extreme in some behavior or attitude than the student was when the student was the sibling's age or when the student was in my class. The differences between the students' ages and their siblings' ages were as little as two years and as much as eight years. This might indicate very informally that differences of the generational type exist between persons whose ages are even two years apart.

When referring to an age group, those persons born within a specified period of time, such as persons born in 1942 or persons born in 1955 to 1960, the term "cohort" is used. Cohort is a much more specific term than generation and can be operationally defined by year(s) of birth. The use of the term and concept cohort facilitates developmental research including the generational factor.

This brings us back to the new model for research into these issues which, though in a state of development, refinement, and controversy, holds much promise. The model, proposed by Schaie (1965), has as its goal to distinguish the contributions of cohort, chronological age, and time (year) of measurement in developmental research. The design is simply shown in Table 7.

There are three types of design within this schema. They are known as (1) the cohort-sequential design, which is formed by the cells that make up the horizontal parallelogram, (2) the time-sequential design, which is formed by the cells that make up the vertical parallelogram, and (3) the cross-sequential design, which is formed by the cells within the square. The elaborate technical aspects of these designs and their analyses will not be dealt with here. From Table 7 one sees that in this cohort-sequential design, one-year age cohorts are followed longitudinally, and that by commencing testing with cohorts on successive years, time of measurement effects can be controlled. Similarly there are advantages from each design over both simple cross-sectional and longitudinal designs.

Table 7. *Schema for Research Design According to Schaie's Trifactorial Model (Entries Are Ages). (From K. W. Schaie, "A General Model for the Study of Developmental Problems," Psychological Bulletin [64], 1965, pp. 92–107. Copyright 1965 by the American Psychological Association. Reprinted by permission.)*

Cohort (Year of Birth)	Time of Measurement						
	'72	'73	'74	'75	'76	'77	'78
1960			14				
1961			13	14			
1962	10	11	12	13	14		
1963		10	11	12	13	14	
1964			10	11	12	13	14
1965				10	11		
1966					10		

Wohlwill differentiated "between age, time and cohort effects in the following terms: Cohort effects represent systematic alterations in the shape or course of the developmental function, while time effects represent temporary variations or aberrations superimposed on the developmental function. Age effects, finally, are those embodied in the generalized developmental function as such, once cohort and/or time effects have been extracted" (1970, p. 173).

Baltes and Nesselroade (1972) utilized the rationale of Schaie's model in one-year longitudinal sequences with 5 cohorts of 1,249 adolescents, 12½ to 16½ years old, in a study of personality development. Using the High School Personality Questionnaire, composed of 14 personality trait factors, they found moderate stability overall, with some personality traits more stable than others, and a pattern in which subjects, with increasing age, exhibit slightly higher stability. The authors have interpreted stability in terms of "the stability of the environmental fields to which individuals are exposed during the time interval considered" (p. 254). Although there were many sex differences on traits, sex and cohort differences in trait stability were not pronounced. It can be concluded that, differentially, the personality traits tested show moderate stability across all cohorts. However, the differential stability of traits in cohorts, i.e., traits changing in different ways from one testing to the other in the various cohorts, imply that "the nature of adolescent trait change appears less dictated by age-related components than by the type of social change patterns which are setting the environmental milieu for adolescents of all ages over a given period of time" (p. 244).

Further, referring to social and anthropological interpretations of adolescence, "the authors feel that none of these theoretical propositions would have assumed that 1-year cohort differences would be of the magnitude reported" (Baltes and Nesselroade, 1972, p. 254). In fact, very few developmental researchers doing cross-sectional or longitudinal research would have assumed 1-year cohort differences of this, if any, magnitude. If the data collected at either the first or second testing were analyzed separately as cross-sectional data, conclusions would have been drawn showing great change and "developmental" patterns. Although "future endeavors aimed at more fine-grained analyses of the mechanisms involved in the developmental linkage of ontogenetic and historical change components" (Baltes and Nesselroade, 1972, p. 255) are needed badly, this study illustrates how the new research strategy may get at personality consistency, and how traditional cross-sectional results have maximized the potential for making adolescent personality appear inconsistent.

In a more recent study, Nesselroade and Baltes (1974) studied 1,849 students, ages 12½ to 17½, who were tested using three trait theory-oriented batteries of ability and personality measures in 1970, 1971, and 1972. They summarized their findings:

In the case of personality dimensions, time difference rather than cross-sectional (cohort) age differences dominated the picture. This finding delegates a lesser role to chronological age in the nature (direction, rate) of adolescent personality development than to the historical time period during which development occurs. . . . It was found, for instance, that all adolescents (largely independent of their age) showed a significant decrement in super-ego-strength, social-emotional anxiety, and achievement from 1970 to either 1971 and/or 1972 and an increase in independence during that same time interval.

With regard to sex difference, male and female adolescents differed on most personality dimensions in the expected directions. However, it was surprising that only a few significant sex by cohort and/or time interactions were obtained, suggesting that most of the sex differences had emerged prior to age 12. There was tentative evidence to indicate that, if further sex-role development occurred from 1970 to 1972 in the 12-6 to 17-6 age range, it was in the direction of increased sex differences.

Examination of various . . . personality stability coefficients indicated that females show higher average stability than males; that there are wide differences among dimensions in the magnitude of associated stabilities with some dimensions exhibiting trait-like features; that stability, by and large, increased with cohort/age; and that the 1971–1972 time period produced higher 1-year stabilities than the 1970–1971 span. These developmental differences in stability, then, were also related to historical time as much as they were to chronological age (Nesselroade and Baltes, 1974, pp. 69–70).

Table 8 shows the data collection and design for the Nesselroade and Baltes (1974) study. The most potent finding in this study, as described in the previous quotations, is that the major differences in personality were found, not between age groups and not between cohort groups, but between *time* of testing groups! In looking at the table, the differences were primarily found between the diagonals, i.e., all those tested in 1970 versus all those tested in 1971, 1971 versus 1972, and 1970 versus 1972. Very clearly the total environment, or specific and unknown events or forces in the environment, had the effect on this sample of adolescents of changing the nature of the pool of personality dimensions. That is, across ages there was a systematic change in certain personality dimensions from one year to the next, and one particular year, 1970–1971, produced more change than the other.

This finding is important, not only for its methodological implications, but because it shows the sensitivity of even personality dimensions, which are like, but broader than, personality traits, to historical time period effects, to "the times."

(In this book, the organization and logic have implied previously that this finding was the case. That is, the first half of the book is an explication of the principles, theoretical laws, if you will, of adolescence, while the last half of the

Table 8. *Short-Term Longitudinal Sequences for the Study of Adolescent Development: Data Collection and Design.*[a] *(Reprinted by permission of The Society for Research in Child Development, Inc., from J. R. Nesselroade and P. B. Baltes, "Adolescent Personality Development and Historical Change," Monographs of the Society for Research in Child Development [39], 1974, p. 12. © 1974 by Society for Research in Child Development, Inc. All rights reserved. Printed in the U.S.A.)*

Cohort	Sex	Age 13	14	15	16	17	18
1959	M	1972					
	F						
1958	M	1971	1972				
	F						
1957	M	1970	1971	1972			
	F						
1956	M		1970	1971	1972		
	F						
1955	M			1970	1971	1972	
	F						
1954	M				1970	1971	1972
	F						
1953	M					1970	1971
	F						
1952	M						1970
	F						

NOTE.—Entries represent times of observation (repeated measurement). Mean testing time (range ± 2 months) is January 1 of the year listed. The broken parallelogram indicates the data matrix used for main analyses reported.

[a] To estimate instrumentation and testing effects (internal validity), a set of randomly selected groups of cohorts 1954–1958 were observed for the first and only time in 1972. In addition, to estimate selective dropout effects (external validity), the core longitudinal sample was contrasted with the dropout sample at the first time of measurement (1970).

book attempts to show these principles in operation within particular time periods, within particular contexts, which are called the situational element.)

At the same time as making the important statements about historical time-period effects, Nesselroade and Baltes (1974) reinforced two other points made in this and the previous chapter. The first is that sex-role development as evidenced through consistent and explicable differences between the sexes "has emerged prior to age 12," and, if anything, becomes more marked during adolescence. The second is that even with the changes attributed to historical time effects, there is great and increasing stability in a number of personality dimensions during adolescence. Overall, ten personality dimensions, the stability coefficients for the years 1970–71, 1971–72, and 1970–72 are .56, .60, and .49 for males, and .60, .65, and .54 for females. Nesselroade and Baltes say, "the average magnitude (.57) is fairly high for personality dimensions. The general pattern is one of increasing stability with increasing age and decreasing stability as the time interval increases" (1974, p. 52).

The numbers illustrating the stability of personality over one and two-year periods in adolescence in conjunction with the findings of historical time effects on stability imply the following: as times change, differing pressures, preferences, freedoms, and restrictions exist and personality dimensions are amenable to change under such conditions; but, by and large, persons will retain a similar ranking relative to other persons on important personality dimensions. That is to say, in a time of high anxiety, the same, or many of the same, people who are highest on anxiety will also be highest on anxiety when the times are less anxious, when many persons exhibit less anxiety. We might say that the adolescent who was a wild extrovert in the mid-1960's, when adolescents in general were more outgoing, would also have been more extroverted than others in the silent 1950s, when he would have been more unusual.

The findings of this study indicate that there are no substantial cohort effects while there are many sex and time effects. This seems to mean, in our context, that the major determinations, adjustments, or assumptions of personality attributes have occurred prior to adolescence, with large sex differences. It further means that the time effects, the historical-environmental effects, have large, almost "across-the-board," effects on personality variables. The implication is that personality consistency over time is not put into question further by these findings. Rather, consistency over time, stability, exists for individuals in relative ranking but "quantity" or "amount" of a variable may alter as a result of time, as a result of "the times."

Adolescents seem, or have seemed, to change more than adults. We have said that there are physical and cognitive developmental reasons for the changes, if they existed, and for the apparent changes as they are viewed. It may be that, as much research shows and as this study begins to show, there is more consistency over time with age, over greater periods of time in adulthood than in adolescence. This may mean that adolescents having not yet come to terms with the wider world are more affected overall than adults.

Consistency: Situation Versus Trait

One aspect of the continuing controversy over the "consistency problem" has been viewed as the situational specificity versus trait-determined influence on behavior.

The question, in general, is, "Are people consistent from one situation to another on a particular personality trait which would support the trait approach if they were, or are people different from one situation to another because of the influence of specific situations on behavior?" Bem and Allen (1974) make the claim that individuals will only be consistent across situations on a particular trait if that trait is important to them (is an integral part of their personality). Therefore, Bem and Allen propose research designs using an ideographic, rather than nomothetic, approach.

To determine the importance and variability of traits among their subjects, they simply asked, "In general, how friendly are you?" and "How much do you vary from one situation to another in how friendly you are?" They found that individuals who said that they did not vary to any great degree from one situation to another did, in fact, vary less across situations than did individuals who said they did vary. And, interestingly enough, variability across situations was not related to self-rated degree of friendliness.

Although they do not take the consistency position rather than the situational position, but "believe in both propositions," their strategy and findings seem, to the author, to support the consistency argument. They say, "In short, if some of the people can be predicted some of the time from personality traits, then some of the people can be predicted some of the time from situational variables" (Bem and Allen, 1974, p. 517). We might say that in situations where a trait that is central to an individual is not central to the situation, the influence of the situation would be greater than the influence of the trait. Conversely, when a trait that is central to an individual is important in a situation, the trait influence would be greater than the situational influence on the exhibiting of the trait.

As this type of research grows it will be necessary to deal with the importance and meaning of situations to individuals in the same way that Bem and Allen have begun to deal with the importance and meaning of traits. Studies of consistency and stability of personality in adolescence will be initially, until research solutions are reached, confounded by the changing, developing meaning of situations for adolescents. We cannot expect that an adolescent in a new school will exhibit important traits to the same degree that he will when he gains a sense of his belongingness in that situation. A conscientious student may not reveal himself as generally conscientious until such time as he is given additional areas of personal responsibility. Do we expect people to be consistent in situations which are foreign to them, which they do not understand? They may have a consistent approach to unknown situations, but it need not be the same as their "normal" behavior. Adolescence, as the one stage past childhood where continuously new situations arise, must be studied with this in mind. An adolescent cannot be consistent in a situation that he does not understand—he cannot know how he could be consistent, be himself, in such a situation. Some good portion of adolescent anxiety and insecurity, as well as inconsistency, may arise when the adolescent does not know how to act—how he, himself, should act—in new and unfamiliar situations.

Before closing this chapter, an important definitional and cautionary note is necessary. At times theorists, and probably all of us, insert the concept and the term "self" in place of "personality." Personality as we have seen is the greater system, organization, set of characteristics—behavioral and attitudinal—which, in toto, is consistent at one time and over time and gives the individual his unique quality. Self is one aspect of personality. According to the Adlerian view we discussed, the lifestyle, or personality, is composed of at least the self-view, world view, and personal goals. Self as a phenomenon is composed of many facets also.

Personality consistency and continuity have been strongly presented and supported in this chapter. Personality, lifestyle, does not change dramatically from childhood to adolescence to adulthood, without therapeutic help or traumatic impetus. The self, in its many facets, may change in many ways, and certainly in adolescence may waiver. Change in self, or sense of self, is an important issue in adolescence and will be discussed in the chapter on Erikson and the "identity crisis," and the chapter on the life-task self.

Theories of
Adolescent Development

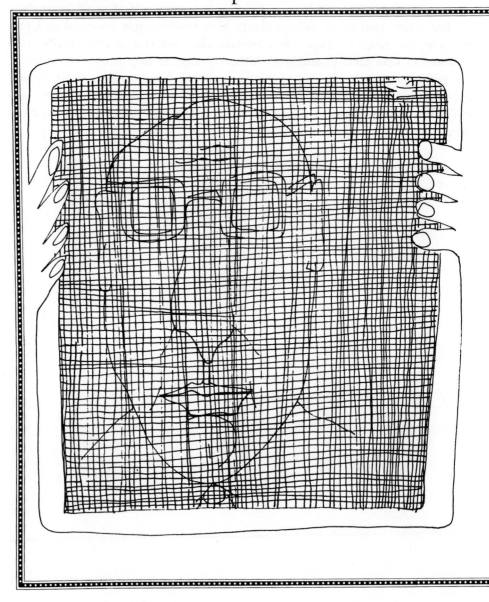

CHAPTER 7

Developmental and psychological theorists may refer to adolescence as it fits their theory or as it presents exceptions to their theory; others have developed theories about adolescence itself. From one context or another, theories and thoughts about adolescence have existed from the early Greeks to the present. By today the list of theories of adolescence is immense. In this chapter three theories are chosen for presentation because of their historical and current importance: personality theory (Freud), social-psychological theory (Lewin), and, most widely used today, the neoanalytic theory of Erikson. Although other and additional theorists might have been covered, an understanding of these three, in my opinion, subsumes the major trends in contemporary thinking about adolescence.

FREUD'S THEORY

Sigmund Freud (1933, 1953) concluded his hypothesized series of stages, in which the child passes through the "oral," "anal," "phallic," and "latency" stages, with the "genital" stage which commences with the onset of adolescence. In this stage, because of pubertal physiological changes, the instinctual balance presumed to prevail during the latency period is upset as the sexual impulses exert themselves, resulting in the "subordination of all sexual component-instincts under the primacy of the genital zone" (S. Freud, 1953, p. 337).

The primary tasks of adolescence, according to Freud and in Freudian language, include the subordination of pregenital part drives (the incomplete, immature childhood drives) to genital primacy, and the resolution of any Oedipal conflicts revived at this stage. The latter demands object loss (detach-

103

ment from parents and their internal representations) and object finding (establishment of mature heterosexual object relations). The primary tasks for the ego in adolescence are modification of the superego, establishment of an ego ideal and more ordered character structure, establishment of sexual identity, and identity formation. Basically, these tasks are necessitated, within the Freudian theory, by the physiological changes at adolescence which unleash the genital sexual instincts that need to be restrained by the person, both to hold himself or herself together and to remain acceptable to society.

Lidz, in describing the psychoanalytic view of adolescence, said, "It has been customary to examine the youth's oedipal transition and to seek to understand his adolescent problems largely as recrudescences of the oedipal difficulties. . . . The intense sexual drives of adolescents tend to follow earlier attachments in seeking outlets, and the oedipal configurations must be reworked and once again resolved" (1969, pp. 105–106). Of course this statement continues the emphasis on sex and the relationships between the sexes which is so central to Freudian theory. It also implies consistency of personality and coping styles from childhood to adolescence. The crux of the task is to "rework" relationships and to try again previously used methods for finding fulfillment as a result of and accounting for the new, revitalized sexuality.

The latency period, the years just prior to puberty and the genital stage, is a period of quietude in the sexual area according to Freud. It is the time when, in the juvenile and preadolescent eras, according to Sullivan, the child becomes social and an orientation toward living is established, norms of behavior in many settings and situations are internalized, and appropriate role behaviors are learned. It is the time for the development of what Sullivan calls a "chum" relationship.

From our discussions of cognitive, moral, and sex-role development we can see the latency period as a time of consolidation. It is the time during which the child "puts it together" concretely. He has the rudimentary capacities for understanding and functioning in his society. This period allows him to build on these capacities, these basic concrete perceptions, and to test them within his somewhat limited world. It is a period of intense but definite, because of the concrete-operational cognitions, socialization. The child can fairly clearly determine what is expected of him, in his various roles, in order to become a part of society. In this period he, again concretely, figures out how he personally is going to meet these expectations— how he is going to fit in.

The latency period is, then, a time during which little physical or cognitive change, as well as little situational or social change, occurs for the child. During this period, the child develops his basic stance and style, his understanding and manner of relating. With the onset of puberty he has to retest his stance and style with his new "powers" and in new settings and social situations. Within the

Freudian framework this need not be that upsetting—indeed, if the previously used techniques work well, it should not be.

However, what of the difficulty inherent in reworking the Oedipal conflicts? Chronologically the last time the Oedipal issue came up was about the time the child started school, i.e., moving out from home into a broader social sphere. It is an issue of power and attachment. The attachment theme is dominant. Who gets, do I, the source of warmth, nurturance, love? In the genital stage, at adolescence, the child again moves into a broader social arena. And again he must ask himself whether he is going to get the qualities of warmth and security he desires and from whom.

At both points in time when the Oedipal issue arises, the child has to look out for himself, his objects of love, and/or his sources of love, when change appears to jeopardize the strength of his attachments to the objects. He is called on to maintain such a source and because of either limited knowledge or limited confidence, he tries to hold on to what he has with the ferocity of a person clinging to the side of a cliff. As the adolescent desires love and support and sex, he or she is very apt to think of mother and/or father as the most likely sources. They have given it before, albeit in ways not wholly consistent with the adolescent's fantasies. But they have probably been the comforters, with hugs and kisses, and encouragers, "we love you, you can do it," and sex symbols of sorts, the only adult of the opposite sex the adolescent has ever seen live, in person, in the nude.

The adolescent can easily fantasize an attachment of a sexual nature with his or her parent(s). In terms of conjuring up an image, it is easier to do with a parent than with someone to whom you never have been, and might never be able to be, close. The fantasy itself may be anxiety provoking because in reality it is taboo. "A family that loves together, stays together" may be a compelling motto for an early adolescent who foresees having to find love outside his home.

The process of detaching oneself from parents (in the sense that identifications are loosened and you see yourself for the first time as an independent self rather than as a filial appendage), is referred to in Freudian jargon as "object loss." Similarly, acquiring new tender love attachments is "object finding." This may be harsh language, but the tension implicit in the "loss" of security and love from home and the need to "find" same as an independent person is clearly conveyed. This Freudian language and these concepts should not be taken literally, but they are helpful as descriptors of an adolescent's movement to independence and mature sexuality with the accompanying potential for distress and confusion.

Included in the primary tasks of adolescence according to Freud were those having to do with ego development. Referring to these tasks in the order they were presented earlier, many behaviors which are strictly forbidden in childhood are open, to some degree, to adolescents. It is incumbent on the adolescent, particularly in the sexual area, to modify the superego, to lessen the severity of the strictures he holds. As he develops a sense of who he would like to be, that is, as he establishes an ego ideal, he is able to modify his superego because he has a high standard set for himself which allows new thoughts and behaviors that he previously did not allow himself.

The ego must incorporate the altered limits and new abilities into a unity that is consistent. This unity must cover the area of morality and character, sense of sexual identity, and a total holistic formation of personal identity. The biological changes of the genital stage require redeveloping stability and order in character and identity.

Freud's importance in psychology and the psychology of adolescence cannot be underrated, even at a time when his followers and revisers, and other contemporary theorists, seem to hold sway. Freudian language, and particularly the Freudian emphasis on the sex drive, do not help the theory's acceptability today. However, the underlying notions in the material just presented continue to be important in understanding adolescents. If we expand motivation, as the neo-Freudians have, to include the full thrust of meanings that moving from childhood imply (physiological—strength, size, looks, and sex; social—all of the new situations), we see the adolescent asserting himself in many ways that are not necessarily sexual in nature.

Freud speaks then, if we accept this elaborated notion of motivation, of accepting one's new sexuality while becoming an increasingly independent individual, who must develop an identity, make new attachments, understand how societal rules apply at this new age level, and resolve the problem of wanting to remain close to one's family of origin while becoming personally more independent. In defining the developmental tasks, Havighurst acknowledged that Freud's insights were integrated into the tasks. Freud's descriptions of the dynamics of the individual adolescent's struggle with these changes remains valuable. That Freud's notions can continue to be modified to contemporary adolescence also speaks to their value.

LEWIN'S THEORY

In the future history of our psychological era there are two names which, I believe, will stand out above all others: those of Freud and of Lewin. Freud will be revered for his first unravelling of the complexities of the individual history, and Lewin for his first envisioning of the dynamic laws according to which individuals behave as they do to their contemporaneous environments. Freud, the clinician, and Lewin, the experimentalist, these are the two men who will always be remembered because of the fact that their contrasting but complementary insights first made of psychology a science which was applicable both to real individuals and to real society (Tolman, 1948, p. 4).

Kurt Lewin was not a psychologist or theorist who concentrated on adolescence. In order to demonstrate his basic theoretical construct, he included adolescence in his discussion. "The field-theoretical approach is intended to be a practical vehicle of research. As is true with any tool, its characteristics can be understood fully only by the use of it in actual research. Therefore, instead of stating general methodological principles in abstractum, I prefer to discuss the problem of adolescence and the definition of a social group as an illustration" (Lewin, 1939, p. 872). Lewin's illustration of his theory through adolescence provides a number of important insights. In order to understand the adolescence illustration, the theory in brief will be presented first.

Lewin called his theory "field theory," stating that "field theory is probably best characterized as a method: namely a method of analyzing causal relations and of building scientific constructs" (1951, p. 45). Lewin's field theory is very technical, with a scientific-mathematical orientation in which the total psychological field— the life space—can be represented in mathematical terms, involving topology theory and vectors. Topology, a branch of geometry, deals with spatial properties and logical derivations thereof without requiring assumptions of quantitative relationships (Cartwright, 1959, p. 59). Lewin (1936) felt that through the topological approach one could determine which events in a given life space are possible and which are not, and with the vector concept which events are more and which are less possible.

Field theory emphasizes a holistic-macro approach. Lewin saw behavior as a dynamic whole, not only the sum of its parts but different from the sum of its parts. Lewin felt that although both the whole and the parts are equally real, the whole has definite properties of its own. He concentrated his efforts on the dynamics of the whole and the interdependence of the parts.

A last general property of field theory is its emphasis on contemporaneity. Although Lewin did not neglect the import of personal history, where relevant, his primary interest was in the interdependence of forces of the present situation, in the dynamics of "contemporaneous properties."

The key to Lewin's theory is the concept of the life space, the psychological field in which behavior occurs. The life space represents "the person and his environment . . . as one constellation of interdependent factors" (Lewin, 1951, p. 240). The constellation that is the life space can be represented by a formula in which B (behavior) is an F (function) of the P (person) and his E (environment). P and E are interdependent variables, and E refers not to the physical environment but to the total psychological, internal and external, environment. Inasmuch as P and E together make up the $L\,Sp$ (life space), the formula is:

$$B = F\,(P, E) = F\,(L\,Sp).$$

Lewin graphically demonstrated the dynamics of the life space in two ways. He mapped the life space showing goals, barriers, etc., i.e., topological representation. He also attempted to show forces acting on a person causing movement toward or away from a goal.

Four directing principles of field-theory analysis have been summarized by Cartwright (1959): (1) only what is concrete can have effects, (2) every concrete aspect of a situation must be included, (3) in any given field, events are interdependent, and (4) only what is present in a situation can influence its outcome (contemporaneity).

One may become confused by Lewin's stress on "contemporaneity" when we have placed so much emphasis on consistency. The notions are not incompatible. In fact, Lewin's position reinforces the consistency argument. He is saying, in effect, that past events do not cause behaviors in the present situation. However, what the individual remembers from the past, the conclusions the individual drew from the past, the beliefs the individual therefore carries into a situation, are concrete aspects of that situation and may thereby affect that situation. An individual's personality, a stable set of characteristics and tendencies, is present in all situations for that person—it is the person's framework for determining life space, for determining what P and E are so that B occurs.

Transition to Unknowns

Lewin calls the period of adolescence a "period of transition," pointing to several ways of characterizing the nature of the transition. Figure 7 shows the clarity of the space of free movement for the child and for the adult as well as the difference in the number of activity regions available to each. The child has far fewer regions accessible to him than does the adult. Lewin says,

> The actual activity regions are represented. The accessible regions are blank; the inaccessible shaded. (a) The space of free movement of the *child* includes the regions 1–6 representing activities such as getting into the movies at children's rates, belonging to a boy's club, etc. The regions 7–35 are not accessible, representing activities such as driving a car, writing checks for purchases, political activities, performance of adults' occupations, etc. (b) The *adult* space of free movement is considerably wider, although it too is bounded by regions of activities inaccessible to the adult, such as shooting his enemy or entering activities beyond his social or intellectual capacity (represented by regions including 29–35). Some of the regions accessible to the child are not accessible to the adult, for instance, getting into the movies at children's rates, or doing things socially taboo for an adult which are permitted to the child (represented by regions 1 and 5).

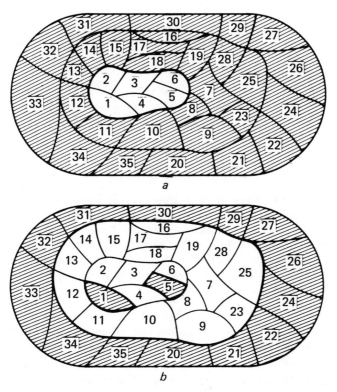

Figure 7. *Comparison of the Space of Free Movement of Child and Adult. (Reprinted by permission from K. Lewin, "Field theory and experiment in social psychology: Concepts and methods,"* American Journal of Sociology, *1939 [44], 868–897. Copyright © 1939. Published July, September, November, 1938; January, March, May, 1939. Composed and printed by the University of Chicago Press, Chicago, Illinois, U.S.A.)*

Figure 8 represents the space of free movement of the adolescent. This figure, or topological map, indicates the growth in the number of activity regions with adolescence and the closing of some regions which had been accessible to the child. The figure also shows the "unknown" quality of the life space of the adolescent. According to Lewin,

> The space of free movement is greatly increased, including many regions which previously have not been accessible to the child, for instance, freedom to smoke, returning home late, driving a car (regions 7–9, 11–13, ...). Certain regions accessible to the adult are clearly not accessible to the adolescent, such as voting (represented by regions 10 and 16). Certain regions accessible to the child have

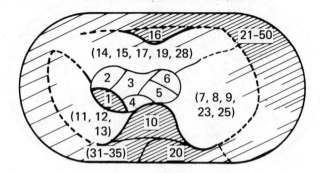

Figure 8. *The Space of Free Movement of the Adolescent as It Appears to Him. (Reprinted by permission from K. Lewin, "Field theory and experiment in social psychology: Concepts and methods,"* American Journal of Sociology, *1939 [44], 868–897. Copyright © 1939. Published July, September, November, 1938; January, March, May, 1939. Composed and printed by the University of Chicago Press, Chicago, Illinois, U.S.A.*

already become inaccessible, such as getting into the movies at children's rates, or behaving on too childish a level (region 1). The boundaries of these newly acquired portions of the space of free movement are only vaguely determined and in themselves generally less clearly and sharply differentiated than for an adult. In such cases the life-space of the adolescent seems to be full of possibilities and at the same time of uncertainties.

As a child, one knows what one is allowed and able to do, and what is prohibited by society or personal ability. An adult, too, understands with considerable definition where he is free and able and where not. The adolescent, moving from the limited activity regions of childhood, finds himself with great "unknowns."

A child belongs to a specific group, child, and probably a small neighborhood school or block group of friends. With adolescence he undergoes "a change in group belongingness." He is no longer, and does not want to be, considered a child, and he physically moves into new schools and neighborhoods coming in contact with, and becoming a part of, new groups. Change in group belonging is always important, to adults as well as adolescents. When, as with many or most adolescents, the change in group belongingness is major and has not been experienced before, it is extremely important.

Referring to Figure 8, Lewin states, "The uncertain character of the adolescent's behavior and his conflicts can partly be explained by the lack of cognitive clarity concerning the adult's world which he is going to enter" (1939, p. 876). The early adolescent may not know what the adolescent world holds as he enters it, much less the adult world.

Lewin points to another area which has been "known" with surety until adolescence brings change—one's own body. "More or less strange and new body experiences arise and make this part of the life space which is so close and vital to the individual strange and unknown" (1939, p. 876).

The time dimension of the life space also becomes an unknown region in adolescence. Until adolescence the child has not had to deal with time to any great degree. His day and his immediate future were set out for him and the more distant future was not even an issue for him. With adolescence, plans for one's activities and life become one's own responsibility. These plans must involve the present, immediate, and distant future in such a way as to satisfy one's own values and goals while still being realistic.

In this regard I will never forget my first day in high school when a staff person asked me to fill out a card showing the courses I wanted to take in my first two semesters. I had no idea what to do and did not particularly care. All I was concerned about was the location of my locker and who I would sit with at lunch. The spring term seemed so far off—as if no action now could affect what happened then.

Marginal Man

Lewin restates his opinion that the child group and the adult group are clearly defined, in contrast to the adolescent group, which is ill defined. The adolescent or youth culture may be seen as a functional attempt to give definition to this group. The issue of whether an adolescent subculture exists will be discussed later, and only slightly reduces the weight of Lewin's argument that "the adolescent does not wish to belong any longer to the children's group and, at the same time, knows that he is not readily accepted in the adult group. In this case he has a position similar to what is called in sociology the 'marginal man'" (1939, p. 881).

The marginal-man position of the adolescent is graphically illustrated in Figure 9. The marginal man is characterized as a person standing on the boundary between two groups, not belonging to either and uncertain about his belongingness. A person in this position, belonging partially to two groups but not fully to either, may exhibit symptoms of emotional instability and sensitivity. He may "tend to unbalanced behavior, either to boisterousness or shyness, exhibiting too much tension, and a frequent shift between extremes of contradictory behavior" (Lewin, 1939, p. 882). Descriptions about adolescents of this type are frequent, but seldom are they within a conceptual framework which explains the forces that cause them. Lewin's description of the marginal man is like the description of a frustrated man on an island in the middle of a lake trying to get the attention of someone on shore to prove he is worthy of being brought in:

(a) During *childhood* and *adulthood* the "adults" (A) and "children" (C) are viewed as relatively separated groups, the individual child (c^1, c^2) and the individual

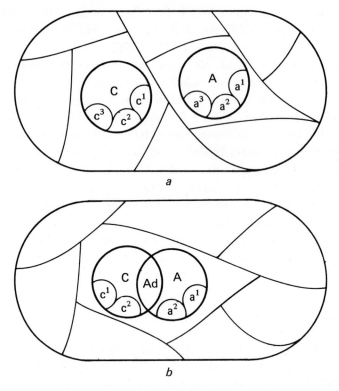

a

b

Figure 9. *The Adolescent as a Marginal Man. (Reprinted by permission from K. Lewin, "Field theory and experiment in social psychology: Concepts and methods,"* American Journal of Sociology, *1939 [44], 868–897. Copyright © 1939. Published July, September, November, 1938; January, March, May, 1939. Composed and printed by the University of Chicago Press, Chicago, Illinois, U.S.A.)*

adult (a^1, a^2) being sure of their belonging to their respective groups. (b) The *adolescent* belonging to a group (Ad) which can be viewed as an overlapping region of the children's (C) and the adults' (A) group belonging to both of them, or as standing between them, not belonging to either one.

Lewin likens the adolescent as a marginal man to the same marginal status of some "members of an underprivileged minority group" thereby preconceiving the "student as nigger" concept by almost thirty years.

Lewin's treatment of adolescent marginality was recently tested by Bamber (1973) with a sample of over 400 14 and 15-year-olds. His adolescent subjects seemed to see three developmental worlds, or circles, in which the overlap is slight between childhood and adolescence and considerable between adolescence and adulthood. Adult subjects, conversely, distinguished greater overlap between childhood and adolescence than between adolescence and adulthood. Adolescents saw their own age period and also adulthood as attractive, while adults did not find adolescence an attractive period. Although Lewin's approach was supported by this work, Bamber "concluded that Lewin's theory of the adolescent marginal man is an oversimplification" (1973, p. 5).

The theory may be too simple to catch the subtleties of the scope of positions adolescents may see and feel themselves to occupy in the many situations they confront. However, the theory and conception of the marginal man describes very well the amorphous world of adolescents as so many feel it. The self-description of this 15-year-old girl illustrates her feelings of marginality, in-betweenness:

> I'm a very impressionable romanticist, and an individualistic realist besides. I'm a mature young woman, and I'm still a little girl. I want so much, yet I quit too soon. I have so many dreams, but I forget to chase them. I'm afraid of people and even more afraid of myself. I love people, and sometimes I kinda like me (Bravler and Jacobs, 1974, p. 204).

Adolescent Extremism: Situational and Cognitive Components

The adolescent stands on the brink of, first, the adolescent, and then of the adult world surrounded by question marks, unknowns, and feeling like a marginal man— a true member of no respectable group. Some symptomatic behavior has been alluded to—how does a young person in this position feel and act? From Lewin's theory there is a logic and lawfulness to the adolescent's reactions to the overall situation of being an adolescent.

The adolescent is moving from one region to another. The very fact of movement and change, particularly the dramatic change at adolescence, makes him more flexible. Lewin says, "A period of radical change is naturally a period of greater plasticity" (1939, p. 878).

The adolescent's movement is to more or less cognitively unstructured regions or situations where he has marginal status, an inbetween-groups position, with baffling changes in his own body and needs. This position is untenable unless the adolescent actively copes with himself and his environment. He is unsure and confused. Of necessity he is open to new ideas and behaviors because he brings a limited, if already patterned, repertoire of coping mechanisms with him into adolescence.

If he sees his life space as described here, he will show "shyness, sensitivity, and aggressiveness, owing to unclearness and instability of ground," be in "more or less permanent conflict between the various attitudes, values, ideologies, and styles of living," and have "emotional tension resulting from these conflicts" (Lewin, 1939, p. 883). He will be ready to take extreme positions and behave outlandishly—this is one way of giving structure and definiteness to his hazy world and partially formed ideas. Extreme attitudes and actions are most likely to bring response from others. The response may not be positive but may help in convincing the adolescent of his existence, if not his value, and in clarifying the limits that are imposed which give structure to his field.

He will also be ready to shift his position radically. Trying to find his place in this unclear field, the adolescent may take an extreme position. Although holding this position may have value, as shown above, the adolescent prefers, as does anyone, to have social support for the position he holds. It may be that one strong friend is sufficient to support his maintaining a radical attitude for a long while. It may also be that he finds that he loses friends, or respect from important others, because of this attitude. It is then quite easy for him to change his position completely to regain lost support—to see if he feels greater belonging when holding this new position.

Great emphasis is placed by adolescents, and most American adults, on belonging to groups, specific groups. To the extent that a group, its leadership or leader, has specific ideals, values, and goals, whether they are overt or simply "understood," it holds great promise for fulfilling the adolescent's needs for structure and belonging. These seem to be "the reasons behind the readiness of the adolescent to follow anyone who offers a definite pattern of values" (Lewin, 1939, p. 881).

The insights conveyed by Lewin's theory to the understanding of the adolescent's tendency to take extreme positions, follow extremist leaders, and make radical shifts in attitude and behavior are immensely important. To show the generality of Lewin's theory consider the persons who assassinated or attempted to assassinate John Kennedy, Robert Kennedy, Martin Luther King, and George Wallace. Although much can be said about each assassin personally, without doubt they were each marginal men, and each one showed extreme behavior and affiliations before attempting the most extreme act of all. Obviously this is not to imply that marginality demands extremism. Rather, marginality makes extremism seem a viable personal option for some persons, their only way of seeking recognition, belonging, and structure in their lives. At times it must seem this way for some adolescents.

ERIKSON'S THEORY

Erik H. Erikson, as a psychoanalyst and cultural anthropologist, amplified Freud's stage theory, attributing the crisis at each stage to the demands of society. Theoretically, Erikson's stages meet the criteria for stage theories in that one must successfully cope with the crisis at one stage in order to be successful at the succeeding stages. However, one can pass through the stages on the negative side. "Resolution of each crisis in ensuing life-stages adds a new quality to the ego—either a positive or a negative dimension" (Stendler, 1964, p. 242).

The stages and areas of development that Erikson (1959) discusses in his most important monograph on the adolescent stage are presented in his worksheet, Table 9. The crucial stage for adolescents according to Erikson is V, Identity vs. Identity (or Role) Diffusion. In this section, the meaning of ego identity and the ego-identity stage as it relates to formal operations will be examined, as will Erikson's concept of the adolescent period as a psychosocial moratorium. Lastly, Erikson's stages will be considered in light of social-class differences.

Ego Identity and Formal Operations

In order to understand Erikson on adolescence, it is important to have a feel for "identity," or "ego identity," and identity formation, as well as how ego identity relates to self. I say "have a feel for" because the differences between these terms, as well as the definitions of the terms themselves, are fraught with subtle distinctions which demand an in-depth understanding of psychoanalytic theory and personology. This "feel for" the terms Erikson uses should be sufficient for our purposes.

Erikson (1959) says that identity relates both to an individual's *unique* development and his link with the *unique* values of the people he sees as *his* people. It is important, then, to an understanding of identity to show concern for an individual's personal uniqueness, emanating from his own personal history as he has perceived and constructed it, and his identification with a group to which he feels he belongs. Erikson's own words for defining identity and his uses of it might best illustrate the multiplicity of views and approaches to the term:

> It is this identity of something in the individual's care with an essential aspect of a group's inner coherence which is under consideration here: for the young individual must learn to be most himself where he means most to others—those others, to be sure, who have come to mean most to him. . . . At one time, then, it (identity) will appear to refer to a conscious *sense of individual identity*; at another to an unconscious striving for a *continuity of personal character*; at a third, as a criterion for the silent doings of *ego synthesis*; and, finally, as a maintenance of an inner *solidarity* with a group's ideals and identity (1959, p. 102).

The simplest definition of identity I know is from Diane Arbus, the late brilliant photographer: "We've all got an identity. You can't avoid it. It's what's left when you take everything else away" (Arbus, 1972, p. 10).

If one looks at ego as the subject and at self as the object, one sees the ego organizing the developing self or selves, and to some extent ego identity subsumes

Table 9. *Worksheet.* *(Reprinted by permission from E. Erikson, Identity and the Life Cycle,"* Psychological Issues [1], 1959, p. 166.)

	A Psychosocial Crises	B Radius of Significant Relations	C Related Elements of Social Order	D Psychosocial Modalities	E Psychosexual Stages
I	Trust vs. Mistrust	Maternal Person	Cosmic Order	To Get To Give in Return	Oral-Respiratory, Sensory-Kinesthetic (Incorporative Modes)
II	Autonomy vs. Shame, Doubt	Parental Persons	"Law and Order"	To Hold (On) To Let (Go)	Anal-Urethral, Muscular (Retentive-Elimina- tive)
III	Initiative vs. Guilt	Basic Family	Ideal Prototypes	To Make (= Going After) To "Make Like" (= playing)	Infantile-Genital, Locomotor (Intrusive, Inclusive)
IV	Industry vs. Inferiority	"Neighborhood," School	Technological Elements	To Make Things (= Completing) To Make Things Together	"Latency"

V	Identity and Repudiation vs. Identity Diffusion	Peer Groups and Outgroups; Models of Leadership	Ideological Perspectives	To Be Oneself (or Not to Be) To Share Being One-self	Puberty
VI	Intimacy and Solidarity vs. Isolation	Partners in Friendship, Sex, Competition, Cooperation	Patterns of Cooperation and Competition	To Lose and Find Oneself in Another	Genitality
VII	Generativity vs. Self-Absorption	Divided Labor and Shared Household	Currents of Education and Tradition	To Make Be To Take Care of	
VIII	Integrity vs. Despair	"Mankind" "My Kind"	Wisdom	To Be, through Having Been To Face Not Being	

self and ideal self. "Identity formation thus can be said to have a self-aspect, and an ego aspect" (Erikson, 1959, p. 149). Certainly self and ego either as felt or as conscious facets of the person exist in some way from infancy. Their developmnt is lifelong and thus identity formation should be considered lifelong. Whether we consider a teenager trying to incorporate new social experiences in high school into his sense of individual identity, or a retiree wrestling with what remains as uniquely *him* after years of feeling solidarity with his work group, the continuous process of identity formation and reformation or refining is evident. As one develops, "it is the ego's function to integrate the psychosexual and psychosocial aspects on a given level of development, and, at the same time, to integrate the relation of newly added identity elements with those already in existence" (1959, p. 115).

Identity, then, incorporates elements which are conscious and unconscious, consistent and changing, general-social and personal-constitutional, and which result from personal internal constructions of reality (effective defenses) as well as social fulfillment through effective coping (successful sublimations). Depending on the manner in which one is studying human behavior, one or more of the elements of identity are considered.

Erikson uses "the term *ego identity* to denote certain comphehensive gains which the individual, at the end of adolescence, must have derived from all of his preadult experience in order to be ready for the tasks of adulthood" (1959, p. 101). At times the adolescent's sense of identity, as internal and external pressures are exerted, becomes conscious, almost to the extreme. Working with himself, to accommodate his felt needs and the demands he perceives (and which may exist) from society, the adolescent may be forced face-to-face with himself, his identity. Very consciously, he attempts to piece it together to make some sense, that is consistent and integrated, of who he is. This total sense of integrated, consistent self or ego identity is what must be gained by the end of adolescence.

However, most of the time one's sense of identity is not conscious. Rather it is a felt sense of adequacy and continuity. "An increasing sense of identity, . . . is experienced preconsciously as a sense of psychosocial well-being" (1959, p. 118). This sense of identity, particularly as a feeling of greater or lesser well-being, is common to everyone at one time or another and is frequent in adolescents. It is hard to describe. Different people feel it in different ways. Many adolescents experience a somatic reaction of real intensity to their sense of well-being in particular situations or in expectation of experiences. Why the somatic reactions appear where they do is difficult to determine. In discussing this point I always tell my classes how, as an adolescent, I felt my qualms or confidence in the pit of my stomach. Although they have suggested some compelling, if not very complimentary, reasons why this prominent portion of my physique should carry such psychological importance, they can also remark on the diverse ways in which they physically felt their growing sense of identity in relation to specific situations.

The adolescent may feel intensely all the setbacks and gains in the process of identity formation. Erikson states, "the end of adolescence thus is the stage of an overt identity crisis" (1959, p. 113). As he explains the tasks of adolescence, he enumerates, in different language than mine, the life tasks which will be expanded on in the latter portions of this book. In the following quote one can see the emphasis on integrating and successfully coping with the life tasks of love and sex, work, friends and community, and the cosmos, in successfully dealing with one's self: "The integration now taking place in the form of ego identity is, . . . more than the sum of childhood identifications with the vicissitudes of the libido, with the aptitudes developed out of endowment, and with the opportunities offered in social roles. The sense of ego identity, then, is the accrued confidence that the inner sameness and continuity prepared in the past are matched by the sameness and continuity of one's meaning for others" (1959, p. 50).

Erikson's emphasis on identity crisis and identity formation in adolescence has been extremely influential. The question posed in this section is whether an identity crisis per se is a "normative crisis" for all adolescents, for some adolescents, or not at all. The question will be attacked from two points of view: (1) in terms of Erikson's "data" and its generalizability, and (2) by differentiating the social or life tasks separately and including the "identity crisis" in the life-task self in adolescence.

Erikson makes use primarily of three kinds of data in building and supporting his theory—biographic, pathographic, and theoretical. Although he has been associated with empirical study of "ordinary" individuals, much of his clinical experience has been with "mildly disturbed young people" who were Harvard students. He has been keenly interested in famous and unusual people. He says, "The autobiographies of extraordinary (and extraordinarily self-perceptive) individuals are a suggestive source of insight into the development of identity" (1959, p. 110). He himself is an extraordinarily self-perceptive person who worked through, with considerable time and psychic energy, his own identity crisis.

From my own experience, which is not to be compared with Erikson's in depth or time, but may be more than comparable in breadth and diversity of types of individuals, the identity crisis—in fact the issue of identity itself—appears minor to many adolescents. This is not to say that the internal dynamic of integrating new abilities and experiences at adolescence does not occur. But rather that this integration is not so difficult as to be disturbing—it falls within the realm of normal day-to-day coping with life's problems. Moreover the struggle that is the essence of the identity crisis as described by Erikson is cognitive. After all, one's self is cognitive; it is one's own mental construct.

It appears to me that the identity crisis of adolescence, as described by Erikson, is to a substantial degree a function of the development of formal operations at its higher levels. The identity crisis is thus a necessary reintegration of the social and physiological development of adolescence. The basic personal constructs about self and the world previously formulated in concrete terms are reinterpreted, that is, restated, to oneself, in the broader and more abstract schema of formal-operational thought. With this view of the identity crisis, it may be that only those persons who reach formal operations to a high degree would find it possible, and maybe necessary, to undergo the reintegration which might cause distress of a crisis nature.

The study cited in the chapter on cognitive development by Arlin (1975), which posits two parts to the formal-operations stage, problem solving and problem finding, may bear on this question. Could it be that the identity crisis in Erikson's sense is a function of problem finding, the second part of formal operations or the stage after formal operations? If that were the case, then only a small, advanced, and older number of adolescents would have identity crises. Does this in turn sound like the differentiation made by Keniston between adolescents and youth dealing with their own identity questions? "The adolescent is struggling to define who he is; the youth begins to sense who he is and thus to recognize the possibility of conflict and disparity between his emerging self-hood and his social order" (Keniston, 1975, p. 9). In this sense adolescents through high school may have a problem-solving struggle with their identity, whereas those who later pass through the period called "youth" find problems with their identity which may cause a crisis.

An identity crisis may be "normative" at Harvard, and among persons such as George Bernard Shaw, Martin Luther, and St. Augustine. But it is not so with the "common" man—with those persons who are not cognitively equipped and/or socially encouraged (note next section on the psychosocial moratorium) to examine themselves in depth in situations of great personal choice, with great potential for personal flexibility of action.

In the section on the life-task self, we will be able to see whether this position is defensible. If, as I hope and believe, it is, it becomes incumbent on educators, psychologists, and counselors to reexamine their use of the identity-crisis concept. It may be that many adolescents are being pushed into introspection when the nature of their problem or crisis is not as deep or extensive as the theory being applied by the educator or "helping" professional would imply.

This brings us to the second attempt to answer the question about the extensivity of the identity crisis. Obviously adolescents have problems. But many of the problems adolescents face are simply the result of ignorance in coping with one or more life tasks. With experience, and counseling—more probably from peers and parents than professionals—they can overcome the problem.

Some adolescents have problems which are neurotic in nature—the way of acting or thinking which they have employed as children is not amenable to functioning as an adolescent and then adult. Either they feel very discomforted by the discrepancy between their view of themselves and the world, how they should behave and see the discomfort as the problem, or else they act as they feel they should and find no approval or acceptance by peers, parents, or adults for their behavior. In either case, the personality, the pattern of behavior and thought, developed to find a place as a child is not suitable for an adolescent or adult. Distress ensues, and professional remediation is called for. This description of neurotic disturbance at adolescence with reference to the life tasks relates well to Erikson's description of the un-successful or negative side of the identity stage, identity diffusion. He says, "A state of acute identity diffusion usually becomes manifest at a time when the young individual finds himself exposed to a combination of experiences which demands his simultaneous commitment to *physical intimacy* (not by any means always overtly sexual), to decisive *occupational choice*, to energetic *competition*, and to *psychosocial self-definition*" (1959, p. 123).

Lastly there are those adolescents whose problems grow from, or are magnified by, the confusion they are having with who they are and what to be. They have an identity crisis. Proportionally, the fewest number of adolescents have problems that are strictly neurotic-personal; a greater number have identity problems sometime in adolescence (which may be when they are in their twenties); and the greatest num-ber of adolescents have difficulties and problems which are the result of limited knowl-edge and experience as they confront new situations. In this last group, unless they are psychologically unprepared, their personality is in conflict with the demands of the new situations, and they learn to cope and grow as a result. It is these problems which are normative. Most adolescents do not get to an identity crisis.

In the introduction to a section of their book of first-person accounts of aspects of their adolescence by college students, primarily from Harvard, Goethals and Klos presented their view of the prevalence of the identity crisis.

> It is our opinion that college students typically do not have a firm sense of identity and typically have not undergone an identity crisis. College students seem to be in the process of identity-seeking and seem to experience identity crisis toward the end of senior year or during their early postcollege experience. A male or female's dis-illusionment with first-job experience or graduate study, or a female's disappointment with being at home with small children is often the jolt that makes them ask what their education was for and why they are not as delighted with their lives as they had been led to believe they would be by parents and friends. . . .
>
> What students often interpret as an identity crisis in college may be more of a crisis of "instrumental competence" or a crisis of "interpersonal competence." A person who is unable to choose his course and then work or who is unable to get along with significant peers may be experiencing a problem of autonomy or of intimacy, in its adolescent sense (1970, p. 129).

In the sense of this discussion of identity and the identity crisis, Goethals and Klos' comments reinforce the notion of the importance of the life tasks. The crisis comes, or is felt to be a crisis, in college within the context of dealing with the life tasks in a transitory situation. The *real* crisis comes when the adolescent encounters the life tasks as an adult. Noncollege youth encounter the tasks earlier and directly from high school, without an extended period removed from home and work. Theodor Reik concluded, "Work and love—these are the basics. Without them there is neurosis." The "identity seeking" in college appears to be a searching for a footing that cannot easily come in a situation where work and love take on the unreal aura they do in American universities.

Psychosocial Moratorium

Erikson postulates adolescence as a second latency period which he views as a "psychosocial moratorium." The adolescent period has been described in many ways but "psychosocial moratorium" is particularly descriptive. Rather than seeing adolescence merely as a period between childhood and adulthood, Erikson's term described society in both a functional and active manner. Adolescence is a period in which society takes a relatively hands-off posture, allowing the adolescent to experiment behaviorally and attempt to find himself and his place. The hands-off posture refers to the laxness of society in enforcing rules on adolescents which apply to adults, as well as a general attitude that diminishes responsibility of adolescents relative to adults. The functional reason society takes this stance is to give adolescents time to mature and experience so that when they are ready to enter the adult world, especially the occupational world, they will be ready, emotionally and educationally.

Erikson's multicultural viewpoint is seen in this quote: "Societies offer, as individuals require, more or less sanctioned intermediary periods between childhood and adulthood, institutionalized psychosocial moratoria, during which a lasting pattern of 'inner identity' is scheduled for relative completion" (1959, p. 111). Differences exist between societies and between groups and individuals within societies in the length of the sanctioned intermediary periods, the psychosocial moratorium.

In our society, the life-task work is a good indicator of the length of the moratorium. It is presumed that when a person stops going to school he or she will take on a full-time career, in or out of the home. There are a great number of points at which individuals stop going to school: they may stop at some point before finishing high school (which includes persons even today in the U.S. who never begin high school); others finish high school, have some college, graduate from college, do some postgraduate study, or complete postgraduate study. The age range of these points is great—from eleven or twelve to the late twenties at least. Individual differences in ability, interest, and personal circumstance influence how much school a person will complete. However, social-class and ethnic-group memberships carry differences in opportunity for and probability of extent of schooling. As an example, statistics show that less than half of the Mexican-Americans in the Southwest complete high school, whereas over half of the middle and upper-middle-class Anglos go on to at least some college. The probabilities then show that, on the average, as leaving school indicates the end of the moratorium, one group will have three to four more years than the other to come to "relative completion" in development of "a lasting pattern of 'inner identity.'"

IDENTITY AND OTHER CRISES
AT ADOLESCENCE

Not everyone has an identity crisis during adolescence, or even young adulthood. We can only hypothesize as to why this is the case. It may be, as has been mentioned, that attainment of formal operations is related to the identity crisis. The identity crisis in this case would be, in a manner of speaking, a crisis of formal operations as applied to oneself.

It may be that dwelling on issues of personal identity is a luxury that comes with an extended psychosocial moratorium. Adolescents who are not pressed into the adult social and occupational world, most probably because they are pursuing courses of higher education, are granted the time, and to some degree are expected, to look closely at themselves and their future.

But not every adolescent by any means is granted this time, or possesses these capabilities. The majority of adolescents come to the end of their schooling with, at most, a high school diploma, and maybe even an additional technical training course of some type. They are pressed into the adult world. They need to find a job. They want to get married and move out of their parents' home. The question for psychologists, teachers, and counselors is whether these adolescents experience an identity crisis, and whether there is any need for them to do so.

It appears to this author that the identity crisis relates to cognitive development, the psychosocial moratorium, and related personal and social variables (such as IQ, SES, etc.), and does not occur for many adolescents, and need not.

In this chapter, the work of Freud and of Lewin has indicated a number of difficulties, of personal and social natures that all adolescents encounter. Overcoming these obstacles, meeting these life tasks, are sufficiently difficult that adolescents at all social, intellectual, and maturational levels may feel the crisis of meeting any one or many of them.

Adolescents may also, and this position is so infrequent in adolescent and psychology texts as almost to be heretical, successfully pass through adolescence, with all of the difficulties mentioned, without crisis. Could it be that many adolescents do cope well with this stage? Could it be that more could? I think this possible.

Might there be an element of delaying the inevitable in this position? That is also possible. Crises in the life tasks may occur throughout life. Does an early crisis preclude a later crisis? Is there an advantage to the early crisis? The theorists presented in this chapter have raised many questions while giving us their perspectives. Some of these questions, as they pertain to the adolescent stage, will be answered in the following chapters.

Adolescent Development
and the Life Tasks

CHAPTER 8

LIFE'S UNIFYING THEME

Adler said:

> For almost every child, adolescence means one thing above all else: he must prove he is no longer a child. . . . Very many of the expressions of adolescence are the outcome of the desire to show independence, equality with adults, and manhood or womanhood. The direction of these expressions will depend on the meaning which the child has attributed to being "grown-up" (Ansbacher and Ansbacher, 1956, p. 439).[1]

When Adler spoke of the "will to power," inferiority and superiority, and social interest, he was speaking, very simply, of the theme which unifies all human life—belonging—to belong, to fit in, to be one with one's fellow man. The notion of compensation refers to the degree to which the individual feels he has to be better than others to make up for the degree to which he feels he is not up to the level of others, i.e., "Someone with my faults and weaknesses must be stronger or nicer or smarter, etc., than the others in order to belong."

The Adlerian position is not too different, or may at least be seen as similar, to that of Erikson or Lewin or certainly Rogers, Maslow, and White. The point in all of these is one of fit and belonging. Fitting for yourself to be yourself, and fitting in with others, belonging with others.

If we take this conception of belonging, of knowing one's place and acting therefrom, as the central theme in life, we should start with the conceptions children have as they move from being children to being adolescents and then adults. When Adler speaks of the major task of adolescence, the major meaning of adolescence for the individual child, he says that the child must prove

1. From *The Individual Psychology of Alfred Adler: A Systematic Presentation in Selections from His Writings*, edited and annotated by Heinz L. Ansbacher, Ph.D., and Rowena R. Ansbacher, Ph.D. © 1956 by Basic Books, Inc., Publishers, New York.

127

that he is no longer a child. Adler is speaking to the problem of learning how to belong to new and larger groups, fitting into new situations, and fitting into new roles.

The conclusion on personality consistency and personality development led us to believe that a child as a unique individual comes into adolescence with certain conceptions of himself and the world, and how he must act in that world. He has had a notion of his body but changes occur in the body of this child as he goes through adolescence. These physical changes he has to cope with. For many children moving into adolescence, the ways in which they think about the world change. They move from concrete to formal operations. The child's ideas on what constitutes right and wrong and the inputs into decisions as to what is right and wrong also change in line with the moral development stages of Kohlberg.

Basically it is these changes which take place within the child, within the developing adolescent. These changes are not purely physical and internal, however. As the child grows into adolescence, as he changes and begins to look like an adolescent and more like an adult, more is expected of him, new ways of behaving, new situations are open to him, and he is expected to act at least like an adolescent and maybe like an adult.

We are brought, then, to the problem of the new adolescent attempting to maintain himself as a unique individual (that is, to hang on to the personality that he has developed as a child) in situations where it is not altogether appropriate still to be a child. At the same time we are expecting him still to be himself, to be the Joe, Tom, Sally, or Meg that he or she has always been and we are expecting; but he is trying to fit in, to belong, in these new groups with his new body and his new thoughts.

The general thrust of Erikson's position, which has been so heavily accepted by people who think about and work with adolescents, is that the overriding emphasis in adolescence is on finding oneself, establishing an identity. The thrust of Lewin's position is one of fitting into groups and, in a sense, seeing oneself and believing oneself to be a part of groups—eventually moving from the adolescent marginal man position to being a full-fledged adult. It is through a combination of personally, individually feeling that one belongs, with accurate perceptions that one does in fact belong, which is the thrust of adolescent development. And it would be remiss not to add the thrust of development throughtout the remainder of the life cycle.

SITUATIONS AND ROLES

With this somewhat strange conception of a changing yet consistent person seeking belonging in new age-graded groups, the next issue has to do with influences on the adolescent in the new situations and roles of adolescence. Lyle Larson, speaking about the variety of influences on the adolescent, and particularly the influence of family, has developed a hierarchical structure of social influence, which is shown in Figure 10. He says,

the basic assumptions of this approach to the structure and process of social influences are summarized below.

1. Role-learning is a lifelong process occurring throughout the positional career of the individual.
2. A hierarchical pattern of influence characterizes all levels of the influence posture (between and within).
3. The influence hierarchy is not static but dynamic and position-situations specific.
4. The influence hierarchy at any given point and time involves the articulation and theoretical integration of the variant structures, processes, and linkages within the influence posture (Larson, 1974, p. 319).

These assumptions and the hierarchical structure in Figure 10 are presented to show the complexity of influences on the individual adolescent. Larson refers to the hierarchical levels as filters. Filters 1–4 are characterized as the secondary system, while filters 5–7 are seen as of primary salience to the individual.

Filters 4–7, as more primary before late adolescence, are the influences about which the child had some awareness and which influenced him for better or worse through childhood. His family, friendship clique in his neighborhood, and his teachers (his reference sets, defined as the base of significant others whom the individual takes into account when he acts [Goodman, 1965]) relate to each other. The child fits in and relates to them. They influence the child and present to him, filter to him, the norms, values, and ideologies of his culture, subsulture, and time in history.

In order to understand the full scope of influences on the adolescent as he comes to assume new roles, meet new situations and the life tasks in adolescence, this hierarchical structure is useful. At the base of the structure "Attributes of individual as final filter—age and personality" is the individual with his own personality—his own approach to belonging. Influencing each individual are the primary groups with their many ways of relating and interrelating. At the secondary normative and behavioral system levels are the influences of social class, race, and education as they filter the dominant culture themes at any and each historical time. There are an incredible number of influences filtered differently at different times by different groups, communities, institutions, families, and *each* individual.

Within this framework, which shows the "big picture," it seems amazing that we know as much about human behavior as we do, still recognizing that we know as little as we do. Clearly, to predict an individual adolescent's successes and failures in the life tasks, his situations and roles, we must know the individual. To predict,

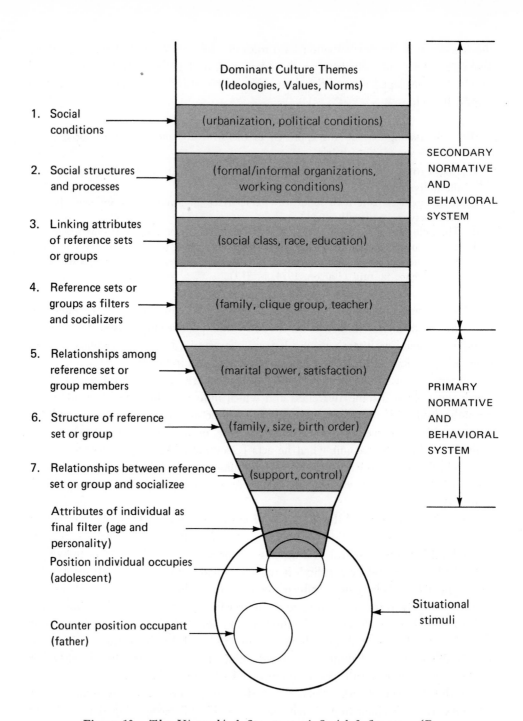

Figure 10. *The Hierarchical Structure of Social Influence. (Reprinted by permission from L. E. Larson, "An examination of the salience hierarchy during adolescence: The influence of the family,"* Adolescence, *1974 [9:35], 317–332.)*

discuss, and understand the problems of adolescents we must deal in probabilities and generalities resulting from empirical research, much of which has classified people according to groupings at the secondary levels.

Therefore, in the remainder of the text we will discuss adolescents, individuals, who are changing in specific ways in line with the developmental criteria, within certain influence groupings at the primary and secondary levels.

SUMMARY OF RELATIONSHIPS IN MACROSCOPIC PERSPECTIVE

Figure 11 sets forth a number of proposed relationships implying probabilities for cognitive development, and associated development and difficulty in adolescence, for persons growing up in differing societal and subcultural settings.

Most of the hypothesized relationships that follow have been suggested in previous chapters. The data cited in these chapters has led to these hypotheses. In time, as they are tested, their validity will be proven or disproven. However, at this point in time in this author's opinion there is justification for presenting the hypotheses, as they can assist in understanding adolescents in general and individually. Nonetheless, as a cautionary note the following "tentative conclusions" by Neimark are presented:

1. There is a stage of thinking beyond and different from concrete operations.
2. That stage is not universally attained by all individuals and may not be stable within an individual over time.
3. Differences among cultures in proportion of the society's members attaining the level of formal operations undoubtedly exist. . . .
4. Within-culture differences undoubtedly exist, also. . . .
5. Among individual-difference variables, general level of intelligence appears to be an important factor. It is probable that a minimal level of intelligence, in terms of mental age, is a prerequisite for the attainment of formal operational thought" (1975, pp. 585–586).

Before explaining the meaning of the relationships implied in Figure 11, an important caution must be restated. All the relationships hypothesized from this figure, as well as most relationships and research findings presented in this book, are based on probabilities determined from group data. Probabilities are a means for understanding group phenomena, for understanding the differences between, and the similarities within, age, class, and national groups. But the reader must be cautioned, we all must continuously remind ourselves, that in human psychology

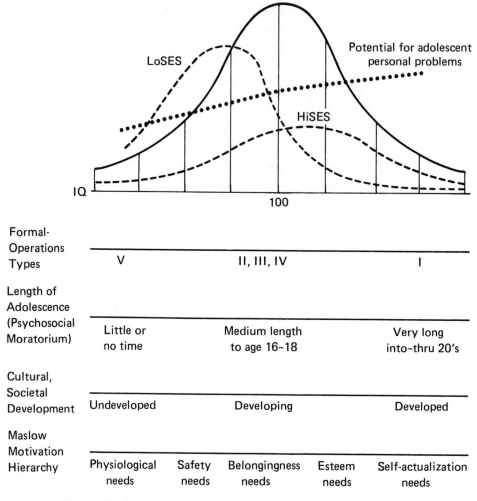

Figure 11. *Relationships in a Macroscopic Perspective.*

there are no perfect correlations, no 100 percent probabilities. The exceptions to the high probabilities, the generally low levels of probabilities and correlations in most studies, should remind us that one never knows an individual from the probabilities revealed in group data. If you find an adolescent to be as, or to put it in the vernacular, where, the theory predicts, you may presume that some of the probabilities have applied. But the probabilities, the predictor variables, did not cause the person to be as he is. The predictor variables tell us about types of persons. No matter how many predictor variables we may apply, no matter how high the probabilities, we may only know and understand an individual in all his uniqueness from knowing him.

Now back to Figure 11. Measured intelligence by definition constitutes a normal curve in the population from which it was derived. The lower and upper-SES groups together form the total population, but the lower-SES groups predominate at the middle to lower portions of the normal curve of IQ while the upper-SES groups predominate from the middle to upper portions of this curve. The five cognitive developmental types in adolescence (see chapter 3) relate to measured intelligence, although at this time the exact nature of the relationship is unknown. Suffice it to say that, in general, the higher an individual's IQ, eventually the more developed will be his formal operations and thus presumably formal operations will be used in more aspects of the individual's thought and life. Conversely, low-IQ persons will not develop formal operations to any extent. The line labeled "potential for adolescent personal problems" refers to the confusions, the affect, and behaviors associated with the development of formal operations. Adolescents at the low end of the IQ scale, with little or no formal operations, will probably have less personal upset than high-IQ, high-formal-operations adolescents who will find their new potentialities upsetting in many facets of their lives. This means also that the upsets related to development of formal operations, such as an identity crisis, should be more prevalent among high-SES adolescents than low-SES adolescents.

The duration of adolescence, although so often assumed to be very long in this country, varies greatly among individuals. We can equate, simply, the end of schooling and the undertaking of job and family responsibilities with the end of adolescence, the end of the psychosocial moratorium. A shorter adolescence is anticipated for persons of low IQ, SES, and little formal operations. They will be less likely to experience the personal upsets related to attaining formal operations, but they will be more likely to have social difficulties resulting from lower ability and poorer coping skills. They may be school drop-outs, un- or underemployed, have delinquency problems, and thus have a shorter moratorium period.

At the other end of the length of the adolescence scale are most probably persons of high intelligence, and more probably of higher social status, who have had the indulgence of the society through a long psychosocial moratorium. They have been given the time and access to the educational and cultural facilities of the society in order to develop themselves in many ways. They have had the time, the inputs from their surroundings, and the cognitive ability to see and meet the personal-emotional challenges of prolonged adolescence. In a sense, the long adolescence, the long period of time of the psychosocial moratorium, allows persons at this end of the scale to meet, anguish over, and then presumably conquer these challenges. Put another way, the long psychosocial moratorium serves to facilitate meeting these personal challenges, whether the person wants to or not.

A central thesis throughout this discussion has been that there exists great variety in the significance of, and necessity for, personal upset in adolescence. It is proposed here that theorists and researchers considering adolescence, and educators and counselors dealing with adolescents, respect these variations and not demand of all adolescents the upsets, thoughts, and feelings associated with high IQ, developed formal operations, and a long psychosocial moratorium. It is as if the unity of the theory about adolescents has the effect of many adolescents being forced through counseling, institutional structure, curriculum geared to presumed problems and an identity crisis, and the attitudes and understandings parents and teachers carry, into a mold or set that is not appropriate for them.

The scales labeled "cultural, societal development" and "Maslow Motivation Hierarchy" are included to place these relationships in a broader perspective and thereby to shed more light on these relationships within the American culture. The scale of cultural development ranges from the least-developed nations and "primitive" cultures to the most-developed, modern nations. The Maslow Hierarchy scale runs parallel to the societal-development scale.

Primitive cultures and very underdeveloped countries are primarily involved in satisfying the basic deficiency needs, the society providing sustenance and safety for its members and citizens, and individuals doing so for themselves. As countries develop, more persons within the country are satisfied in their basic deficiency needs and are able to confront the issues of belonging and love, and then move to the growth needs. In the most developed countries, the great majority of normal adjusted adolescents and adults are thought to be satisfied in their deficiency needs and to be dealing with their growth needs. The emphasis on esteem needs and, particularly, self-actualization needs is feasible to more persons in developed than in succeedingly less-developed cultures. As Nehru said, "Poetry and culture have little place in a poor man's hut; they are not meant for empty stomachs. It is an insult to talk of culture to people who have nothing to eat." The differences in the level of the hierarchy at which the majority of persons, or large groups of persons, are involved in the various societies relates also to the development of a middle and upper-middle class in the society; the more developed the society, the greater the middle class.

It is important to note that even in the most developed countries, such as the U.S., there is great variability in the needs levels among the population. "In our society [physiological] needs are seldom dominant, at least in the greatest segment of the population. That is to say, they are chronically gratified; few people fear starvation" (Cofer and Appley, 1964, p. 676). But many people are concerned about where their next meal is coming from, and fear for their personal safety. These persons, at the lowest socioeconomic levels of our society, are surely far less involved in personal issues of esteem and self-actualization.

Persons at the lowest socioeconomic levels of our society, in some ways like persons in underdeveloped societies, are shown to have probable deficits in three of the four influences on cognitive development: maturation of the nervous system, active experience, and environmental effects. The fourth influence, equilibration, is a dynamic which functions in all persons though on different contents and cognitive structures.

The maturation of the nervous system, and as we have seen related physiological maturation, influence and correlate with cognitive development. There is strong, but hotly debated, evidence that genetic influences account for much of the difference in intelligence scores between social classes. In addition, however, there are presumably nutritional and other bases, that may be subsumed under the physiological and safety needs, which influence cognitive development. Persons at the lowest socioeconomic levels of developed, as well as less developed, countries are more likely to have deficiencies in the physiological and safety needs and therefore to be deficient or slow in the maturation of the nervous system.

Active experience with a variety of stimuli is the second influence on cognitive development. One of the primary reasons for the Headstart program has been the wealth of material showing that low-SES children do not get this active involvement, particularly with some structure. This was evident in the many children who entered inner-city schools who were not able to count or discriminate among colors. Children in the lowest strata of undeveloped countries have active experience within a very limited range, with limited structure, and are also therefore deficient in experience by comparison.

Lastly, the lower strata in countries at any stage of development have more limited contact with the cultural and educational opportunities of the country, the variety of environments, and the breadth of language styles and nuances.

The three influences on cognitive development are less satisfied or available to persons at the lower socioeconomic levels of undeveloped and developed countries. This position, in general, is accepted as it applies to children. This discussion implies that the influences continue through adolescence and have a proportionally greater effect as they limit both potential for future activities and opportunity in wider environmental spheres.

Let us construct a hypothetical, but typical, lower-SES youth with measured intelligence in the normal range but below average. In early adolescence, say at 15, he has attained at best little formal operations, in limited areas of his experience. His high-school achievement is barely adequate and he is encountering greater academic difficulty as his courses introduce more abstract concepts, which seem vague and irrelevant to him. Some kids he knows are leaving school, some are trying to finish high school, a few are hoping to attend college. He would like to have more money to take out his girlfriend and would love to have a car. His father has had a variety of laboring and semi-skilled jobs and the son aspires to at least a skilled job, but he does not know what.

He has limited ability and has, fairly realistically, limited his occupational aspirations. He may have other cultural or artistic interests; he may have other dreams. But probably not. He has not been exposed to these areas; the concrete possibility has not presented itself. And he does not have the cognitive ability to explore possibilities for himself which do not have tangible referents in his reality.

The genetic-maturational, experiential, and environmental influences served to limit his cognitive development. His cognitive-developmental level and his intelligence limit both his potential and his aspirations. As he fulfills his potentials and aspirations, his experiences and environment will probably not expand to any great degree beyond what he has known. Therefore there will not be experiences or environmental influences to foment further cognitive development; there will be little "external disturbance" to upset his cognitive equilibrium.

This hypothetical case may look like the proverbial dead end for persons without ability and status. In some sense it is true, and change agents are being sought, although the person described does not necessarily feel unhappy with his life and situation. However, this section attempts to place these relationships in a macroscopic perspective.

There is an adaptive value to differential cognitive development across social classes and, similarly, across countries varying in development. No society, to this time, has been able to develop or accommodate all its members at the highest cognitive-developmental level. Quite simply, the cognitive abilities of formal operations are necessary for certain levels of occupations, such as those in higher management and government, professorial and the professions. Formal operations are not required to any degree for the majority of workers at lower bureaucratic jobs and semi-skilled and laboring jobs.

As societies develop, as the need for a middle and upper-middle class grows, the society needs more persons at higher cognitive levels. As the society develops, nutrition and education improve and facilitate cognitive development among at least certain portions of the populace.

On the individual level, there is a question as to whether persons with higher cognitive abilities and more education are satisfied with occupations and lifestyles which do not involve these abilities. That is to say, within a population those persons who are "overeducated" for the job they hold, with growth needs probably unfulfilled, would presumably be dissatisfied with their life situation. It is therefore more functional, both for the personal satisfaction of individuals and satisfaction of the ability needs of the society, that the cognitive ability "pool" within a society relates in size directly to the needs of the society at its stage of development.

Thus, taking a macroscopic view, the adaptive value of differential cognitive abilities within a society is understandable. However, this is in no way presented to deprecate the possibility of a society of the future in which deficiency needs are met and a happy and satisfied populace functions at the formal-operational level.

DEVELOPMENTAL CHANGE, BEING AN ADOLESCENT, BEING ONESELF

In 1872, Herbert Spencer wrote in his *Principles of Biology,* "Life is the continuous adjustment of internal relations to external relations." Cognitive development, moral development, sex-role development, personality development, and physical development are all internal changes. If the adolescent lived in a world that was otherwise unchanging, these internal, personal changes would demand adjustments. If the adolescent's view of himself, the world, his body, and right and wrong changed and nothing else around him changed—he went to the same school, played the same games with the same friends, was expected to function interpersonally and heterosexually as he had as a child, etc.—he would have difficulty adjusting to the internal changes. If the adolescent's internal relations did not change—there was no developmental change with adolescence—but he was asked to change schools and friends, to begin to decide on a vocation, to develop heterosexual attachments, to think of the meaning of life, and to begin a transition to adulthood, he would have difficulty adjusting to the external changes.

There is a logic to much of the external change in adolescence to conform with the internal change. Dating and expectations of more intimate heterosexual relations accompany physical changes and heterosexual interests. Adult-like strength and abilities occur as they are needed for work. Many laws allowing assumption of civic responsibility are timed to coincide with assumption of other responsibilities. Recognizing that society, too, is changing, it just may be doing so to become compatible with generalized changes among adolescents. At any one time, aspects of external demands may be out of step with internal changes occurring in large numbers of adolescents. But in the main it must be assumed that the changes society expects from adolescents during their adolescence are functional, assist them on the road to adulthood, and smooth the path.

This kind of analysis may satisfy the academician, but it does not make adolescence satisfying for the individual adolescent. He must cope with both internal and external changes, and still be himself, cope as he knows how for him. The remainder of this book explains how adolescents in general adjust their new internal relations to their new external situations. Generalization follows generalization. That is the best we can do, both because that is as far as the science has moved, and because *each* adolescent does it his own way. "No two human beings have made, or ever will make, exactly the same journey in life" (Sir Arthur Keith).

PART II
Life Tasks

Love and Sex

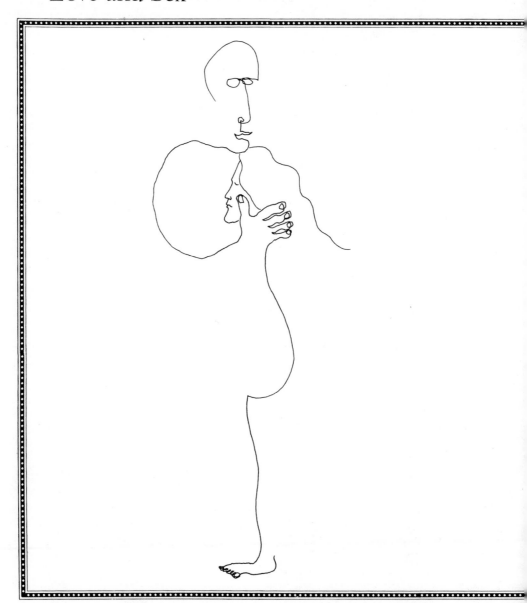

CHAPTER 9

THE TASK

Sex is a pleasure that has a biological function as well. At least sex *can* be a pleasure. But psychologically it has other meanings and offers other goals. It may serve many different personal psychological functions. Culturally and socially, sex may serve various functions and is limited and sanctioned in many ways. If a person is confident, content, and knowledgeable about himself, and has made his peace, with knowledge, with the expectations and demands of his society, sex is easy, natural, and a pleasure. Unfortunately many adolescents have serious doubts about themselves and ignorance of the physical and social facts and attitudes about sex. For them the whole question of sex is anything but easy, natural, or pleasurable.

Love is a word which describes a crucial and necessary quality of relationship. Love may be natural and pleasurable, although maintaining a love relationship is seldom easy. Love, like sex, may have a variety of meanings and functions psychologically and socially.

Sex and love have a place in the lives of children. They are quite separate in childhood and in a sense removed from the child's control. That is to say, the child is severely, and probably properly, limited in his contacts with others to first his family and neighbors. Should love and warmth not be forthcoming from his parents and family, he does without and holds dearly to whatever little passes for love and interest in him.

With adolescence, the young boy or girl is faced with new demands, new situations, in which the task of love and sex must be faced. A few points need to be made. First, life for anyone is fuller, brighter, and means more when one has a "loved" one or ones. The capacity or ability to love serves also to fill and broaden the potential for enjoying one's life. A person who is unable to love—for whatever psychological or social reason—is deficient. In the parlance of youth, love most commonly refers to romantic love. In its fullest meanings love refers to the selfless and complete relating of one person to another and must therefore include love of parent for child, and vice versa, love between friends, and may include love of God and country. However, as we are speaking of youth and the life task, love and sex, heterosexual love and sex will be our primary topic. The development of the capacity to love and to enjoy sex is the global task.

The old song said, "Love and marriage go together like a horse and carriage." In this day of the horseless carriage, love and marriage may constitute the romantic ideal but are not by any means the universal situation. Love and sex may go together, too, but not necessarily. It is said that this life task in adolescence involves the development of the ability to integrate love and sex. Ideally and traditionally, this may have been true. However, it would appear, as we examine the evolving attitudes and behaviors in this task, that three related capacities may be developed: the capacity to love, the capacity to function and enjoy oneself sexually, and the integrating aspect, the capacity to love someone with whom one enjoys sex. It seems that this separation allows for both the traditional and new forms of love and sex relationships accepted by adolescents of differing social-class levels, subcultures, and sexes.

The developmental tasks associated with each life task overlap and interrelate, as do the life tasks themselves. Many of the developmental tasks may be associated with the life task love and sex, particularly because an adolescent's sense of self, ethics, friends and community, all impinge on his ability, knowledge, and freedom in love and sex. However, the three primary developmental tasks relating to love and sex are achieving newer and more mature relations with agemates of both sexes, preparing for marriage and family life, and achieving emotional independence of parents and other adults.

It may be, if the reader is disenchanted with the institution of marriage and is doubtful about its future, that preparation for marriage and family life appears to be a false goal, or an unnecessary task. As Havighurst says, "Marriage is not becoming less important. . . . It is being readjusted, as an institution, to the changing economic and social and religious characteristics of the society" (1972, pp. 60–61). It is hard to imagine that the institution will change to the degree that maintenance of a long-term and secure heterosexual relationship and at least some responsibility for rearing children will not be a basic part of marriage.

It may also seem curious that achieving emotional independence of parents and other adults is presented as being essential in the love and sex task. Certainly it is important in the establishment and maintenance of friendships also. Without emotional independence, an adolescent or an adult cannot establish an active love relationship or a sexual relationship, or both, that is his own. When an adolescent who is emotionally dependent on one or both parents attempts to form a love relationship, he feels severe limitations because his source of support and fulfillment is not his partner but his parent. He must view his partner through his parents' eyes and evaluate his payoff from the relationship as much or more in terms of the quality of life at home as in terms of what he feels and experiences in the relationship. His behavior is reactive—a reaction to real or expected behavior from his parents, and the love relationship cannot be what it could be.

On the other hand, the adolescent who develops a sense of emotional independence from parents and other adults but who does not develop a close heterosexual relationship with an agemate feels very much that he has missed out and is at loose ends. Emotional independence from parents fosters the need for the interdependence of a love relationship.

This, then, is the task. What is the situation?

THE SITUATIONAL ELEMENT

Sex, like all human social behavior, becomes patterned. Individuals as members of groups of various sizes need to know what is expected of them culturally, how others will act, and how they should act. The expectations in an area of behavior, such as love and sex, are determined by many factors, historical and cultural, immediate and social, personal, psychological, and biological. These factors interact with and influence each other.

The pattern of approved, usual, or normal sexual behavior in adolescence in America at this time, or at any time, will be static or changing in conjunction with changes in the influencing factors. At this time the ages of biological development at adolescence are changing, as we have seen. This is surely not the sole cause of the current changes in behavior in this area, but may well be influential. So, too, the great social changes, the loosening of tradition, may be influencing changing attitudes and behaviors in the love and sex area. With these great changes, the adolescent finds himself in immediate social situations which would not have occurred before, or at so young an age. His adaptation to these new situations as part of his total life situation, in view of all the pressures he feels, becomes the current norm.

Much of what is called here "the situational element" is substantially obvious to anyone who has lived through it himself. As this part of the book is written primarily about adolescents in the U.S., the overall situation should be familiar to most American readers. The situation should also be highly similar to that in many developed Western nations, and to that among the middle and upper classes of many developing nations (albeit with specific cultural differences, such as, say, chaperoning in Latin cultures).

As a child comes through puberty and shows development in secondary sexual characteristics, and as this occurs among the child's peer group, the child is expected to show heterosexual interest. These expectations may be more or less obvious to the child as they are conveyed by his peers, older siblings, parents, as well as by the institutions in which he participates. As examples, the child who has been used to choosing one or two activities from a list made up for children of his age by his local YMCA, church, or park district will find that included in the "age twelve list" may be social dancing, boy-girl parties, or even a sex-education class. Birthday parties he attends may be boy-girl parties and the party games may be, for him, shockingly heterosexual. Parents may suggest that an agemate of the opposite sex be invited to accompany the family on an outing. From a much earlier age the child may have been teased about "loving" or being "loved" by an opposite-sex agemate. But now it has more meaning and may be less a tease than a compliment.

The child does not succumb to social pressure and express heterosexual interest. That is not what the preceding paragraph is meant to imply. Rather, depending on the individual child and his rate of physical development, interest in sex and sexual feelings develop naturally. The social pressures and opportunities for expression of heterosexual interest facilitate finding outlets for the interest and means for learning how to express this interest.

There are probably as many variations and themes in sexual patterns of behavior around the world as there are cultures and subcultures. What is considered natural in one culture for people of a certain age is considered unnatural in another. The following poem from Ghana, called "Life in Our Village," by Matei Markwei, shows both the patterning of sexual behavior which is inherent in all cultures and the behavior of adolescents which, in the last analysis, is inherent in mankind:

> In our little village
> When elders are around,
> Boys must not look at girls
> And girls must not look at boys
> Because the elders say
> That is not good.
>
> Even when night comes
> Boys must play separately,
> Girls must play separately.
> But humanity is weak
> So boys and girls meet.

The boys play hide and seek
And the girls play hide and seek.
The boys know where the girls hide
And the girls know where the boys hide—
So in their hide and seek,
Boys seek girls,
Girls seek boys.
And each to each sing
Songs of love.[1]

We probably can gain no greater consensus than to state that in one way or another, at one age or another, sex, meaning sexual intercourse, regardless of what comes before or after, is practiced in all viable societies! We may want to go a step further and state that with the onset of puberty it is acknowledged in all cultures, maybe through encouragement or maybe through discouragement, that the ability to have sexual intercourse and interest in relationships with the opposite sex develop and exist at this time. This book is intended to pertain primarily to American adolescents. Therefore, the behavior patterns relating to sex and love that exist in the various subcultures and regions of this country (and to some degree in other developed nations) will be explored herein.

It is probably appropriate that a chapter titled "Love and Sex" should exhibit the confusion that exists in the scientific literature, both theoretical and empirical, on this topic. It is probably appropriate that the love and sex life task, which is the most private of the social tasks (the self and existential life tasks being more personal), should be the least clearly defined and allow the least firm conclusion. It is probably appropriate that the love and sex life task which is lived at the most individual and personal level by the adolescent, although still being influenced at all levels in the hierarchy in the fullest historical and contemporary context, should be confusing. And most important, this life task probably raises the greatest confusion and anxiety for the adolescent as he lives it.

For one adolescent, love, sex, and the social structure, the system called dating, which allegedly supports these behaviors, may fit together comfortably and efficiently. For another adolescent, these behaviors may not mix well at all, to the extreme situation in which they may be almost mutually exclusive. That is, in the extreme case an adolescent may be dating for purely social, fun reasons; have sex in an illicit and separate portion of his life; and love, if he loves at all, an unattainable person at a distance. Certainly this extreme is not a comfortable, nor ideal, way of

1. Taken from *An African Treasury*, Articles/Essays/Stories/Poems by Black Africans, selected by Langston Hughes. © 1960 by Langston Hughes. Used by permission of Crown Publishers, Inc.

dealing with the life task. In the main, however, there is a merging of love and sex within a loosely established system. Due to the obvious overlap it is difficult to speak of the areas of love, sex, and the system for facilitating heterosexual interaction, the dating system, exclusively. It is more difficult to speak of them at the same time, which is why the remainder of this chapter will be broken down into separate sections on dating, sex, and love. But we cannot forget that the adolescent is living these all at the same time. He must, says Offer (1966/1967), "plow his own way through the maze of adult double standards" (p. 311) and wrestle with the direct and indirect influences from friends and family. As he balances these influences with his feelings, his experiences provide the testing ground for matching feelings and fantasies with the external world.

Dating

"Dating" is a system whereby the adolescent may enjoy himself in heterosexual relationships while learning his strengths, weaknesses, and coping strategies in social situations and whereby he determines his preferences for choice of qualities in a mate. By saying that dating is a system, we do not assume that this means only the formal aspects of the system. Dating is an evolution from previous courtship practices which were very formal, with clearly proscribed manners. The formal element in current dating practice still includes the boy calling the girl and asking her if she will accompany him, at a specific time, to a designated event, movie, party, meal, what have you. The girl accepts or rejects the offer and, if she accepts, a date has been made and they go on said date. But this is only the formal portion of the whole arena that allows boys and girls to be together.

This capsule statement of the dating system seems simple and sweet with obvious differences in the sex roles within the system. There probably are places in the U.S. where this simple-sweet system operates in the idealistic, encapsulated form just presented. But by and large this "system" is much more complex, not as sweet, and predicated on assumptions of sex differences and sex-role differences which may be seen either as changing, as having changed, or for that matter, never having existed.

Lynn (1962) postulates differences in the process whereby boys and girls acquire sex roles as well as basic differences in the nature of the sex roles acquired. Lynn assumes that initially males and females identify with their mother, while females continue this process throughout adolescence but males shift to other models (Lynn, 1959). The male turns to his father as model as well as receiving cues about the masculine role from the fuller cultural environment. This process requires generalizing, abstracting, and exploring the environment. Lynn believes that boys learn their sex role within a "problem-solving" context whereas girls learn their role as a "lesson" from their mother's behavior. Lynn asserts that males surpass females in problem-solving situations and that females are more receptive to and controlled by the standards of others. Lynn's position relates closely to that of Douvan, in which she concludes that

> . . . girls are consciously less concerned about developing independent controls than boys are. They are more likely to show an unquestioned identification with, and acceptance of parental regulation. They less often distinguish parents' standards from their own, and they do not view the parents' rules as external or inhibiting as often as boys do. . . . More important, perhaps as evidence of their involvement in building controls, we find that boys tend to conceive parental rules as distinctly external, and, to some extent, opposed to their own interests. . . . In answer to all of our questions about parental rules, boys repeatedly revealed greater differentiation between their own and their parents' standards. . . . Moreover, dependence on external standards is the norm for girls in adolescence (1960, p. 209).

The nature of the differences in sex role and corresponding character differences between the sexes would lead one to predict more divergence or greater latitude in the behaviors of the love and sex life task for boys than for girls. But we might also speculate that when changes in the parental standards occur, either explicitly or implicitly, a rapid change in the behaviors of female adolescents would occur. That is, in conjunction with the more explicit and open portrayal of heterosexual and purely sexual relationships in the media, and presumably more honest and open communication in the area of sexual experiences from parent to adolescent, particularly mother to adolescent girl, rather dramatic changes in the nature of heterosexual relations and sexual relations in adolescence should occur.

This change could occur as the reward system in our culture begins to lessen the discrepancy between the positive reward for the acquisition of the male role versus the female role. Brown (1958) summarized several studies which demonstrated that between 20 and 30 percent of the female sample, but only 2 to 4 percent of the male sample, had ever been aware of the desire to change their sex. Rudy (1968) tested ninth and tenth grade students in a New York metropolitan area and found support for the hypothesis that males view masculine traits as more desirable than females view female traits. Although the masculine role is still more highly rewarded in this culture, it is a more rigidly defined role, whereas the feminine role is more flexible. Heilbrun (1968) found support for this in his study, which showed that better adjustment for females is not correlated with maternal identification, whereas father identification in boys correlated with good adjustment.

The female adolescent, it would appear, is more likely to be socialized into a flexible role with a clearly identifiable model and a clearer set of standards for her behavior that is approved by her peers. The male role, on the other hand, although highly rewarded, is fairly specific and includes a greater number of potential models and more leeway for deviation from parental standards. Thus, for the male, although the potential for conflict with parents exists through deviation from their standards, and the potential for conflict exists with peers through deviation from peer standards, there also exists great potential for conflict with and punishment from the culture as a whole for deviation from the specific male role. For these reasons one would assume that males would experience a great deal of anxiety in the area of sexual behavior, which has been confirmed by Gray (1957) and Webb (1963).

In our culture today, with the continued assumption of changing sex roles propounded in all facets of the media, adolescent boys and girls must have a less precise view of how to proceed as males and females than did their adolescent predecessors. This is not to say that it will be more difficult to proceed through adolescence and life, as a human being, but merely that less clearly defined sex-role standards are of less assistance to the adolescent in the process of identity development. Moreover, the dating system cannot function as clearly, formally, simply, or sweetly, as in the past.

According to Staton (1963), there are developmental stages of heterosexual maturation into which the dating system fits. These are:

> (1) sexually undifferentiated behavior, (2) sexual segregation, (3) heterosexual group activities and associations, (4) tentative pairings-off within the group, (5) double dating, (6) dating numerous people for various types of activities, (7) going steady and becoming engaged, and (8) marriage (p. 397).

Hurlock (1967) presents a kind of stage theory to explain the transition from sex aversion in childhood to a merging of sex and love, as in marriage. The first stage in this progression, according to Hurlock, is the crush—a strong emotional attachment directed usually toward an older individual of the same or opposite sex. The crush is the beginning of the movement of affection outside the home and thus the beginning of independence. Crushes also function as a step in the development of a permanent identity through the process of choosing a person one would like, a person one would like to be like. Girls tend to form crushes earlier in keeping with their earlier maturation and earlier development of heterosexual interests, and to maintain them until boys of their own age group are ready for heterosexual relationships or until they develop relationships with older boys who are already interested.

According to Hurlock, the first heterosexual relationships with agemates are of the type often referred to as puppy love. These awkward, playful, sexually tinged, aggressive, short but intense affairs provide the adolescent with the opportunity to appraise members of the opposite sex, to begin to learn self-confidence in heterosexual relations, and to discern the patterns of heterosexual behavior which are positively sanctioned in his peer group.

The next stage is dating. This evolves through the stages mentioned by Staton, from heterosexual group activities, through pairing-off in a sort of informal dating structure, then double dating and dating numbers of people, and then the more intense relationship of going steady, which is Hurlock's following stage. Hurlock lists twelve functions which dating serves. These can be summarized by saying that dating allows the adolescent to learn about himself in relation to a member of the opposite sex, to clarify sex roles, to experience different situations, to experiment socially and sexually, to unromanticize some of his ideas about sex and love, and to have a good time socially. Lowrie (1951) identified three main theories concerning the functions of dating. The first, which is highly negative, sees dating as a competitive dalliance relationship participated in by people too young to be formally committed to marriage and therefore a system which produces thrill seeking and exploitative relationships. The second theory, which is very positive, sees dating as a system for fun maximization in which no commitment is involved except the expectation that it will be enjoyable for both parties. The third orientation, also favorable, sees dating as an educational experience in which the parties develop needed social skills.

An elaborated framework for analyzing dating was also delineated by Skipper and Nass (1966). In their analytic framework, they saw four functions of dating placed on a continuum from most instrumental to most expressive: (1) a form of recreation, (2) a form of socialization, (3) a means of establishing status and achievement, and (4) a form of courtship. They saw the functions of dating on this continuum as expressive of the primary motivation of the individual involved in the process of dating.

Moreover, Skipper and Nass developed the notion that there is a relationship between the place on a continuum from instrumental to expressive in the primary motivation for dating and the degree of involvement in dating and relationships themselves. This notion relates well to the conception of sex-role differences that has been developed. Males would be seen as more likely functioning in dating situations at the more instrumental side of the continuum, recreation and socialization, whereas females would be seen as functioning at the other, more expressive extreme, seeing dating as a form of courtship. Also, then, males would be less likely to be emotionally involved in the dating system, whereas females would be more involved.

With the exception of the refinement in the functions of dating determined by studies in the 1960's, Moss, Apolonio, and Jensen (1971) imply that there has been little recent research progress in understanding adolescent dating attitudes and behavior. By placing dating into a more global category of "the premarital dyad" which includes dating, courtship, and mate selection, the importance and overall function of dating is more readily understandable. However, in speaking primarily about adolescents through high school we are severely limited because most of the studies of dating, and particularly studies of courtship and mate selection, have been carried out at the college level.

It seems worthwhile to list the specific findings that describe the state of the art on adolescent dating attitudes and behaviors as they existed at the beginning of the 1960's and continued to exist at the beginning of the 1970's:

(1) the dating period covers approximately 6 to 8 years and generally begins between ages 14–16 for both sexes; (2) transition from single-sex associations to the courtship continuum has probably become less abrupt and traumatic as heterosexual relationships have begun developing earlier in life; (3) though the transitions may be easier, anxiety is still prevalent for many youths and is not limited to initial dating experiences; (4) conflict between adults and youth concerning dating and courtship probably peak somewhere along the continuum and then decline as adult norms seem to be more influential at the beginning and ending of the experience; (5) age appears to be the most influential factor in dating frequency, but the consequences of variation in age at initial dating and going steady seem unclear; (6) it appears that there are at least two kinds of going steady experiences (steady and steady dating) with differing antecedents and consequences which need to be examined; (7) the effects of varied dating patterns are unclear and await the evidence from more comprehensive and longitudinal studies. Though some support for the educational value of dating appeared, so did evidence associating early age of dating and accelerated heterosexual activity with early age of marriage and possibly greater marital stability (Moss, Apolonio, and Jensen, 1971, p. 1).

This listing, interestingly enough, includes some reference to conflict and anxiety as well as a framework for forecasting some lessening of conflict and anxiety. Having a "steady" and "going steady" imply an intensity to the relationship and a commitment to continue that relationship for some period of time in the "steady" situation, while implying also a greater future orientation in the going-steady situation. A growing acceptance of the steady relationship as well as the earlier commencement of heterosexual relationships and activities would seem to point to a greater acceptance of a natural meaning to the dating system. The conflicts and anxieties which dating arouses in the adolescent can easily be seen from the perspective of (1) the individual fighting for greater independence from his parental home, yet concurrently concerned with giving up some of that independence in a relationship; and (2) the adolescent approaching the whole area of sexual relations which, despite the frequent and constant demands for and offering of more and more sex education, seems to perpetuate itself as an area which holds the aura of the unknown no matter how much is known.

Husbands (1970) suggests that the American dating system is dysfunctional. Frequent turnover of partners and the superficial nature of the relationships, in always trying to make good impressions, lessens ability to learn about personalities, increases the tendency to be dissatisfied with partners, and reduces "opportunity to experience the open expression of sexual antagonisms" (p. 460).

If Husbands is referring to the dating system or the "dating" stage separately from the later stages of going steady and engagement, or without regard to the dating system as part of a total premarital dyad, which includes courtship and mate selection, he is probably fairly correct. It would appear that in dating, prior to the commitment implicit in going steady or engagement, a greater degree of dallying, fun for its own sake, and education in the broadest social skills, is occurring. Much of early going steady includes a tendency to break off the relationship if things are not going just the way you want them to and before you openly express yourself. However, it may be, as we look at the section on sexual relationships, that more future oriented, more open and intense relationships are developing among adolescents today, and that these orientations are active within dating.

Sex

Any young adult or adult in this country who can look back five, ten, twenty, or thirty years can see the tremendous increase in the visibility of sex as a topic for discussion and as entertainment in all the media and probably in day-to-day life as well. In this section, we will look at the change in attitudes of adolescents toward sex, assuming that all will agree that the changes in attitudes are dramatic. However, prominent researchers in the field of sexual behavior such as Packard (1970) and Simon and Gagnon (1970) seriously question whether there has been change in actual behavior in the sexual area in recent decades. A noted authority, Reiss (1966), stated:

> There is a widespread belief that much has changed in terms of premarital sex behavior in the last twenty to twenty-five years. However, the evidence from all the available major studies is in strong agreement that although attitudes have changed considerably during this period, that many areas of sexual behavior, such as premarital coital rates, have not . . . (pp. 125–126).

There is then some difference of opinion as to whether behavior change in premarital sex has occurred in the same way as attitude change. Conger (1973) states that there are proponents of both sides of the behavior question. Although most agree that attitudes and values are changing, particularly among higher SES, urban, and suburban youth, the data and opinions about sexual behavior changing is not agreed on or conclusive. Some observers maintain that the openness and freer attitudinal and verbal expression by today's teenagers is not matched in their sexual behavior—which is essentially the same as that of their parents at the same age.

Others feel that significant changes have occurred in sexual behavior as well as attitudes.

In 1964 Ehrmann, reviewing marital and nonmarital sexual-behavior research from the beginning of this century, took the position that a sexual revolution had occurred over these years in which both men and women, and particularly women, were participating much more in premarital coitus. Much of the dramatic change in frequency of premarital coitus seems to have occurred between the generations that would be today's adolescents' parents and grandparents or between the generations of today's adolescents' grandparents and great-grandparents. However, to determine the current situation regarding sexual behavior of adolescents, and the degree to which the change is felt as change, research over the last twenty years is probably most pertinent.

Research into premarital and adolescent sexual attitudes and behaviors since World War II includes a few studies at the high-school level and many more at the college level. For our purposes here, to understand the love and sex life task for adolescents through high school, the paucity of research in this life-task area on this age group demands that we infer to some degree from studies of older adolescents both in college and noncollege. In order to make these initial inferences, an analysis of the make-up of high-school-age youth into subgroups may be of assistance.

Thornburg (1974) divides adolescents into three distinct peer groups: high-school youth, noncollege youth, and college youth. In fact, in order to understand adolescents through high school, it is more accurate and more valuable to think of this age group in terms of three subgroups: (1) those who are not in school—a drop-out group (with whom we are not dealing specifically here), (2) those who are in high school but will not go on to college, and (3) those who are in high school and who will go on to college. Nationwide, approximately 50 percent of high-school graduates go on to college. Therefore, data representing college youth and noncollege youth, at post-high-school age, should represent the attitudes and behaviors of these two groups at the later, post-high-school, developmental stage. In inferring back to high-school age youth overall, therefore, where socioeconomic differences or educational-plan differences are not noted, we would expect the attitudes and behaviors for high-school-age youth to fall somewhere between those attitudes and behaviors noted for the college and noncollege youth. This conclusion must be tempered by the obvious fact that the attitudes and behaviors of younger adolescents as a group appear to be more conservative and less permissive than those of older adolescents, as a group.

In comparing college and noncollege youth, Thornburg summarized the findings of a 1969 CBS News survey titled "Generations Apart":

It could be said, as compared to college youth, that noncollege youths are (1) more conservative, (2) more prone to traditional values, (3) more religious, (4) more respectful, (5) more work-oriented, (6) more money-oriented, (7) more patriotic, (8) more concerned about moral living, (9) more conforming, (10) more accepting of the draft and war, (11) less activism-oriented, (12) less sympathetic with activists, (13) less drug-prone, and (14) less sexually permissive (1974, p. 336).

Although Thornburg concludes that noncollege youth are less sexually permissive than college youth, Kinsey's 1948 data showed that lower-class males, who were far more likely to be noncollege, had a much higher incidence of premarital intercouse than did college males. Of the drop-out group—males not going beyond grade school—50 percent had experienced intercourse by age 15 and three-quarters had experienced intercourse during adolescence, whereas only 10 percent of college-educated youth had experienced intercourse by age 15 and not even half had experienced intercourse throughout their adolescent years.

However, Reiss (1967) feels that a sampling bias in Kinsey's data might have accounted for much of the difference between socioeconomic and education-level groups, in that many of the lower-class interviews in Kinsey's sample were with prisoners, and Kinsey's upper-class sample was predominantly conservative. Reiss found no relationship between sexual permissiveness and socioeconomic status. Conger (1973) concludes that although, historically, working-class youth had the highest incidence of premarital intercourse at any given age, over the last two decades tremendous increases in intercourse among college-educated youth, and most particularly among the college-educated girls at the liberal elite coastal colleges, has lessened if not erased the social-class differences. The difference between male and female incidence rates is smallest at these "prestige" institutions, but there, as everywhere, the male incidence rate is still higher than the females'. However, the male-female difference is lessening dramatically.

Lastly, and this is important for inferring from college-age studies to high school students' attitudes and behaviors,

> . . . among college-educated persons, the higher incidence of premarital intercourse among today's youth, in comparison to those of their parents' generation, is accounted for largely by the age at which it occurs (as well as by its greater openness). After all, the incidence among college girls currently is no higher than it eventually was for their mothers, but among the latter it began at a later age, and usually only with their future spouses (estimates of the mean age of first coitus among contemporary American college students range from 19–22 for females, and 18–20 for males) (Conger, 1973, pp. 262–263).[2]

Cannon and Long, reviewing a great number of studies of premarital sexual behavior in the sixties, concluded that "apparently there is not a single major study

2. J. J. Conger, "Adolescence and Youth: Psychological Development in a Changing World." Harper & Row, New York, 1973.

that has been made in the late 60's that has found premarital coital rates that were the level of those found in the late 50's and early 60's" (1971, p. 40). Using comparable samples of college females for the years 1958 and 1968, Bell and Chaskes (1970) reported that, in a dating relationship, 10 percent of the girls in 1958 and 23 percent of the girls in 1968 had premarital coitus. The proportion of girls having premarital coitus while going steady moved from 15 percent in 1958 to 23 percent in 1968, and, while engaged, from 31 percent in 1958 to 39 percent in 1968. Bell and Chaskes also reported significant reductions at each dating level in guilt connected with coitus.

Christensen and Gregg (1970) studied changing sex norms in the U.S. and Scandinavia, using comparable samples from universities, in 1958 and 1968. Looking only at the data for the U.S. sample, which is referred to as the intermountain sample (a Mormon sample) and the Midwestern sample, we note a sizable increase in coitus rates from the 1958 and 1968 samples. In analyzing the comparisons of 1968 with 1958, Christensen and Gregg produced additional generalizations, which pertained to the American samples and to the Scandinavian (Danish) sample. In the American samples, the incidence of premarital coitus among males remained about the same, whereas the rate among females increased dramatically. This suggests a convergence between the sexes in behavior as well as attitudes. A sharp rise in premarital coitus for both sexes, slightly higher for females, in Denmark brought the rate of incidence to 95 percent with 100 percent of both sexes approving such behavior.

Table 10. *Percentages Expressing Approval of Premarital Coitus and Percentages with Premarital Coital Experience. (From K. L. Cannon and R. Long, "Premarital Behavior in the Sixties,"* Journal of Marriage and the Family, *February 1971, pp. 36–49. Copyright 1971 by National Council on Family Relations. Reprinted by permission.)*

	Intermountain		Midwestern	
	Males	Females	Males	Females
Approval of premarital coitus:				
1968	38.4	23.5	55.4	37.7
1958	23.3	2.9	46.7	17.4
Have premarital coital experience				
1968	36.5	32.4	50.2	34.3
1958	39.4	9.5	50.7	20.7

Analyzing their data in light of Reiss's (1969) conclusion that America is moving toward the traditional Scandinavian pattern of "permissiveness with affection," or permissiveness with commitment, Christensen and Gregg conclude that "while the emerging American pattern seems to be toward the traditional Danish norm of premarital sex justified by commitment, the emerging Danish pattern may be away from both commitment and restriction, toward free and promiscuous sex" (1970, p. 625). From this cross-cultural data one is inclined to conclude that as far as regional, religious, socioeconomic, etc., differences are concerned, Conger's (1973) statement about adolescent sexual attitudes and values pertains to behaviors also— "the differences between some subgroups of youth appear wider than those between youth in general and adults in general" (p. 254).

Influences on sex behavior. The influence of friends, parents, significant others, and reference groups on adolescent sexual behavior may be a key to particularizing that behavior, thus promoting greater subgroup differences. Mirande (1968), testing among college students the hypothesis that "the sexual behavior of an individual will tend to be a function of the reputation of his peer reference group, irrespective of the direction of influence" (p. 573), found a close relationship between the students' sexual behavior and that of his two best friends, his reference-group standard. This relationship is even more significant for females than for males, upperclassmen than lowerclassmen, and fraternity and sorority-affiliated students than non-affiliated students, leading the author to suggest that "they tend to seek our groups which reinforce their psychological predisposition . . ." (p. 577).

Kaats and Davis' (1970) data illustrates both the influence of significant others and reference groups or selective perception on the part of the adolescent. They found significant differences regarding the amount of disapproval the adolescents felt from close friends, fathers, brothers, and clergymen according to whether the adolescents were virgins or nonvirgins.

Reiss (1967) developed the proposition that "there is a general tendency for the individual to perceive of his parents' permissiveness as a low point on the permissive continuum and his peers' permissiveness as a high point, and to place himself somewhat closer to his peers, particularly to those he regards as his close friends" (p. 139). In Reiss's study, 66 percent of the students perceived their sexual standards to be similar to their parents' standards, 77 percent perceived their sexual standards to be similar to their peers', and 89 percent saw their standards as similar to those of their very close friends. Davis' (1970) study shows the interrelationship of personal attitudes and reference-group influence. He found that girls who believe sexual intercourse to be acceptable when in love, who were very much involved in a dating relationship, and who considered that several of their girlfriends had had sexual intercourse, were much more likely to have had sexual intercourse themselves (only 21 percent had not); whereas of those girls who did not believe that premarital sexual intercourse was acceptable even when a person is in love, were not involved in a dating relationship, and did not think that several of their girlfriends had had sexual intercourse, all were still virgins.

Reiss (1967) shows a clear relationship between the stage of a dating relationship, the degree of affection or commitment, and the level of intimacy that is acceptable to students. Approval of petting when there is no affection in the relationship is 34 percent for males and 18 percent for females, whereas when the couple is in love and possibly engaged the percent of males approving of petting is 83 percent and for females is approximately 78 percent. When there is no affection in the relationship, 21 percent of the males and 11 percent of the females approved full sexual relations, whereas when the couple was in love and possibly engaged, almost 50 percent of the males approved of full sexual relations and approximately 41 percent of the females approved.

This brings us, then, to two aspects of sexual attitudes and behaviors. This discussion has centered primarily on premarital intercourse, which may be seen as the culmination, or an endpoint of sexual relations as evidenced by the acceptable adolescent terminology for sexual intercourse—"going all the way." The directionality from more superficial or introductory sexual behaviors to "going all the way" is illustrated by Luckey and Nass (1969) in the following types of sexual behavior experienced by both adolescent males and females in roughly descending order from most to least frequent: light embracing or fond holding of hands, casual goodnight kissing, deep kissing, horizontal embrace with some petting but not undressed, petting of girl's breast area from outside her clothing, petting of girl's breast area without clothes intervening, petting below the waist of the girl under her clothing, petting below the waist of both boy and girl under clothing, nude embrace, coitus. The permissiveness with affection or commitment concept appears to pertain, particularly as it relates to college-age males and females in America today. Approximately 70 percent of college males having intercourse and 77 percent of college females having premarital sexual relations are doing so with only one partner with whom they are emotionally involved.

> These and similar findings suggest that the sexual behavior of a majority of today's middle class adolescents is consonant with their expressed values, and that for most youth of both sexes, but especially for girls, the element of emotional closeness and shared experience appears at least as important as the specifically sexual satisfaction involved (Conger, 1973, p. 261).[3]

If emotional involvement and affection are primary reasons for participating in premarital intercourse, it would seem logically to follow that an absence of affection

3. Conger, "Adolescence and Youth. . . .

would be the primary reason for not participating in more intimate heterosexual behavior. Ehrman (1962) rank ordered reasons for not going further, in all heterosexual behavior, with acquaintances, friends, and lovers, for both male and female adolescents. The major reasons for control, for not going further in heterosexual behavior, among the females in their relationships with acquaintances and friends, was that they were just not interested, had no desire, in sexual behavior with these categories of persons. On the other hand, moral restraint, morals, was the most important reason for control with lovers. The second most important reason for females not going further with lovers was fear, whereas the second most important reason for not going further with acquaintances and friends was morals. In contrast, the two most important reasons given by males for not going further in all heterosexual behavior were "date would not" and "respect for date."

Ethnic and SES differences. A number of the issues that have been discussed were investigated in a recent U.S. national probability sample survey of 15–19-year-old females by Kantner and Zelnik (1972), which revealed that premarital intercourse is beginning at an earlier age and is becoming more widespread. Ninety-two percent of the total sample, which included approximately 2,800 white and 1,400 black girls, had not been married. The likelihood that a never-married woman has experienced coitus rises from 14 percent at age 15 to 46 percent at age 19, and about twice as many never-married blacks have had intercourse as whites. The differences between blacks and whites were not striking with regard to frequency of intercourse and number of sexual partners. The permissiveness-with-affection concept seemed borne out in that sexually experienced female teenagers did appear to have relatively stable sexual relationships as judged by the number of partners, restricted in over half the cases to the man they intended to marry. Furthermore, they experienced coitus with relatively moderate frequency, two times or less in the month prior to the interview. Poverty status seemed to have an effect on black females under 18 who were more likely to have had premarital sexual experience than those who were less poor. This effect did not pertain to whites. Reiss (1968) also found that his data indicated that white youths are more restricted sexually than black youths, though Dreyer (1975) points out that the differences in sexual behavior are lessening between the races, as well as the sexes and classes.

Broderick (1965) studied 10–17-year-old black and white adolescents living in the same urban industrial community on an index of social heterosexuality which permitted interracial comparisons by sex and by age. He concluded that

> . . . the most striking difference between the races occurred during the preadolescent and pubescent ages of 10–13 years. At these ages, the white children showed the traditional pattern, with girls far more romantically oriented than boys, although at about the same level in terms of actual heterosexual interaction. Negro boys, however, showed none of the heterosexual reserve of the white boys. They did not

trail the Negro girls on any item except attitude toward marriage, and in fact, showed a higher level of heterosexual interaction at 12–13 than the girls did. This high level of preadolescent heterosexual interest and involvement among Negro boys, together with an apparent progressive disenchantment with marriage, suggests that the pattern of socio-sexual development in the Negro subculture may differ markedly from that of the dominant culture (p. 203).

To further confuse this pattern, a study by Harrison, Bennett, and Globe (1969), comparing premarital permissiveness among Mississippi and Virginia adolescents, indicated that both white and black adolescents in Mississippi tended to display more permissive attitudes, especially regarding the acceptability of premarital intercourse. These were rural groups, who are usually considered to be more conservative in the area of premarital sex. They found the permissiveness by affection or commitment rule to hold, in that affection was seen as a prime factor in determining acceptability of advanced sexual activity, and neither racial group appeared to be particularly promiscuous. Although blacks were considered to be somewhat more permissive by the authors, this difference fit the condition of permissiveness in engagement or love. Sex differences by race showed white females to be less permissive than white males, with no sex differences among blacks.

Vener, Stewart, and Hager (1972) looked for a revolution in sexual behavior to correspond with the revolution in adolescent attitudes toward premarital sexual permissiveness among middle-American boys and girls, and did not find it. They concluded that coital rates among adolescents have been essentially stable since World War II. However, more recently, Vener and Stewart (1974) resurveyed a representative school system (Community "B" in Table 11) in a white, nonmetropolitan community, ranging from upper working to upper-middle status levels, comparing them on measures of adolescent sexuality over a 3-year period, 1970–1973. Their findings are significant because they studied levels, or types, of sexual activity by sex and age. They take the position that statements about adolescents' sexual activity must detail the specific level of sexuality being considered in order to determine the nature of stability or change in these activities. Table 11 shows the levels of sexual activity by sex, comparing the 1970 and 1973 samples, in which only the last two levels show statistically significant percentage increases over these years. The value of looking at the levels is noted in that the 1973 replication shows again that males are not necessarily more sexually involved than females in that girls report slightly higher participation in the first four levels of sexual activity than do boys. But the bottom portion of Table 11 seems to indicate that the fifth level, light petting, is the level or stage at which the sex differences associated with the traditional double standard of morality emerge.

An analysis of incidence of involvement at different levels of sexuality by sex and age does not show marked, statistically significant, increases, but rather shows

Table 11. *Heterosexual Activity—By Community and by Sex. (From A. M. Vener and C. S. Stewart, "Adolescent Sexual Behavior in Middle America Revisited,"* Journal of Marriage and the Family, *November 1974, pp. 728–735. Copyright 1974 by National Council on Family Relations. Reprinted by permission.)*

Levels of Sexual Activity	Percentage of Students Who Have Participated in an Activity At Least Once		
	All Students 1970 (4220)	Community "B" 1970 (1909)	Community "B" 1973 (1976)
I. Held Hands	88.8	88.4	88.9
II. Held Arm Around or Been Held	83.2	82.6	83.1
III. Kissed or Been Kissed	80.0	79.0	80.5
IV. Necked (Prolonged Hugging and Kissing)	65.3	65.6	63.9
V. Light Petting (Feeling Above the Waist)	51.3	53.7	55.1
VI. Heavy Petting (Feeling Below the Waist)	37.5	39.6	43.2
VII. Gone All the Way (Coitus)	19.3	22.2	27.7
VIII. Coitus With Two or More Partners	9.0	10.2	14.0

Levels of Sexual Activity	Percentage of Students Who Have Participated in an Activity At Least Once			
	Boys		Girls	
	1970 (989)	1973 (937)	1970 (924)	1973 (1035)
I. Held Hands	87.6	88.5	89.2	89.4
II. Held Arm Around or Been Held	80.5	81.7	84.6	86.5
III. Kissed or Been Kissed	76.6	79.7	81.6	81.2
IV. Necked (Prolonged Hugging and Kissing)	63.3	63.7	67.8	64.1
V. Light Petting (Feeling Above the Waist)	57.3	59.0	49.7	51.4
VI. Heavy Petting (Feeling Below the Waist)	45.1	49.3	33.6	37.5
VII. Gone All the Way (Coitus)	27.8	33.4	16.1	22.4
VIII. Coitus With Two or More Partners	14.2	19.4	5.7	8.9

certain trends in that an increase of incidence at all levels of sexuality is apparent for boys between the ages of 13 to 15, whereas some increase occurs for girls at ages 15 and 17. Considering that the sample is entirely of in-school youth, Vener and Stewart find the coital rates at age 17 in 1973 "startling": both sexes report essentially the same rates of coitus—boys, 34 percent; girls, 35 percent. "This finding portends similarity of male-female coital incidence rates with increasing age" (p.732). These findings are consistent with those of Kantner and Zelnik's (1972) national-probability data, but are lower than those reported by Sorensen (1973). Sorensen found that 44 percent of the boys and 30 percent of the girls in the 13–15-year-old age group had experienced sexual intercourse at least once, whereas 33 percent of the boys and 17 percent of the girls in this age group in the Vener and Stewart study reported incidence of coitus.

Vener and Stewart's conclusions, which follow in length, seem to describe well the current situation in adolescent sexual behavior, the pervasiveness of this new morality or, at least, the relationship between sexuality and other areas of behavior.

Our 1970 findings, in comparison with Ramsey's (1943) and Kinsey's (1953) did not offer evidence that a long-run, major revolution in the sexual behavior of adolescents had occurred. However, the short-run comparison of the findings of our 1970 and 1973 studies, for both boys and girls, do show moderate degrees of significant increases at ages 14 and 15 at the more involved levels of sexuality (levels VI–VIII). This may or may not portend greater levels of sexuality over a longer time span, i.e., a decade. The possibility exists that this short-run increase may represent cyclical fluctuations and not adequately reflect the linear increase over an extended time period. Despite this precaution, we believe that the increases are indicative of an upward, long-run evolutionary change.

Apparently the relative permissiveness of sexual attitudes over the past several decades has provided the moral support base which enables the adolescent to engage in higher levels of sexuality. This new morality is not limited to sexuality, but extends to the broader context of youthful behavior. For example, higher correlations were found between sexuality and the use of illicit drugs, alcohol and cigarettes. Therefore increases between 1970 and 1973 should also be evidence for these activities. This was, in fact, the case. The rate of reported marijuana use in 1973 was more than 3 times that of 1970. Psychedelics increased in frequency over this 3-year period by more than 2½ times. Similarly, the use of hard drugs almost doubled and the consumption of liquor showed an increase from 25.2% in 1970 to 35.6% in 1973. Significant changes were also found in the reported consumption of amphetamines and beer as well as the use of wine and cigarettes.

The findings underscore our initial impression that substantial change has occurred in the social climate of the school system over the 3-year period. This was especially discernible in the high school. Dress and adornment were more casual. Less deference was shown to teachers and administrative officials. Much more informal student interaction both between and during class was observed. These apparent changes were not in the form of revolution where generational hostility and the rejection of traditional authority hold sway; but rather reflected increased egalitarianism and mutual respect.

As in the 1970 study, the current findings offer further support for the notion that boys are not necessarily more sexually active than are girls. In both studies, level V, light petting, represented the stage where the earliest manifestations of the traditional double standard appear. Differences attributable to the double standards between levels V–VIII are most clearly in evidence at the younger ages. However, the 1973 findings show that by the age of 17, the impact of the double standard seems to have become attenuated. Whereas in 1970, there was a difference of 11% between the reported coital incidence of boys and girls, in 1973 they reported equivalent percentages.

Both the 1970 and 1973 researches were purposively designed as middle American studies. Communities were selected because they were white, ranging from upper-working to upper-middle socioeconomic levels, and were not part of a large metropolitan complex. It was felt that these communities were representative of only about 40% of the country. We believed, therefore, that projections of the findings to the American population as a whole, should have been done with prudent forethought. The similarity of our findings with those of Kantner and Zelnik (1972), who employed a national probability sample of blacks and whites, lessens this precaution (Vener and Stewart, 1974, pp. 734–735).

We have seen in this section that sexual attitudes and particularly sexual behaviors are related to age, to sex, to religiosity, to political and social attitudes, to parental–peer–best-friend attitudes and perceptions, to societal mores and norms and their change, to personality, and to geographic differences; in fact, sexual attitudes and behaviors in adolescence are related to inputs and influences at all levels of the influence hierarchy. This makes for enormous individual variation within communities and between communities and geographic areas; and yet we see national trends in change to a more permissive standard.

Sex behavior and moral development. From a developmental point of view, it appears natural that with greater age adolescents would exhibit more sexual behavior, both for social reasons as they become more independent, and for biological reasons. There has also been a certain natural logic to the double standard in the pre-pill days, as well as social-class differences in sexual behavior. Younger marriages among lower socioeconomic groups, persons who would be classified as noncollege youth or drop-out youth, might be construed as justifying or allowing more premarital sexual activity. Allen and Martin (1971) report that 30 percent of the brides from families earning less than $3,000 per year go to the altar pregnant. The poor cannot afford birth-control devices or abortion, and free services are not being adequately delivered. The greater availability of birth-control devices, abortion, and sex education to the middle-American adolescent could in itself almost portend the diminution of the double standard among older middle-American adolescents as we have seen in the Vener and Stewart study. A recent study of the effects of moral development on the selection of premarital sexual standards carried out at eight coeducational colleges in the northeastern region of the U.S. adds a significant dimension to our understanding of adolescent sexual attitudes and behavior.

Jurich and Jurich (1974) related Kohlberg's moral-developmental levels, tested with two of Kohlberg's moral-dilemma situation stories and two additional stories dealing with premarital and marital sexual problems, to five classifications of premarital sexual standards, four of which had been developed by Reiss (1960) and a fifth which they found empirically in piloting their study. Reiss's four standards are (1) the traditional standard (supported by law and church, dictating total sexual abstinence before marriage); (2) the double standard (allowing males sex before marriage but total sexual abstinence for females); (3) the sexual-permissiveness-with-affection standard (linking the morality of premarital sex to the existence of love between the partners); and (4) the permissive-without-affection standard (a hedonistic standard dictating that sex is legitimate with anyone at any time under any circumstance). The fifth is the standard developed by Jurich and Jurich, labeled nonexploitive permissiveness without affection (which allows premarital sex, including intercourse, for both sexes without love, but includes the proviso that any sexual exploitation by either partner is immoral).

Jurich and Jurich found that subjects who held the nonexploitive permissiveness-without-affection standard were at the highest level of moral maturity among subjects in their sample. The subjects who held to the permissiveness-with-affection standard had moral maturity scores significantly lower than those with the non-exploitive permissiveness-without-affection standard, but their moral maturity scores were significantly higher than those of the subjects who held the other three standards. Those subjects who advocated the double standard, the traditional morality standard, and permissiveness-without-affection standard did not significantly differ on moral maturity among themselves.

Jurich and Jurich interpret their findings in terms of the level of intellectual sophistication necessary to function at any of the sexual standards. The permissiveness-without-affection standard can be applied to all people in all situations and requires no sense of reciprocity, no sense of a moral order. The traditional morality standard demands only a desire to maintain the social order but may otherwise be applied to everyone in all situations, and therefore may be seen as a slight progression in the level of moral and intellectual sophistication necessary. The double standard demands an evaluation of whether one's partner fits the moral order, is good or bad, and therefore whether the standard applies in the particular situation. If the female partner is deemed "bad," the relationship with her will take on the aura of the permissiveness-without-affection standard because this evaluation and decision must be made in each new relationship and situation. The double standard also requires a slightly more sophisticated moral and intellectual approach.

A major step in level of cognitive moral sophistication is needed to adhere to a permissiveness-with-affection standard. In this standard, the individual must evaluate for himself and his partner whether there is a mutuality of feelings which can be considered in both cases to be love. These determinations are very difficult and subtle, and require an empathy and honesty which is not always within the capability of even more intellectually sophisticated adolescents.

Allen and Martin (1971) show how the pursuit of this standard is often erroneously construed by adolescents in the quest for sexual gain and the confusion of love and sex. Allen and Martin say that love is taught to adolescents to be a marvelous thing that "happens." When it occurs, it brings unqualified happiness and changes sex, which until then was considered bad and forbidden, to a "good" and "right" thing. A developing adolescent begins to experience sexual desires and wants to express his sexuality. However, he has learned, and it is well known to him, that sexuality without love is bad. Therefore, the adolescent decides that his feeling of desire is naturally love and proceeds as if he were functioning on the permissiveness-with-affection standard. These evaluations are extremely difficult.

The adolescent has grave difficulties distinguishing between the state of being "in love" and the interpersonal feeling of "loving" another person. Adler pointed out that the healing power of love is severely limited if it exists at all. Were the healing process not much more difficult, "it would be enough to surround every problem child, the neurotic, the alcoholic, the sexual pervert, with love in order to cure him" (Ansbacher and Ansbacher, 1964, p. 306). Adolescents often look to "love" to heal their wounds, to cure their hurts. So little in the scientific literature investigates love in adolescence, yet so much of the literature of adolescence is about love. The popular music of adolescents is a training program in winning and losing in love. And the panacea for the problems of adolescents, to many, is to be "in love." To be "in love" means all is right with the world, the sky is blue and the clouds are pink, there is Muzak in the park, and nothing else matters. To "love" someone means an enduring and deep emotional regard for someone; it may rain, there may be troubles, life goes on, but through it all, the regard, the "love" prevails. Adolescent experimentation in the full bloom of being "in love" leads to the realistic ability to "love," mature love. Trying to determine whether applying the permissiveness-with-affection standard is built on "love" for the other person or on being "in love" is a sincere problem for the adolescent. And it is sometimes useful for immediate purposes not to make that distinction.

The highest level of sophistication is needed to pursue the nonexploitive permissiveness-without-affection standard. To function at this level, the person has to determine before engaging in premarital intercourse for each person in each situation whether there is any way in which participation is exploitive of the partner and thereby invalidates or makes the sexual act immoral. In terms of intellectual sophistication this standard requires the highest level and the most effort. One always has to ask the question why, both for himself and for his partner, and cannot rely on consensual love.

Phyllis was sixteen, and I was a freshman at college. Sexually she was much older than I. She was no virgin. She didn't do it for anybody as the rumor stated, but she had "been around." She just did it for love. It took her two dates to love me . . . (Goldburgh, 1965, p. 26).

As a conclusion and a caution Jurich and Jurich state,

. . . the present study has given evidence to support the description of the logical prerequisites required for the formulation of each sexual standard. This is not to say that one standard is more moral than another but that certain standards require a greater level of cognitive moral development. Although they are different in a systematic way, that does not imply that a sexual standard requiring a high level of cognitive moral development is better or more functional than a standard requiring a low level of moral maturity. In fact, a low level of moral development may be highly functional in a specific environment. Therefore, no value judgment shall be placed upon this ordering of premarital sexual standards (1974, p. 740).

The influences which have been seen to bear on sexual behavior in adolescence all filter through that final influence, the individual. In a longitudinal study of high-school students, Jessor and Jessor (1975) looked at personality variables and views of the environment (sense of control and beliefs related to the environment). They hypothesized that there would be differences between virgins and nonvirgins on these variables, and that the differences toward the nonvirgin position would be evidenced by virgins in the testing before they became nonvirgins. In fact, among the high-school students they found both a pattern of differences among the virgin and nonvirgin groups, and the pattern was found "to obtain prior to the initiation of sexual intercourse experience and to constitute therefore a transition-proneness that significantly predicts becoming a nonvirgin during the subsequent year" (p. 480).

The nonvirgins, and those high-school students who were more probably to become nonvirgins in the coming year, showed less conventional values and outlook in their immediate environment, parents and peers, which supports and facilitates the changing status. Moreover, "the nonvirgins—and those virgins who are going to have sexual experience in the subsequent year—consider independence important, have loosened their ties to the family in favor of greater reliance upon friends, and have also engaged more in other nonconventional or transitional behavior" (Jessor and Jessor, 1975, pp. 480–481). This study strongly supports the notion that the various influences on sexual behavior obtain through the attitudes and decisions of the individual adolescent.

Homosexual Experiences and Homosexuality

Maybe the last sentence on value judgments reminded me to say a few words about homosexuality in adolescence. Even though spokesmen for Gay Liberation feel that considering homosexuality "abnormal" is a harmful label to apply to "normal" people, homosexuality is not practiced nor accepted to the extent that it is usual, normal behavior. In a 1971 poll of sex preferences on campus, 1 percent of males and 2 percent of females gave their preferences as exclusively "same sex." Ninety-three and 91 percent of the males and females, respectively, gave "opposite sex only" responses. Six percent of the males and 7 percent of the females indicated that they preferred either sex, although they had leanings in one direction or the other in almost all cases. In the same survey, one-third of the college men revealed that they had had a homosexual experience in which orgasm was obtained by themselves or their partner (Homosexuality, *Playboy*, 1971).

Homosexual experiences in adolescence are not infrequent, yet they are not the norm. These experiences are not "abnormal." They may provoke crises in cases where adolescents worry that they will become homosexuals, but for the vast majority of adolescents the crisis as well as the homosexuality passes.

As Kiell (1964) noted, in general, homosexual activities in adolescence are normal with elements of experimentation and represent single or short-time occurrences with little or no long-term psychological effect. In fact, he says, rather than forecasting homosexuality in later life, homosexual activities in adolescence are usually not present in the life histories of adult homosexuals.

A vast array of psychological, social, and physical factors are hypothesized by different theorists to influence or cause homosexuality. Most of this theorizing weights childhood and early childhood heaviest in determining future homosexual tendencies. Although adolescence may be a particularly difficult period for the adolescent who does become a practicing homosexual in adulthood, homosexuality is not truly developed in adolescence.

Homosexual experiences in adolescence are within the domain of this book. To understand their occurrence, two factors seem crucial: (1) the intensity of, and need for, the same-sex friendship group as a support and base from which to move into the greater adolescent, heterosexual social world; and (2) the influence of cognitive development to formal operations with its extensions of possibilities for thinking about oneself, i.e., "maybe I am homosexual," "this is a way to act that can also be considered."

Even from Otto Fenichel's (1945) psychoanalytic perspective, the strong social component in these behaviors is apparent. He says that homosexual gatherings are preferred by many as a social outlet to avoid the excitement and temptation of the other sex. However, the sexual component asserts itself within these groups, too.

In arguing against a hereditary explanation of homosexuality, Adler points out the frequency and normalcy of homosexual experiences which are almost forced in some settings:

An argument against the hereditary view of homosexuality is the frequent occurrence of noncompulsive homosexuality, that is, casual homosexual experiences, in childhood, in boarding schools, on long journeys as in the case of sailors, or in the life of soldiers and of prisoners (Ansbacher and Ansbacher, 1956, p. 425).[4]

In settings that the adolescent devises and in others over which he has little control, i.e., same-sex settings of longer duration, homosexual experiences may occur. For the teacher, parent, or even the adolescent, without denying the self-questioning that may occur at the time (although the experience may be the result of the questioning rather than the opposite, I think), we may tell the adolescent, "This is nothing to worry about." And the worry, if it occurs for the homosexual, should not be about the label "abnormal" itself, but about the long-range effects of behaving in a way which is negatively sanctioned by our society (no matter how unjustly), as well as the effects of limiting one's potential for heterosexual life and having a family with children.

An example of the view that homosexuality in adult males emanates from childhood perceptions, experiences, and conclusions is seen in the following early recollections of adult male homosexuals. Although these recollections were gathered in my psychotherapy practice and may not be representative of the life views of "well-adjusted" adult homosexuals, they also show that early on these patients found, or gave themselves, reasons for avoiding the opposite sex. One young man said his earliest recollection, at age 5 or 6, was:

I was lying on the floor and made a caustic remark, and she [mother] kicked me in the crotch. It hurt—but she apologized. It was an enraged kick—but she immediately became soft.

Another said that at age 4:

Mother was cleaning the house. I picked a thing off the floor. I went to blow into it. I thought it was a balloon. She was furious and hollered. It seemed like a long time, on and on. I couldn't understand how, over a balloon, but I knew there was more to it. Now I know it was a prophylactic. Whenever they are mentioned I think of this (Manaster and King, 1973, p. 29).

4. From *The Individual Psychology of Alfred Adler: A Systematic Presentation in Selections from His Writings,* edited and annotated by Heinz L. Ansbacher, Ph.D., and Rowena R. Ansbacher, Ph.D. © 1956 by Basic Books, Inc., Publishers, New York.

Homosexuality does present problems, such as avoidance, as these recollections imply, but it appears to be under individual influence. It originates in childhood, although, obviously, it is evidenced later. Homosexual activities in adolescence are not of this nature.

In saying "not to worry" the pervasiveness of the notion of the normalcy of homosexuality in adolescence is illustrated in the following quote from the auto-biography of Kenneth Clark, the guide and author of the television series *Civilization*:

> And here I must make a confession that psychologists and advanced educationalists will regard as shameful. I have never felt the faintest inclination to homosexuality. I realize that it is natural for young people to form emotional and sometimes physical attachments to members of their own sex, partly out of fear of the unknown, partly from the structure of our educational system. For some reason I never did so. I was not one of those plump and pretty boys who attract the attention of their elders, and I never fell in love with my contemporaries. I do not think this can be explained by emotional poverty or lack of vitality, but by the fact that my premature devotion to the girls was so strong as to fill my fantasy-world and leave no room for homosexual attachments (Clark, 1974, p. 73).[5]

Possibly the adolescent who feels no homosexual interest should also be cautioned "not to worry."

SUMMARY

The life task love and sex brings together the full scope of influences on the individual in an area that is extremely personal. We have seen that the pressures to conform to expectations of parents and peers interact in this area, yet the adolescent chooses carefully the information he wishes to utilize. The adolescent chooses to follow the lead of those he or she feel have the most to offer on the question at issue. In particular, we have seen that as the adolescent's attitudes change, and the influences felt are not as dependent on less mature emotional attachment to parents, the likelihood of more intimate sexual behavior follows.

The adolescents of today in high school hold more sexually liberal attitudes and are more sexually active at a younger age than their parents were. In part this relates to the more open attitude toward sex that is prevalent throughout the society. But this also relates to new moralities available to the adolescent as a result of cognitive and moral development.

5. Kenneth Clark, "Another Part of the Wood." Harper & Row, New York, 1974.

Sex differences (notably absent in the most recent high-school data of Jessor and Jessor [1975]), race differences, and socioeconomic-status differences appear also to be decreasing. All in all, the responsibility for sexual behavior and attitudes seem to be on the individual adolescent, which is where it should be, if the adolescent has the facts and maturity to handle it.

Some letters from the problem columns of recent magazines for teenagers illustrate the continuing pressures adolescents feel in this task (and how similar the problems are to those adolescents have felt in the past):

Dear _____,

How can you tell whether a boy really likes you? I mean he's the best and all the girls follow him and talk to him and he's so considerate and friendly with everyone. I don't want to be a jealous fool, but how can I be sure it's me he likes?

Dear _____,

I have a girl friend but I don't know how to ask her for a date or kiss her. So, how does a guy get started?

Dear _____,

I'm 14 and all my friends are having sex with boys except me. I'm really scared to! There's one boy who likes me but the thought of him even kissing me makes me tremble. What should I do?

And most interesting, particularly for those of you who anticipate glaring differences between the races in approaching the life tasks, the first two letters were written to teen magazines for blacks. The influences may differ in the various subcultures but the problems for the individual adolescent are the same.

School

Miss Van Buren's
7th Grade Class
C. A. Riley Jr. H.S.

CHAPTER 10

This chapter on school and the next chapter on work together deal with the life task which emphasizes contributing to the welfare of others through one's efforts. School prepares one, hopefully, to make his or her contribution. The full scope of learning that should occur in school from the formal basics through the learning of social behaviors and social-institutional living, add to the individual's ability to make it, for himself and for others.

Time spent working constitutes the major single portion of time in an adult's life. That is to say, if an adult works a 40-hour week, with the exception of sleeping, there is no other single activity which takes as much time. For adolescents, although schooling probably in and of itself does not take 40 hours a week, schooling with extracurricular activities related to school constitutes the largest portion of time in the adolescent's life also. School is not only the major time consumer in the adolescent's day, but it is also the societal mechanism for assisting him to become a productive, contributing member of the society. Although there are exceptions—the drop-out who is very successful in business or the immigrant with little or no education who is very successful—there is a strong, long, and consistent relationship between success in school, number of years of schooling, and economic success. High school appears for the many who graduate and go directly into work to be education for a job, while high school for the college bound is preparation for additional education which may then be education for a job or education for a broader and fuller life, or both.

It becomes clearer over the years that school is not solely for the purpose of "education for a job." Regardless of the intent in the various schools in the country, school and its surrounding formal and informal activities is a major socialization agent. Whether intended by the school authorities or not, it is where adolescents learn a great deal about the other life tasks also, sometimes through curriculum, but greatly through interpersonal associations formed in

171

organized and unorganized activities in and around the school. The developmental tasks, achieving assurance of economic independence, and selecting and preparing for an occupation, are still at the base of American schooling. The tasks relating to civic competence and socially responsible behavior may be taught but are equally a part of living a good part of one's life, i.e., many full school days, in a larger group, an organization, or an institution.

The task of becoming a socially responsible citizen contributing to others both as a citizen and economically independent worker is the forerunner of becoming such a person as an adult. Therefore, for adolescents, because of the length of the moratorium, the time given to learn and develop the ways in which they can succeed in these life tasks, school is the adolescent's form of work. It is from this perspective, school as the adolescent's work, that this chapter will proceed. We will look at school achievement in relation to personal, peer, family, and social influences and then attitudes, aspirations, and expectations in the occupational realm in light of these same influences will be looked at in the next chapter.

THE SITUATIONAL ELEMENT—THE SCHOOLS

In the United States schooling is mandatory for all children up to at least age 15 or 16, and most high-school graduates finish at about 18 or 19. With the exception of extremely rare, usually isolated, schools where students remain in the same school from age 5 or 6 until school-leaving age, children go to at least two schools, grammar and high school, or three schools, grammar, junior high/middle, and high school. There was a time, 25 years ago and more, when schools across the United States were much more uniform in organizational structure and curriculum than they are now. What has become known as the "traditional" school was then the standard. Moreover, the neighborhood school at the grammar-school level, and the local high school, combining the students at high-school age from a number of neighborhood grammar schools, was also normative. This structure produced de facto racial segregation in great portions of the country, whereas de jure segregation was practiced in other portions of the country. The attempt to eliminate racial segregation, which continues today, as well as the institution of a multitude of educational structures, teaching approaches, and curricula have produced a situation where generalizations may be made but exceptions proliferate. Evaluations and conclusions are more prevalent of the exceptional programs, making generalizations to the greater high-school scene tenuous.

Schools have traditionally differed in "quality," some considered better and others worse for reasons such as monies expended per student, quality of facilities, aspects, innovativeness of programs, success of graduates. Many of these differences in "quality" have related directly to the social class and ethnicity of the student body. Moreover, schools have differed in the curriculum content, that is, vocational or college bound, or, unfortunately, custodial, with related prestige attached to the various curricula. Schools also vary in size and location and thus in community impact or involvement.

As schools vary greatly, teachers vary every bit as much. In grammar schools, pupils traditionally spent the day with a single teacher and evaluated school each year on their feelings about that teacher. More grammar schools are moving to a team-teaching, open approach, so pupils have the chance to interact daily with more teachers. In junior high, middle schools, and high schools, a student generally has a number of teachers each day. Attitudes toward school are related on a day-to-day basis to attitudes toward certain teachers, but the qualities of a "good" teacher can be, and are, disputed. The teacher I think is good, that I like, may not be the teacher you think is good, that you like. And probably we are each right for ourselves.

All these factors, listed as contributing to the quality of a school or teacher, may be thought of as the school-related influences on the student's attitude and success in school.

The schools are under constant criticism and have been for many years. At a recent school-board meeting in the author's city, the schools were criticized for being too conservative and for being too liberal, for being too narrow and academic, and for being too social, and proposals were brought before the board to reinstitute "traditional" grammar and high schools, as well as proposals to make the schools more open, flexible, and progressive.

Education involves far more than just schooling. Yet, as Coleman (1972) points out, although schools may attempt to deal with nonintellectual learning, we have at present a system of schools. Until explicit planning and organization of the other parts of education take place, we cannot be said to have a system of education.

Ivan Illich speaks of "de-schooling society" (1971). Yet Silberman reminds us of de Tocqueville's observation: "All the abuses then removed call attention to those that remain, and they now appear more galling. The evil, it is true, has become less, but sensitivity to it has become more acute" (1970, p. 20).

It was easier to note the strengths and faults in the educational system when it was more uniform nationwide. Today, when a myriad of attempts are being made to improve the education of our young people, recognizing that many of these attempts will fail, prove fruitless, or be downright silly, there is no reason to believe that education for young people is any worse today than ever. It may, in fact, be better and fuller. De Tocqueville's quote reminds us that when we have one or two rooms in our home newly painted, the rest of the house looks drab. In some ways, it was more comfortable having the whole house with drab walls, but now that some improvement has been made, we feel called upon to complete the refurbishing. The gigantic American system of schools is in the process of refurbishing. How successful is this change so far?

The 1970 census tells us many things about our education, such as:

A greater proportion of Americans than ever before is going to school.

We are starting school at an earlier age and staying in school longer.

For the first time, the average American adult has completed high school.

People who live in urban areas have a higher level of education than those in rural areas.

Although a higher percentage of whites finish high school than blacks or those of Spanish ancestry, these minorities are closing the gap.

There is a definite relationship between level of education and the kinds of jobs people hold, and how much they get paid (We the Americans: Our Education, Bureau of the Census, 1973).

Silberman pointed out that "Three students out of four now finish high school; in 1929, three out of four did not go beyond the eighth grade" (1970, p. 17). According to the 1970 census, "Across the nation, 15 percent of young men between 16 and 21 have not graduated from high school and are not going to school—1.3 million whites, 340,000 blacks, and 103,000 of Spanish heritage" (We the Americans: Our Education, Bureau of the Census, 1973, p. 11). The drop-out rate was 14 percent in rural farm areas, 20 percent in small towns, 11 percent in suburbs, and 16 percent in central cities. About twice as many blacks and youths of Spanish heritage had quit high school than whites in the same age group in both rural and urban areas, with about one-quarter of the black and Spanish heritage youth in urban areas dropping out. Although the success of the schools as measured by at least completion of high school is definitely improving, it is obviously far from ideal. The proportion of high-school-age youth, 14 to 17 years of age, enrolled in school, most of them in high school, was 79 percent in 1940, 83 percent in 1950, about 90 percent in 1960, and more than 93 percent in 1972 (We the Youth of America, Bureau of the Census, 1973).

At the most basic level, success of the school might be evaluated by analysis of illiteracy rates nationwide. From the first question asked in the 1840 census, at which time over 20 percent of the population admitted being illiterate, the illiteracy rate declined. Although these questions were dropped in the 1940 census,

. . . recent studies show that, although the proportion of the population unable to read or write is small, the number of persons still may be quite large. A 1969 national survey showed 1 percent of the population over 14 years old to be illiterate. . . . The largest group of illiterates was made up of elderly persons (We the Americans: Our Education, Bureau of the Census, 1973, p. 11).

In answer to the question "How functionally competent are U.S. adults?" the authors of a recent national survey report "not as competent as we thought. Overall, approximately one-fifth of U.S. adults are functioning with difficulty" (Adult Functional Competency, 1975, p. 6). Knowledge and skill competencies in areas such as consumer economics, government and law, community resources, reading, and problem solving were ascertained. The results further caution us in our optimism regarding advancements and improvements in education.

Across a broad educational spectrum, the Educational Testing Service analyzed approximately 200 studies in which the same or comparable tests were given to large, approximately representative national samples of students at two different times since World War II. These comparisons showed, in over 90 percent of the cases, that the second testing, the group tested more recently, had higher scores than the group in the first, earlier testing, with an average increase of about 20 percent in their scores (Toward a Social Report, U.S. Department of Health, Education, and Welfare, 1969). Conger (1973) answers Silberman's question, "The critical question is whether students are learning any more as a result of their longer exposure to the public schools" (1970, p. 18), by saying, tentatively, "yes." Although it can be concluded that adolescents are learning more as a result of their schooling, Havighurst (1966), acknowledging the truism that "everybody has unrealized potential," points to three specific groups who are not being served by the schools as well as they might: the socially disadvantaged and educationally maladjusted adolescent, the underdeveloped and underachieving adolescent, and the potentially superior but uncommitted adolescent.

Each adolescent, as he proceeds through the junior high or middle school and high school, is exposed to some combination of all the factors mentioned hereto, and these in interaction with his personal attributes and other influences on him culminate in his attitudes and success in school and to some degree in his occupational life.

Adjustment When Changing Schools

One potential trauma, although usually not traumatic, or at most a gentle readjustment, for children moving into adolescence is the transition from grammar school to junior high school or middle school and again from those schools to the high school. Although efforts are oftimes made to soften the effects of these transitions through orientation meetings and social functions, a number of influences may affect the quality of this transition.

Family and socioeconomic influences may include transition from a school in which one is primarily similar to the other children in the school in socioeconomic status or race to a school where one is less similar to the majority. The new school may be located some distance from the child's home and bring him into an area which is more foreign to him than was his grammar-school area. The transition may be more difficult because zoning regulations or busing procedures for integration disrupt existing peer relationships and bring a student to a new school without a core friendship network. The new school may be organized differently, be much larger than the school the student was used to, be more demanding. Yet through it all the student brings one constant to the new situation: his own conception of himself and his abilities and strategies for coping with new situations. Recently I saw a college freshman who utilized none of these strategies for introduction into the greater college scene, including orientation week, fraternity rush, organized campus activities, and consequently he had a very difficult and lonely first semester in college. He slowly developed his own group of acquaintances and friends and with the mutual support of these friends moved into some of the more formal campus activities. He reported that prior to attending both junior high school and high school, he was very anxious and cried at night, not knowing why, for two weeks before attending both schools. His personal strategy for becoming a part of a new institutional organization was to remain isolated so as to be selective in choosing friends and associations. This was a difficult and discomforting strategy which put him through a period of unhappiness but eventuated in a good adjustment.

The study by Simmons, Rosenberg, and Rosenberg (1973) of disturbance in the self-image at adolescence, suggested that environmental variables may have a stronger effect than age in producing greater instability of the self-image and somewhat lower self-esteem in early adolescence. "Children who had entered junior high school appeared more disturbed along these lines than their age-peers still in elementary school" (Simmons, Rosenberg, and Rosenberg, 1973, p. 553).

The difficulty in adjustment, in adapting, to any situation is in the final analysis most directly a function of the individual's coping strategies and coping style. "Coping strategies are the child's individual patternings and timings of his resources for dealing with specific problems, or needs or challenges" (Murphy, 1962, p. 274). "A given child may develop a large range of coping devices and strategies or he may limit himself to very few. The total range determines his coping style" (Murphy, 1962, p. 321).

Coelho, Silber, and Hamburg (1961) define "coping behavior" from a personality-social viewpoint, as having two broad components. The first component of coping behavior has to do with the effectiveness of the behavior in accomplishing specific tasks. The second component has to do with the "cost to the individual" in dealing successfully with these tasks. If a behavior accomplishes, or increases the likelihood of accomplishing, a task within limits that are tolerable to the individual and tolerable, in the sense of successful, to the group in which he lives, then it may be said to "serve coping functions," i.e., be successful coping.

The coping strategies, the coping style, developed through childhood, have been aimed at dealing primarily with family first, then peer and grammar-school associations. The first encounter of these strategies with a broader and possibly very different situation is in the movement to new schools. The schools may or may not be terribly different; the peer and family influences may be supportive; and a child with poorly developed coping strategies may still make a smooth transition to middle school or high school. Conversely, all the factors influencing this transition may be negative, may make the transition potentially more difficult, and yet a child with a large range of coping devices and strategies may make this transition smoothly. And lastly, as in the case cited above, the transition may not be smooth because of the nature of the individual's coping strategy and therefore be very costly to the individual, but may in the long run be very effective.

For the most part, adolescents like school. Utilizing data from the Purdue Opinion Poll, Leidy and Starry (1967) found that from 1953 to 1967 the percentage of children who stated that they disliked school was in the area of 25 to 27 percent; there was a decline in those stating that they like school very much, from 32 to 16 percent, and an increase in those who said that they liked school "most of the time," from 43 percent to 57 percent. Although this shows a change in exuberant liking for school, the vast majority of teenagers still stated that they liked school. Eighty-four percent of the high school and college students interviewed in a recent *Life* survey stated that, in general, they were satisfied with their educational experiences to that point (The Un-Radical Young, 1971). This survey also showed that over 66 percent of the high-school students wished to continue their education in college. Interestingly, Gesell (1956) shows that liking for school drops most sharply at ages 12 and 15, approximately the ages at which school transition occurs.

In general, adolescent girls (as well as boys) have a very positive attitude toward school (Konopka, 1975). If they have been treated badly because of racial discrimination or having been labeled delinquent, their attitudes are more negative. But many girls enjoy school. When asked "what they expect of school, they spoke of friendship and understanding, but also of learning. Often the subjects they preferred were those we consider difficult" (Konopka, 1975, p. 4).

With all of the criticism, all of the problems, all of the trauma and potential for trauma and personal difficulty in school, with unrealized potential great in some groups but existing in all, by and large children go through school liking it, wanting more, and benefiting from their achievements therein.

This fourteen-year-old-boy's statement seems typical:

When it comes to school, I can honestly say I don't like it a whole lot, but I don't hate it. I like coming back and seeing people I haven't seen all summer, and I like getting into a class that is really interesting and there's a good teacher. He or she will help you and kid with you, and you look forward to that class and really get something out of it. I try harder in a class that's interesting (Bravler and Jacobs, 1974, p. 137).

With all the faults in our society and its schools, achievements are immense, and achievement in the society is related to achievement in school for most people. In attempting to understand adolescents within the school and work tasks, I am afraid that we will have to concentrate on what *is* rather than what *might be*, although I would also hope that ideas for what *might be* would be generated from an understanding of what *is*.

SCHOOL ACHIEVEMENT

School achievement has been used as a criterion variable in innumerable researches. Lavin (1965), in his book *Prediction of Academic Achievement*, lists 29 types of variables which have been used as predictors of school achievement in over 300 studies published during the period 1953–1961. Although there is a group of school critics who contend that schools overemphasize achievement, the reason for this great interest in school achievement and in predicting school achievement seems to be twofold. First, school achievement is a standard, however reliable, in an individual grade or even in a grade-point average, which is accessible for all children in our country. Second, it is also, for the vast majority of children, a stressed and understood goal. It may be said that with very few exceptions parents would like their children to do well in school. They may not convey their desire to their children to the same degree or in an equally effective manner. However, school achievement is generally a desired goal of all parents for their children. School achievement is therefore the one quantitative indication we have of results of behavior that are sought after, at least the ideal, for all children.

The Personal, Self-Influence

In Lavin's review of measures of self-image as predictors of achievement, which includes such terms as self-acceptance, self-image, self-esteem, and self-confidence, he concludes that "Although research findings below the college level are spotty, the studies suggested a positive self-image is associated with higher performance" (1965, p. 92).

The self-concept construct has been utilized by several psychologists in research related to academic underachievement and overachievement in education. Though their studies are based on different assumptions and hypotheses, it is not difficult to find some logical truth in the belief that certain types of self-regarding attitudes may affect academic performance. For example, if the child perceives himself to be able, confident, adequate and a person of worth, worthy of respect rather than condemnation, he has more energy available to spend on academic achievement. On the other hand, if he perceives himself as worthless, incapable to cope with life's problems, he may not find it convenient or possible to identify with academic achievement and may fail in spite of being intellectually capable of achieving more (Bhatnagar, 1966, p. 178).

One aspect of the self that necessarily has a strong personal influence on achievement is intelligence. Regardless of whether or not you believe that intelligence is primarily a function of heredity or environment, by the time an individual reaches puberty and adolescence, his measured intelligence is very stable and will change by little more than the amount expected from measurement error over the course of the remainder of his adolescent and adult years. One would expect that adolescents of very high or low measured ability would have correspondingly high or low achievement levels in high school in the great majority of cases. "Studies suggest that for the high school level, ability and grades are correlated at about .60" (Lavin, 1965, p. 56). Curry (1962) showed that deprived home conditions have a more serious effect on school achievement as intellectual ability decreases. That is, when the child or adolescent has above-average intelligence he can more probably overcome a deprived environment. Lavin's and Curry's conclusions lead one to believe that the ability-achievement relationship would hold true to extremes of intellectual ability regardless of social class.

Manaster (1969), using a sample of 10 and 14-year-olds of average intelligence, removed the effects of intelligence in predicting achievement and found a significant relationship between sense of competence and achievement. Sense of competence as a construct may be seen as falling within the global self-concept, or self-regarding, attitudes. Sense of competence, as developed by White (1964), is considered to be the individual's subjective perception of his ability to solve problems in general or to solve specific types of problems—his perceived ability to overcome the obstacles encountered in life. Although self-concept and the self-regarding attitudes are more global conceptions, whereas sense of competence is a more discrete, particularized concept, there is considerable overlap. Ruth Wylie states, "Most of the hundreds of researches aimed at studying self-regard are apparently based on the assumption that individual differences exist in an overall or global self-evaluative attitude" (1961). However, Shibutani's use of self-esteem is much closer to the way in which Manaster used sense of competence; Shibutani says, "Much of what a person does or refuses to do depends upon his level of self-esteem" (1961, p. 433).

Purkey (1970) arrived at a definition of self which stresses its organized and dynamic aspects, in which self is "a complex and dynamic system of beliefs which an individual holds true about himself" (p. 7). The organizational aspect of the definition of the self allows one to conceptualize and study the most global, all inclusive self-concept, a concept such as sense of competence which is more particular but still global, or any of the specific beliefs that an individual has about a certain aspect of himself. All of the specific beliefs about particular aspects of the self add to, weighted for their own importance to the individual, the total self-concept and constitute the organizational element of the definition.

One such specific belief, or aspect of the total self-concept, is "self-concept of ability," which we will define and examine to understand the "dynamic" quality of an aspect of self-concept. Brookover, Erikson, and Joiner (1967) saw self-concept of academic ability as "behavior in which one indicates to himself (publicly or privately) his ability to achieve in academic tasks as compared with others engaged in the same tasks" (p. 8). This definition indicates the organized aspect of self-concept while implying that other concepts of self refer to other areas of behavior.

In the next quotation, Brookover, deriving his use of self-concept from the symbolic-interactionist framework of human behavior, in which self-concept is an intervening variable, illustrates the dynamic quality of self-concept, self-concept of academic ability:

> We postulate that the child acquired, by taking the role of the other, a perception of his own ability as a learner of the various types of skills and subjects which constitute the school curriculum. If the child perceives that he is unable to learn mathematics or some area of behavior, this self-concept of his ability becomes the functionally limiting factor of his school achievement. "Functional limit" is the term used to emphasize that we are speaking not of genetic or organic limits on learning but rather of those perceptions of what is appropriate, desirable, and possible for the individual to learn. We postulate the latter as the limits that actually operate, within broader organic limits, in determining the nature or extent of the particular behavior learned (1967, pp. 11–12).

Brookover's findings support the general conclusion that "overall, the research evidence clearly shows a persistent and significant relationship between the self-concept and academic achievement" (Purkey, 1970, p. 15). However, there is a qualifier to this statement in that this relationship has appeared to some researchers (Bledsoe, 1967; Campbell, 1965; Fink, 1962) to be more clear for boys than for girls. Nonetheless, Brookover found that self-concept of ability is significantly related to achievement for both boys and girls. When the effects of intelligence were removed, the relationship still persisted. Brookover's conception of self-concept of ability, providing a "functional limit" on achievement, was supported and it was concluded that self-concept of ability is a better predictor of academic achievement than is global self-concept.

One interesting finding of Brookover's is important in understanding the dynamic quality and the extent of the influence of self-concept in achievement. He found that students with low self-concept seldom achieved at above-average levels, but a good number of students with high self-concepts of ability do not perform at high or above-average levels as would be expected. This means that students who do not believe that they can do well will not, but that students believing they are able to do well will still not necessarily do well. Brookover put this in the form of a "necessary but not sufficient" hypothesis, in that high self-concept of ability is a necessary but not sufficient influence in determining academic achievement.

Self, Subgroup, and Achievement

Patterson explains the self-concept of academic ability dynamic with particular emphasis on its meaning for black adolescents:

> Once a child is convinced he cannot learn in school, the task of educators becomes almost impossible. He may well make trouble for his classmates, his teachers, and himself. A negative self-concept is just as crippling and just as hard to overcome as any physical handicap. In fact, a negative self-image may be even more crippling, because it is often hidden from the view of the naive or untrained observer. Most children who hate themselves act out this self-hatred by kicking the world around them. They are abusive, aggressive, hard to control, and full of anger and hostility at a world which has told them that they are not valued, are not good, and are not going to be given a chance. Such attitudes often continue to cripple an adult life (1965, pp. 4–5).

This description of the dynamic effect of low self-concept on achievement and school behavior is extreme for most cases but is illustrative of the extent to which some psychologists and social scientists view the influence of self-concept. When Patterson states, "The child with the negative view of self is a child who will not be able to profit adequately from school" (1965, p. 4), he is in essential agreement with Brookover.

Although the dynamics of self-concept influencing academic achievement are apparently generally understood and accepted, conflicting views remain of the specific effects of this relationship when analyzed separately by sex and race. Whereas the assumption of the Conference on Negro Self-Concept introduced by Patterson (1965) was that Negro self-concept would necessarily be lower because of the press of the American color-caste system, and therefore would result in "defeated behavior" in academic spheres, Coleman et al. (1966) indicated high self-concept and achievement motivation for both black and white students. Zirkel and Moses (1971) reported that black students had even higher self-concepts than whites, although the difference was not significant. Soares and Soares (1969, 1970) also found that disadvantaged children had higher self-perception than did advantaged children and concluded that "despite their cultural handicap, disadvantaged children do not necessarily suffer lower self-esteem and a lower sense of personal worth" (1969, p. 43). Wylie (1963), investigating self-concept of academic ability, found that black students modestly estimated their abilities for college as compared with white students, but more blacks expressed the desire to go to college than did whites. However, the black-white difference disappeared when socioeconomic status was controlled. Wylie suggested that the lower level of black students' estimates of ability might be a function of their relatively low socioeconomic status overall.

It might be suggested that some of the conflict in these findings relates to the generality of self-concept being investigated. That is, an adequate-to-high global self-concept is a reflection of the individual assessment through experience of his ability to get on in general and an assessment of how he compares overall with his peers. Among lower socioeconomic groups, regardless of race (although it must be remembered that black and Spanish heritage groups have greater proportions at the lower socioeconomic levels), where emphasis on educational achievement is less than in the higher-status groups, global self-concept need not be greatly affected by one facet, self-concept of academic ability, which might be less important to the individual child or adolescent. Studies such as Wylie's (1963) support the notions or socioeconomic effects on self-concept, the greater predictability of achievement from self-concept of ability measures, and the overall difference between black and white achievement related to self-concept as based on the prior two findings.

Kleinfeld (1972), recognizing that "academic self-concept has been found to be strongly related to school achievement for both white students and Negro students" (p. 211), investigated the relative importance of teachers and parents in the formation of Negro and white student academic self-concept. Although Brookover et al. (1967) had found that white students' parents' perceived evaluations were more strongly related to the students' academic self-concept than were the perceived evaluations of their teachers, Kleinfeld considered that "since Negro parents are less likely than white parents to be highly educated and expert on academic matters, their views on their children's academic potential may have less credibility than the evaluation of the teacher" (1972, p. 211). Her findings confirmed Brookover's for the white sample, and her notion that Negro students' academic self-concept would be more strongly related to the teachers' perceived evaluation than their parents' was also confirmed. "The difference in the strength of the relationship between parents' and teachers' perceived evaluation and students' academic self-concept reached significance for the Negro females but not the Negro males" (Kleinfeld, 1972, pp. 211–212). Here we see sex differences operating more strongly on influences related to girls' self-concept of ability for blacks than on boys' self-concept of ability. This area is not at all clear, but it may be that girls' self-concepts are more malleable and generally higher (Baum et al., 1968) than boys'. Whether the predominant influence of females in American schools affects these sex differences is not known, but the entire question of the influence of sex on self-concepts at present, in a time of changing sex roles, is an area greatly in need of investigation.

Boys do appear to suffer with lower grades, even when IQ's are comparable. Teachers seem to be more harsh with boys and to be less accurate in their estimates of boys' achievement (Arnold, 1968). It may also be that since boys exhibit greater independence, are more restless, less conforming, and more assertive, they do not fit the model of orderly, disciplined, quiet behavior emphasized in most schools, and teachers may therefore underestimate their efforts and interests (McCandless, 1970).

A study by Gawronski and Mathis (1965) and a review by Taylor (1964) indicate that a great number of motivational, interest, work-habit, and personality characteristics combine in various ways to determine school achievement. Overachievers, students whose achievement exceeds that predicted on the basis of their IQ scores, were found, in comparison with normal achievers or underachievers, to have better work habits, more interest in school, to be more persistent, more grade conscious, more responsible and conscientious, well organized, have higher self-esteem, greater acceptance of authority, more positive interpersonal relationships, a more realistic goal orientation, and better control over anxiety. Underachievers, on the other hand, combine some of the following characteristics: inability to delay gratification, greater impulsivity, less inhibition, poorer interpersonal relationships with peers, lower self-concept, low academic orientation but high social, pleasure-seeking orientation, and either unrealistic long-term goals or none at all. As is unfortunately the case when dealing with personality traits, the traits hang as separate and discrete labels of specialized aspects of behavior and do not cohere, or form a dynamic whole to allow explanation and understanding of real people in real situations. The above listings are descriptive, but only of general trends. Some overachieving students may be overcompensating for feelings of inadequacy and inferiority. Some underachieving students may be disinterested, and achieve when school catches up to them.

"Success in school depends less on the school than it does on what the youngsters bring to school with them (intelligence, ability to attend, perhaps degree to which they have developed inner control systems)" (McCandless, 1970, p. 277), and we should add, although this is obviously related to development of internal control, a conception of their ability to succeed academically and an adequate or positive sense of competence.

This conclusion, which stresses the personal or self-influences on school success, was reached by McCandless after reviewing the various contributing factors in this area. Among these is a most interesting relationship or nonrelationship between attitudes toward school and achievement. Lahaderne (1968) found no relationship between measures of students' attitudes toward their schools, school work, teachers, and their scores on standardized achievement tests. Lahaderne described the typical classroom of her study, concluding, "In short, pupils were coaxed and compelled to adhere to a code of conduct that supported the order of the classroom. Thus, regardless of how he felt about school, the disgruntled pupil had little chance to do anything about it in the classroom" (1968, p. 324). She seemed to conclude that no correlation was found between school attitudes and achievement because bright children would be bored in such a classroom and slower children would be "bewildered."

Jackson and Lahaderne (1967) found that teachers were not at all accurate in assessing whether or not their pupils had positive attitudes toward school, schoolwork, or themselves, the teachers. To paraphrase P. G. Wodehouse, the teachers couldn't tell whether the students were actually disgruntled, but knew they were far from being gruntled. The assumption and logic of the argument in these two studies is that pupils have to present themselves in a manner that coheres to the orderly norms and standards of the classroom, that teachers in this setting cannot discriminate their pupils' satisfaction or dissatisfaction with school, and that the press to achieve is cloaked by this orderly behavior pattern.

> An alternative explanation might be that the individual brings a set toward satisfaction or dissatisfaction to the institution—that it is a reflection of a more pervasive personal orientation and that success or failure experiences within the institution have a limited influence upon it (Jackson and Getzels, 1959, p. 295).

Jackson and Getzels tested this alternative explanation on a large group of adolescents (whereas the Jackson and Lahaderne studies used sixth graders) using an instrument called the Student Opinion Poll. They determined two experimental groups—(1) the dissatisfied, and (2) the satisfied—which were made up of students who were considerably above or below the mean scores for the entire sample of 531 on this Student Opinion Poll instrument. The experimental groups were compared on a number of intelligence, achievement, personality, and teacher rating instruments. They also found that attitude toward school in neither group related to either intellectual ability or scholastic achievement. However, they did find that on each of the instruments which assessed psychological health or adjustment, the "satisfied" group attained "better" scores, i.e., the score indicating a higher or more adequate level of psychological functioning. In addition, teachers rated the "satisfied" boys higher than they did the "dissatisfied" boys; however, this did not appear to be true for girls. This perhaps supports the popular expectation that girls are less likely to express negative feelings publicly than are boys. Jackson and Getzels summarized by saying that, in order to understand dissatisfaction with school, data on psychological health may be more relevant than scholastic-achievement data. In addition, the girls who feel dissatisfied with school may be more likely to be feeling personal inadequacy whereas dissatisfied boys may be characterized as having feelings which are critical of school authorities.

This section has shown the continuing importance of self-concept and other variables pertaining to self and personality in relation to school achievement. However, the section has also shown that as aspects of self and personality are related to variables such as sex, race, socioeconomic status, etc., the relationship of self-concept and achievement may be obscured. The interaction between the variables, that is, the ways in which the variables influence each other, in this instance, make less clear the major individual relationships with school achievement.

An adolescent who thinks well of himself and who has developed healthy and efficient coping strategies will probably be more successful in school than others. But influences on him not to succeed, such as low expectations of parents, peers, and teachers because of his race and/or class can take their toll. However, the influence of the individual himself on the outcomes of his life, his achievement, are generally stronger than the other influences.

In the early sixties I began teaching the fall semester in a school located in the center of a public-housing project on the west side of Chicago. The area was the most heavily patrolled in the city as it had the highest rate of violent crime. Almost all of the students qualified for free meals. We had a short written assignment the first day of class, and I was particularly taken with the paper by one young fellow. The theme was how he intended to make it to college and become an engineer. That first day, as he sat with a sparkle in his eye dressed in a clean white shirt, I felt there was no stopping him, he would make it.

As the semester went on, the quality of his work never wavered. His attendance was perfect. Although he did not have the needed supplies, all the teachers in the school bought supplies for the kids who could not afford them. Occasionally he dozed off in class. And his white shirt became progressively grayer. We spoke about life and his life, and eventually I had to request that outside agencies be brought in to help him. His mother worked the streets at night, slept during the day, and was seldom sober. He did not know who his father was, had no other relatives to turn to, and was locked out of the apartment most of the time. He had not slept in a bed for the first three weeks of school—he slept in hallways and stairwells. He was a poor, black, essentially parentless, urban ghetto kid. He had a sense of commitment, a desire, a feeling that he, himself, could make it. The year I knew him he did.

This young fellow, on the basis of ethnicity and socioeconomic status, illustrates the following points, which cannot be overstressed:

The socioeconomic status of students calculated on the basis of parent occupations and education almost invariably has a strong association with attainment of education and societal goals when the average attainment of large student aggregates is examined. On the other hand, using SES to predict an individual student's prospects for academic achievement, or future employment, is very liable to error.

Students' ethnicity, especially their majority or minority ethnic status, relates strongly to the life prospects of aggregates of students, but again the prediction of individual achievement on this basis could easily be wrong (Grannis, 1975, p. 1).

At the other extreme, while making the same point—and moving to the section on school influences—George Bernard Shaw said:

"I was never in a school where the teachers cared enough about me, or about their ostensible profession, or had time enough to take any such troubles; so I learnt nothing at school, not even what I could and would have learned if any attempt had been made to interest me. I congratulate myself on this; for I am persuaded that every unnatural activity of the brain is as mischievious as any unnatural activity of the body, and that pressing people to learn things they do not want to know is as unwholesome and disastrous as feeding them on sawdust." He further asserted that even "experience fails to teach when there is no desire to learn" (Pearson, 1942, p. 14).

School Differences and School Influences

In the preceding section, we have seen the substantial degree to which individual differences and scholastic achievement are related to individual differences in motivation, ability, and sense of self-adequacy. In the sections that follow, we will examine and see relationships between influences such as peers, family, and socioeconomic background as they relate to scholastic success.

In this section, we will explore the influences of particular facets of schools on achievement and pupil participation within those schools. This is a somewhat different perspective than is taken in most of this book. As adolescents develop, they are confronted with the life tasks which present themselves differently and have potential for many successful outcomes for each adolescent. However, the life task as it applies to schools for adolescents is the one standard instance in which all adolescents confront the issues of their potential for contributing to their own lives and to mankind in a single, nationally similar, institution.

In America, for all intents and purposes, every adolescent goes to school. There may be some differences between schools to accommodate particular handicaps, strengths, or interests of adolescents, but all adolescents go to school. Some adolescents, possibly because of other interests, but most usually with below-average ability and background factors which lessen or impede success in school, drop out of high school, but the great majority finish. These statements seem simplistic, but are stressing an important and oftimes overlooked fact. Compulsory education has been with us for many years; universal literacy has almost been reached. Although critics galore will disagree, the paucity of findings showing impressive school effects on achievement may be the result of our having reached a plateau of good basic education for most of our adolescents. This is not to say, nor even to imply, that higher plateaux cannot be reached through improvements, innovations, and change in education. Rather it is to say that maybe the inequities and differences between schools and school systems are not sufficiently great to allow empirical research findings which differentiate school effects.

What, then, are the findings on school effects? Coleman et al's (1966) large-scale study of equality of educational opportunity carried out on behalf of the U.S. Office of Education concluded that: "Variations in school quality are not highly related to variations in achievement of pupils. . . . The school appears unable to exert independent influences to make achievement less dependent on the child's background" (p. 297). Having reviewed studies at both the university and public-school level, Nichols (1973) concludes:

> The largely negative results of studies of school effects suggest that in the United States, where some sort of education is available to everyone and the mass media continually bombard us with seductive conceptual material (in other words, where very few suffer really drastic educational disadvantage), the family factor and the genetic factor are likely the major sources of individual differences in ability (pp. 138–139).

Johnston and Bachman (1973) say:

> . . . after several years of intensive analysis, . . . [we] are forced to a conclusion similar to Coleman's. There are differences between schools, to be sure, in terms of educational and occupational aspirations, test scores, values and attitudes, affective states, and so on. But when we ask what produces these differences, we find almost invariably that they can be attributed to individual differences in background and basic abilities (pp. 236–237).

They conclude:

> In retrospect, the overall lack of differential school effects is not necessarily proof that schools are generally ineffective. It could just as well indicate that our schools, in conjunction with aspects of our culture, are succeeding in making equally rich educational opportunities available to nearly all who desired them. Perhaps a more realistic conclusion involves a balance between these two interpretations (p. 237).

It may be that the key term in the previous quotation was "in conjunction with aspects of our culture." Differences between achievement levels of various minority groups have been attributed, at least in part, to differences in importance of education, attitude toward education, and view of what education may provide them, as in better jobs or a fuller life. These attitudes at specific levels pervade thinking within a subculture and affect the achievement levels reached by great numbers of pupils within the subculture. So, too, the meaning and role of education as seen by vast numbers of the youth at any one time may be different from these views at another time.

When schooling is seen as a way of broadening oneself and an avenue for securing a better job and better life by the majority of adolescents and adults, one would expect achievement levels nationally to be high or rising, with the most able, motivated, confident pupils still achieving above the average. However, during times when schools are under fire, either from critics or literally, when the national economy is declining, when myths of national glory, of equality, are being shattered, one would expect achievement levels nationally to be lowering—but the higher achievers will still be the individual students who are most motivated, with most ability, and most self-esteem.

Time (Learning Less, March 31, 1975) asked, "Are U.S. public school students learning less now than they did a decade or even a few years ago"? Citing three separate national studies, *Time* answered "Yes," saying, "Whatever the cause, it is clear from all three studies that the cure lies in the classroom."

One of the studies conducted by the College Entrance Examination Board using the Scholastic Aptitude Tests shows that SAT scores have been falling every year since 1962 and that this trend is continuing. The second study by the National Assessment of Educational Progress reported that students knew less about science according to the 1973 testing than they did in a 1970 testing. The third study, supported by the U.S. Department of Health, Education, and Welfare, showed the reading levels of public school students falling ever since the mid-1960's.

There have been many innovations in public school education in the last 12 to 15 years. A good number of these have stressed nonacademic facets of education. Have these innovations or changes in educational practice negatively affected the achievement of students in reading and science nationally? Were these changes instituted consistently across the country in all school systems and are they so now? I think not in both cases. To some degree there may be a lessening of academic emphasis in the public schools by teachers, administrators, and policy makers. However, the students who are being tested today and those who have been tested through the sixties must all have been greatly affected by the events, changes, and atmosphere of the times, at least as much as by changes in educational practice. These "aspects of our culture," or influences of the times, may greatly influence national trends, changes, in achievement levels. Would another Sputnik affect achievement levels in science positively? Will a prolonged economic slump inspire students to perform at higher levels? The answers to these questions are certainly not clear. But the findings on school effects make illogical the conclusion that schools are suddenly nationally less effective and therefore producing lower achievement scores.

Efforts to determine the most effective organizational, structural, and personal attributes of school districts, schools, classrooms, and teachers have been extensive. The scarcity of findings relating these variables to student achievement is not for a want of looking. Some examples of studies and conclusions regarding school districts, school, and teacher characteristics as they relate to student achievement follow and may assist in providing a better understanding of the immensity of the problem.

Bidwell and Kasarda (1975) used a "social-ecological" approach to ask whether, and how, various aspects of the organization of school districts in relation to environmental or demographic characteristics of that district (what they called "environmental inputs") affect academic achievement level in the school districts. This approach had not been well developed and previous research was uneven. Using data from 104 school districts in Colorado, they looked at the environmental conditions: school-district size, fiscal resources, percentage of disadvantaged students, educational level of adults in the school district, and percent of the school district population classified as nonwhite. These they related to organizational attributes (seen as the intervening variables): pupil-teacher ratio, administrative intensity—that is, the ratio of administrators to classroom teachers, professional support components, and the percent of the total staff who held at least a master's degree. Both the environmental and organizational variables were studied for their effect on reading and mathematics achievement. They found that, as pupil-teacher ratios declined, as there were fewer pupils per teacher, achievement scores tended to rise. On the other hand, as administrative intensity rose, as there were more administrators relative to teachers, pupils' achievement scores went down. With better qualified teaching staffs, both math and reading achievement is higher. But administrative overhead seems to divert resources from teaching and instruction and has a negative effect on achievement.

In view of our previous conclusions regarding the paucity of findings on school effects on achievement, Bidwell and Kasarda's findings are especially striking. They clearly show that there are "certain ways in which the structure and staffing of school districts appear to transform inputs to school districts into outputs of student achievement" (1975, p. 68). It appears from this study that, by examining dependencies among the environmental and organizational aspects of school districts, particularly concerning qualifications of teachers, revenue, and size of the district in conjunction with pupil-teacher ratio, effects of school on achievement may be seen.

The idea that "big is good" has long been a prevailing ethic in America (and an author writing in Texas must certainly be aware of that ethic). It has been incorporated into the thinking of educators, since it has been assumed that larger school districts, and presumably larger schools, are better equipped to be effective and have more and more varied resources for instruction (Conant, 1967). Gump (1966) specifically asked the question of whether increasing school size produced a corresponding increase in variety of instruction. He very definitely confirmed this relationship; however, he found it less than economical. It takes an increase of 100 percent in size to realize a 17 percent increase in variety. "Since size increase, by itself, pays relatively poor dividends" (Gump, 1966, p. 1), he suggests that educational planners look at strategies other than increased size.

From the perspective of behavior-setting theory (Barker, 1960), school activities may be seen as behavior settings—ecological-behavior units characterized by time and place, arrangement of people and objects, and patterns of behavior. Wicker (1968) summarizes recent work by Barker and his colleagues which indicates that the number of students in a high school relates to both the behaviors and subjective experiences of the student in extracurricular activities of the schools. He concludes that students of small schools are more likely than students of large schools to become involved in more different kinds of activities, attain more responsible positions in the activities they enter, describe school activities in more varied ways, achieve more satisfaction, involvement, challenge, and feelings for moral and cultural values, and feel and report internal and external pressures—feel obligated—to attend, participate, and support activities.

Wicker conceives of the differences between large and small schools as relating, although not perfectly, to undermanning and overmanning of behavior settings. Undermanning was determined by calculating the number of students who performed in a particular high-school activity, divided by the number of students who attended a setting, activity, of that kind. The activities used for analysis were available at most high schools of any size—activities such as varsity basketball game played at home, class or club business meeting, school play, informal evening dance, class or club money-raising project, and school-sponsored or organized trip away from school. It seems clear that in a large school unless it has an incredible number of activities, the number of students who are truly active in each setting would be a smaller percentage of the total group in attendance than would be the case in a small school, but more students would be available to participate in the large school. Wicker found "for five of the six kinds of behavior settings, undermanning is significantly greater in small than in large schools" (1968, p. 256). This conclusion means that in large schools most behavior settings, most activities, are overmanned and some few are undermanned, whereas the opposite is true of small schools. In overmanned settings fewer students participating will be performers, whereas in undermanned settings more students are likely to be performers. The average student, then, in a large school, would have fewer performances and experiences in activities than would the average student in a small school. Through participation, the small-school student may feel greater confidence, importance, depended on, a sense of obligation and responsibility for success, closeness with others, and a feeling of accomplishment. Clearly, Wicker is supported in his feeling that school size, because of its effect on under or overmanning and opportunity for student performance, is an important influence on the experiences of students.

Teacher Influences and Characteristics

Buxton (1973) studied four school systems in his analysis of adolescents in school. He refers to his conclusions as "sober" and "concerned," though some may consider them depressing.

> What has determined the mismatch between adolescents and schools is to a large extent the unwillingness or incapability to adapt of the junior and senior high schools and the communities in which they serve. I have also come to feel that less than new "programs" or facilities, a massive change in attitude of all persons concerned with the schools is necessary (Buxton, 1973, p. 123).

Although he finds that, on the whole, students are indifferent to school, he also finds, in one of the few hopeful notes, that "It is typical for a student to believe that schooling can make a difference in his future" (p. 121). Another hopeful finding, which he found surprising, was that "On the whole, teachers are liked in every school, more by girls than by boys, and rather unclearly so by the more advanced students. . . . It nevertheless now suggests that teachers may be a positive resource for change" (p. 120). A most important aspect of studies of school effects or studies of teachers is teacher characteristics as they relate to students' attitudes and achievement. It is to this feature of school effects that we now turn.

An extensive research literature into the relationship between teacher characteristics and student achievement exists, covering more than 50 years. By and large, significant relationships have not been demonstrated, but belief that a relationship exists continues. We all, from our personal educational experiences, can identify teachers we have had who are "better" and "worse," teachers from whom we have learned more, and teachers from whom we have learned less than average.

Heath and Nielson (1974) assessed a good number of reviews of the teacher-characteristics literature, citing Brim's (1958) conclusion, reiterating that reviews of the vast body of research on the relationship between teacher characteristics and effectiveness do not show any consistent relation between any teacher characteristic and teaching effectiveness. Getzels and Jackson (1963), reviewing teacher personality and characteristics studies, concluded that in spite of the importance of the problem and the enormous amount of research effort, "very little is known for certain about . . . the relation between teacher personality and teaching effectiveness"

(p. 574). Mood (1970), in the same vein, concluded, "We can only make the very useful observation that at the present moment we cannot make any sort of meaningful quantitative estimate of the effects of teachers on student achievement" (p. 7). Heath and Nielson (1974), citing background variables that we have not yet discussed, conclude, "Given the well-documented, strong association between student achievement and variables such as socioeconomic status and ethnic status, the effect of techniques of teaching on achievement are likely to be inherently trivial" (p. 481).

And yet the belief that a relationship exists between student achievement and the characteristics and behaviors of teachers continues. Rosenshine and Furst (1971) propose 11 teacher-behavior variables they consider to be most promising after reviewing some 50 studies in this area. The variables they propose are (1) clarity, (2) variability, (3) enthusiasm, (4) task-oriented behaviors, (5) opportunity for students to learn material, (6) use of student ideas and general indirectness, (7) criticism, (8) use of structuring comments, (9) types of questions, (10) probing, and (11) level of difficulty of instruction. Hamachek (1972) reviewed teacher variables related to motivation and learning and concluded that, in fact, there are characteristics which, at least, appear more consistently in teachers who are "high" or "low" in motivating students to learn.

Hamachek lists characteristics which seem to be exhibited by teachers who are superior in "encouraging motivation and learning in students":

> . . . (1) willingness to be flexible, to be direct or indirect as the situation demands; (2) capacity to perceive the world from the student's point of view; (3) ability to "personalize" their teaching; (4) willingness to experiment, to try out new things; (5) skill in asking questions (as opposed to seeing self as a kind of answering service); (6) knowledge of subject matter and related areas; (7) skill in establishing definite examination procedures; (8) willingness to provide definite study help; (9) capacity to reflect an appreciative attitude (evidenced by nods, comments, smiles, etc.); (10) conversational manner in teaching—informal, easy style (1972, p. 237).

Klausmeier and Goodwin (1966) summarized their review of teacher characteristics and pupil learning, saying:

> Efficiency of pupil learning . . . is enhanced when guided by a teacher who is intelligent, well prepared in the subject matter, a high achiever while in college, and well educated. . . . High interest in students and subject matter, favorable attitude toward students and subject matter, and a stable personality are associated with successful teaching. Other characteristics also are important. For example, teachers above age 60 experience more difficulty than do younger teachers. Male teachers seem to get along better with boys than do female teachers. Although middle class teachers may secure better results with children from the middle social class, we have not found out which teachers work well with students from the lower social class (pp. 158–159).

Excepting a few crucial cognitive and personality attributes that directly relate to the learning process, Ausubel (1968) is not at all enamored with the extensive research on personality characteristics as he sees a broad range of these characteristics as "compatible with effectiveness in teaching." He comes down hard on what he sees as an overemphasis on teacher characteristics presumed to relate to student mental health and personality development. It appears that for some teachers and teacher educators today the sole standard and purpose of teaching are improved interpersonal relations and the development of positive self and other attitudes. Teachers should not be selected for personality characteristics which theoretically relate to personality or mental-health development. Their selection and evaluation should be according to "their ability to stimulate and competently direct pupil learning activity" (1968, p. 450). Ausubel goes so far as to cite evidence that pupils are primarily concerned with their teacher's ability to teach, and not merely concerned with having kindly, sympathetic, and cheerful teachers (Taylor, 1962). Recognizing the full scope of the teacher's role as socializer and "facilitator of personality development," Ausubel analyzes teacher characteristics as they relate to achievement within a perspective that sees it as "undeniable that the teacher's most important and distinctive role in the modern classroom is still that of director of learning activities" (1968, p. 450).

Teachers in this country, by virtue of their training and selection within the training institution, are generally above a certain minimal level of intelligence which is necessary to be an effective teacher, and therefore the relationship between teacher effectiveness and teacher's intelligence is found to be low because of the limited and higher range of intelligence of teachers. Certain aspects of the teacher's academic preparation as well as their orderliness and systematic approach to running a classroom and teaching have been found to relate at relatively low levels to student achievement, although some presume that they have a somewhat larger effect.

But from all the teacher characteristic variables that have so far been investigated, and probably from the extensive number of variables which have not yet been investigated, the relationship with effective teaching produces at best low correlations. "The two principal exceptions to this generalization are warmth and understanding, on the one hand, and a tendency to be stimulating and imaginative, on the other" (Ausubel, 1968, pp. 453–454). These two exceptions fit well with Ausubel's statement, "Perhaps the most important personality characteristic of teachers influencing their effectiveness is the extent of their personal commitment to the intellectual development of pupils" (1968, p. 455). Teachers committed to student learning may not always appear warm and understanding to even a trained observer. But students in interaction with their teachers day after day come to know who is really interested and willing to make the effort and sacrifice to help them. This commitment, I believe, reaches the adolescent as warmth and understanding even if masked by a cold exterior. Commitment to the student's intellectual development, not commitment to a particular teaching style or commitment to maintaining one's personal status and protecting and defending one's self, demands being flexible. Commitment to the student's intellectual development demands of the teacher who feels it that he or she try everything within his ability and bag of tricks to stimulate and encourage the imagination and ability of his students. As Ausubel laments, however, commitment is a difficult factor to measure and no objective evidence exists of its generally acknowledged value. Nonetheless, we must agree with him as to its crucial importance. Students who are bound and determined to learn will probably do so regardless of their teachers. But teachers bound and determined to teach may do so even with students less interested in learning.

Social-Class Influences through Family and Friends

The concept of social class is global. It cuts across other social groupings in our society, such as racial, ethnic, and religious groups. We may think of American society in toto as composing a single culture, the American culture—the attitudes, beliefs, and behaviors which are common to or most typical of Americans. But there is enormous variation within this culture. It is composed of subcultures which may be considered horizontal and vertical. By virtue of shared attitudes, beliefs, and behaviors, subgroups based on ethnicity, race, or geographic area may be seen as comprising the various subcultures which cut vertically across the American culture. We see these subcultures as vertically cutting across the horizontal layers, the ranked, structured, hierarchical levels of social classes. Ethnic, racial, and geographic-area subcultures cut across all levels of social class. Catholics, Protestants, and Jews, Polish-Americans, Italian-Americans, Irish-Americans, whites, blacks, and Chicanos may be found at all social-class levels from the lower to the upper. The relative distribution, or proportion, of each subcultural group in the various social classes may differ for historical and other reasons. Conversely, each social class—working, middle, and upper—cuts across the racial, ethnic, religious, and geographic subcultures.

> Social classes constitute subcultural groups. When people from the same social class meet and converse, they soon find they have much in common, even though they may come from different ethnic or religious backgrounds or from different sections of the country. They will find that they live in much the same kinds of neighborhoods, have similar eating habits, dress in pretty much the same ways, have rather similar tastes in furniture, literature, and recreation, and have about the same amount of education (Havighurst and Neugarten, 1967, p. 9).

Try to visualize any axis at which a vertical subculture such as Italian-American meets the horizontal subculture of social class. There are ways in which the persons at that axis are similar in beliefs, attitudes, and behavior to all other Italian-Americans up and down the vertical ethnic subculture lines. So, too, these Italian-Americans are similar in beliefs, attitudes, and behaviors to most other persons falling along the horizontal social-class subcultural line. The combined wisdom of social-class studies in this country and across countries indicates that persons of the same social class, differing in ethnic, religious, etc., subcultures, will be more similar in their general way of life to the others of their same social class than they will be to members of their same ethnic, religious, or racial subcultures of other social classes.

Social stratification, the ranking of people hierarchically within a society according to their degree of economic and political power, and social prestige, is recognized if not readily accepted, by most people. They may with little difficulty, as Warner et al. (1960) illustrated, rank themselves and persons near them or of whom they are aware, as being at the same level or higher or lower than they are in power and prestige on a social ladder, creating thus a social scale.

The major dimensions underlying the social-class structure in America have been defined by Kahl (1957). They are: prestige (as shown in the amount of respect and deference a person receives), occupation (considered higher or lower on the basis of contribution to the welfare of others, particular or special abilities, and extent of reward), wealth (income or holdings), social interaction (whom one usually socializes with, one's own kind), class consciousness (seeing oneself or feeling oneself as working class or middle class, union/labor or management), shared value orientations, and the actual or perceived ability to control the actions or outcomes for other people (power or clout). In itself, occupation is probably the single best indicator of an individual's status. Occupation, like all of the dimensions, may be studied independently, but all are in general related. Persons high or low on any one dimension are likely to be similarly positioned on the others. This similarity across dimensions constitutes social class.

In respect to the dimensions of social class delineated by Kahl, children and adolescents cannot be said to possess most of the characteristics of the dimensions on their own behalf. They come, through the process of learning and socialization, to develop a class consciousness to some degree, value orientations, and interact socially with "their own kind." But in the main, children and adolescents derive their status and are members of a social class, through their parents. The child and adolescent becomes a part of, learns to be a part of, the social class of his parents and experiences their mobility or lack of social mobility. The child and adolescent may be said to have

> . . . the experience of growing up in a certain social class. The existence of a social structure based largely on occupational differentiation gives all people common perceptions of society and of the occupational and personal characteristics that determine status in that society. The membership of a person in a particular social

class, then, gives him certain attitudes toward education, property, family relations, and certain occupational aspirations that he shares with people of similar social class in other societies (Manaster and Havighurst, 1972, p. 4).

The adolescent in and from his family is part of a fairly clear social class. His associations and interactions with friends are more intimate, more comfortable with his "own kind," with other adolescents of his same social class. The pervasive and multidimensional quality of social class makes it a difficult but important concept to use in explaining school achievement and family and peer influences on school achievement.

Swift (1967) has suggested that the use of the concept social class is too crude to explain home-environment differences and differences in school achievement. However, research over the last 40 years has consistently emphasized that educational achievement of middle-class children is superior to that of working-class children, and correlations of the order .30 to .35 between social class and academic achievement are customarily found. A study by Miller (1970) attempted to get at factors, clusters of variables, that would suggest explanations for social-class differences in achievement. Moreover, Miller hypothesized that these factors, derived from variables thought to differentiate between social classes, would be more directly associated with academic achievement than would the global concept social class. Almost 500 children from the top primary classes of 10 primary schools, 5 from middle class, and 5 from working-class districts, completed an inventory designed to elicit their own perceptions of their environment. Five of the 8 factors derived from the inventory responses may be considered to help "explain" social-class differences in educational development and achievement. The factors labeled "desire for education," "intellectual enterprise," and "confidence and parental support" correlated positively with social class and with academic achievement, whereas the factors labeled "general deprivation" and "dominant parent-submissive child" were negatively correlated with achievement.

The variables generally found in the middle to upper social classes favor school achievement, whereas the variables found in the lower occupational levels are negatively correlated with achievement. However, as Miller states, "this is only a weak tendency" (1970, p. 267). That means that a family of higher social class may have characteristics which have been found to relate negatively with school achievement. In like manner a low socioeconomic family may exhibit those characteristics positively correlated with achievement.

This is an important point. In this study, as in so many others, social class is assumed to be different from the variables which make up social class. However, the differentiation is by no means perfect. As in any comparison between groups, particularly on global measures such as social class, we analyze degree of relationship or degree of difference. Almost always groups overlap, which in this instance is confirmed by Miller's statement that a family of high social class may have characteristics that are negatively associated with achievement, that more usually would be associated with families of lower social class and vice versa. Miller concludes on the basis of his findings that there is a more direct association between the environmental factors and achievement than with social class, that the factors themselves have higher correlations with academic achievement than has social class, and that social class is of less importance in predicting or determining achievement—it is too vague a concept to be explanatory. Nonetheless, the notion of social class, with its easy access and general understanding by educators and to some degree the lay public, is valuable for predicting and understanding achievement. The more specific variables or factors would almost by definition be more clearly related to academic achievement, but would be much more difficult to determine in the individual case than would social class.

People working with adolescents, particularly teachers and others related to education, become very aware of differences in attitudes toward school, work habits, sense of competence or self-concept of academic ability, educational and occupational aspirations, as they differ by social class and relate to differences in academic achievement. These educators become equally well aware of exceptions to the "social class by academic achievement" relationship. It is thought by many that the expectations of teachers for students of differing social classes may influence the students' achievement. Conversely, however, the adolescents themselves are aware of and hold, with the variations within social classes of which we have spoken, expectations and aspirations for their own behavior and success that they think is appropriate to their own social class. Parents of middle and upper-class children have traditionally been more interested in and more encouraging of their child's career in school and afterwards, than have parents of children in lower socioeconomic groups. Parents at the lowest, the lower-lower social-class levels, have been by far the least encouraging and expected the least of their children. School success has long-term implications for higher education, future occupation, future associations, and maintenance of social status or upward mobility. In addition to the direct influences on achievement resulting from class consciousness, varying satisfaction of basic needs (health care, home stability, etc.) related to social class may also influence achievement.

A study by Harrison (1968) investigates social class/home background, school success, and attitude of adolescents. This study assumed and found expected social-class differences while pursuing further the question of students whose performance is not as expected. Harrison started with the proposition that most students who succeed in school come from advantaged home backgrounds, whereas most students who do not succeed are from disadvantaged home backgrounds. But there are students who do not fit, are inconsistent with, this proposition: advantaged students with expectations for school success who are not successful, and disadvantaged students who are successful.

It was hypothesized that the attitudes of the inconsistent students would be incongruent with those of their associated majority group who, for the advantaged, non-successful students, were the advantaged, successful students, and, for the disadvantaged-successful students, were the disadvantaged-non-successful students (Harrison, 1968, p. 334).

The hypothesis was confirmed. The attitudes of the inconsistent students were not congruent with those of their like-majority groups, advantaged-successful, disadvantaged-nonsuccessful. With the exception of attitudes toward education, which did not distinguish between advantaged and disadvantaged students or successful and nonsuccessful students, but was positive for all, the attitudes of the successful students were similar and the attitudes of the nonsuccessful students were similar regardless of advantaged or disadvantaged position. The successful students' views were more positive for the scales investigated, with the disadvantaged-successful students expressing the most optimistic view of the future of all groups.

On the scales investigated in this study, view of the environment (that man can gain control of his environment), attitude toward education (that it is of little/real value), attitude toward school groups (that association with school groups may be a waste of time/real value), and peer-group attitude toward education (that the student's peer group did not/did value education), there are social class, advantaged-disadvantaged, differences in attitudes and related differences in school success. Seemingly a student with the preferred, positive attitude will be successful in school regardless of advantaged or disadvantaged status, whereas a student with negative attitudes will not be successful. But the fact remains that the attitudinal differences usually coincide with social-class differences and school success.

An interesting presentation of socioeconomic or social-class factors in school achievement was included by Havighurst (1964) in his survey of the Chicago Public Schools. He listed 39 schools in rank order according to the schools' socioeconomic ratio (SER) in Table 12. SER was calculated by determining the occupational level of the adults in a school-attendance area and following the formula: number of adults with upper-middle-class occupation $\times$ 2 + number of adults with lower-middle-class occupation $\div$ number of adults with upper-working-class occupation + number of adults in lower-working-class occupation $\times$ 2. Essentially this is a weighted ratio of white-collar to blue-collar workers, middle and upper-middle versus working-class adults, in a school's attendance area. The percentage of ninth and eleventh graders in the top three stanines on standard reading achievement tests were given for each school. Looking at schools 1, 11, 21, and 31, from highest

Table 12. *Socioeconomic Area and Pupil Achievement in High Schools. (Robert J. Havighurst,* The Public Schools of Chicago: A Survey by Robert J. Havighurst. *Chicago: Board of Education of the City of Chicago, 1964, pp. 208–209. Reprinted by permission of the Board of Education of the City of Chicago, May 14, 1976.)*

School Number	SER[1]	Achievement[2]	Say Will Enter College[3]	% Negro
1	290	52	94	0
2	229	49	88	0
3	199	54	91	0
4	180	54	81	2
5	123	40	71	26
6	109	47	67	0
7	97	36	74	0
8	83	32	57	0
9	82	29	55	21
10	82	29	55	0
11	79	36	74	0
12	75	27	57	0
13	74	41	49	0
14	69	32	52	0
15	68	33	52	0
16	68	25	73	87
17	66	28	48	0
18	61	32	46	3
19	54	11	46	28
20	54	43	70	3
21	53	21	76	88
22	53	26	39	11
23	53	25	42	19
24	52	17	78	98
25	50	23	41	0
26	49	23	44	0
27	39	22	38	1
28	34	16	35	1
29	27	27	44	0

[1] Socioeconomic ratio of adults in attendance area in 1960. See Appendix 1 for details. Certain schools are not representative of adults in area because there is a selective factor in school attendance. This is true of School 20, for example, where the school represents a higher socioeconomic group than the average for the attendance area.

[2] Percent of ninth and eleventh graders in top three stanines on standard tests of reading. For city as a whole, 23 percent are in the top three stanines.

[3] Students who will graduate in June are asked in the spring whether they expect to go to college. Composite of data from 1962, 1963, and 1964.

Table 12—*Continued*

School Number	SER[1]	Achievement[2]	Say Will Enter College[3]	% Negro
30	24	8	53	100
31	23	11	36	9
32	22	10	65	100
33	22	4	53	94
34	20	10	65	80
35	20	14	39	44
36	19	8	61	99
37	17	4	51	91
38	14	4	53	100
39	11	6	53	100

socioeconomic ratio in descending order, the percentages of students with high reading achievement are 52 percent, 36 percent, 21 percent, and 11 percent.

Havighurst typed the schools in Table 12 as the high-status high schools (the first 10 or 12 in the table and possibly schools 13 and 20), the common-man schools (12 to 15 of the middle range of the table), and the inner-city schools (the bottom third of the table). The high-status schools all have high achievement, and 50 to 94 percent of the seniors plan to go to college. The common-man schools' students are about average in achievement and roughly half intend to enter college. The students in the inner-city schools are well below average in achievement, have high drop-out rates, and although a surprisingly high percentage say they will enter college, this is not very realistic, in part because of their grades but also because these schools have very inadequate college-preparation curricula.

The conclusive and pervasive influence of social class on adolescents in school is well summarized by Charters:

> To categorize youth according to the social class position of their parents is to order them on the extent of their participation and degree of "success" in the American educational system. This has been so consistently confirmed by research that it now can be regarded as an empirical law. . . . It seems to hold in any educational institution, public or private, where there is some diversity in social class. . . . Social class position predicts grades, achievement and intelligence test scores, retentions at grade level, course failure, truancy, suspension from school, high school dropout, plans for college attendance, and total amount of formal schooling. It predicts academic honors and awards in the public school, elected school officers, extent of participation in extracurricular activities and in social affairs sponsored by the school, to say nothing of a variety of indicators of "success" in the formal structure of the student's society. . . .

The predictions noted above are far from perfect. Inasmuch as the social class position rarely accounts for more than half the variance of school "success," the law holds only for differences in group averages, not for differences in individual success (1963, pp. 739–740).

Home background and socioeconomic influences on academic achievement in high school may be compounded by achievement itself when the adolescent considers future educational plans, educational aspirations and expectations. A recent study by Schwarzweller and Lyson (1974) investigated educational plans of American and Norwegian rural youth as affected by their social-class background and the support they thought they received from their parents—the perceived parental interest. They found that the educational plans of girls were only slightly affected by parental interests, whereas for boys, parental interest played an important part in influencing educational plans. They point out that much research has shown social class to be an important determinant of educational mobility, educational plans. The data from their study is in keeping with this finding both in the United States and Norway. In the United States more students go on to college than in Norway, but the "pattern of class effect is essentially similar, cross-culturally, and its magnitude is substantial" (p. 452).

Parental interest plays an important role for boys, but not for girls, in influencing educational plans. And most interestingly they found that academic performance, in and of itself, influences educational plans, at least for boys. In America, particularly for boys, high academic achievement serves to neutralize the class effect on educational goals. When a lower-class boy does especially well in school and shows that he could go on to college, his family and peers are likely to encourage him.

The considerable influence of social class of origin and parental interest on educational plans in Norway, particularly for boys, is somewhat unexpected because in Norway adolescents with strong academic ability and potential are virtually assured of college scholarships. In the United States, where this assurance of subsidy for post-high-school education does not exist, it would be expected that to a greater degree educational plans would be dependent on socioeconomic background and support from the family. These expectations would appear to be well justified in the United States. According to Sewell's longitudinal research on inequalities in opportunities for higher education,

. . . using such measures of socioeconomic status as parental income, father's and mother's educational attainment, and father's occupation—either singly or in combination—we have found enormous differences in educational opportunities among the various socioeconomic groups and between the sexes. These differences are great regardless of what socioeconomic indices are used and regardless of how restrictively or broadly opportunity for higher education is defined—whether it is taken to mean college entry, college graduation, professional or graduate study, or simply continuation of any kind in formal education beyond high school (1971, pp. 794–795).

SUMMARY: WHAT'S IT ALL ABOUT, ALFIE?

The concentration in this chapter has been on academic and achievement aspects of school. There are no answers at this time. There are influences which are relatively more and less important, as has been shown. And probably most important for the prospective teacher, the teacher, the prospective parent, or the parent, is the enormous variation, the individual ways of responding to all the influences that have been mentioned. It seems clear that adolescents from homes which foster educational achievement by virtue of parental interests and encouragement both personally and materially will more probably have higher aspirations and expectations, a more positive sense of their own abilities, a more positive self-concept, and more success in high school. The school an adolescent goes to may, because of an achievement ethic fostered by a high-achieving, higher social-status student body, have some positive effect on academic achievement. But one student, regardless of socio-economic background, regardless of parental encouragement or the nature of his home life, regardless of biases and discriminations against him or her on the basis of sex, ethnicity, or race, may still regard himself as an adequate and able person and, if he has the ability as well as this conception of his ability, will be successful.

Although this section has dwelled mainly on academic achievement, the schools that adolescents attend are also the setting for good portions of their activities in the other life tasks. In and around schools, friends are made and lost, organizations and extensions of activities into the community are joined and developed, stronger love attachments begin, exposure to persons of differing religious and philosophical orientations occur, and the individual—the self—reacts to and develops with all of these. As confusing as the information given on the adolescents in school has been so far, imagine how confusing school is for the adolescent.

The confusion, contradictory valences, and overlappings or interacting of the life tasks seem well represented in the following game. "The High School Game" was developed by Karen Mays[1] in my adolescent course at The University of Texas at Austin a couple of years ago and she has kindly given me permission to use it here, for which I am very grateful.

1. Used with the kind permission of Karen Mays.

To actually play the game one would need a game board with 88 squares numbered from 1–88, and a single die. Each player in order rolls the die and moves the number of squares the die indicates. The squares alternate, the even-numbered squares having an academic meaning and the odd squares designating social aspects of life in high school. By following the symbols and statements for each square at the roll of the die, one moves through high school.

Symbols

★ = roll again
△ = go back
□ = lose a turn
➤ = advance

(The number of symbols equals the number of times the player follows the symbols order, i.e., two ★ ★= roll again twice. If there is no symbol, next player throws and moves.)

The Squares

1. Go. First day of school.

2. Your parents went to college. ★ ★

3. First same-sex friend goes steady, breaks up clique. □ □

4. Art history course.

5. First football game of season.

6. You test out of Spanish. ★

7. Your first offer of marijuana. ★
   Odd, race ahead. Even, relax here a turn.

8. Hard geometry homework. ★

9. Learn to water ski. ★

10. You make an "A" on a pop quiz. ★ ★

11. You are offered a part-time job.

12. Study hall.

13. First kiss. ★ Float ahead this number.

14. Home with the flu. △

15. You make friends with a football hero. ★

16. You do a football hero's homework. □

17. You lose debate for your team. □

18. 1500 word term paper. ★ Odd, advance. Even, go back.

19. Vice-principal's office. ☐

20. You fail an elective. ☐☐

21. You get a new car. ★ ★ ★ (Use now or later)

22. Fire in chem lab. No class. ★

23. Your sister gets married. ☐ Stay home to cry.

24. You spent last night at movies. △

25. You cut school but aren't caught. ★ ★

26. Read *Pilgrim's Progress*.

27. You have a new stereo system. ★

28. You publish a story in *Harper's*. ➤ to 51.

29. First time your father offers you a drink. ★ ★

30. Trip to Europe. ➤ to 51.

31. Classmate O.D.'s. ☐

32. American history exam.

33. Best friend snubs you. ☐

34. Part-time job curbs your studies. △

35. Find a hall pass. ★ (Use now or later)

36. You fall asleep in class. ★ Odd, advance. Even, stay here.

37. You're sent to vice-principal. △ to 19.

38. Oral report on Hamlet. ➤ Five squares.

39. Childhood friend gets married because pregnant. △

40. You lose French homework. ☐

41. You elope. ★ Odd, stay in school. Even, drop out (leave game).

42. You make honor roll. ★ ★

43. Face breaks out. △

44. Achievement tests all day. No class.

45. You feel sulky. ☐

46. You are tired. Go to study hall (12). △

47. You are elected homeroom president.➤ to 51.

48. You don't read *Silas Marner*. △ to 26.

49. Picnic at the lake.

50. Visit counselor to plan next semester.

51. Your picture in school paper. ★★★

52. You forget your books. ☐

53. Best friend moves. ☐☐

54. Go to study hall (12). △

55. You're grounded. ☐ Roll a "2" to get out.

56. The Lit teacher screams at class. △

57. You're tardy. Go to vice principal (19). △

58. Year book day. No classes.

59. You drop out. Leave game.

60. College of your choice wants you. ★★

61. You make tennis team. ★

62. Typing class.

63. Fight with your folks. △ Go back to square you just left.

64. Someone else is top student. △ to pout.

65. Your mother waits up for you. △

66. No exam in government. ★

67. You are suspended for smoking. Roll odd to get back in play.

68. You are suspended for cheating. Roll even to get back in play.

69. The coach knows your name. ★

70. You tutor a friend. ➤ Advance 2 spaces.

71. You discover the office can't hurt you. ★★

72. You win a scholarship. Graduate now.

73. Go to the beach. Spring vacation.

74. Go to the beach. Spring vacation. ★

75. Go to the beach. Spring vacation.

76. Go to the beach. Spring vacation. ★

77. Begin hunting for summer job.

78. You decide to join the army. ★

79. Your steady breaks a date at the last minute. □

80. You finish classes. ★

81. Graduation party.

82. You find out your grade point average. ★
    Odd, it's good. Even, you fail. Leave game.

83. You know it's love. △

84. You decide on a career or a college. ★

85. All night "slumber" party. □ to sleep.

86. Get advanced placement credit in college. ★

87. You get "nice" graduation gifts. △

88. GRADUATION.

The game has somewhat of a middle-class bias, but I think and hope it shows that high school "can be a mess." There is so much going on—so many successes and failures in all life tasks which occur in and around the high school.

Work

The life task work "means contributing to the welfare of others" (Dreikurs, 1953, p. 4). The variety of ways in which one can work for the welfare of others is immense and probably endless. The connection between formal work, a job, and its contribution to the welfare of others may sometimes be indirect and obscure. As one produces, serves, as one's efforts culminate in the maintenance of life or improvement in the quality of life, one's work can be said to be contributing to the welfare of others. Concurrently, as one benefits from his work, carries his own weight, he is not a burden on others and in most cases is contributing to the welfare of those close to him. A person who works, therefore, contributes to both the greater good of society or those further from him as well as those close to him. Women who choose to be housewives contribute most directly to the welfare of others while maintaining a home and providing security, nurturance, and raising children. The person who makes no efforts to maintain and advance lives of others in his immediate environment, of his family, or in his society in general cannot be said to work. "If you're not part of the solution, you're part of the problem." Fulfillment in the life task work is crucial as one lives his life until his life is over. As Erikson has shown, fulfillment in the life task work is crucial in the life stage "generativity," when the older person reviews his life to see where and how he has left his mark.

WORKING HIGH-SCHOOL STUDENTS

Our major interest in this text is adolescence through high school. Early adolescents are not likely to work for many reasons, not the least of which are state laws which prohibit adolescents below certain ages from working. The Department of Labor, Bureau of Labor Statistics, generally considers 16 as the earliest age at which persons work, and its data begins with that age. Examining the 16 and 17-year-olds as of October 1973, there were 7,236,000 people in this age group who were enrolled in school, and 959,000 who were not enrolled in school. Of those 16 and 17-year-olds enrolled in school, 2,978,000, or 41.2 percent, were in the labor force, with all but 15 percent of these employed. Of the 2.5 million employed 16 and 17-year-olds in school, presumably some sophomores but mostly juniors and seniors, 55 percent were male and 45 percent were female. For both sexes combined, the major occupations in which they were employed were service workers, except private households (30.5 percent); laborers, except farm (17.2 percent); craft and kindred workers (13 percent); operatives and kindred workers (11 percent); and sales workers (10.9 percent) (Employment of School-Age Youth, October 1973, Bureau of Labor Statistics, 1974). This data shows what has been a continuing trend, that somewhere in the area of 50 percent of high-school seniors and a considerable proportion of high-school juniors work for pay during the school year. However, the work they do is not necessarily directly related to the work they will do when they finish their education, either high school or college, or to their career, the work that they will do for most of their lifetimes.

Noblitt and Asher (1971) investigated the characteristics of senior high-school students who work for pay. Using approximately 800 subjects from Project Talent, they developed a profile of the working high-school boy—lower academic achievement, poorer reading skills, lower IQ, greater interest in vocational education, more likely to have use of a car, and to date more often. The working high school girl takes fewer English classes, shows less interest in further education, earns her own spending money, and saving part of that money is more important to her.

Work for pay for high-school students may provide experience which allows and facilitates more sophisticated occupational decision making. But most high-school students who work are doing so, it would appear, to promote values as found by Coleman (1961), wherein high-school boys highly value auto ownership and girls value physical beauty, social success, and nice clothes. Moreover, girls who work may be attempting to ensure economic security in order to marry early.

Rice (1975) gives seven reasons why the work experience in adolescence is helpful:

By working the adolescent learns that work is an important and necessary part of life. . . . Working teaches the adolescent responsibility, cooperation, punctuality, and industry. . . . Working helps the adolescent learn social skills and how to get along with many different types of people in a variety of situations. . . . Through working, the adolescent develops autonomy and independence. . . . Working helps the adolescent develop self-assurance, a feeling of self-worth, and to develop his own concept of self. . . . Work enables the adolescent to earn money for things he needs now and in the future. . . . Properly selected work can provide relevant training for the adolescent for a future career (pp. 400–401).

This list bears most strongly on the value of work in adolescence, summating in a young adult who is prepared and knowledgeable to work. Job experience has been shown to relate to satisfactory vocational choice (Hurlock, 1975). These values of work also begin the process of developing vocational values which continually evolve throughout an individual's working years. By the time one is in the late twenties, primary vocational decisions have been made and stability of vocational choice increases thereafter. Sometimes people change jobs because their interests change, but by and large job changes are within the same general vocational categories. The adolescent who works seemingly has an advantage in having begun to appraise his occupational values and develop skills related to working.

The degree to which the reasons given by Rice for adolescents' work experience are helpful can be seen to overlap with, and ease the burden of, the following list of factors which makes vocational choice difficult:

The ever-increasing number of different kinds of work from which to choose.

Rapid changes in work skills due to increased use of automation.

Long and costly preparation which makes job shifts impossible.

Unfavorable stereotypes of some occupations.

A desire for a job that will give an individual a sense of identity, rather than one that makes him feel like a cog in a large machine.

The individual's ignorance of his own capacities due to lack of job experience or vocational guidance.

Unrealistic vocational aims carried over from adolescence.

Unrealistic vocational values, especially concerning prestige and autonomy (Hurlock, 1975, p. 233).

Comparing these two lists, one can see that the adolescent who works and develops skills related to work, social skills, independence, self-assurance, and understanding of some occupations eliminates a number of the factors which make vocational choice difficult. This adolescent could then confront the difficulty factors that are inherent in the magnitude of occupational choices open to persons in a dynamic, developed, changing society.

VOCATIONAL CHOICE AND VOCATIONAL-DEVELOPMENT THEORIES

We cannot hope in this section to do more than introduce some examples from the multitude of theories of vocational choice and development. There are theories of vocational choice grounded in economic, cultural, sociological, psychological, and interdisciplinary theories.

In keeping with the influence-hierarchy model is a cultural and sociological theory of vocational choice described by Super and Bachrach (1957), in which the individual is seen at the center of a series of concentric circles, which represent the social systems with which he interacts. These systems influence his occupational decisions and choices, and may be seen as comparable to the influence hierarchy by Larson presented in Chapter 8. Moving from the most distant circle to the social systems closest to and most directly affecting the individual's decisions are the general American cultural variables, subcultural forces, community variables, and finally home, school, church, etc. At the center of the circle is the individual with his personality—seen in terms of traits or reality testings and subdecisions, perceiving the social systems or influences on him from his personal and biased apperception. And somewhere, probably clouding this entire picture, is serendipity. The system in all its complexity is presented in Figure 12.

Luck, fate, chance, and accident are the reasons given by most laymen for their vocational choice. This popular notion, called the accident theory of vocational choice, may be defined as "chance factors are the fortuitous, unplanned, unpredicted events which affect a person's vocational choice" (Crites, 1969, p. 80). But not only laymen subscribe to this theory—Miller and Form, occupational sociologists, studied the occupational background of a large sample of young people, concluding:

> One characteristic is outstanding in the experience of most of the case histories that have been cited. In their quest of a life work there has been a vast amount of floundering, and chance experiences appear to have affected choices more than anything else. It is the compounding of various experiences and influences which has finally crystallized into a wish for a certain occupation. Chance experiences undoubtedly explain the process by which most occupational choices are made (1951, p. 660).

The social or behavioral scientist aspires to an understanding of any facet of human behavior within a framework, theoretical and then verifiable, of laws or rules which account for as much as possible of the variance and variability in the behavior in this area. A theory in the area of vocational choice based on accident or chance is alien to and discomforting for most behavioral scientists. However, each of us, within our own experience, is aware of the operation of the accident theory personally and among friends. You can think of people you have known in this situation and I will give you some examples of persons I have known. I know a highly successful businessman who left a university where he was a promising anthropology student, on the death of his father, because he had to support the family; a clergyman who, when "turned on by a campus minister," had changed

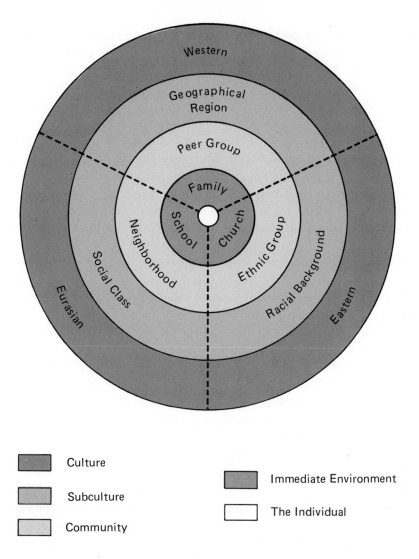

Culture

Subculture

Community

Immediate Environment

The Individual

Figure 12. *Cultural and Social Systems Hypothesized to Be Related to Vocational Choice. (From* Vocational Psychology: The Study of Vocational Behavior and Development. *Copyright © 1969 by McGraw-Hill Inc. Used with permission of McGraw-Hill Book Company.)*

his major from pre-med; a bartender whose part-time bartending job became his career and who never returned for his second year in law school; a high-school honor graduate who gave up a college scholarship and became an apprentice in a building trade when his father's bowling-team partner told him of an opening; a female M.D. whose uncle said he would pay for her schooling if she would become an M.D., an option she had not previously considered; a talent agent whose connections and experience in this field began when she represented her first lover, an entertainer, to the media; etc., etc. And I know a young fellow who had been offered a job as a truck driver who turned it down until the day he fell in love with a car in a used-car lot. That day he dropped out of high school, took the driver's job, put a down payment on the car, and has been driving and out of school since.

"If I knew then what I know now" often prefaces an explanation or lament of a vocational decision which in retrospect an individual considers wrong for him. This may mean that as an adolescent this person did not understand the economic and status aspects of the job chosen, although in the main, adolescents seem to rank occupations accurately, as adults do. Of course, there may be something peculiar to a particular job which made it a bad choice for the individual. The statement that began this paragraph reflects an individual's acknowledgment that the job chosen does not "fit" his personality or interests; that he is more (or less) able, competent—has a higher or lower sense of competence, self-concept—than he thought or felt when he chose the job, and/or that he has changed, developed, since that vocational choice. Psychological theories of vocational choice emphasize personality and personality trait, matching of interests and abilities with choice, self-concept commensurate with choice, and development of rationales and reality testing for making vocational decisions.

The idea behind all psychological theories is that the individual systematically chooses the occupation to enter. Even in analyzing the examples proposed above of the accident theory of vocational choice, the psychological theories presume that an individual would not make the decision that the individuals portrayed above made, except as each individual's interests, values, sense of ability and competence, led him to respond to the change factor in the manner in which he did.

The trait and factor matching theories of vocational choice, generally accepted in this country until the early 1950's, were first explicated by Parsons (1909) in a 3-step process for choosing a vocation which a person was said to go through: with a clear understanding of himself and his aptitudes, abilities, strengths, and weaknesses, and knowledge of all aspects of various occupations, the individual is said to make his decision through the third step, "true reasoning on the relations of these two groups of facts" (p. 5).

In a general way, the notion that, by matching his abilities and dispositions with the demands of a particular occupation, an individual makes his occupational choice, underlies the thinking of laymen and many counselors in explaining and understanding occupational choice. Unfortunately, the research relating occupations to the personalities of the members of those occupations have not supported this theory. Super and Crites (1962) observed that the assumed relationships between particular personality traits and choice and adjustment in certain occupations, as in, "social dominance and selling, submissiveness and bookkeeping" (p. 516) have rarely been found.

Borow (1973) points out that the trait-matching approach has proved static and does not account for the psychology of motivation and human development. The traits exhibited by a high-school freshman which might be thought to relate to a particular vocational choice may not be the same trait exhibited by that student as a high-school senior, and ambitions and aspirations may also change. One wonders whether the traits appropriate to the conductor of a major symphony orchestra are more easily specifiable than the traits appropriate for being in sales—whether selling door-to-door, representing a corporation, or being a sales engineer for international conglomerates. Contemporary trait theory presumes that "The more generalized the activity, on a scale ranging from specific position, to job, to occupation, to occupational group, the larger is the number of (trait) patterns applicable to the activity" (Super and Bachrach, 1957, p. 102).

The psychodynamic and developmental theories of vocational choice elaborate on both the factors preceding choice and the changing factors or considerations in choice. The theories developed by Roe, Holland, Ginsberg, and Super are most prominent and illustrative of psychodynamic and developmental theories of vocational choice.

Some short indication of the content of these most influential theories of vocational choice follows. The validity of the theories is not sufficiently established to allow one to conclude that there is *a* way of assisting adolescents in their career choice. However, counselors and parents are called on to give advice in this area. And teachers, explicitly and implicitly, offer advice in this area all the time. When a teacher turns on a student to a particular subject, a career option may be opening. When a teacher encourages a student by rewarding a set of behaviors, the student may begin to work on the notion that this is something he can do well. And of course when a teacher expresses a value judgment on the status of a job, or the sex-role appropriateness of a job, the teacher may be influencing the students' choices. Lastly, when students seek advice from teachers rather than presenting purely personal opinion, a sense of the field may be helpful to the teacher. For these reasons the following theories are presented.

Roe's Need Theory

Roe's theory (Roe, 1956, 1957; Roe and Siegelman, 1964) is a need theory of vocational choice, one in which the desires and wants of the individual lead to preference for one occupation or another as the primary focus of the theory. Emanating from inherited tendencies interacting with childhood experiences and environment, a style or pattern develops for expending psychic energy and satisfying specific needs or levels of needs that the individual has developed. To some degree unconsciously, without conscious thought, the individual learns to satisfy the needs he feels, needs which have not been satisfied for him. In the process of satisfying his own needs, specific interests, attitudes and values, and abilities are developed and pursued.

Roe uses Maslow's needs hierarchy to define level of needs from the lower-order needs (food, safety, love) which must be satisfied before the higher-order needs (understanding, beauty, self-actualization) may be pursued or become effective. Osipow (1968) presents three specific propositions from Roe's theory:

> . . . (1) Needs that are routinely satisfied do not become unconscious motivators. (2) Higher-order needs, in the sense of Maslow's self-actualization need, will disappear entirely if they are only rarely satisfied; lower-order needs, in the Maslowian sense, will become dominant motivators if they are only rarely satisfied; in the event they become dominant motivators, they will block the appearance of higher-order needs. (3) Needs that are satisfied after unusual delay will become unconscious motivators under certain conditions (p. 18).

These propositions from Roe's theory seem to bear particularly on social-class differences in need satisfaction. Although Crites (1969) assumes that in modern society lower-order needs are usually satisfied "for most people most of the time" (p. 97), it would appear that there are major differences between the lower, or lower-lower socioeconomic groups and the upper-middle and upper socioeconomic groups in satisfaction of the lower-order needs. In groups where there is economic insecurity, hostility and violence in the environment, and greater family instability, many children and adolescents will not feel that their lower-order needs are being satisfied, regardless of an objective determination that they are well-off relative to their peers in Ethiopia or Indochina. Roe concludes, and it must be remembered that her work began with studies of scientists and has continued primarily on professionals and university students, that the self-actualization need is paramount in the choice of a vocation, saying: "All that a man can be he must be if he is to be happy" (1956, p. 29).

Although the research evidence does not strongly support Roe's theory as "an adequate representation of the crucial features of vocational development" (Osipow, 1968, p. 33), a generally unrecognized aspect of her theory is conceptually stimulating and possibly useful for counseling. The theory does not connect specific needs to specific occupations, but points out how any occupation may satisfy needs at some level. The theory "pertains to the relationship between levels of need and occupations, not kinds of needs and occupations" (Crites, 1969, p. 97).

This notion seems crucial. An adolescent may have, or see himself as having, a need to satisfy higher-order needs and do so as a craftsman, a farmer, or even on a production line. So, too, lower-order needs may be satisfied in occupations which presumably demand a human orientation and fulfill self-actualization needs but which also very highly satisfy the lower-order needs, as in such occupations as doctor, lawyer, and psychologist.

The realization between self-actualization and work is illustrated by Hugh Prather (1970) in his *Notes to Myself*:[1]

> Today I want to do things to be doing
> Them, not to be doing something else. I
> Do not want to do things to sell myself
> On myself. I don't want to do nice things
> For people so that I will be "nice."
> I don't want to work to make money,
> I want to work to work.
>
> Today I don't want to live for,
> I want to live

Clearly one must feel very satisfied at the lower-order needs level to be able to make the above self-actualizing statement.

Holland's Personal-Orientation Theory

Holland's theory (1958, 1964, 1966) is one in which a personal orientation, the style or pattern of dealing with the environment in preferred ways, should match the occupational environment (in a sense a matching-occupation orientation) for appropriate occupational choice and adjustment. He proposes that to the degree that a person has a stable personal orientation, a well-integrated and consistent orientation, he will have clarity in vocational choice and stability in vocational behavior. The orientations developed by Holland are realistic, intellectual, social, conventional, enterprising, and artistic. The literature contains some confirmatory evidence for Holland's theory. It is a more sophisticated version conceptually, but less precise in some ways, of the trait-matching theory. However, Holland does not speak to the issue of development of personal orientations and therefore adds little to developmental information.

Ginzberg's Developmental Theory

Ginzberg's theory (Ginzberg, 1972; Ginzberg et al., 1951) is a developmental one which has evolved considerably to its most recent form. Ginzberg proposed movement through three primary psychological periods, a fantasy period, tentative

1. H. Prather, *Notes to Myself*. Moab, Utah: © Real People Press, 1970.

period, and realistic period. The fantasy period covers childhood up to about age 11. Children by the age of 4 or 5 are able clearly to state vocational preferences, which I am reminded of since my 6-year-old son declared yesterday that he wants to be a farmer, to me a clear come-down from the astronaut he wanted to be last week. Through the fantasy period, because of insufficient information and a sense of inadequacy in their own childishness, children "play" at work and assume made-up work-role identities. In this play and in their acting out of occupational roles children do not consider the various presses of occupations such as abilities, training, economics and opportunities, potentials, and time perspectives.

The next period, the tentative period, is said to last from approximately age 11 to age 18 and is divided into three stages. The interest stage, ages 11 and 12, finds the child recognizing the need to consider and identify a career area, and the interest is shown through identification of activities and areas which are liked or disliked, enjoyed or not enjoyed. In the capacity stage, ages 12 to 14, the adolescent begins to put together the notion of ability, necessary and relevant aptitudes and education, with their areas of vocational interest. In the value stage, ages 15 and 16, issues of service to society, personal goals, and need satisfaction at all levels that the adolescent feels and is cognitively aware of, come into play. At about age 18 or 19 the adolescent moves into the transition stage, during which the individual confronts the necessity of making concrete and realistic decisions about his vocational future which will have immediate and direct consequences for him.

The realistic stage begins at about 18 and although Ginzberg earlier stated that it concluded as late as age 24, he concedes that realistic vocational choices and decision making may occur throughout one's lifetime. During the realistic stage, the adolescent is, in a sense, forced, either through termination of schooling or choice of the continuation of schooling, to make efforts to resolve his questions of vocational choice. He attempts to coordinate the self-knowledge in the area of vocation that he has developed to this point with his knowledge of the openings and opportunities in the social and economic world. From his earlier interpretation, which viewed the adolescent as compromising with reality, Ginzberg now sees the adolescent as attempting to optimize personal satisfaction through career decision.

Although Ginzberg divides the realistic stage into further periods, these periods pertain to post-high-school adolescence but do not differentiate between college students and nonstudent youths. Ginzberg's studies were mostly carried out on upper-income adolescents, primarily boys. He did investigate the applicability of this theory among underprivileged boys and using a female sample. He concluded that, in general, underprivileged, lower socioeconomic boys' and females' vocational development paralleled the development of the boys on whose data the original stages were built, through the fantasy and tentative stages. At the realistic stage, however, there is divergence from his male highly privileged sample. It appears that the variance in role and educational patterns that differentiate upper middle from lower socioeconomic males and males from females, upsets the progression of periods within the realistic stage. Moreover, the underprivileged boys' sample parallels the privileged boys' through the interest and capacity stages, but this parallel was obscured in the value stage of the tentative period and during the transition period. The value stage and transition stage would presumably be more difficult and more clearly defined for adolescents into, or well into, formal operations, and also more demanding for them in terms of their consideration of options and their greater potential occupational options. The particulars of Ginzberg's theory possibly overdefine the sequence and timing of the stages and thereby may limit its value. But the general theory is receiving some support in the research literature.

Super's Self-Concept Theory

Super's theory (Super, 1957, 1973; Super et al., 1957, 1963) is the most extensive of the psychological theories of vocational choice and development. The theory is based on the notion of the self-concept which the adolescent brings with him into adolescence. In adolescence there develops a vocational self-concept, which is part of the individual's global self-concept but is particular to, and developed in contrast and in evaluation with, others in the vocational world as perceived by the individual adolescent. The vocational self-concept is similar to the self-concept of academic ability spoken of earlier. However, the self-concept of academic ability was developed through childhood as the child was participating in and able to measure himself in the academic arena. The vocational self-concept does not really spring to the fore until adolescence when issues and press for a vocational decision begins. Super says that the adolescent has to "translate" his self-concept into occupational terms to develop the vocational self-concept.

Super has elaborated the concept of vocational maturity and defined it normatively as the correspondence between the vocational behavior exhibited by an individual and the vocational behavior expected for an individual at that age. Super specifies five vocational developmental tasks which are: crystallization of a vocational preference (14 to 18 years), specification of a vocational preference (18 to 21 years), implementation of a vocational preference (21 to 24 years), stabilization within a vocation (25 to 35 years), and consolidation of status and advancement (35 years plus). The ages given are typical of the age range at which these developmental tasks are reached and passed through, but are not rigidly defined.

Implementation of vocational preference, which includes obtaining a first job in the preferred vocation, cannot without considerable wasted time occur for the high-school graduate in the age range typically stated for it. The high-school graduate who obtains a first job in the vocation preferred would probably do so at age 18 or 19. This age flexibility in the theory allows investigation of movement through the stages according to differing career-development patterns, and is a real advantage of this theory. Most recently, Super (1973) has presented a problem-solving sequence, developed to foster understanding of computer-system use in vocational counseling. The general model of problem-solving steps to vocational choice which follows may be seen elongated or shortened according to the press for decision making on the adolescent. That is, the high-school graduate who is not going on to college needs to reach the stage of implementation more quickly than the college student. The sequence is:

- Anticipation
- Awareness of the need to choose among alternatives
- Acceptance of responsibility for choice
- Awareness of factors to be considered
- Knowledge of sources and resources
- Crystallization
- Use of resources for exploration and information
- Clarification
- Awareness of the consequences of choice
- Specification
- Synthesis of information and the choice
- Implementation
- Action on the choice

Super feels that this sequence may be potentially useful in guidance and counseling. In fact all of these theories have been useful in guidance as employed by trained counselors utilizing the measuring instruments developed for each. Super's sequence, above, illustrates the steps the adolescent goes through, but adds to its utility as it indicates for the teacher or advisor differing kinds of information the adolescent should be offered. It also appears that there is a parallel between the kinds of information and decisions an adolescent who is not going on to college makes in relation to a job and the kinds of information a college-bound adolescent makes use of in choosing a college. Super's sequence appears worthy of study for both of these purposes.

Blau's Conceptual Framework

A "conceptual framework" integrating economics, psychology, and sociology, developed by Blau et al. (1956), places the vocational choice in a broader perspective, particularly as it reminds us that entry into an occupation is not solely determined by the preference of the individual, but is dependent too on the appropriateness of the individual for a job as determined by an employer and the availability of such jobs as determined by economic conditions. Occupational entry is seen as an inter-action of vocational choice and occupational selection. "In choice, the individual compromises between preferred and expected occupations, whereas in selection the occupation compromises between ideal and available workers" (Crites, 1969, p. 110). Blau sees the determinants of occupational choice, selection, and entry divided be-tween those factors which are influential prior to the time of entry into an occupation and those factors which are operative at the time of entry into an occupation. Blau therefore sees occupational choice as a long-term developmental process in which there are antecedent conditions for the individual (biological conditions: native endowment, socialization, and personality development); antecedent conditions for the occupation; the selection agency (the physical-economic conditions and historical change); and both the individual and agency antecedent conditions interact with the social structure.

> Within the limits set by his native endowment, the individual responds to the social structure within which he lives, particularly the family unit and the educational system, and forms various typical reaction patterns, which together constitute his personality. As he makes decisions about occupations at various points in his life, his personality influences his thinking. . . . Similarly, the interaction of social insti-tutions with technological advancements affects the composition and nature of occupa-tion and brings about changes in them over periods of time which are reflected in their demands and rewards for individuals with certain qualifications (Crites, 1969, pp. 110–112).

The more immediate factors influencing the selection agency at the time of proposed entry into an occupation by an individual are the socioeconomic organiza-tion (division of labor, distribution and turnover, policies, stages of the business cycle), and the agency's demand, requirements, and rewards for a potential em-ployee. The more immediate factors influencing the individual at this time include his sociopsychological attributes (knowledge, abilities, education, social position, aspirations, expectations, and motivations) and his immediate preparedness and appropriateness in terms of qualifications, characteristics, and values for that job. As conceptualized by Blau it is within these three nonstatic processes—vocational choice by the individual and occupational selection by the agency—in interaction at one point in time that occupational entry by an individual is determined.

Correlates of Vocational Aspirations and Choice

The story of how a little kid from anywhere grows up to be the holder of a particular occuptional role is a fantastically complex one, as the theory section should have indicated. The full range of influences is operative on the child's and then the adolescent's aspirations, preferences, expectations, and choices. According to which measuring instruments are used, the sample, the geographical region, the specific hypotheses of the study, etc., the empirical findings are in agreement or conflict. Research in this area in general has been going on throughout this century. It is therefore at this point mammoth. In this section, conclusions that are generally agreed upon as to the influence, or relationship, between factors and their vocational aspects will be considered.

Intelligence has been shown to be related to vocational choice (Holden, 1961), and vocational preference (Porter, 1954). Perrone (1964), using Roe's system for determining vocational preference, concluded that "The most significant finding of this study is that boys with similar scores on cognitive measures tend to indicate a preference for similar occupational groups" (p. 978). Stubbins (1950), on a sample of over 200 male World War II veterans, obtained a correlation of .43 between intelligence and aspiration. Although for some reason he considered this a rather low correlation coefficient, it is in comparison with most correlations in this field rather high, and provides ample indication of the relationship between aptitude and aspiration.

A number of aspects of personality (personality viewed from a number of positions) has been shown to be related to vocational choice. Super's hypothesis that "in choosing an occupation one is, in effect, choosing a means of implementing a self-concept" (1951, p. 92), has been tested and in general supported by a number of studies of education majors (Englander, 1960), nursing and education majors (Morrison, 1962), and twelfth-grade boys (Blocher and Schutz, 1961). Oppenheimer (1966) tested Super's hypothesis, using yet another measuring instrument, and concluded that "people prefer occupations perceived as congruent with their self-concept" (p. 194). Studies by Schutz and Blocher (1961) and Stockin (1964) lend support to the thesis in Holland's theory that a relationship exists between vocational choice and self-evaluation, which is defined broadly as including status needs, sense of competence and potential competence, and interpersonal evaluation of work. A study by Osipow, Ashby, and Wall (1966) among college students lends support to Holland's other major thesis that personality types relate to vocational choices.

A recent study by Manaster and Perryman (1974) analyzed early recollections in order to differentiate between persons choosing different occupations. College majors in teaching, counseling, nursing, biological science, and accounting were used. The early-recollection technique asks the subject to recall and relate the earliest scenes that can clearly be remembered. Differences found point to long-term, deeply embedded personality differences of a global nature between persons choosing different types of occupation. For example, the nursing and counseling majors were most similar in having a higher frequency of mentioning "mother" in their early recollections than did the biological science, teaching, and business groups. If a person has a lifestyle in which the "mother-helper-supporter" image is important, the fields of nursing and counseling seem natural occupational choices to manifest that lifestyle. The teaching, biological science, and accounting groups showed more neutral affects in their early recollections than did the nursing and counseling groups. There were indications that the counseling group showed more positive affect than the other groups and that the counseling and nursing subjects showed more negative affect than the other group. These findings

are consistent with the affective differences that might be expected to exist for people in these occupations. People choosing to be counselors and nurses live in a more "emotional world," i.e., more open to and active with emotion. On the other hand people choosing to be biological scientists, teachers, and businessmen might be expected to see life in less emotional terms (p. 236).

Manaster and Friedman (in press) analyzed questionnaire data collected from a large sample of high school graduates who had indicated that they would be pre-medical students when they enrolled in college. The data was collected in the summer prior to fall entrance to the university. Of this large pre-med group, 52 stated they wished to be surgeons, 29 pediatricians, 18 psychiatrists, and 43 intended to specialize but had not yet decided on a specialization. Differences between self-assessment, future priorities, and recollections of early experiences were found between these future specialists—and it should be pointed out that at the very least, it would be seven years until they began their specialization training. The future psychiatrist was seen as reflective, confused, and less emotionally stable, with lower self-confidence than surgeons who were seen as emotionally stable and saw themselves as well-suited for their chosen specialization. The future pediatricians remember their mothers as having stable dispositions and are the least complaining of any unsatisfactory family life. The psychiatrists, whose memories of their families were less favorable, were uninterested in family practice, whereas the pediatricians whose memories were most favorable obviously intended to go into family practice. Interestingly, and in keeping with earlier statements about needs and satisfaction available at different levels and different types of jobs, the group of future specialists who were undecided on a specialization appeared much more susceptible to external influences on their career and had the highest desire for status and monetary reward from their specializations.

Research on personality and vocational choice, etc., is fraught with contradictory findings and inconsistencies. Nonetheless, the field of research flourishes. It appears to be that with sensible and sensitive selection of personality variables and occupation, and/or broad open instruments which allow subjects to show their personality characteristics, strengths, and predispositions (rather than the variables the researcher wants to look at), the personality-by-occupation relationship will be more strongly supported.

Family Influences

The last two studies, particularly through analysis of early recollections, early family life, and personality, illustrate again what every student of psychology must by now know, the relationship between family (at least as perceived by the individual) and personality.

We keep coming back to the direct and subtle ways in which parents and family influence adolescents in all of the life tasks. In the choice of occupation, parents' direct influence, direct in the sense of open, overt, may have a decided effect on the adolescent's vocational choice. If at 21 you can expect to be vice-president in charge of anything in your father's company, which will some day be your own, you well may have your vocational choice made for you. Over 90 percent of farmers' sons choose to go into farming (Gottlieb and Ramsey, 1964). Parents in craft unions are often able to wangle apprenticeships for their children and their children often take them.

Parents may steer, or try to steer, their child into a particular occupation by providing encouragement and training in the relevant area. They may go further. One thinks of extremes such as Shirley Temple or Judy Garland, whose parents chose their occupations for them when they were children, with, as history shows, mixed outcomes. Or watch when Jimmy Connors plays championship tennis on television. The camera pans to his mother in the crowd, and the broadcaster mentions, "She forced a tennis racket in his hand when he was four."

In terms of vocational interest and vocational choice, "identification with both parents influences the formation of vocational interest patterns, but identification with the father is more important than with the mother" (Crites, 1962, p. 269) for boys. The quality of the identification, in nature of attitudes toward parents, is seen in differences between occupational groups. Segal and Szabo (1964) found that accountants had more positive attitudes toward their parents, other people, and were more accepting of authority and rules, than were creative writers. Their interpretation was that the accountants' positive attitudes toward others were generalized from their attitudes toward their parents. Segal (1961) had earlier hypothesized a "seeking for the completion of multiple identification in creative writing students" (p. 208) which may be a function of the more negative identification found for this group. Either positive or negative identification, acceptance of the identification relationship, or rejection of the role model may equally well influence career decisions and patterns: "Their importance may be more similar than it has been commonly realized. Each may serve as important occasions for self-definition" (Bell, 1969, p. 34). Permutations of "My Son, the Doctor" could include "My Son, the Doctor, is a Bum" or "My Son, the Bum, is a Doctor." Parents influence adolescents in the models they present for them and their wishes for their children, their hopes and aspirations for their child, their motivational influence.

Parents, particularly father for son, may be a very concrete role model as evidenced when son follows in the father's footsteps. Although this occurs more frequently than would be the case if occupations were chosen randomly, there are great variations in the literature as to the extent of this practice. More importantly, adolescents tend to choose, enter, and remain in occupations at the same socioeconomic level as their fathers or one level above. This may be more a function of socioeconomic status of family of origin, does not seem to account for family differences within socioeconomic levels, and will be mentioned again in the section on socioeconomic status influences.

Parental motivation, the support, encouragement, and ambitions that parents have for their children, influence the ambitions and aspirations of the adolescent regardless of the adolescent's ability and social-class status (Douvan and Adelson, 1966; Simpson, 1962). Simpson (1962) found that ambitious middle-class boys and ambitious working-class boys received far more parental support than unambitious working-class boys. He pointed out that parental support, parental motivation, may be a more accurate indication of the adolescent's ambition than socioeconomic status alone.

Peer, School, and Subgroup Influences

The influence of peers, teachers, and school on vocational interests and choices involve each other, as well as family of origin and social class, to such an extent that a mixed, or composite, statement may be most informative. Armour, in his *A Diabolical Dictionary of Education* (1969), defines peer group as "in education, a peer group is a group of students of about the same age and ability who, also being about the same height, can peer at each other on equal footing. In this sense the 'peer' goes back to the Latin *par* meaning equal" (p. 87). As is so often the case, there is a strong element of truth in humor. In this humorous definition there is the implication that peers, a group of friends and associates, stick together because they are on an equal footing, or stay on an equal footing in order to stick together.

The peer group, *in toto*, in the school characterized by a similarity of socioeconomic status among the majority in that school, conveys the dominant values for that school and total peer group. If the dominant values are upper middle class, even the working-class adolescents in the school will be affected in choice of occupation by that dominant value climate. And this operates in reverse fashion if the dominant group is a working-class group. "The dominant climate of opinion within a school makes a significant impact upon students' occupational goals . . ." (Wilson, 1959, p. 844). High-school students who intend to go on to college are influenced in their vocational choice, in the form of college major, particularly, by favorite teachers or those few teachers whom they get to know well (Carlin, 1960; E. G.

Johnson, 1967). Although peer influence is notable, parental influence is more important overall than peer influence (Simpson, 1962).

The composite situation appears to be this: the adolescent will approach school and vocational choice in all probability with the expectations appropriate for, or held in common by, the majority of his socioeconomic status group. If his parents have been particularly encouraging and ambitious for him, or the reverse, his expectations and aspirations will be accordingly higher or lower than the norm for his own socioeconomic status group. If the majority group in his school is of the same socioeconomic status as his own, his tendency will be to adhere to the norms for expectations and aspirations as that dominant group. If the dominant group is different from his, there will be a tendency, particularly if supported by parental encouragement, for him to move toward the norms of the dominant group. In a mixed socioeconomic school there would appear to be more leeway, more potential for movement, in ambitions and choices according to the level of ambition promoted by parents and assumed by the adolescent.

Studying academic achievement among working class Mexican-Americans in junior high schools, Manaster and King (1972) predicted that the "clannishness," the sticking together, commonly attributed to Mexican-Americans, would operate to a greater degree when the Mexican-American students were a minority in a school than when they were equal to or greater in number than the other students in the school. They found that there was a tendency for students, when a minority in a school, to show smaller variance on GPA. When the Mexican-American students were about equal in number to the others there was no difference, but when they were a majority their variance was larger. It appears that for this particular ethnic group, with the social characteristics attributed to it, minority status in a school has the effect of closing doors, closing opportunities, to students, while accentuating peer influence, thus eliciting stricter adherence to group norms. Cherry (1974) found:

> . . . the effect of school composition on "ambition" is relevant to decisions about comprehensive education and the catchment area for local comprehensive schools. Children from working class homes in schools with mainly working class pupils appear to have less interest in breaking with working class occupational traditions than do similar children mixing with pupils from more varied home backgrounds. Social class and the parent interest in education are shown to be of substantial importance in determining the ambition of children at non-selective schools. If the school is to counter the effect on job choice of poor family circumstances, the area from which it draws its pupils may be important in determining the acceptability of occupational information and guidance (p. 29).

If the schools, or the society, take the responsibility for instilling in children and adolescents the motivation to achieve vocationally at higher levels, then the effects and influence of socioeconomic status and sex on aspirations and expectations must be countered. Children and adolescents are socialized into the roles they occupy and the roles that surround them in the society. To a great degree, adolescents come to a common orientation of what is important, common values, and common aspiration and expectation levels appropriate to (by virtue of being common to) the members of their class. So, too, still today, the vast majority of boys and girls develop the values, aspirations, and expectations traditionally appropriate in the vocational arena for their own sex. Aspiration level has been shown to be related to family socioeconomic status and a variety of environmental correlates of family SES (Hollingshead, 1949; Thomas, 1956; Tseng, 1971; Youmans, 1956), as well as sex (Seward and Williamson, 1969), although the relationship between aspiration level and sex may be in the process of change (Seward and Williamson, 1970; Steinmann, 1963).

At a time in history when change appears so rapid and all-encompassing, many people, and especially many young people, tend to notice and pay more attention to the changes than the constants. For that reason, it seems worth noting a series of studies which indicates the continuing and pervasive influences of socioeconomic status and sex on occupational aspirations and expectations.

In investigating occupational aspirations and expectations, some form of measuring device must be used, and there are many such devices available, which in essence ask the questions, "What job, kind of job, prestige level of job, would you like to have?" and "What job, kind of job, prestige level of job, do you expect to have?" The researcher must then, depending on the measuring instrument, calculate the occupational-prestige level of the answers to both the aspiration and expectation question. The concept of level of aspiration, as in idealistic goal, and expectation, as a realistic goal, is well established in the literature (Haller and Miller, 1963; Stephenson, 1955). In order for the findings from investigations of occupational aspirations and expectations using these devices to be valid, to make any sense at all, the subjects taking the tests must understand the occupational-prestige hierarchy. Tseng (1971), in a study of middle, lower, and lower-lower-class high-school students, found "that as the social class of the group shifted away from the middle class toward the lower socioeconomic levels, the S's perceptions of occupational prestige hierarchy became significantly more distorted from a national norm standpoint" (p. 90). This finding may be a function of the inclusion in the sample of lower-lower-class students. There have been other studies in which lower-lower-class, and particularly lower-lower-class minority, high-school students' perceptions of the occupational prestige hierarchy and their place and potential within that hierarchy were distorted and unrealistic.

It appears that adolescents from the lower working class up are fully capable of understanding the occupational-prestige hierarchy and responding sensibly to questions of occupational aspiration and expectation. In a major cross-national study (Peck et al., 1973), in which over 10,000 upper-middle class and upper-lower, skilled working class ten and fourteen-year-olds were tested, generally accurate and adequate understanding of the relative positions of occupations on the occupational-prestige hierarchy was found for children and adolescents in Brazil, England, Italy, Japan, Mexico, and the United States. The United States data, collected in the Chicago area and Central Texas, and made up of approximately 1200 white ten and fourteen-year-old, male and female, upper-middle and upper-lower-class students in each locale, found in both areas males' aspirations and expectations were higher than females', and middle-class children's aspirations and expectations were higher than upper-lower-class children's. In studies of the same socioeconomic, sex, and age groups in Puerto Rico and Mexico (Manaster and Ahumada, 1970) and in India (Manaster, Ahuja, and Pannu, in press), socioeconomic-status differences of the same direction and order were found for both occupational aspirations and expectations. Although due to a peculiarity in the Indian sample the Indian females had higher occupational expectations than did the Indian males for the total sample, in Puerto Rico and Mexico females' aspirations and expectations were lower than those of the males. In both studies the aspiration and expectation discrepancies between males and females was greater at age 14 than at age 10, leading to the conclusion in the Indian case that "males who stay in school longer, the fourteen-year-olds in this sample, have higher aspirations and expectations than the younger males. Females who stay in school longer have lower aspirations and expectations than the younger females." The data, collected within the last six or seven years, in ten countries around the world, reinforces the enduring influences of socioeconomic status and sex on occupational aspirations and expectations, and presumably, therefore, occupational choice.

Vocational Choice, Sex, Ethnicity, and the Future

It would be a joy to be able to say that the strictures, biases, and prejudices which have excluded females and minority-group members from particular occupations and occupational prestige levels have vanished. It would be a joy to be able to say that "cultural pluralism" at its best is operative in America today. ("At best, 'cultural pluralism' means that the separate groups coexist harmoniously, secure in their distinctive biological, religious, linguistic, or social customs and equal in their accessibility to natural resources, civil rights, and political power" [Havighurst and Dreyer, 1975, p. 269].) Clearly we have not moved that far.

It would be equally erroneous to say that the barriers to equal occupational opportunities exist to the degree that they have in the past. "Cultural pluralism" at its worst is not operative. ("At worst, 'cultural pluralism' means that the separate groups compete with each other for economic, social, and political power, regarding each other suspiciously as threats to their own survival and well-being" [Havighurst and Dreyer, 1975, p. 270].)

Income and occupational status for minority-group members and females is still considerably lower than that of majority-group males. Sufficient statistics abound indicating that the situation is improving. That it has not improved enough to satisfy many and exhibit cultural pluralism at its best is obvious. Organized efforts of representative groups from these populations as well as the continuing efforts of governmental agencies hold promise of further improving the situation in time.

Yet the theme running through this book has been that in the final analysis the individual, regardless of race, creed, ethnicity, or sex, has potential and responsibility for his or her choices, achievement, and way of life. The group figures, the probability statistics, are merely that. But they indicate the greater or lesser difficulty that might be expected of adolescents from particular backgrounds in meeting the life tasks, which ultimately are individual life challenges.

Women whose career choices are influenced by what they think men feel are appropriate women's jobs (Hawley, 1971), and/or who maintain preferences for typically feminine occupations even when this is contrary to their interests and potentials (Harmon, 1971), are clearly not meeting their individual potential. They are not taking full responsibility for their decisions and future. The obstacles they see in the society are there. However, their efforts to remove these obstacles may take the form of choosing and working for the occupation and way of life they desire, as well as working in the more organizational process mentioned above.

The efforts of readers of this book, the future parents, teachers, counselors, and scholars, must be to support the individual children and adolescents with whom they work to realize, both in the sense of understanding and fulfillment, their potential. This means your efforts must be toward equality in the greater society *and* in your dealings with individuals, while also encouraging individual children and adolescents. Encouragement engenders the sense of competence needed for them to make their own decisions. And encouragement suggests presenting them with the most enriching experiences which in turn allow them to choose occupations without regard to sex typing or the traditional domination of that occupation by a certain group (Almquist and Angrist, 1970). The future is bright to the extent that we make it so for ourselves and make it so that others may brighten their own futures.

Family, Friends, and Community

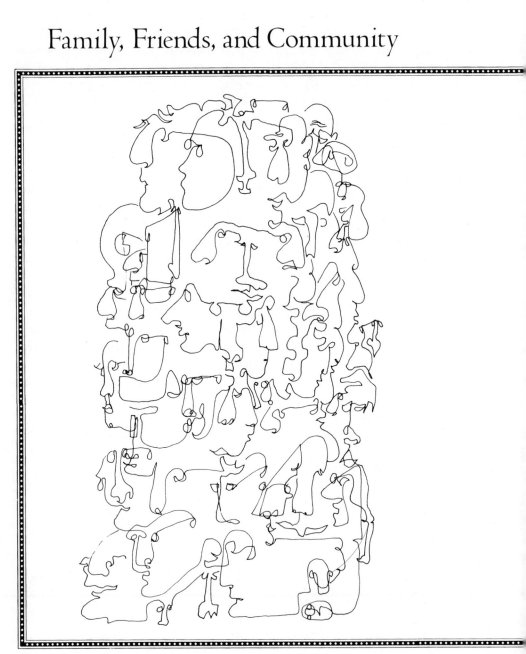

CHAPTER 12

The life task of family, friends, and community is an evolving one. That is, when a child is preadolescent, his community and friends are severely limited, the family being the center of his life. In adolescence, the movement is essentially one from major emphasis and influences of family to greater influence and emphasis of friends and movement into the greater community.

The developmental tasks that fit within the friends and community life task can be seen as evolving in this same order—family to friends to community (Havighurst, 1972). They are, first, "achieving emotional independence of parents and other adults (p. 55); second, "achieving new and more mature relations with agemates of both sexes (p. 45) and "desiring and achieving socially responsible behavior" (p. 75).

The nature of the situation or what we called the situational element for this life task may therefore be broken down into these three major areas: the relationship and the relative influence of family; the relationship and relative influence of peers as individuals and groups; and, lastly, the movement, participation with large groups, small groups, and intimate friends, i.e., being integrated as a member of the total community.

THE FAMILY

The nature of the American family has, in the eyes of many social scientists and social philosophers, changed considerably in this century. Certainly we are a more urban people, and more dependent on each other, major institutions, and governmental agencies and institutions. There is no doubt that in many of our cities, and in many of our suburbs, there is a degree of personal isolation

231

and therefore dependence on social institutions which is much different from the close-knit interdependent family that existed in the past. But nonetheless the family in America today is still central in the lives of almost all children; it is still a crucial factor in emotional and social development. It cannot and should not be forgotten that the family is by no means lost in the modern technological society.

The family in America, by virtue of differing in socioeconomic status, ethnic and cultural background, rural, suburban, and urban setting and geographic area, is extremely diverse. In this chapter we will not differentiate to any degree according to these differences, but rather we will attempt to look at the adolescent's movement from and problems within the family as he attempts to achieve independence, as evidenced in studies which investigate something of the dynamics of family and peers. A quote by Martineau (1966) indicates, I believe, how the influence hierarchy affects parents in responding to the dictates and contradictions of society and funnels the influences through to the child. Martineau says that "To one degree or another [the adolescent] absorbs the contradictory feelings that the parent has about his social status, his income, his jobs, his friends, and applies them to himself" (p. 277).

So too, Lidz (1969) sees the development of children into adolescents as an additional influence on parental behavior and interaction. The impact on the parents of the onset of adolescence in a son or daughter may be intensified due to the confrontation of the parents with the full spectrum of middle age. At this time the parents attempt to come to terms with the limits of their own lives, their accomplishments, the frustrations they have met in meeting or not meeting their own ambitions and ideals. The adolescent at this same time confronts them with adolescent insecurities, rebelliousness, and resentments. From Lidz's point of view, the male adolescent seeks to assert himself and wants to be more instrumental in the decision making of the family. If the parents are unable to surrender some of their prerogatives, the adolescent's drives are turned toward disruption of the family system. The female more likely seeks to live out the expressive-affectional role in the family. Rebellion in this instance may take the form of open hostility or incitement of siblings to defiance. This bears a strong relationship to Parson and Bales' (1955) view of the male instrumental role and the female expressive role, and we may look to see whether we find in our development of the parent-peer conflict in adolescence an instrumental-expressive dichotomy.

Two studies by Cameron (1970a, 1970b) present evidence that youth envy adults their power and wealth, and that adults envy youth their sexual vitality and prowess. Conflict between generations on the basis of unfulfilled needs in each generation is evident here as it is in Lidz's work.

Attaining Autonomy

In attempting to look at the movement toward independence of the adolescent, from the family to an independent member of the community, we will look at it from within the framework of family or parental power and influence versus the adolescent's power and influence. The idea is that the more power that is asserted over an individual, the less his independence, and the adolescent's battle is therefore to move to an independent position from beneath others, parents', power. The adolescent wishes to develop a modicum of control over his own actions and, in the process of developing this control, to exercise some power of his own. At the same time he realizes, probably through his anxiety, that he is not intellectually, psychologically, or emotionally ready to deal with the world or to exercise power in a mature, adult-like manner. Lastly, his anxiety continues because he is fearful of too much separation from his parents. So the movement to independence is not like walking out of the house with head up, fully confident that "now as an adolescent I am a powerful, autonomous human being." Rather, a conflict exists within the adolescent between being fully autonomous and being able to rely on the protection of his parents. Thornburg (1970) says, "The ambivalent conflict is affected by the need to relinquish childhood ties on the one hand and to find sufficient independent behaviors that do not overpower the adolescent on the other" (p. 474).

In one way the adolescent feels, maybe knows down deep, that he cannot handle, and does not want, too much independence and power, so he attempts to stay within the aegis of his parents; but at the same time he tries to demonstrate his independence and fights, or at least exerts himself, to wrest more independence from his parents. The parents then are put on the spot. How much independence to grant? The more independence, the more power over his own life, they grant to the adolescent, the more power they lose over the adolescent.

Salzman (1973) points to this problem from the perspective of parents who must be seen within the influence hierarchy as being influenced both from higher levels of the hierarchy and also from their children, their adolescents, at lower levels in the hierarchy. Salzman points to an implicit demand on the part of parents that youth conform to the standards set for them by their parents because the parents have raised them, are responsible for them and their further socialization and development. If the standards of the adolescent differ excessively from the parents' standards he will, from the parents' point of view, not be accepted by society. It is the responsibility of the parent, as the parent views it, to see that this does not happen. Moreover, the parents fear that if their child participates in behaviors that are not in keeping with the parental standards, and thereby deviant, it might have an adverse effect on the parents, emanating from the possibility of their being labeled as failures as parents. Salzman says, therefore, that parents are very hesitant to relinquish any of their power over their child and to grant their child independence, for if this independence is misused, it will reflect negatively on the parents. This is not something that parents readily admit, both because it reflects badly on their child and because they fundamentally wish to have their children grow to be independent, responsible adults.

There is then this two-way problem or conflict within both parents and their adolescent children. There is hesitancy on the part of the adolescent to accept too much independence and power over his own life, although he outwardly demands it. There is hesitancy on the part of the parents to give this power and independence, for the reasons Salzman states, though the parent wants to give his child power and independence to enable him to grow and develop according to the best standards of the society as the parents perceive them.

In a study of freshman college students and their parents, 184 nuclear units, Lerner and Knapp (1975) assessed the comparability of their attitudes toward contemporary societal issues. They found that, although parents and adolescents were fairly accurate in assessing the attitudes of each other, there was a tendency for parents "to minimize discrepancies between themselves and their children, and a tendency for the adolescents as a group to magnify such discrepancies" (p. 35). In terms of attitude consistency between parents and adolescents, the youth seem to feel that the difference is greater than it is, whereas the parents feel the opposite. That may be a good guide for parents and teachers. As large as you feel the gap is, the adolescents think it is larger.

Goodman (1969) spoke to the issue of this conflict when he developed three stages in the growth of autonomy: the "they-me" of infancy and childhood, wherein the child is subservient and dependent, powerless against "they"; the second stage, "I-me," occurring during adolescence, wherein the individual attempts to acquire power over his own self and his own behavior; and the third stage, the mature stage, called "I-them," wherein control over others has developed from control over oneself. Studying the adolescent in terms of parent, teacher, and friends reference groups and home, family, school, and peer areas of behavior, Goodman hypothesized that in order to express a degree of autonomy and power the adolescent calls upon a different subgroup of his total reference group when interacting with each subgroup. The adolescents conformed more with parents in the peer role and more with their peers in their family role. In this way the adolescent was able to show his independence from parents by depending on and exclaiming norms of his peer group in the family-behavior area, while conversely calling on the norms of his parents when interacting with his peers. This very interesting juxtaposition of norms and behaviors is cunningly safe for the "marginal man" adolescent. Remembering Lewin's thesis that the adolescent is marginal in not being a part truly of either the child or adult group, Goodman's study shows how the adolescent can keep his foot, so to speak, in both camps. The adolescent does so by being defiant of his parents when in their presence and under their direct control but still maintaining their protection by comforming to their expectations when he is out of their sight, out of their direct control.

When it is said that the influence of peers is greater in adolescence than in childhood, people often construe this to mean that the peer influence is so great as to exclude previous and current parent and family influence. The dynamics of the movement out of the total power scope of the family in adolescence certainly does not mean that the adolescent jumps completely into another realm of influence. Talk of the generation gap has implied that this kind of total jump has been made; that the adolescent's values, views, norms, attitudes, etc., are completely opposite from and opposed to those of their parents and all people over thirty. A short review of recent evidence looking at differences in values and norms between parents and adolescents may give us some additional perspective on the nature of the "generation gap," of the relative influence of parents and peers.

Solomon (1972) argues that a sense of family identity is a necessary aspect of a healthy adjustment to maturity. He says that autonomy is not reached until part of the parental image has been internalized. The values and norms held by the parents thus must in some way be internalized in order for maturity to be reached, and one would expect some congruence between parents and adolescents in terms of these norms and values. In Havighurst's (1972) description of the developmental task "achieving emotional independence of parents and other adults," he says the goal of the task is "to become free from childish dependence on parents; to develop affection for parents without dependence upon them; to develop respect for older adults without dependence upon them" (p. 55). Solomon and Havighurst are in accord in seeing that, in the process of maturing, the adolescent takes the values and norms from his parents which enable him to function as an adolescent and will enable him to function better as an adult. The "childish" dependence on parents is what needs to be eliminated in the process of achieving this emotional independence. Solomon would therefore be correct from Havighurst's point of view in seeing a more mature interdependence evolving through a congruence between parents and adolescents in norms and values.

A pertinent question at this point would seem to be, "Where do adolescents stand in relation to parents and peers on various values, norms and attitudes?" Meisels and Canter (1971) asked adolescents to judge issues such as the Vietnam war, marijuana, modern art, etc., in terms of their own views, those of their friends, and those of their parents. The mean "self" scores placed the adolescents between their parents and their peers. They viewed themselves as somewhat more progressive than their parents but not as progressive as their peers. Munns (1972) compared male adolescent self scores and perceived scores for parents and peers on the Allport-Vernon-Lindzey study of values. The boys' self ratings and ratings for peers were quite similar for all value categories, while the ratings for fathers were similar on four of the six values. However, the mothers' values were seen as quite different. Although Munns does not make this point, on three of the six values the male adolescents' mean scores were between those for parents and peers and, on two additional values, were between those for mother and peers. Both studies seem to indicate that adolescents see their values as falling between those of their parents and those of their peers. It is as if they want the best of both worlds, which certainly reflects on the power-independence conflict.

Two recent studies indicate that parents' influence over their adolescents is dependent to some degree on the use of parent power. Permissiveness and parent tutoring in political areas were found to be important in transmitting a political role to adolescent children (Thomas, 1971), and control that is combined with affection was found to be influential in transmitting a "proper" societal role (Jessor and Jessor, 1974). Baruch (1972), studying the influence of the mother on attitudes toward women and work held by their adolescent daughters, found a tendency for daughters of nonworking mothers to devalue women's competence in competing with men. These studies show the influence of parents on the values related to roles taken by adolescents, thereby integrating the previous few studies which looked at influences on values and influences on roles separately.

In a study by Gray and Gair (1974), adolescent girls rated themselves as they would like to be, and this ideal self was rated also by their two best friends and their parents, i.e., the friends' and parents' ratings indicated how they believed the subjects rated themselves. The parents and peers agreed with each other and with the adolescents' ideal self ratings, which would seem to indicate a good deal of understanding and empathy between the generations.

Nowicki and Segal (1974) showed that adolescent males and females perceived themselves as having approximately the same locus of control, the same sense of personal control over the outcomes of life situations, as their parents had. This seems to indicate the kind of influence that parental self-concept, or sense of self, has on the child's sense of self or self-concept.

In a study by Brittain (1967), the hypothesis was tested that adolescents would respond to parent pressures versus peer pressures, what Brittain called parent-peer cross-pressures, as a function of the content of the alternative presented by parents or peers and as a function of the specific situation in which the cross-pressures were presented. His ideas were supported and Brittain offered some hypotheses to explain the pattern of responses produced in the study. The first hypothesis stated,

> . . . the responses reflect the adolescents' perception of peers and parents as competent guides in different areas of judgment. The general social orientation of adolescents is of a dual character. Choices tend to derive meaning from either of two general reference groups, or both; the peer society in which many status and identity needs are gratified, and the larger society in which the status positions which one can aspire to as an adult are found. When choices pertain to the latter, parents are perceived as the more competent guides. . . . Two, the responses reflect concern to avoid being noticeably different from peers. . . . Three, the responses reflect concern about separation from peers. . . . Four, a fourth hypothesis overlapping but different from those above is that the choices reflect perceived similarities and differences between self and peers and self and parents. Adolescents, for

example, perceiving themselves to be more like peers in regard to tastes in clothes and in regard to feelings about school, find peer-favored alternatives in these areas psychologically closer and more acceptable. But in other areas the greater perceived similarity is between self and parent (p. 389).

Brittain's study is particularly significant in the context of the previous articles which show the continuous strong influence of parents on values, norms, and roles of adolescents. The findings of this study point clearly to the areas of values and behaviors where there are more probably disparities, and I think that the furor over hair styles, dress, music, etc., in the last few years points to this disparity. Parents, and maybe adults in general, seem to become more upset about hair styles and clothes than many other aspects of the adolescent's life. It would appear that this is because, using Brittain's rationale, these are areas where the adolescent's reference group is his peer group and he is more influenced and more conforming to the values and norms of his peer group. It is therefore an area in which parental power is minimized.

Munns (1971) queries the issue of the generation gap and takes the position that what is seen as a conflict between the generations is in actuality the result of the adolescent making efforts to understand, explore, and define his own system of values. This, as we have seen, is the goal of Goodman's "I-me" stage. It would also seem to bear on Erikson's emphasis on the search for identity and the identity and role confusion in adolescence. From Munns' point of view, the adolescent is not as much concerned with values and identity in the sense of "who am I?", but is deeply concerned with the questions "which way can I be?" or "which ways can I be?" According to Munns, the problem in the search for identity lies in the self, an abstract concept, which demands in its fullest development the attainment of formal-operational thought which, as we have seen, is not yet or may never be developed for many adolescents. This may therefore produce "muddled self-concepts." In view of the studies presented, it would appear that the great generation gap is really not very great at all. Moreover, it appears that because of social pressures, the "marginal" position, and the cognitive-developmental stage, or "between stage" of adolescence, the generation gap appears and feels to adults and adolescents alike to be greater than it is. And adolescents sometimes feel the need to show their peers where they stand—on the adolescents' side of the generation gap. "A 1972 teenager found it pertinent to say to his parents: 'I hope you'll understand . . . some friends are coming over and I have to pretend I don't like you. . . .'" (*Individual Psychology News Letter*, 1973, p. 55).

The variety of child-rearing and parent-personality influences and variables which might influence an adolescent in his attitudes, values, behaviors, and norms is immense. In this chapter (and in this book) we are not getting into issues relating to specific personality types, specific child-rearing patterns and their relationship to specific adolescent behaviors. It is important, I think, at this point, to interject some negative findings as well as some more sociological variables into the issue of attitudes and values in general, and the issues of compliance or conformity to parents or peers.

Spencer (1972), in a survey of attitudes and values of over 500 14–15-year-old boys in school in England, found no support for two hypotheses that appear generally supported in the literature elsewhere. These are, first, that the social class or origin of the adolescent or the type of school that he attends provide criteria for determining the pattern of attitudes and values, what might be called "the subcultures," of these boys. Second, Spencer found no anticipatory socialization; that is, he did not find the adolescents adopting attitudes and values that are appropriate for the socioeconomic status that the adolescent expects to enter. In this book we attempt to look at influences which affect adolescents in general, but have numerous times referred to the importance of the individual. Spencer believes that his negative findings are in a sense accounted for by the importance of this individuality. Social surveys use broad variables such as social class and type of school. As we have seen, this necessitates omitting the particular, individualistic aspects of these variables. This results, according to Spencer, in patterns of low correlations, such as he found, being "elevated into the position of being evidence of the role of family, or school, as a socializing agent" (1972, p. 10).

And yet it is through the social survey, and the kinds of generalizations and models they generate, that we are able to develop general pictures of what is distinctive in adolescence. We may then apply this knowledge and understanding in planning day-to-day activities with individual adolescents in which their specific personality and characteristics prevail.

A cross-national study by Thomas and Weigert (1971) investigated the hypothesis that conformity to significant others, i.e., best friend, mother, father, and priest for middle-class Catholic male and female adolescents would increase as one moved across four selected samples from New York, St. Paul, San Juan, Puerto Rico, and Merida, Yucatan, Mexico. Their data indicated "that it is primarily conformity to the expectations of authoritative others that is inversely related to the development of industrialization-urbanization" (p. 844). This type of conformity, conformity to authority, is differentiated from the other conformity, to the expectations of best friend, that was also studied. "This type of conformity (category of best friends) is not consistently related to industrialization-urbanization" (p. 844). Thomas and Weigert seem to be showing a relationship between modernization and a decrease in conformity to authoritative others. This relationship may be predicated on the greater number and diversity of authoritative others who would exist in a more modern urban setting. However, they do not find that conformity to the category of best friends, peer compliance, is consistently related to the differences in modernization and urbanization of their four samples.

Brittain (1969), comparing rural and urban adolescents with respect to peer versus parent compliance, analyzed items pertaining to dating, to dress, to glamour roles in the peer society, and to informing, or communication with, agemates. Significant differences between the rural and urban adolescents were found: the urban group was more peer-compliant than was the rural group. In speculating about the interpretation of this difference, Brittain recalls the distinction Coleman "makes between the influence of peers as individuals and the influence of the peer society. It may be that there is a rural-urban difference with respect to the latter and that this difference may or may not be obscured, depending on how the data were analyzed" (p. 66).

These last three studies have been interjected, in a sense, to confuse the issue. The hierarchy of influences is always operative. From Thomas and Weigert's study we can see the macroscopic cultural influences on conformity to, or compliance with, the expectations of parents and other significant figures in the adolescent's life. From Brittain's study we get an indication of the importance of geographic, which may be considered subcultural, influences on the adolescent's relationships vis-à-vis parent and peer. And although Brittain, citing Coleman, points to the influence of a peer society, Spencer does not see what are generally considered important influences—school and social class—as being sufficiently precise to help explain the development of adolescent subcultures. All of this is to say that the issue is anything but resolved.

Returning to the issue of the struggle for independence by the adolescent as a power struggle between parents and adolescents, Smith (1970) delineated the conditions which promote or deter parental influence, using a social-power model. Five types of power were developed based on the kinds of resources the influential authority possesses:

1. Reward-Resource is ability to dispense rewards
2. Referent-Resource is previously established orientation on the part of the other person to turn to him for guidance
3. Coercive-Resource is punishment or threat of punishment
4. Expert-Resource is supposed to possess useful knowledge
5. Legitimate-Resource is granted the right of power by either obligation or social norms accepted by the other person

Smith combined the first two types of power, reward and coercive, calling them outcome-controlled power, in studying the influence of parents using these types of power. He predicted a relationship between the type of power used and the influence obtained. He found that legitimate power correlated with influence more consistently than any of the other types of power among college freshmen studied. Expert power correlated with influence except over grooming and dress with males. Referent power was similar in strength to expert, whereas outcome-control had the least degree of strength. There is a striking resemblance between Smith's classification of power types and Kohlberg's stages of moral development. Smith's findings therefore lead us to look at the relationship between power and moral development, or moral development and conformity or compliance.

Saltzstein, Diamond, and Belenky (1972) investigated the relationship between Kohlberg's moral-developmental stages and conformity behavior, assuming that children would conform to individuals whom they viewed as having moral authority. The type of conforming behavior anticipated to relate to the various stages was identical to that described by the power types presented by Smith. In a group-pressure situation study to measure conformity in seventh graders, although Saltzstein et al. found little overall conformity, the stage-three moral-development subjects, good-boy morality subjects, conformed the most to their peers, as would be expected. The stage-four and five subjects conformed the least, thereby demonstrating their own growing autonomy. This study seems to support the relationship between moral development and the kinds of power or parental influence that will be effective with the adolescent.

Weisbroth (1970) investigated the proposition that individuals with close parental identification would attain a higher level of moral judgment. She found that identification with parents was significantly related to a high level of moral judgment for males and that identification with the father was significantly related to a high level for females. Her position was that close parental identification contributes to personal and social adjustment, thereby giving adolescents the opportunity to develop positive self-evaluations and feelings of self-worth. This theorizing points again to the effectiveness of parental use of the various types of power.

Remembering Munns' hypothesis that generational conflicts are related to a lengthening of time before adolescents reach Piaget's formal-operation stage of cognitive development, and the relationship between Kohlberg's moral-development stages and Piaget's stages, and remembering also the relationships between development of and search for personal identity and intellectual or cognitive development, we are brought to the following attempt to summarize the material on parent versus peer relationships and compliance. Shainberg (1970) points out that identity formation often demands a fit between the real self and the ideal self, because the individual is tied to concrete-operational thinking, and therefore cannot free his ideal self as an abstract concept. The individual is therefore trapped in Goodman's "I-me" stage of autonomy formation with its emphasis on the concrete. To progress to the "I-them" stage requires the ability to abstract a "them" from the situation, over which the individual can then exercise some personal control. It would appear that before development of formal-operational thinking, the adolescent is unable to abstract the standards of his various reference groups from given situations and make them a unified part of his moral principles. He is still tied to Kohlberg's third stage of maintaining good relations and is under the influence of referent power. The movement through the stages of the growth of autonomy according to Goodman, going from dependence, in the "they-me," to conformity to reference group, in the "I-me," and finally to personal control, in the "I-them," stages bears a close relationship to movement toward more autonomy and the highest level of moral development, the level of conscience, in Kohlberg's stages.

In summing up this section we see a logic along the following lines. A conflict arises between parents and adolescents over the degree of autonomy the adolescent will be permitted to have. The adolescent will respond to his parents' use of authority on the basis of numerous influences including the mode and manner of exertion of that parental authority. He will also respond in relation to his stage of cognitive development, his stage of moral development, and his stage of autonomy development.

PEERS IN GROUPS AND AS FRIENDS

Peer groups and peers as friends provide the adolescent with the arena for much of the learning and developing that occur in all the life tasks. In general, friendships, the close friendships that an adolescent has, will be with some one or some few adolescents who are also members of his peer group. Differentiating between the functions of the peer group and of friendship presents a false dichotomy. This dichotomy must be viewed as two points on a social-interaction continuum, the adolescent learning and developing in two social areas, i.e., finding his place and interacting with a group of people, and learning how to interact more intimately with individual people. The remainder of this section will be broken down into functions of the peer group, structures of the peer group, and the functions and manners of friendship. The issue of conformity, to peers in groups and to peers as friends, will be related in both portions of the section.

Ausubel (1954) saw peer groups in adolescence as performing several functions. Probably the most important of these is to provide the adolescent with the chance to demonstrate his competence, which Ausubel calls "providing primary status." Primary status is considered such because it is the status that the individual adolescent earns through his own efforts, exerting his own abilities, and is different from the status he had as a child which was termed "derived status," the status granted him by virtue of being his parents' child. Elkind (1969), in the Piagetian tradition, views adolescents as being in a stage of egocentrism in which they are so preoccupied with self-definition and self-interest that all friendships and social interactions are based on these egocentric needs and perceptions. So, too, Erikson's (1968) continued view of the identity crisis shows the importance of the many aspects of identity formation, including the nature of relationships. This is put succinctly by Oshman and Manosevitz (1974):

> During the identity crisis the emerging adult is confronted with the task of reformulating all that he has been into, all that he wishes to be. This reformulation demands a relinquishment of infantile sources of gratification, a transmutation of notions of youthful omnipotence, a selective assimilation of meaningful occupational and ideological alternatives, and a synthesis of childhood identifications. In this way, an individual can develop a sense of ego identity which will permit him to establish a symbiotic relationship with the society and preserve a sense of continuity for himself (pp. 207–208).

These views relate well to the need for status, for gaining primary status, as a type of self-definition during adolescence and the assumption that the identity, or self-definition, is garnered through interaction with external sources.

In addition to the first function of the peer group, providing a source for developing primary status, Ausubel offers several other functions of the peer group. These additional functions are interrelated and lead to the development of the first function, primary status. Ausubel says that peer groups facilitate emancipation from home and parental influence and furthermore give focus to the adolescent's resistance to adult standards and authority. A study by Phelps and Horrocks (1958) adds weight to the notion of this function. They found, in a study of 200 adolescent boys and girls using a questionnaire about group membership, attitudes, feelings toward the group, activities with the group, and satisfaction with the group, that "the degree of emancipation from adult control appears to be a most important influence in the formation of patterns of informal group activities and attitudes" (p. 86).

The other side of this emancipation from parental influence is the focalization of resistance against adult standards and authority. Sherif and Sherif (1964) concluded, on the basis of numerous observations of adolescent groups, that group members often engaged in behavior that was not only socially unacceptable but was in fact in violation of the law. These behaviors included drinking of alcohol, traffic violations, destruction of public property, carrying illegal weapons, and buying and smoking cigarettes, which was illegal for minors in most communities. Douvan and Adelson (1966) found that even though adolescents stated that the reason for membership in many peer groups might be emancipation and resistance, they did not change greatly their emotional attachment and dependence on adult standards. The question of degree of resistance and emancipation from parental standards and authority has been referred to in the previous section. The Phelps and Horrocks and Sherif and Sherif studies show that the adolescent peer group supports this function and facilitates the movement to greater autonomy.

Relating to this support, the next function of the peer group that Ausubel discussed is that of the peer group providing certain norms for governing behavior. As the study by Dunphy (1963) presented later will show, the norms are intended and function to provide guidelines for learning different types of behaviors, values, etc., as the nature of the peer groups and the nature of the adolescents' interests change through the adolescent years. Sherif and Sherif show that peer-group members develop common practices, common evaluations, and shared tastes which become standards by which the adolescents appraise their own and their peers' behavior.

It seems crucial to consider the norms of the peer group as providing the adolescent with alternatives to the parental norm. We should try and view the adolescent as moving from a limited world of family and small community into a world with much more varied behavioral and attitudinal options. The adolescent takes giant steps as he moves away from the normative standards of his family. Accompanying these steps, logically, is considerable anxiety. By moving into and forming peer groups which set their own standards, the adolescent is able to deviate from parental standards and norms while still having support from other persons. It is hard to stress enough this difficulty for the adolescent. If we try to think of the mass and maze of possible behaviors, attitudes, and values the adolescent sees around him personally, in his greater community, in school, and in the media, and try to see through his eyes the extreme difficulty of choosing values, attitudes, and behaviors which might feel consistent and coherent for him, we begin to grasp the nature of the adolescent's dilemma. If next we try to envision the adolescent constructing a coherent and consistent set of attitudes, values, and behaviors on his own, and then acting out this pattern on his own, we may be able to conjure up the frightening, even awe-inspiring, range of social and personal difficulties that might be encountered. If one has to choose his own way of thinking and his own way of behaving, and it would seem that one does have to, how much easier and how much safer this is as part of a group which has norms for values and behaviors for people like oneself.

The last function of the peer group presented by Ausubel that will be discussed here describes the peer group as an arena allowing latitude for the adolescent to test himself in a variety of roles, to test the range of his abilities and emotions, and to test these within a peer group which conceptually, at least, will be more open and empathetic to the problems, the extremes, and the anxieties of adolescence. Gottlieb and Ramsey (1964) also see the peer group as providing opportunity for trying out different abilities and testing one's skills in a variety of roles, including the leadership role. They consider the peer group as a critic of the adolescent's role-playing ability and to be the adolescent's most important critic. By viewing and talking about the reactions his peers have to his ways of behaving, the adolescent is able to construct definition and/or extend the boundaries of his self-concept and range of behaviors. With the approval of his peer group, he may exhibit behavior, attitudes, and values which he would be unlikely, and discomforted, to otherwise exhibit at all. Certainly the first time the adolescent shows new ideas and behavior to his parents and other adults, the support of a peer group is helpful and maybe necessary.

In sum, the adolescent peer group functions to provide the adolescent with an arena that is sufficiently supportive, rigid in the sense of providing alternative norms from those of his parents, but flexible in providing opportunities for trying out new roles, skills, attitudes, and values, so that the adolescent may begin to answer the question, "Which ways can I be?", can begin to derive his own "primary status."

Peer-Group Structure

Turning now to the issue of the structures of peer groups, we see that they have been variously described, starting with the "subculture" conceptualization which received impetus from the work of Coleman (1961), observations of agemate reference groups (Sherif and Sherif, 1964, 1965), and analysis of the social structure of peer group developmentally by age (Dunphy, 1963).

Is there a youth culture? Are there youth subcultures? There is no universally accepted answer to either of these questions. Elkin and Westley (1955) believed that they had destroyed the myth of the adolescent subculture through their survey study which showed that an adolescent middle-class sample complied with the norms of their parents and held no hostile or resentful feelings against their parents. Berger (1963) concluded that what Elkin and Westley had "actually done is present evidence that certain adolescents do not share the norms of youth culture" (p. 319). Berger suggests that the characteristics associated with youth culture refer to a system that is normative for youthful persons. There may be young persons who do not adhere to the system and older persons who do. "Whatever it is that is normatively distinctive about youth cultures is probably not characteristic of all or even most adolescents" (Berger, 1963, p. 319), but the term and idea have value.

Elkin and Westley's explosion of the myth of the adolescent culture relates directly to the previous section which showed adolescents seeing themselves as somewhere between their parents and peers on many issues, closer to their parents on important issues, and closer to their peers on issues that fell within a "youth culture" purview. Berger's position is that most adolescents spend little if any time or energy involved with facets of behavior which might be considered part of the "youth culture." But he does say that the youth culture is attended to by certain youthful people and there is not an age bar to participation in youth culture. Funnily enough, and very funny indeed, on one episode of the television show "The Odd Couple," Felix felt he was old, over the hill, so he and Oscar went to a purely "youth culture" discotheque. In support of Berger, not only did they not have the appropriate clothes and the appropriate language, but they did not have the essential ingredient of youthfulness. The audience enjoyed their time at the discotheque but Felix and Oscar did not.

"Youth culture" sometimes is perceived as monolithic, singular. The following quotation from Berger shows the multiplicity of ways in which youth cultures exhibit themselves:

> The flower has many blooms; the varieties of youth cultures are as wide as the variety of cultural contexts and opportunity systems offered by a pluralistic society. At its broadest and most innocuous, the youth cultures of the young touched the fringes of what is called "teenage culture": popular songs, rock and roll, disc jockeys, juke boxes, portable phonographs, movie stars, dating, and romantic love; hot rods, motorcycles, drag racing, sports car, panty raids and water fights, drive-in hamburgers and clandestine drinking, football games, basketball games, dances and parties, and clubs and cliques, and lover's lanes. At its delinquent extreme, youth culture is black leather jackets, gang rumbles and switchblades, malicious mischief, and joyriding in stolen cars. Politically, it is expressed in sit-ins, freedom rides, peace marches, and folk songs; it is jazz at Newport, vacations at Fort Lauderdale— and their attendant riots. And it is also Bohemians and beatniks and beards and hipsters, and coffee shop desperados plotting everything from literary magazines to assaults on the House Committee on Un-American Activities (Berger, 1963, p. 182).[1]

James Coleman's (1961) widely acclaimed and widely criticized study helps put the issue of subcultures into the framework of the influence hierarchy. Coleman's position, in generalized form, was that our society, changing rapidly, highly rationalized, can and does no longer rely on the family in the "natural processes" of education. These processes are now the business of formalized institutions, the schools, which are set apart from the rest of the society and which take longer to educate the child and adolescent in the fullness of contemporary education than the family did in the narrower life of the past. As a result of this institutionalization of education, society is no longer confronted with individuals to be trained or socialized into adulthood, but is rather confronted with "distinct social systems" in which adolescents to be trained offer a united front to the efforts toward their education made by the adult society. He said that adolescents' peers are as important, or more important, in the adolescents' decision making as are their parents. Although the adolescent subculture bears a strong resemblance in its major characteristics to the adult society, there is nonetheless superimposed on this subculture variations in its character which are due to factors that differ from school to school and from community to community. Sampling from ten high schools, a nominational procedure was used for identifying the "leading crowd" and the persons most outstanding in athletics, popularity, and activities in the school. The leading crowds in the

1. B. M. Berger, "On the Youthfulness of Youth Cultures," *Social Research*, 1963, Vol. 30, No. 3.

various schools were similarly composed, with emphasis on the athletes and the popular girl and far less emphasis on the brilliant student. More differences were found for girls, in that girls who were activity leaders from higher socioeconomic schools and girls who were popular in lower socioeconomic schools were more likely to be in the leading crowd.

Being an athlete and being in the leading crowd are of great importance in making a boy popular. In general, the boys in Coleman's study felt that school-related activities other than athletics are of considerably less importance in being popular with girls than they are in being popular with other boys. Just as athletics for the boys shows a high relation with actual popularity so do activities for the girls, particularly in higher socioeconomic schools. Remembering that this is a 1961 publication and attitudes may have changed, the role of girls as objects of attention for boys is seen as very important by the adolescents as exhibited in their values in the schools studied.

However, a recent replication of Coleman's study by Eitzen (1975) indicates that athletics are still of primary importance to adolescents and their status within their high schools. He did find that differences exist between schools which might suggest that in the future athletics will be of less importance in more urban, higher-SES schools. But in the years since Coleman's study, with the influence of his findings on educators, athletics have not diminished appreciably as the major source of status within our high schools.

To the question "What does it take to be important?" the answer "good grades, honor roll" was ranked fourth out of the six items used for boys and fifth out of the six for girls for all schools. Regardless of this overall low standing, its position differs considerably in the different schools. Coleman continually illustrates differences between the schools based on school size, SES, urban, suburban, country setting, etc. But his point is that the "value climate" of the school is more than all of these.

The general picture one constructs from Coleman's work is one in which boys do not try for academic success as they might since it cannot get them status by itself. Girls try to do well enough to please their parents but not so well that their social status is jeopardized. And the leading crowd of a school, as the norm setting for that school, adds to more than the sum or consensus of the values of the student body with an extra middle-class weighting. The leading crowd appears to support the important background characteristics representative of the school and to accentuate these characteristics whether they be lower or upper socioeconomic characteristics.

Acknowledging the influence of the school and school differences, and acknowledging the differences in value climates between schools, one must still remember the extent of diversity in personality and group types within schools. Reister and Zucker (1968) analyzed the informal school structure of a high school and found a number of more or less distinct groupings. One clearly defined group, the "collegiates," appeared active, social, establishment oriented, what might be seen as the classic all-American high-school student. Equally extant and equally a tradition in American high schools was the group called "the leathers." These are kids who act rougher and tougher than the others and who might at one time or another have been thought of as hoods. Another group, which was small at the time of this study, was called "true individuals." They would be primarily identified by their clothes and hair and called variously over the last 20 years "beatniks," "hippies," or "freaks." Reister and Zucker noted three other less distinct but still identifiable groups of young high-school people with the following patterns of behavior:

1. "Quiet kids," who seem more independent, go their own way and may in fact belong to an identifiable grouping but outside the school,
2. "Intellectuals," students who were serious about their studies and interested in many or deeply interested in at least one topic or area of study, and
3. "Kids going steady," who spent a great deal of time with each other and maybe with other couples similarly involved with each other.

The geographic, and urban-rural, effects on the values and social groupings in schools are evident to anyone who has traveled and, particularly, taught in various regions in the country. As I write this in Austin, Texas, I am aware that the high-school students in the city could do a ranking of high schools on the basis of how many and how valued the "kickers" group is in each school. Kickers are either future cowboys or highly westernized ranch, rodeo-oriented people. What they "kick" is implicit in the nature of their preferred environment.

Although heading toward an understanding of the ways in which schools and adolescent peer groups are structured, it is clear from these materials that the influences which make for differences in the structure of the groups in different areas do not overwhelm individual differences. As an example confirming this, Roff and Sells (1965) studied the relation between intelligence and socioeconomic status in groups differing in sex and socioeconomic background. They concluded that above-average intelligence in a peer group is an asset to the adolescent in a wide variety of social groups.

Peck and Galliani (1962), studying intelligence, ethnicity, and social roles in adolescents, found for both Anglo-American and Latin-American adolescents in three Texas communities that intelligence was related positively to peer nomination as "brain," "wheel," "big imagination," and "average one," and related negatively to nomination as "day dreamer." Intelligence was not related to being labeled "quiet," "left out," or "wild one." "The intellectually above average individual tends, generally, to be more visible among his age mates than his intellectually less able fellow" (p. 70).

Recognizing now that (1) there are a variety of types of adolescent agemate or reference groupings; (2) that these groupings are influenced in norms and behaviors by family and background variables as well as value variables inherent in particular communities and schools; and (3) that the choice, either by individual adolescents or by peers, of inclusion in a particular group is related to personal interest and ability, i.e., personal characteristics of the adolescent and characteristics of the peer group, the peer group itself is of interest.

After many studies of adolescents, and especially an intensive study of 24 groups of boys in several cities, Sherif (1966) concluded that adolescent goals and attitudes are strongly affected by the status structure and norms of their group as well as the interaction process within the group. While functioning as a group member, or acting with the internalized norms and goals of the group, the adolescent is still bombarded with influences, competitions, and conflicts within the context of other social ties and from other peer groups and adult authorities.

Clearly Sherif and Sherif are impressed with the complexity and multiplicity of influences and interactions in the functioning of agemate groups and the development of adolescent attitudes, goals, and behaviors. Equally important is their conclusion on the generality of groups:

> We were impressed once again with the generality of group formations in all walks of life in this age period. . . . All have differentiated patterns regulating their interpersonal relations. All have rules, customs, fads—in short, norms—regulating behavior in their activity. These are the minimum essentials of a group. . . .
>
> These groups of adolescents were formed, or joined, on the members' own initiative, through interactions among individuals sharing the dilemmas of status and motivation common during adolescence in this society. The status differentiation which developed was not imposed on them; the norms were not considered arbitrary impositions on the members.
>
> The individual had a hand in creating the properties of the group, or had selected it. The group was his—a context where he could have personal ties with others, could amount to something in ways not available elsewhere, could accomplish things as a person. It contained others whose acceptance he wanted, whose yardsticks were his personal gauges for success and failure, whose approval brought inner warmth and whose disapproval left him miserable.
>
> Psychologically, therefore, the basis of group solidarity, of conformity to group norms without threat of sanctions, of the binding nature of group rules even when they conflict with those of parents and officials, lies in the personal involvement of members (Sherif and Sherif, 1965, p. 286).[2]

The functions of the peer group as explained by Ausubel are clearly seen in the generality of group formations found by Sherif and Sherif.

In addition to the striking similarity in peer group make-up among these different groups, Sherif and Sherif found a considerable amount of similarity in

2. M. Sherif and C. W. Sherif (eds.), *Problems of Youth*. Chicago: Aldine Publishing Co., 1965.

attitudes and behavior across groups from different socioeconomic classes. They all held highly an image of individual success in adults as symbolized through the media, they were all strongly oriented toward agemates as their reference sets, and they all held an intense interest in the opposite sex. Moreover, all of these groups were able to distinguish very clearly what adult authority considered to be right or wrong, while "the finding most common to all was the boys' insistent desire to do things on 'our own,' without adult programming or supervision" (p. 316). In analyzing the differences between the groups, the direction of differences in achievement, ambition, and adherence to middle-class values were as expected between the upper-middle, lower-middle, and lower-class adolescents. However, the conclusion was not that the middle-upper-class youth were more ambitious or achievement oriented, but rather that the lower-class youth were as ambitious "relative to their own ideas of achievement, and even more ambitious relative to their own parents' achievement" (p. 318).

A most interesting and important aspect of the Sherifs' findings relates to the issue of conformity in adolescence. In analyzing their data, the Sherifs were surprised to find that in the schools serving high socioeconomic areas there was the least diversity of individual values and goals. Much greater heterogeneity was found in the values and goals of the student bodies of schools in the middle and lower socioeconomic areas. Only on questions that were strictly financial such as income, spending money, and the like, was homogeneity, or like-mindedness, found in the schools serving lower socioeconomic groups to the degree that such like-mindedness was found in the high socioeconomic schools. Sherif and Sherif say, "These findings have led us to suspect that some theorists on lower class life may have overlooked the actual diversity within lower class settings, perhaps because of their preoccupation with specific social problems" (p. 321).

The greater homogeneity in upper-middle-class schools and upper-middle-class reference groups may be attributable to greater similarity of personal aims and goals, i.e., more likely to go to college, more likely to have upper-middle-class jobs and live in particular places. The middle and lower socioeconomic groups will be made up of adolescents for whom upward mobility is differentially important and the tracks or ways of attaining desired mobility would be more varied. Also for those who feel unable to move upward in the social system, the variety of ways to entertain themselves, enjoy themselves, or hold the status quo must be greater than for the people who are trying to move up.

Dunphy (1963) studied the social structure of urban adolescent peer groups. His findings helped provide a framework for considering why there may be greater diversity within adolescent subcultures or large adolescent groups than might previously have been thought, as well as providing a picture of the general trend in the changes in the social structure of peer group developmentally, through the adolescent period. According to Dunphy, the social structure of adolescent peer groups is composed of two basic types of groups—crowds and cliques. The crowd is larger and is essentially an association of cliques, ranging in size from 15 to 30 members or up to 4 cliques of 3 to 9 members each. He found no cliques with more than 9 members, which points strongly to the intimacy involved in a small group. Although they were the basic units of crowds, not all cliques were associated with crowds. One could be a member of a clique without being a member of a crowd but clique membership appeared to be a prerequisite of crowd membership.

This is very interesting, and functional for adolescents. The adolescent becomes a member of a small group, which Dunphy is calling a clique, composed of three or more individuals, up to 9, with similar interests. They may be close friends from childhood days or newly found friends, but they have a strong feeling of "we," with strong emotional involvement individually among members, and a strong attachment to the clique by each of the members. The aim of the individual adolescent, both as an adolescent and in terms of socialization into adulthood, is to be able to function comfortably and successfully with people in groups from small to large sizes. Therefore, a possible aim for most adolescents is to become part of a crowd. A crowd is larger, less closely knit, and more impersonal than the clique, although the crowd is made up of people who are more similar in terms of backgrounds, interests, likes, and dislikes. The crowd is most likely to function through particular kinds of activities which may be of a sport or social nature providing the opportunity for interaction between the sexes. If we try to envision an adolescent moving into a new community or moving into a new school or merely progressing in the usual way from junior high school or middle school into high school, he encounters by himself many people he does not know and we start, I think, with a fairly lonely character. Not only would the average adolescent be too anxious and unsure of his social competencies to attempt to plunge directly into membership or association with crowds, but this movement does not, I believe, fit the logic of movement into crowds at any age level above adolescence. Clique membership comes first.

The clique, the making of 2, 3, 4, 5 friends, gives the adolescent the chance to establish some degree of companionship, security, and acceptance, a place of belonging where he need not be as anxious, before attempting any kind of movement into a larger social scene. Moreover, the clique allows him to try out social skills, evaluate his own behavior, and have others evaluate his behavior, and gives him some standards for behaving which, because of the relationship between the clique and the crowd, allow him to gauge his potential for success and acceptance in the crowd. The clique allows the adolescent to blow off steam and act differently than he might otherwise, since he can rely on the closeness of the clique, while simultaneously he can develop skills and have support for moving into the wider arena of the crowd.

There are potential disadvantages, or what are considered by some to be disadvantages, in both the clique and the crowd. Primarily, these center around issues of exclusiveness. The clique or crowd may become snobbish and not include certain other cliques or individuals as members which may be difficult for the excluded. The clique or crowd may become of such importance to the adolescent that it causes tension with his family and a tendency to neglect other responsibilities. These problems are probably more crucial in the upper-middle-class areas where there is less diversity and the standard of clique and crowd behavior is more commonly accepted. In such a setting adolescents who are, or who feel, excluded would conceivably have fewer options for other directions of behavior and other types of cliques and crowds to join. However, group membership and the variety of groups that exist in a community and in a school relate to a broad range of individual difference and individual choice. We can consider that the clique/crowd manner is facilitative and satisfying for many.

The differing functions of the clique and crowd also lead to a tendency for their settings and activities to be distributed differently throughout the week. Most of the crowd settings occur on weekends while most of the cliques meet on weekdays. The crowd settings, social activities, parties, and dances are by nature more organized and therefore have to fall into "free time." The predominant activity of cliques is talking. Analysis of the incredible amount of conversation that occurs within a clique shows that it has an instrumental function in organizing and publicizing crowd activities, and evaluating them when they are over.

A superordinate grouping occurs in some high schools where certain crowds or combinations of crowds are distinguished according to a particular status within the youth hierarchy. These larger groupings are called "sets." Sets are usually based on their members' social background, ethnic background, personality type, or some combination of these. For example, churchgoers may form a set, college-bound youth another, playboys and playgirls—a highly social group—may form another. Sets rarely overlap, and even if an individual qualifies for two or more sets he is generally assigned by his peers to the set for which they think he is most suitable (Stone and Church, 1968).

Another form of peer group which should be mentioned is the gang. Gangs may be differentiated from cliques and crowds in that they seem to have regular leaders, well-defined membership, and a clear-cut organization. Whereas clique members have greater mutual affection and spend more time interacting with each other as individuals, gang members seem to focus more on the activities of the group and goals of the group. The gang member is more likely than the clique member to play a well-defined role and to adhere more closely to the more structured, intense rules of the gang which tend to be rigidly enforced. Although gangs vary greatly among themselves and generalizations are difficult to make (Rogers, 1972b), research suggests that organized gang behavior is traditionally more a part of particular subcultures and found only in specified slum areas in larger cities (Thrasher, 1936). Gangs are viewed by many as being abnormal to the American adolescent experience, although successive migrant groups and minority groups in urban centers have and still are forming and participating in gang behavior. Gangs seem to function in approximately the same way as other peer groups with clique-type subgroups either forming the gang or together making up the gang. However, gangs are typified as being antisocial, and many members of gangs are individuals who have antisocial attitudes and behavior and are often poorly adjusted in school. The brighter, better adjusted individuals in these same communities are not usually attracted to gangs (Crane, 1958). Gangs are more likely to be same-sex groups with the opposite sex, female, group participating as tangential cliques, or auxiliary units, to the gang.

Dunphy shows, and this is illustrated in Figure 13, the structural changes in the typical make-up of adolescent peer groups through adolescence. Particularly note-worthy is the development from unisexual peer groupings and relationships to heterosexual peer groupings and relationships, as well as movement from smaller to larger groups, thereby in combination allowing the adolescent in late adolescence to function with members of both sexes in large and small groups. We will allow Dunphy to explain these structural changes in his own words:

> The initial stage of adolescent group development appears to be that of the isolated unisexual clique: i.e., isolated in terms of any relationship with corresponding groups of the opposite sex. This primary stage represents the persistence of the preadolescent "gang" into the adolescent. Stage 2 introduces the first movement towards heterosexuality in group structure. Unisexual cliques previously unrelated to cliques of the opposite sex now participate in heterosexual interaction. At this stage, however, interaction is considered daring and is only undertaken in the security of a group setting where the individual is supported by the presence of his own sex associates. Interaction at this stage is often superficially antagonistic. Stage 3 sees the formation of the heterosexual clique for the first time. Upper status members of unisexual cliques initiate individual-to-individual heterosexual interaction and the first dating occurs. Those adolescents who belong to these emergent heterosexual groups still maintain a membership role in their unisexual clique, so that they possess dual membership in two intersecting cliques. This initiates an extensive transformation of group structure by which there takes place a reorganization of unisexual cliques and the reformation of their membership into heterosexual cliques (stage 4). While the cliques persist as small intimate groups, their membership now comprises both sexes. Stage 5 sees the slow disintegration of the crowd and the formation of cliques consisting of couples who are going steady or engaged. Thus there is a progressive development of group structure from predominantly unisexual to heterosexual groups. In this transition the crowd—an extended hetero-sexual peer group—occupies a strategic position. Membership in the crowd offers opportunities for establishing a heterosexual role. The crowd is therefore the most significant group for the individual, but crowd membership is dependent on prior membership in the clique. In fact, the crowd is basically an interrelationship of cliques, and appears to consolidate the heterosexual learning appropriate to each stage of development. The majority of clique members, therefore, possess a determinate position in an extended hierarchical arrangement of cliques and crowds,

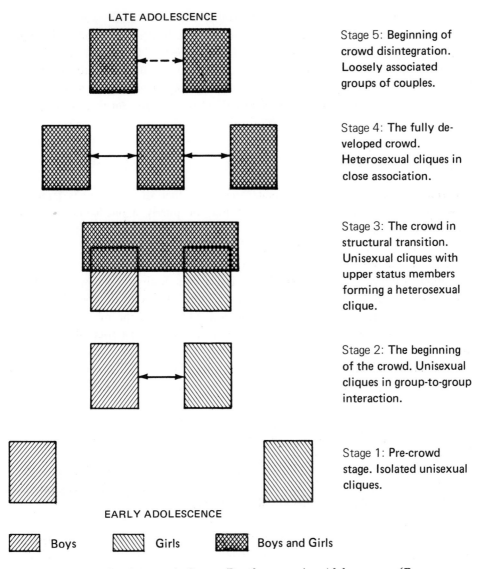

LATE ADOLESCENCE

Stage 5: **Beginning of crowd disintegration. Loosely associated groups of couples.**

Stage 4: **The fully developed crowd. Heterosexual cliques in close association.**

Stage 3: **The crowd in structural transition. Unisexual cliques with upper status members forming a heterosexual clique.**

Stage 2: **The beginning of the crowd. Unisexual cliques in group-to-group interaction.**

Stage 1: **Pre-crowd stage. Isolated unisexual cliques.**

EARLY ADOLESCENCE

Boys   Girls   Boys and Girls

Figure 13. *Stages of Group Development in Adolescence. (Reprinted by permission from D. C. Dunphy, "The social structure of urban adolescent peer groups," Sociometry, 1963 [26:2], 230–246.)*

in which high status is accorded to groups most developed in heterosexual structure. The course of the individual's social development appears to be strongly influenced by his position within this structure (Dunphy, 1963, pp. 235–237).[3]

3. D. C. Dunphy, "The Social Structure of Urban Adolescent Peer Groups," *Sociometry,* Vol. 26, No. 2, 1963.

Dunphy reports that in Sydney, Australia, where his study was carried out, about 70 percent of the boys and 80 percent of the girls at ages 14 and 15 belonged to peer groups similar to the types he has described. He sees these groups as extending the socialization process begun in the family, including the differences between instrumental and expressive lines of behavior, movement to more complex systems of relationships, and the personality development inherent in this movement.

Friends

The smallest, closest, and most intimate peer group that an adolescent is a member of is his friendship group, which in fact may be purely a one-to-one friendship group. In this section, as the movement from family to community is viewed, the recurring issues are "What can I do?", "How many ways can I be?", or "What can I be?", and "How can I find this out?" Put differently, the issues are identity formation in the process of growth into a larger community, and how social facilitators enable and encourage this growth. Cliques and crowds and their interrelationship just described operate as facilitators. However, the most crucial facilitator is friendship. Mussen et al. (1969) state in this regard that friendships perform a special function for adolescents.

Friends are people who will like you anyway. They will like you regardless of your success or failure, of your victories or losses, of your social finesse or social faux pas.

> Friendship engages, discharges, cultivates, and transforms the most acute passions of the adolescent, and so allows the youngster to confront and master them. Because it carries so much of the burden of adolescent growth, friendship acquires at this time a pertinence and intensity it has never had before nor (in many cases) will ever have again (Douvan and Adelson, 1966, p. 174).

So often in therapy one sees adults who have missed in the process of adolescence the close and open communication of a friendship. They have missed a learning that is essential to growing into a healthy functioning adult. They do not know that other people are concerned about small and everyday occurrences and therefore they either overlook much of what happens in their day-to-day life or worry excessively that they are different and are the only ones to worry in this manner. I once saw a client who was acutely embarrassed when, on entering the office, he had difficulty taking off his overshoes. When I remarked that this kind of difficulty bugged me also, he was amazed. He said, "I didn't know you should even think about these things." In an adolescent friendship, the satisfaction and also the crucial importance of the friendship is in being able to share, to reveal one's feelings and thoughts about the most mundane to the most important events and considerations in the adolescent's life. "My parents make me mad when . . .," "Would he/she like me if I . . .," "I don't know if I can . . .," "Do you think I should . . .," "Do you ever feel . . .," "Do you ever think . . .," etc., etc., etc. The questions, the concerns, the intimacies are endless. In the process of helping each other, each adolescent helps himself. As friends, "They explain themselves to each other, and in so doing, each explains himself to himself" (Osterrieth, 1969, p. 19).

The adolescent wants and needs friends, as does everyone. The friends he chooses will most likely share common interests and personal and social characteristics, and although some of these may be complementary rather than similar (Byrne and Griffith, 1966), in general the friendship will be built more on similarity of characteristics than on differences (Douvan and Gold, 1966). But in the process of demanding that he make his own friends, the function of the friendship comes second to learning to make friendships themselves. Since "the adolescent insists upon choosing his own friends, he often makes mistakes . . . the friendship is broken, and the adolescent is then disillusioned" (Hurlock, 1967, p. 130). With age and experience, obviously, most adolescents become more critical and successful in their choice of friends.

There are sex differences in adolescent friendship patterns. Generally, girls' friendships are more frequent, deeper, and more dependent than are those of boys, and girls' friendships are more intimate and provoke more upset when they appear to be faltering (Douvan and Adleson, 1966). The nature of girls' friendships would appear to be more expressive in much the same way that the nature of girls' roles in peer groups was more expressive. Boys, on the other hand, tend to stress, relatively more, the results of their friendship, as in having a companion with whom one gets along while participating in activities of common interest (Douvan and Adleson, 1966). Again this seems to show the instrumental perspective of boys in friendships as we have previously seen in social roles. The sex difference in perspective on sexual matters may influence the quality of same-sex friendship. Boys are more likely to see sex as a motive relatively specific and independent of love, whereas girls are more likely to integrate the sexual and love aspects of heterosexual relationships (Bardwick, 1971).

Douvan and Adleson (1966) characterize the changes in function, quality, and content of friendship through adolescence as proceeding from more superficial friendship in early adolescence to the intense sharing of middle adolescence and then a more realistic, both interdependent and independent, relationship in later adolescence. This movement may be seen as relating to the development of formal operations and the tremendous experimenting with possibilities that characterize middle adolescence. The early adolescent's more superficial friendship is based on concrete activities, sharing things rather than thoughts, sharing time and the doing of favors. The friendship of middle adolescents is characterized more by trying on of roles, styles and feelings, testing the limits of personal abilities, friends' and society's endurance and tolerance—a movement into the area of hypothesis testing—"What ways can I be?" By late adolescence the individual has come to better define himself and therefore does not need the continuous support of a friend for all and sundry feelings and behaviors. Therefore, the friendship can be built with greater emphasis on the friend's personality and talents, on what the friend brings to the relationship and a greater degree of tolerance for individual differences (Douvan and Gold, 1966).

Rogers (1972b) says that the intimate friendships of adolescence serve the following purposes: (1) they permit an opportunity for exploration and extension of the self that kinship intimacy does not; (2) they help in establishing an identity that the person feels confident with; (3) they serve to relieve guilt, provide reassurance, and establish controls; and (4) they provide a transition to heterosexuality and a heterosexual adult sex-role identity. These purposes, and in fact this entire discussion of friendships in adolescence, point to the transitional character of the extreme, intense, adolescent friendship, and the socialization function of adolescent friendship to bring the adolescent into adulthood where he may have friendship, yet be "himself" in a great variety of other social roles.

Conger (1973) speaks of the emphasis by contemporary adolescents, both early and late adolescents, on the need for more true friendship and love in a world that is generally viewed as impersonal, competitive, and constantly changing. He cites a 1971 Harris survey in which 9 out of 10 adolescents expressed agreement about the importance of more friendship and love between people. Conger feels that the reason for this emphasis may be, first, the difficulty adolescents have in the current social climate with developing open, honest, warm relationships even with peers; and second, that despite their concern for this type of relationship, many adolescents have difficulty in practicing what they preach or at least what they desire. A third reason that he gives has to do with the meaning and definition of close and meaningful friendship according to the subjective requirements of today's adolescents. These requirements may be more demanding and more stringent than those of adolescents, or for that matter adults, in earlier generations. Wolf (1974), in a discussion of why Reich's *Greening of America* was not the answer to the problems of our young, speaks to this question. Adolescents began to feel that the essential ingredients of proper friendships and relationships were as follows:

> . . . the only true connection with others was that which Martin Buber called the "I-thou" relationship, in which one authentic self and another meet without hiding anything. This relationship one should have with every other man, not only friend with friend, or lover with lover, but businessman with clerk, and passenger to conductor, and student to janitor. Everything must be fully human (p. 19).

Wolf explains why this demand for authenticity in relationships goes unmet.

The I-thou relationship is very hard. Our young were mistaken when they thought it could be maintained all the time, that one could be utterly open and available to every other human being. It is possible only to pretend to speak openly for hour after hour, to listen openly hour after hour, to treat every person as if he were your beloved, or as if he were your self. Buber has told us that one inevitably moves in and out of I-thou relationships. And so one goes back into the world of I-it. We cannot always treat the janitor as if he were our friend; we must learn how to treat the janitor as if he were the janitor (p. 20).

Development into a stage of realistic friendship in late adolescence, as explained by Douvan and Adleson, is often, it would seem today, not reached by many adolescents who require friendships of the type and level described by Conger and by Wolf. It seems that we can ask a great deal, and adolescents expect a great deal, in friendship, but an adolescent can ask no more of friendship than a friendship can provide and still remain himself. A fifteen-year-old girl wrote:

A friend is a person who you can:
   1—trust
   2—put a burden upon
   3—share happiness
   4—share sadness
   5—depend upon
   6—love

I've really never experienced the feeling of having a friend whose personality made all of the above possible. I thought I had such a friend once, but it turned out that just like all other people I know, he was an acquaintance. I hope someday I'll find a real friend I'll want to feel close to (Bravler and Jacobs, 1974, p. 56).

Conformity

In friendships, cliques, crowds, and sets, adolescents have been seen to choose and more than likely be with people who are more like themselves than different from themselves. A solid degree of veracity in the statement "birds of a feather flock together" is acknowledged by almost everyone. The similarity in friends, cliques, and crowd members in adolescents has been seen to occur in a broad spectrum of demographic variables such as socioeconomic status, ethnicity, etc. Attitude similarity as a determinant of attraction would appear to underlie many of the similarities in friendship patterns. Much research has shown that degree of attitude similarity relates to degree of attraction, and that proportion of similar attitudes relates almost linearly to attraction, i.e., the more attitudes we agree on the more we are attracted

(Baron et al., 1974, p. 41). This relationship has been seen to hold for people of all ages and across nations.

It makes very good sense within this framework to see adolescents who have the opportunity to make clear and unencumbered choices of friends and associates, albeit somewhat limited in distance, to associate with people who are similar to them. What then appears to be conformity behavior within the peer groups could be, and no doubt to some degree is, a function of the similarities in attitudes which promoted the development of attraction and establishment of the peer group. However, conformity in adolescents is even greater than these factors might indicate. A number of social-pressure experiments, experiments in which adolescent subjects were influenced in some subtle manner to see whether they would change behavior or attitudes to go along with, to conform to, the other people in the experiment, give support to a long-held notion "that a rigid, 'slavish' type of conformity characterizes early adolescence and diminishes in the later adolescent years" (Landsbaum and Willis, 1971, p. 334). The explanation for this finding is most generally based on socialization theory.

> With the onset of pubescence, the child becomes acutely aware of his social peers and relies on them for many of his external behavior patterns. . . . Therefore, the child at the pubescent stage displays much uncertainty with his own judgment and mirrors the behavior of his peers. By the post adolescent and the early adult stages, the individual has learned that there are both situations which call for conformity and those which call for individual action (Costanzo and Shaw, 1966, p. 974).

In a study with subjects ranging in age from 5 to 19 years, Collins and Thomas (1972) found that the degree of conformity to peer pressure, "the degree of yielding increased from the early childhood to the middle childhood group, decreased in the preadolescent group, then increased to a maximum in the adolescent group before decreasing in the later adolescent group" (p. 85). The increase in yielding or conformity to peer pressure in middle childhood is explained as a result of the child's learning about social pressure. The spurt in yielding in adolescence is said to result from an increase in peer-group power. The adolescent conforms, yields, because he "is ready to rely on his social peers or yield to their pressure" (p. 85).

We have learned from Brittain's work earlier that the adolescent is more likely to conform in areas such as fashion, haircut, and manners, those areas in which the adolescent might consider his peer group has more expertise than his parents, and we can see that conformity or yielding to peer pressure could increase as an individual moves into new areas where he is not sure of his stance. Both of these socialization factors could account for much of the increase in the conformity in adolescence.

However, the additional influences of moral development, and cognitive development as related thereto, may contribute to conformity behavior in adolescence.

It seems safe to say that in the process of developing from concrete to formal operations, and until such time as formal operations are established, an adolescent may be less sure of himself in terms of his rationale for decision making than he would be either formally in concrete operations or formally in formal operations. So too, in developing through the moral-development stages of Kohlberg, the movement, particularly in the last three stages, is from clear-cut, more precise, acknowledgment of the forces influencing judgments to more complex and involved judgmental processes. Fodor (1971) discusses this, showing that on Kohlberg's moral-judgment scale,

> . . . stages three and four, for example, imply a degree of submissiveness to the social influence of others, whether they be peers or authority figures. The greater preponderance of principled moral reasoning (stages five and six), therefore, the less susceptible should one be to various forms of social influence (p. 122).

Fodor found that "subjects who successfully resisted attempts by the interviewer to induce them to reverse their moral decisions were found to be more advanced in moral development as measured by the Kohlberg interview" (p. 124). Although there is not sufficient research to back up this conclusion, it would appear that moral and cognitive development in adolescence may account for some of the rise, the spiking effect, in conformity behavior in early to middle adolescence. One might also wonder whether the differences in cognitive development and moral development between the lower and upper-middle socioeconomic status groups might account for the greater homogeneity found amongst upper socioeconomic groups than lower socioeconomic groups.

The Life-Task Self

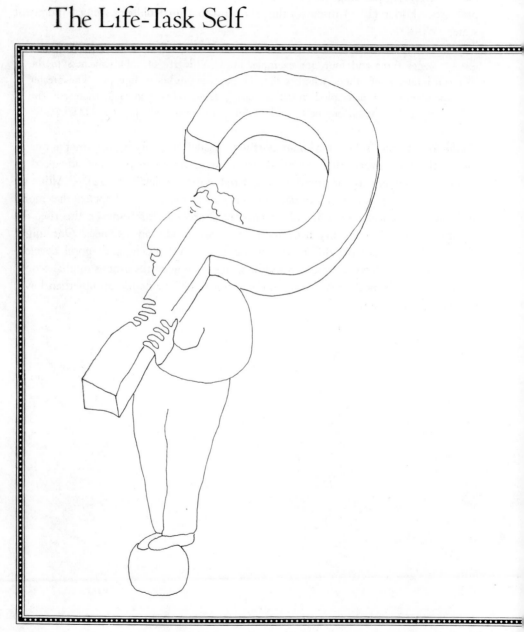

CHAPTER 13

The term self or self with a hyphen, self-, is so frequently used by everyone, including psychologists and educators, that it demands definition wherever it is used. This is because self has very different meanings to lay people and psychologists and philosophers of different schools.

When my daughter, at three, kept the entire family waiting because "I want to do my buttons myself," she expressed not only her competency need and ability to control but also her sense of unity of self. When a truant is brought to the principal's office and says, "I didn't want to stay away but my friends made me," he is expressing a duality—as if his mind-self said go to school, but his body-self, his behavior, was controlled from outside. (This brings to mind comedian Flip Wilson's line "The Devil made me do it.") As Royce (1973) recently pointed out, psychologists and all of us, as the inheritors of certain strains of Western philosophy, tend to utilize the mind-body dualism as a construct in thinking of man and ourselves. But common sense and empirical observation tell us:

> The self . . . is not a mental construct, but a living organism, a person. When I say that I cut myself shaving this morning, I do not mean that I cut a mental construct. Likewise, if you hit ME, that "I" who got hit is not some "ego" of Freudian theory. We are talking here not about one's self-concept or self-image but about the existing reality. And this reality is the same referent when we say "I understand," or "I choose," or "I run" (Royce, 1973, p. 885).

Cooley's (1902) definition of self was "that which is designated in common speech by the pronouns of the first person singular, 'I,' 'me,' 'my,' 'mine,' and 'myself' " (p. 136). We all use the first-person singular and have a sense of self—a sense of oneself as knower and as an object, as known (James, 1910). We may grant, then, that persons have a feeling or a sense of self and that "the self is the person" (Royce, 1973, p. 886). If the self, then, is the person, and you all will agree intuitively that you (the person) are yourself; and if personality is, as Maddi (1968) said, "a stable set of characteristics and tendencies that determine those commonalities and differences in the psychological behavior (thoughts, feelings, actions) of people that have continuity in time . . ." (p. 10); then what of "self"—what aspect(s) of self—may be relevant in a discussion on development, and dealt with as part of a separate life task?

The constructs made up of self with a hyphen, most importantly self-concept, form the nucleus of the personality (Lecky, 1945). The position being taken here is that a holistic, phenomenologic view envisions the person and self as the same, while, as stated in an earlier section, personality describes the set or organization of an individual's ways which make him uniquely himself and which are consistent, to a large degree, over time. The self-concept, which is a key element in the nature of one's personality, is a concept which implies active intellectual awareness and control. Therefore the self-concept, and related self-constructs, may be seen as possessing possibilities for developmental change in conjunction with intellectual and environmental change and may be thought of as part of the life-task self, over which one may assume active control, may have an effect.

Two definitions of self-concept should assist us in seeing the cognitively active nature of the construct. Rogers, who defined the self as "an organized, fluid, but consistent conceptual pattern of perceptions of characteristics and relationships of the 'I' or the 'me,' together with values attached to these concepts" (1951, p. 498), includes in the self-concept only those aspects of himself that the individual is aware of and feels some control over. In Snygg and Combs' (1949) definition of self-concept, "those parts of the phenomenal field which the individual has differentiated as definite and fairly stable characteristics of himself" (p. 112), the operative word is "differentiated," illustrating cognitive activity.

McCandless (1970) conceives of self-concept, which is an extremely complex construct, as including three major components: structure, function, and quality. Within his conceptual framework, in the structure of the self-concept, such terms as rigid or flexible, congruent, simple or complex, broad or narrow, apply; in the function of the self-concept, such things are included as self-evaluation, and prediction of success or failure; and in the quality of the self-concept, the primary components are high or low self-esteem and self-acceptance versus self-rejection.

Within this very useful framework, the function of the self-concept is a theoretical given. That is to say, theoretically the self-concept operates in certain ways, functions in certain ways, regardless of the rigidity, congruence, complexity, or narrowness of the structure of an individual's self-concept, or the approving or disapproving, accepting or rejecting nature of the quality of an individual's self-concept. The self-concept functions as a standard for evaluating and predicting one's performance or potential performance socially (as others might see it), objectively (if there is an objective measure of the behavior), and personally (as it relates to the structure and quality of one's self-concept), and it functions to limit performance for the purpose of maintaining and enhancing itself, i.e., a person behaves as he thinks he can or should for the person he thinks he is.

Epstein (1973) sees the self-concept as a "theory that the individual has unwittingly constructed about himself as an experiencing, functioning individual" (p. 407). The functions of the self-concept or self-theory, as Epstein says (1973), are "the maintenance of a favorable pleasure/pain balance, the assimilation of the data of experience, and the maintenance of self-esteem" (p. 411). The functions of the self-concept must be remembered as operating as the self-theory of individuals. For the youth who feels himself neglected, average performance in scholastic or sporting competition may best fit his self-theory and its functions. By receiving "C" grades or running in the pack in a long-distance run he maintains a pleasure/pain balance that is favorable for him—he need not be picked out or picked on for running first or last. The "C" grade and running in the pack fit his expectation for himself and therefore are easily assimilated pieces of data and serve to maintain the level of self-esteem he has developed.

Waterbor (1972) and Epstein (1973) both speak of development of sense of self, or self-theory, as sequential. Waterbor (1972) classifies three groups of theories of self which he suggests may form a developmental sequence. They are, in developmental order, those theories, or aspects of self, which stress the continuities of body awareness, the continuities of social life, and, lastly, the continuities of valuing. Epstein's developmental aspects of the self-theory begin first with the child's learning that he has a *body self* by virtue of simply recognizing that his body is one of many human bodies but is separate, distinct in certain ways, and his. The development of a body self requires only a low level of cognitive ability, whereas the next development, of an *inferred inner self*, requires a somewhat greater and abstract level of cognitive ability. Epstein shows that as one sees others who are behaviorally as well as physically identifiable, feels continuity in one's own experience, and feels emotions, needs, and defensiveness about aspects of one's own being, one concludes, or infers, an identity, an inner self, of his own. Lastly, in response to social demands, at a simpler, lower cognitive level when young and at a more abstract, higher cognitive level when older, one develops a *moral self*.

It is, I hope, obvious from this discussion of the self and self-concept that the biological changes at adolescence may potentially upset or alter the aspect of the self-concept called the body self and thereby make the self life task difficult. Cognitive, moral, sex-role development at adolescence may have effects on aspects of the self-concept. And, as has been shown in earlier chapters, as these developments differ among groups of adolescents, the teacher, parent, or psychologist may anticipate differing types of self problems according to the group membership of the individuals with whom they deal.

THE SITUATIONAL ELEMENT

Erikson (1959), as we have seen, supposed that adolescents experience an identity crisis in late adolescence. Tanner (1971) points to effects hormonal and other pubertal physiological developments may have on the self-concept in early adolescence. Offer's (1969) study found both parents and adolescents agreeing that the adolescents experienced their greatest personal "turmoil" between the ages of 12 and 14.

It would appear, then, that as developmental changes occur in a youth's body or thought, there is the potential for upset in youth's thoughts about himself, his self-concept. Moreover, events which occur with some frequency for large groups of adolescents, or all adolescents in a particular culture, may have the effects of creating upset or "turmoil" in self-concept also, of fulfilling the potentiality. It is these events that are here being termed "the situational element."

A very good illustration of the situational element in the self life task is a study by Simmons, Rosenberg, and Rosenberg (1973), in which they first investigated whether there is self-image disturbance in adolescence; if there is, at what age, or ages, does it occur, and, finally, what "triggers" the disturbance.

They studied a random sample of 2,265 pupils in grades 3 through 12 in Baltimore. The sample was 63 percent black and more heavily working class than the national average and reflected the population of Baltimore. They noted the fact, which from our discussion of group differences would have concerned us, that the study was cross-sectional and did not include drop-outs as members of the older student population. They studied self-consciousness, stability of the self-image, global self-esteem (a general, overall feeling toward oneself), and specific self-esteem (an average of self-assessment on eight characteristics such as smart, good-looking, helpful, honest, etc.).

Simmons et al. found a marked change for the worse on all measures between the 11 and 12-year-old groups. In general they found the 12-year-old group much lower than the younger groups on all self-image measures, with some further deterioration thereafter leveling off around 14 for self-consciousness and specific self-esteem and improving after 14 on stability of self-image and global self-esteem. From these findings one might conclude that puberty is the chief determinant of self-image disturbance. However, Simmons, Rosenberg, and Rosenberg went on to analyze the effects of changing schools, and moving into a junior or senior high school, on children of the same age. Their conclusion points to the importance of a situational factor influencing the rate or amount of upset youth feel toward themselves. They say:

> In sum the data indicate increased self-image disturbance associated with the transition from elementary to junior high school. The reason does not appear to be

solely the age change (with its associated biological changes); for at ages roughly equivalent, the seventh graders still show greater disturbance. Nor does it simply appear to be the shock of transferring to a new school; furthermore, the transition from junior to senior high school shows no such effect. Perhaps puberty does not in itself disturb the self-image but heightens vulnerability to environmental circumstances which threaten the self-concept (1973, p. 564).

The situational element, going to junior high school from elementary school, may disturb the young adolescent's self-image. Simmons et al. do not find that moving on to senior high school is similarly disturbing. This would seem to point to the value of the junior high school in preparing its students, through organizational and social structures, for senior high school. But also one must remember that the students who remain in school until the end of high school and beyond have better coped with the school and are continuing to do so. In part they will be coping better with school because of their abilities and higher IQ and because of their sense of self and sense of competence which will facilitate achievement (Manaster, 1972).

What other "events" occur for most, or all, American youth? There are situational elements which affect self-concept in the life-task areas school, friends, and love, as we have seen. But in the continuity of self there are no events which hold for all youth except in interaction with other life-task areas because of differences in the paths that people take through life. Therefore this discussion will continue first by expanding on the cognitive-developmental effects on self-concept in adolescence, and then looking at sex, and social class and race differences in self-concept in adolescents.

"NORMAL" SELF-CONCEPT DEVELOPMENT IN ADOLESCENCE

It must be repeated and remembered that probably the most frequent and continual description of adolescence is as a time of stress and upset. The classic psychoanalytic theory, as expressed again recently by Anna Freud (1969), predicts that disturbance in the ego-defense system, the maintenance and protection of self, will occur with the biological and sexual developments at adolescence. McCandless (1970), too, says that ideas about oneself, particularly heterosexually, change dramatically with adolescence. And Erikson and Lewin, as we have seen, stress the same phenomenon of a normative crisis for adolescents. As this treatise is attempting to show, there are very usual, normal reasons for upset in the life-task areas in adolescence, many of which are situationally fomented in interaction with developmental change.

But how does self, or self-concept, itself develop in adolescence? Monge (1973) studied the "connotative structure" of adolescent self-concept using seven-point semantic-differential scales to rate the concept "My Characteristic Self (yourself as you most often feel about yourself)" on 21 polar adjective pairs, such as smart-dumb; confident-unsure; relaxed-nervous; rugged-delicate; etc. Monge's idea of "connotative structure" includes comments that McCandless would refer to as structure and quality. It may therefore be thought of as the connotative structure, referring to the elements which make up the structure and quality components of the self-concept.

Looking at over 2,000 male and female public students in grades 6 through 12 in central New York State, Monge was interested in the continuity or discontinuity of the structure of the self-concept over these years. Although he found self differences, an issue we will discuss later in this chapter, he found that "there was a very high degree of structural simplicity across grade and sex in the ratings of self-concept as shown by the emergence in all of the analyses of the same four factors" (Monge, 1973, p. 391). The four factors were named (I) Achievement/Leadership, (II) Congeniality/Sociability, (III) Adjustment, and (IV) Masculinity/Femininity. Granting the problems for inference caused by the cross-sectional design, drop-outs from the older grades, and limited prepubescent data from girls because they mature earlier, Monge concluded, "The evidence for a restructuring of the self-concept around and after pubesence was very slight for boys and modest for girls" (p. 391). Monge, then, does not agree that major discontinuities in self-concept and psychological development occur around pubescence.

This finding is important but may be influenced by the method used. Factor analysis determines which variables, or items on a test instrument, go together. This "going together" is determined statistically, through the factor-analytic statistical technique, and the researcher decides that the factors produced statistically are conceptually meaningful. It is possible using factor analysis to determine, as in Monge's study, for a specified number of items making up a test, the most meaningful number and character of factors for subjects of various ages and grades, for the whole sample, and to determine the match between the factors for age and grade samples. This is what Monge did. He did not find striking differences across the subsamples; he was not really looking for them, but he did not find them.

Mullener and Laird (1971) were specifically looking for changes in the organization of self-evaluations, in a sense changes in the structure of the quality component of self-concept, and chose a method that would help them find such changes if they existed. They hypothesized that "with age, individuals reveal an increasingly differentiated use of categories of personal characteristics when evaluating themselves" (Mullener and Laird, 1971, p. 233). Their sample was composed of 24 students in a seventh-grade honors program, 24 college-prep high-school seniors, and 24 evening-college students. From a 40-item questionnaire in which the subjects evaluated themselves on a 6-point scale in each of 5 content areas, evaluation scores were determined, as was a variance score which was taken to measure differentiation in evaluation of self, i.e., more variance = more differentiation. To test the intellectual level of the subjects, the Shipley Institute of Living Scale was given and showed mental ages of 16.7, 17.3, and 17.7 for the seventh grade, twelfth grade, and adult groups, respectively. The mental ages of the groups were then roughly equivalent and the seventh-grade group was really (considering their age) brighter than the older group. So if intellectual level was the crucial variable in differentiation, no differences would have been found. However, these are not average groups and the relationship that might be found between intelligence and differentiation using the full range of intellectual levels could not be illustrated with this study.

But Mullener and Laird (1971) found that with age "there was a change from relatively global to relatively differentiated self-evaluations, changes that have been shown to characterize development of other cognitive products" (p. 235). They also found that subjects who did not differentiate as much, who had low variance scores, had higher evaluation scores than did those subjects who had high variance scores. So as well as finding greater differentiation at higher ages, greater differentiation was related to lower self-evaluation.

The differentiation of self-evaluation was measured by Mullener and Laird within five areas at all ages. These five areas were achievement traits, intellectual skills, interpersonal skills, physical skills, and social responsibility. In a general way, these areas resemble the factors of achievement, sociability, adjustment, and masculinity-feminity found across ages by Monge. It is as if Mullener and Laird assumed structural similarity of self-evaluations across ages and investigated differentiation within this structure.

Mullener and Laird referred to the general conception that greater cognitive differentiation occurs with higher levels of development, which is a conception based on the work of Piaget and Werner. Achenbach and Zigler (1963) studied the self-image disparity, the difference between the real self and the ideal self, using a developmental rationale. They predicted a positive relationship between self-image disparity and maturity level, assuming that (1) with greater maturity a person will make more demands on himself because he will see and feel more demands from society and will feel more guilt when he cannot fulfill those demands; and (2) with greater maturity a person will differentiate more within his real-self concept and thereby see more ways in which he does not measure up to his ideal self. They found the relationship they predicted with adults. Katz and Zigler (1967) explored the same hypotheses in greater detail with children and their findings are more important to this discussion.

Katz and Zigler's (1967) sample was made up of 120 fifth, eighth, and eleventh-grade students, half of whom, at each grade level, were low IQ (means 91, 93, and 94 for the three grades in ascending order) and half of whom were high IQ (124, 127, and 125 for the three grades, respectively). Looking at the disparity between real and ideal self they found that "real-self scores are more negative than ideal-self scores. The magnitude of this difference between real and ideal scores is influenced by both age and IQ" (p. 344). There were "greater differences between real and ideal scores at grades 11 and 8 than at grade 5. The high-IQ subjects exhibit a greater discrepancy between real and ideal scores than do low-IQ subjects" (p. 344). They then looked at the real-self scores separately. They found the real-self ratings more negative at grades 11 and 8 than at grade 5. For the real self, the high-IQ subjects had more positive feelings than the low-IQ subjects in fifth grade, the real-self ratings were similar in the eighth grade, and by eleventh grade the low-IQ subject ratings were less negative than for the high-IQ subjects. For the ideal self it was found that "the older or brighter the child, the more positive was his ideal-self" (p. 345).

These findings support the hypothesis that there is an increase in self-image disparity with increasing maturity since a positive relationship was found between self-image disparity and chronological age and IQ. By comparing and analyzing the scores on the various instruments used in the study, Katz and Zigler concluded that support was also found for the developmental rationale "that self-ideal disparity is a function of two underlying factors related to maturity level, namely, capacity for guilt and cognitive differentiation" (p. 350).

By asking adolescents to describe "The Person I Would Like to Be Like," researchers have found a sequence of categories which indicates the developmental maturity of the ideal self. Manaster, Saddler, and Williamson (1976) hypothesized that development of the ideal self, and therefore presumably other developmental changes in the self in adolescence, is related to, is a function of, cognitive development. They analyzed written passages for cognitive-developmental level, from concrete to formal operations, and The Person I Would Like to Be Like for over 200 12 and 13-year-old (the younger sample) and 15 and 16-year-old (the older sample) working and middle-class boys and girls in the north of England.

Table 13 shows the findings of a regression analysis in which the variables age, sex, SES, and cognitive-development score were used to predict ideal-self score. Whether all subjects were combined in a single analysis, the entire sample, or the younger and older samples were analyzed separately, as can be seen in Table 13, the cognitive score is the most significant predictor of ideal self. In a general sense adolescents who are still in the concrete-operations stage are more apt to think of their ideal self in terms of their parents or heroes or other glamorous adults. But adolescents who have moved to formal operations may begin to think of who they might be in terms of combinations of imagined or real persons.

Using these studies, what might we say in general about the development of the self-concept in adolescence? The basic structure of the self-concept remains pretty much the same throughout adolescence for individual adolescents; those with higher IQ become able to differentiate more about the many facets of their self, and also become able to refine their ideal self as they differentiate their perceived world.

Table 13. *Age, Sex, SES, Mean Cognitive Development Score as Predictors of Ideal Self Score: Stepwise Multiple Linear Regression Analyses. (From Manaster, Saddler, and Williamson, 1976.)*

Predictor	DF	R^2	R^2 Change	F-Ratio	Significance
		Entire Sample			
Cognitive Score	1; 221	.089	.089	21.56	p < .0001
Sex	2; 220	.112	.024	5.88	p < .02
SES	3; 219	.113	.001	f < 1	p > .70
		Younger Sample			
Cognitive Score	1; 132	.043	.043	5.93	p < .02
Sex	2; 131	.058	.015	2.03	p > .10
Age	3; 130	.067	.009	1.31	p > .20
SES	4; 129	.068	.001	f < 1	p > .70
		Older Sample			
Cognitive Score	1; 87	.14	.14	14.28	p < .0001
Sex	2; 86	.19	.05	5.29	p < .03
Age	3; 85	.21	.02	1.65	p > .20
SES	4; 84	.22	.01	f < 1	p > .40

This may result in greater anxiety, as the disparity between real and ideal self grows, and general concern as the adolescent perceives many smaller, differentiated, areas in which he varies from the global way he has seen himself before. The anxiety need not be debilitating; it may be healthy. And whatever "crises" occur may be the same. Yet the potential for such a crisis is much greater in the older and brighter adolescent, as we have seen. Such a crisis or set of concerns may never occur in the vast number of average or below-average intelligence adolescents. As Katz and Zigler (1967) have shown, by late high school the low-IQ students had higher real-self ratings than the high-IQ students and lower ideal-self ratings. Quite logically they have no need for a crisis if they feel fairly positive overall about themselves and are more closely the kind of person they would like to be.

This section has alluded to the effects of intelligence, cognitive development, and age on development of the self-concept in adolescence in a manner similar to that in Chapter 8. In a sense it has pointed to two extremes in the development of self-concept.

At one extreme are adolescents who are younger, less bright, less cognitively developed. They, at that time in their own development, do not seem to differentiate to any great degree in their thinking about themselves, have a relatively lower opinion of themselves, but also have a relatively lower opinion of the self they would like to be. As they grow older they may differentiate more, but still not to a great extent, and their self-concept relative to others is higher. The sense of who or how they would like to be does not rise appreciably, and therefore the real self–idealself disparity does not grow. It may be that with cognitive development in adulthood they become more like the other extreme group, but knowledge in the field on these issues is limited. It may be that little or no additional development occurs for these people in this area.

Is this first extreme group typified by the child who did not do very well in grammar school, and possibly in high school either (remember the relationships of both self-concept and intelligence with school achievement), but who later developed an area of competence that was satisfying? In grammar school, low achievement in the basic academic areas was part of an undifferentiated, or less differentiated, self-concept. As he or she ages (and finds competencies as a working person, in a craft, with secretarial or clerical skills, socially and/or around the home) the global self-concept reflects this feeling of competency, of adequacy. And this less differentiated feeling of adequacy is not too distant from the conception he or she has of the person he or she would like to be.

Adolescents in the other extreme group are brighter and experience greater cognitive development as they age. When in grammar school, achieving at higher levels, they feel pretty good about themselves. In the same way as the first group, their self-concept at that age is not very differentiated and their achievement is reflected in their self-concept. However, as adolescents in this hypothesized group develop, they differentiate more aspects, or subsets, of self and more possibilities for how they could be. They see areas in which they are very distant from their heightened level of ideal self. These feelings may promote the massive reformulation of the many selves which are seen as an "identity crisis." As the persons in this group are more likely to attend college and thereby have a prolonged adolescence, a longer psychosocial moratorium, they may be the group which composes, or experiences, the stage called "youth."

Normal Problems/Normal Crises

Adolescents have problems. Some adolescents have crises. But let's face it: everyone has problems, and at one time or another everyone faces crises. Yet to many contemporary adolescents their "self" is a problem. Chabassol and Thomas (1969) compared studies of adolescents in the U.S. and Canada carried out in 1936, 1959, 1961, and 1968, in which subjects ranked 15 items as greater or lesser problems to them. A most interesting change from 1936 to 1968 for both males and females was found. In 1936 males ranked mental hygiene 13, and females ranked mental hygiene 9.5, of the 15 problems. In 1968 males ranked mental hygiene 3, and females ranked it 2. Clearly, mental hygiene (concerns with one's self and personal adjustment) is an increasingly important problem for college-age youth. The five most prominent problems for males in 1968 were, in order, money, study habits, mental hygiene, personal and moral qualities, and philosophy of life. The five most prominent problems for females were money, mental hygiene, personal attractiveness, study habits, and home and family relationships.

Allport (1964) discussed "crises in normal personality development" using his undergraduate class as subjects. His approach and conclusions seem relevant to high-school-age youth also. He said a crisis "is a situation of emotional and mental stress requiring significant alterations of outlook within a short period of time" (p. 236). The changing role prescriptions that accompany the move from high school to college are more extreme than those that accompany the move to high school, but the crisis potential is similar. Allport notes that the freshman in college does not sense the feeling of crisis as much as in the sophomore year, because as a freshman the youth is trying to please the folks back home. But in the sophomore year "suddenly it becomes no longer tolerable to live one's life for the edification of the people back home" (p. 237). The youth feels at a crossroads between the past and the future and for many the choice is clear. So, too, high-school teachers know the reticence of some early students to participate, and they find that when these students are truant they may be found "hanging around" their old junior high school or grammar school. The junior-high-school and grammar-school teachers, initially quite happy to be visited by a former student, often find the student unhappy and tearful as he or she reminisces about the good old days, the sure, secure days of junior high or grammar school. The student may also be returning to where he is still a "big man."

Allport speaks of four areas of conflict, four crisis areas. The first is the intellectual crisis, which comes in high school for superior students who are bored and unchallenged, or who, in moving to a new school level, find suddenly that they are not able to maintain their superiority academically and are devastated by the competition. Next are the crises of "specific inferiorities" in which "besides the sense of intellectual inferiority . . ., we encounter deep disturbance due to physical handicaps or to plain physical appearance" (p. 238). The individual will have made adjustments and developed strategies for dealing with his real or felt inferiority or weakness in previous environments. Through adolescence new situations may arise in which he feels unable to cope because of his perceived inferiority and this may spark a crisis. Allport speaks, too, of crises due to religious and ideological conflicts, sexual conflicts, and family conflicts. These areas of conflict are analogous to the life-task areas, and the "specific inferiority" area, the "inferiority complex" area, is analogous to the life-task self.

Adolescents differentiate their "self" into more discrete units, life-task area situation-specific units. Some will differentiate more than others. Presumably cognitive-developmental differences will effect differentiation. That is, brighter and higher cognitive-level adolescents may construe their "selves" in a greater variety of ways than less able adolescents. Also adolescents with more life options, because of their own abilities or background, SES, which opens more options, may differentiate their "selves" to match, compare with, the attributes they think important to these options.

To some extent on entering adolescence, self-concept and certain facets of the "self" appropriate to the life tasks exist along with a global self-concept. Children have a body concept, a self-concept of their own body. However, the physical changes at puberty and after demand a reevaluation of body concept. "All the changes in the body, not only in sexual development and function but also in physical size and strength, necessitate modification of the earlier established mental images of the body" (Committee on Adolescence, 1968, p. 74).

The modification for each adolescent would depend on the perception of change by the adolescent, which would relate to actual change, and the importance of the body concept to the individual. But every adolescent's body changes, and the potential for difficulty, or crisis, exists for every adolescent in dealing with his body concept. If the "normal problem" of body change and adaptation of body concept becomes a "normal crisis" for an adolescent, more change, or effect, on the global self-concept, or other aspects of self-concept, would be presumed. A social, popular child who is a late developer, or feels changed to a relatively ugly adolescent from a cute or pretty child, or a relatively weak adolescent from a strong child, may no longer (or for a period of time) feel adequate socially or completely and have a lower global self-concept.

As adults, most of us probably get up in the morning, wash up, throw on some clothes (which hopefully go together and look alright), and proceed with our day. Maybe during the day, because it is convenient or even necessary, an adult might glance at himself or herself in a window or mirror and tidy up. What does a typical adolescent do? He or she probably spends considerable time early and throughout the day checking his or her carefully selected outfit, combing, recombing, and restyling his hair, and examining "how he looks." Are there any new pimples, new hairs?

For adults, the question "How do I look today?" can generally be answered, "Like I looked yesterday." For adolescents, it is a real question, which they answer by frequently inspecting and modifying the way they look, and incorporating this information into their changing body concept.

The self-concept and its differentiated parts may be affected by adolescent situations and affect feelings about self and performance in these situations. The new situations of love and sexual behavior, new and lesser known social situations in a wider community, a larger, more distant school with greater variety of course offerings and required skills, demands of occupational and educational choice, are all problems and potential crises for most adolescents. The adolescent's self-concept affects his coping with these problems, and the effectiveness of this coping in turn affects his self-concept.

Contemporary "Normal Problems," Activist Example

This section emphasizes the continuing normalcy of problems and crises in American adolescence. From the Chabassol and Thomas data we might expect that problems and crises of the "self" are increasing, but Allport's view points to the continual presence of the usual human, life-task conflicts. In the 1955 study, "Youth's Outlook on the Future," Gillespie and Allport compared the attitudes of youth in a number of countries and concluded that American youth were more self-centered and more privatistic, i.e., less interested in or evading issues of, wider ideological and international concern. In replicating portions of the Gillespie and Allport study some 20 years after the original data were collected, Kleiber and Manaster (1972) found considerable change over time and also greater differences within their sample.

Kleiber and Manaster divided their sample into activists and nonactivists on the basis of participation in demonstrations or confrontations and found that "while there was a general trend away from conservatism and traditional values in all our subjects, the activists reflected far greater changes" (p. 232). The activists were more involved with social problems than the nonactivists, who seemed to be content with primary involvement in their own personal lives and futures. The nonactivists were more similar to the 1950 sample, whereas the activist group seemed to be moving away from privatism. From this we might conclude that the wider issues and therefore the life tasks other than self are taking on greater import for American youth, but we must still realize that this change is negligible in the majority of nonactivist traditional college and certainly high-school youth.

Although the majority of youth in the 1960's and certainly in the early 1970's were not practising activists, the activist's role is open to today's youth. This same situation pertains to other lifestyles also.

We live in an age of extraordinary culture contact and conflict. The electronic revolution, coupled with the revolution in transportation, enables us to confront alien values within our living room or to immerse ourselves physically in alien cultures after a flight of a few hours. The days when one could live in parochial isolation, surrounded only by conventional morality, are fast disappearing. Conflict of ideologies, of world views, of value systems, of philosophical beliefs, of aesthetic orientations, and of political styles confront every thoughtful man and woman, wherever he lives. If such confrontations stimulate moral development, then we live in an era in which technology and world history themselves provide new facilitation for moral growth. We are all today a little like Redfield's peasants who move to the city, living in a world where conflicting cultures and moral viewpoints rub against us at every turn (Keniston, 1970, pp. 588–589).

Whether the technologies of today along with the abrasions of culture contact and conflict are positive in the sense of developing higher-level morality in larger numbers of young people is a moot question. There is no question but that Keniston is correct in pointing out that parochial isolation is dead. We are all, and all youth are, made continually aware of the vast spectrum of ideologies, political and social, mechanisms and strategies, i.e., activists' outlets and options, available in pursuit and support of such ideologies.

Block, Haan, and Smith (1973) discuss adolescent political-social behavior in terms of two dimensions: The "degree of involvement" of a youth with political and social issues, ranging from the uninvolved, apathetic youth to the involved, active youth, and acceptance or rejection of the traditional values and the authority of society's institutions, ranging from the adolescent who is accepting and conforms to society's values and institutions to the adolescent who outwardly rejects society's authority. There has long been in this country the option for adolescents and adults to be distant from the political process and political issues. They may have been apathetic or they may have been mildly interested; however, their involvement was minimal. The option of being more involved was, of course, always open. Although the option of rejecting the society's values and institutions was open, it was seldom taken, and when it was, it was seldom publicized except in the instance of behaviors that were thought to be traitorous. For whatever reasons, and Keniston's are as compelling as any, the rejection of society's values, institutions, and lifestyles occurs among far more young people today than it has in the past, and we all, including young people, know it.

Block, Haan, and Smith review the literature on activism and apathy in contemporary adolescence. They pose a number of types of youth who fall in some combination on their degree of involvement and acceptance or rejection dimensions. In very simplified form it appears that there are youths who are active and rejecting in keeping with the values of their parents, or supported by the values of their parents, just as there are youths who are active in rejecting society as well as actively rejecting their parents. There are youths who are uninvolved and accepting, the politically apathetic youths who make up the majority of contemporary youth, and youths who are uninvolved and rejecting, the alienated youth. Interestingly, Kerpelman (1970) noted a similarity between activists on the right—active and accepting—and activists on the left—active and rejecting—in that both were high on "autonomy." "All activists—left, middle, and right—were found to need less support and nurturance, to value leadership more, to be more socially ascendant and assertive, and to be more sociable than their ideological counterparts who are not politically active" (Block, Haan, and Smith, 1973, p. 325). This picture of the activist, regardless of political persuasion, is one of a self-confident, high-self-concept person. There is, of course, the question of support from family and peers in choosing a political and social position at the extremes of involvement and rejection or acceptance. But it can be seen that in many individual cases, the autonomous, self-confident adolescent is willing to take the extreme position with minimal, but some, support.

We should also remember that in any group movement there are followers as well as leaders. The excitement, the notoriety, and the sense of community in mutual commitment provide ample support for the less self-confident, lower-self-concept, youth in activist roles.

> *Why strip naked and bellow words of four letters in public?*
> *Poor young things, can it be none of you have any friends?*
> *(Auden, 1972, p. 50).*[1]

These findings and thoughts about activist youth have pertained primarily to college-age youth. Although it is clear that activism and protest increased in the high schools through the 1960's, and is still with us to some extent today, there have been virtually no research studies on activist adolescents below the college level. My first experience of the filtering down of activism and protest to the high-school and junior high-school level occurred a few years ago. A strongly worded, but I think humorously intended, petition was circulated by University of Chicago Laboratory School students to the administration and around campus. The petition stated that "little people have rights, too," and demanded that all doorknobs and urinals in the school be lowered.

Almost the only study of high-school student involvement in social-political activism is by Leming (1974). The activist sample consisted of students taking an elective course in community involvement, and a second group known as the "Memorial 100," a group of 100 students who had been suspended by the administration of the high school in Madison, Wisconsin, where this study was undertaken, when they demonstrated inside the school against the war in Vietnam. Leming looked at moral reasoning in relation to activism because some studies have indicated higher moral-judgment levels among left-oriented activists and because activists generally protest most loudly their own morality. Comparing the activist group with nonactivist adolescents in the same high school, Leming found little difference in their moral reasoning. Most of the students were at level two, Kohlberg's conventional level of moral reasoning; but more activists were at stage three, the good

---

1. From *Epistle to a Godson and Other Poems,* by W. H. Auden. Copyright © 1972 by Random House, Inc., New York.

boy/nice girl orientation; and more nonactivists were at stage four, the law and order orientation.

The activist group was composed of two differing types of activists, the community-involvement course group who were not rule or law breakers; and the "Memorial 100" group, who had shown themselves to be rule and law breakers. Twenty-two percent of the community-involvement group and only 4 percent of the "Memorial 100" group were at stage four, the law and order orientation. Twenty percent of the "Memorial 100" group could not be scored on the moral-reasoning global score. That is, no predominant level or stage of moral reasoning was found in these students' responses to the Kohlberg moral-judgment stories. Leming considered that this indicated that these students were in a transitional period and were uncertain about their moral views.

In the "Memorial 100" sample, 65 percent were at the stage three level of moral reasoning. As "a particular mode of reasoning determines how we perceive or interpret the world around us, clearly this 65 percent see right and wrong actions predominantly in terms of peer-group or good-boy orientations" (p. 524). Within the operation of this orientation, acting as a good boy should, these adolescents, adhering to the norms of their peer group, must therefore include an activism component. Leming's data clearly indicates that among some adolescent groups at least, and presumably among many, there is a norm for activism. This norm operates as an option among the value and behavior potentials for high-school youth. Of the activist group in Leming's study who protested beyond the bounds of law, fully 85 percent either judged the morality of actions on the basis of good-boy orientation or without a clear orientation. Yet there were twice as many principled reasoners—level-three activists as there were nonactivists. One wonders, but feels intuitively that he knows, who the leaders were in the activist group.

A discussion of activism as it relates to adolescence through high school is necessarily short because so much is not known and so little is known. The purpose of this exposition was to illustrate how adolescents differentially involve themselves in phenomena and behaviors that are not inherent in the life tasks, but are to be considered and accepted or rejected by all youth in contemporary culture. The data does not indicate the relationship between self-concept and activism. But it does indicate that, at least for moral development, those adolescents who feel that going along with the crowd, being a good guy, is right behavior, and those adolescents who do not have a clear orientation, clear perspective, on right behavior are apt to behave as activists when the times seem to call for it. If going along to be a good guy or because you are not sure what else to do, from a moral-judgment viewpoint relates to the same kind of thinking relative to self-concept, the appropriateness of this discussion would be assured. I feel justified in this conjecture, even if it is not validated by the data.

In a sense adolescents are called upon to make decisions of "degree of involvement" and "acceptance or rejection" in their behaviors in all of the life-task areas. In love and sex, friends and community, school and work, we have seen that the sense of oneself affects degree of involvement and acceptance or rejection of the traditional and normative ways of behaving. In each of these life tasks problems and crises may arise. But for the adolescent today, even in high school, questions regarding social-political activism, drugs, alcohol, lifestyle, etc., are all encountered and must be answered by and for each adolescent. The process of answering may relate quite significantly to self-concept considerations and may feel like a major problem or crisis to the adolescent. And the answer of the individual adolescent may, too, provoke a crisis.

Problems and Sex Differences in Self-Concept

Issues, problems, of the type just described are particularly noteworthy in considering self-concept as we consider personality in adolescence. These types of problems appear to ebb and flow. They become more or less popular among adolescents, and receive greater and lesser news and media coverage accordingly. Remembering the discussion of personality consistency and research strategies in developmental psychology in Chapter 6, these problems would seem to affect more adolescents during periods when they are popular and newsworthy. During these times, and across time, these issues would show themselves in the time effect in cross-sequential developmental studies.

Some problems seem to be with adolescents continually. Fleege (1945) listed the major problems confronting the adolescent in the conclusion of his extensive study of adolescent boys. His list, starting with most frequent and intense, included sexual adjustment, vocational choice and decision, feelings of misunderstanding and lack of understanding from adults, few social opportunities, financial difficulties, and difficulties with school. In Meissner's (1961) study, "the results indicate that the major sources of worry and anxiety for the high school boy of middle class background are school, sex, unpopularity, immoral activity, religion, vocation, and his future life" (p. 73). Adams (1966) asked 4,000 boys and girls, ages 10 to 19, to identify their own personal problems and those of their peer groups. School, interpersonal relationships, family and money were the most frequently reported problems. Boys more frequently mentioned school and financial problems; the girls mentioned interpersonal and family problems more than did the boys.

Morgan (1969) reviewed studies of junior high-school and senior high-school students with the Mooney problem checklist. At the junior high-school level, school problems were most frequent and problems concerning money, work, and the future, self-centered concerns, and interpersonal relationships followed. At the senior high-school level, adjustment to school and work was the most frequently mentioned problem, followed by personal-psychological relations and current and future financial, vocational, and educational problems. All these problems may be seen as fitting neatly into the life-task areas.

Although there is overlap and interrelationship among the other four life-task areas, the life-task self affects, aids, or interferes with, feelings about and success in the other four life tasks. Therefore, in the other four life-task chapters, there are discussions of how the self, self-concept, interacts with them. Hurlock (1975) notes four conditions which influence the self-concept of the adolescent which are covered in the life-task chapters, and three conditions which influence the adolescent's self-concept which are not. She notes that appearance, interest, and behavior of the adolescent which are sex appropriate help in achieving favorable self-concept; a close relationship with the same-sex family member facilitates sex-appropriate self-concept; peers influence self-concept; and the adolescent's level of aspiration also does. Names and nicknames, given to the adolescent either by family members or peers, may be a source of embarrassment and the adolescent may feel ostracized and ridiculed when the name or nickname is used. Age of maturation may have a positive effect on self-concept when those maturing early are treated more like adults, but a negative effect on self-concept when late maturers are treated like children. Appearance is particularly important to adolescents, and being or feeling that you are different in appearance may influence the level of an adolescent's self-concept. "Being different in appearance makes the adolescent feel inferior, even if the difference adds to his physical attractiveness. Any physical defect is a source of embarrassment which leads to feelings of inferiority" (Hurlock, 1975, p. 197).

> Adolescent self-consciousness centers about appearance and to a lesser extent about personality, athletic prowess, and social skill. The concern of adolescents about acne, body odors, superfluous hair, and body proportion is hard to exaggerate. Although it may seem silly to adults it is very important to young people. The hours spent before the mirror, the money spent on salves and creams to hide acne and to deodorize, and the excruciating diets and body building exercises engaged in by adolescents all attest to this tremendous preoccupation with the self and to a heightened self-consciousness. They also explain the young person's hypersensitivity to any even slightly derogatory or teasing remark about his face or build. In general this hyper self-consciousness diminishes as the adolescent grows older and becomes more adapted to his changed appearance (Elkind, 1971, p. 111).

Of the many changes which become issues or problems for adolescents, whether affecting or affected by the self-concept, they are all social and/or cognitive with the exception of the concern with appearance which is a function of physiological change.

We usually think that while adolescents are all more concerned with appearance and attractiveness than adults, adolescent girls are even more involved in this concern than boys. Both the Douvan and Adelson (1966) and Coleman (1961) studies support this notion. However, Maccoby and Jacklin (1974), in their study of the psychology of sex differences, "encountered very little additional evidence for or against this view, except for the isolated fact that girls and women are somewhat more likely to want orthodontic treatment" (p. 160). They point out that the traditional stereotype of girls in front of mirrors, thinking about clothes and the way they look for hours at a time, if it were ever valid, is now probably changing very rapidly. Although they cite some evidence that girls may be more interested in physical attractiveness than boys, they point to the unisex movement, men's hair stylists, curlers, and dryers, and the colorful, varied, and showy clothes that men and adolescent boys now wear.

In fact, in their study of sex differences, Maccoby and Jacklin find remarkably little difference in self-esteem between the sexes across all age levels through adolescence. In our discussion of self-concept earlier we observed its relationship to sense of competence in much the same way that U'Ren (1971) does—"a sense of competence, a sense of doing or achieving something that is valued, is crucial for the development and maintenance of self-esteem" (p. 470). From this position we would hypothesize that both males and females, having, as we have seen, essentially equal self-concept, would show an equal degree of self-confidence and sense of competence in approaching task situations. But Maccoby and Jacklin present 15 studies in which confidence in task performance was measured. There was no difference between the sexes in four of the studies, whereas men and boys had more confidence in their task performance in the other 11. It appears that through high school, boys and girls do not differ consistently on locus of control, but in college, girls tend to become more external. Looking beyond the locus-of-control variable as early as the grade-school years, males exhibit a greater sense of personal strength and potency. By the college years, Maccoby and Jacklin see a "male cluster" in which there is greater self-confidence in task performance, higher sense of potency, and a greater personal sense of internal control. The "female cluster" is "amorphous" but describes women as more competent socially, more attractive, acceptable to others, and less shy. It is as if men and women, boys and girls, have carved out for themselves, or had presented to them as appropriate and more rewarding, the traditional sex roles and stereotypes, which do give some satisfaction. And the sexes do not differ in self-satisfaction. Within the areas which are more important to them, the male and female "clusters," each sex may have a higher feeling of self-worth but in toto there is no difference.

It is particularly interesting, and in fact exciting, to be able to conclude that there are virtually no sex differences in level of self-esteem, of self-concept, through adolescence and early adulthood. It is as interesting and exciting, in the discussion that follows, to be able to conclude that differences between the races in level of self-concept may not be as marked or in the direction that we have thought them to be. These discussions of sex and race comparisons of self-concept draw us toward the conclusion that evaluations of self are made within one's own group. They do not reflect societal prejudice and discrimination, but rather personal and individual comparisons and evaluations with individuals, and types of individuals, one knows best.

Race Differences in Self-Concept

It had long been considered, and a review of the literature to the early and mid-sixties concurs, that in studies comparing the self-concept of blacks and whites, blacks had lower scores. More recently, there is a growing body of literature which not only denies the earlier studies but even shows positive and high self-concept scores for those black, Mexican-American, and Puerto Rican children and adolescents who are disadvantaged (Carter, 1968; Havighurst and Dreyer, 1971; Powell and Fuller, 1970; Soares and Soares, 1969, 1970/1971, 1971; Trowbridge, 1970a, 1970b). Trowbridge (1970a) found that regardless of whether schools were more or less equally integrated or predominantly black or predominantly white, and regardless of SES or neighborhood, disadvantaged boys and girls had consistently higher self-concepts than advantaged children. Powell and Fuller (1970) tested 617 students and found the higher self-concept scores for black students in all black, or predominantly black, schools. Black boys had higher self-concept scores than white boys regardless of the racial composition of the school. Soares and Soares (1971) found that

> . . . (a) disadvantaged children view themselves and think that others (i.e., their classmates, teachers, and parents) look at them more positively than do advantaged children; (b) elementary school children have higher self-images than secondary school students. Therefore, in comparison to elementary school children, both disadvantaged and advantaged high school students showed a diminishing self-image (p. 428).

As we have noted numerous times, personality characteristics and self-concept are founded on perceptions and conclusions of the child. The child comes to the initial conclusions about himself, his initial self-view, and self-concept within his home, immediate neighborhood, and early school. The people, the children, around the child are most likely to be similar to him in SES and race, for a variety of social, historical, and economic reasons. His early perceptions, his models, his significant others have probably not reflected prejudices against him as being different or inferior because of class or caste membership. Rather he most probably has been among equals and the self-concept he develops is reinforced by those with whom he is closest and has most in common. "At first the child sees only that part of life and of the human community which is bounded by his environment, the family in which he is living. To him this environment means 'life' and the members of the family seem to be 'society' and he attempts to adapt himself to them" (Dreikurs, 1953, p. 43). The family is the first and most important set of significant others. According to Derbyshire and Brody (1964), the significant others in his immediate environment partially define an individual's self-image for him. Carter (1968), in his study of Mexican-Americans, felt that they did not have lower self-concepts than Anglos because they had their own peer group and ethnic group against which to evaluate themselves and develop their self-concept.

Within any group (sex, race, or ethnic) there is no reason for development of low self-concept relative to another group. However, as groups define themselves and are socially defined, they may differ in areas of strength and weakness, areas of high and low self-concept. We have just seen this between the sexes in the "clusters" of attributes which are most important to each. Even between socioeconomic classes, the important, relevant issues for status within that class and self-esteem of its members are available to all—individual differences in the creation of self-concept account for the differences. "There is no indication that the distribution of self-acceptance in a group is related to the social prestige of that group in American society" (Rosenberg, 1965, p. 56). However, as has been illustrated numerous times, there are group differences in aspects of self-concept and these aspects of self-concept in relation to attitudes and behaviors in the life tasks. The point here is that the importance and relevance of an aspect of an individual's self-concept to some degree reflects the importance and relevance it has for the individual's group and that the related behaviors have for the group.

How can this chapter be concluded? Some adolescents, more intellectually able, develop views of their selves in more abstract, wider frameworks. Most adolescents further differentiate facets of their selves as they are forced into a wider world where they must "measure up" in new ways. Each new situation and new option may provoke a "crisis" of fit—"Am I up to it?", "Is this right for me?" And for many adolescents their self fits their world and their future so that crises are few.

From within any group, and for any person, high self-esteem, self-confidence, is possible. The low-self-concept person will try to avoid areas of failure but agonize when he cannot avoid such situations. The high-self-concept person need not avoid tough situations and may provoke them to prove, or prove again, his own worth to himself.

Self-concept pervades all life tasks. Adolescence is the time to test it. Many adolescents do. Françoise Mallet-Joris illustrates this beautifully in "the saga of Daniel," her son:

At fifteen there was a rock-'n'-roll phase. . . . At sixteen he began to display a lively interest in the opposite sex. Young ladies whose Christian names I didn't even know were always disappearing into his room, . . . like ladies in B-feature movies.

He began playing the clarinet. And drinking a little.

At seventeen he became a Buddhist.

He began playing the tuba. His hair got longer.

At eighteen he passed his baccalaureate. Shortly before that, there was a period when he was always covered in jewels, like a Hindu prince or a movie extra. . . .

The jewels disappeared. He began playing the saxophone and the guitar. He hitchhiked 2,500 miles. . . .

He returned home more or less without shoes. . . . He cut off his hair and began studying for a degree in economics. That is the saga of Daniel.

Where is the upbringing in all that? If Daniel, who will be twenty-one this year, is a good son, a good-looking boy, serious yet with a sense of humor, endowed with both imagination and common sense, did I have anything to do with making him so? No, nothing, nothing. And yet yes, something, one tiny little thing, the only thing perhaps that I have given him, yet the only thing too, I sometimes tell myself with pride, that it was important to give him: confidence (Mallet-Joris, 1971, pp. 81–82).[2]

2. From *The Paper House*, by Françoise Mallet-Joris, translated by Derek Coltman. Copyright © 1971 by Farrar, Straus & Giroux, New York.

The Existential Task–
Religion

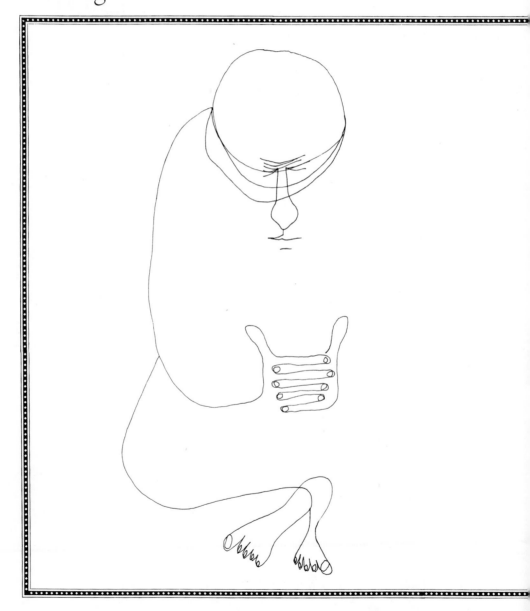

CHAPTER 14

The existential task cannot be described with the precision that describes the love, friends and community, or work and school tasks. The existential task concerns the questions of the meaning(s) of life and from what or whom the meaning is derived. Probably daily we confront issues which bear on the first three life tasks and evaluate our decisions and indecisions in light of our self and our understanding and evaluation of our self. But we probably do not daily, or weekly, or even monthly, reflect on the meaning of life. This may be because we have given up attempting to figure this out, or it may be that we have already come to some conclusion that is sufficiently satisfying that we can proceed with life. Adolescence is the time when the question becomes most pertinent, for social and developmental reasons, and the time when it is most often asked, pondered, and answered, to the degree that it can be.

The framework for regarding the question of what it is all about is religion. Though the questions may be asked outside of this framework, and are, social scientists have not been able, or at least have not, investigated this manner of questioning to any extent. It is within the context of adolescents and religion that an understanding of the existential task must be developed.

> With each year we know more about when the adolescent enters cliques, whom he admires among his peers, what affects his performance in school, which occupations he aspires to, why he becomes delinquent. . . . But what he thinks about his religion and the degree to which he observes its rules and why, is possibly one of the least researched areas in contemporary American life (Rosen, 1965, p. 2).

Rosen's words are as applicable today as when they were written.

THE SITUATIONAL ELEMENT

"As the adolescent moves toward independence, he feels compelled to examine and reconstruct the religious beliefs given him by his family" (Knight, 1969, p. 39). The wording of this quote is particularly pertinent to the thesis being presented. The adolescent "moves" toward independence. On the one hand, this movement is of his own choosing and a function of his biological and psychological development. On the other hand, this movement is not of his choosing, but is determined by the course of social development in the society.

The world, in a sense, has been for the child the world that he was exposed to, the world as given to him by his family. As he moves into and through adolescence, his world broadens—he is exposed to more and new viewpoints. The world he now lives in will in some ways not fit the world he was told existed. In terms of his religious upbringing, whether from a deeply held and/or formally religious home, he will become acquainted with peers whose religious upbringing differed from his. The pattern of religious observance practiced in his home may interfere with other things he may want to do. The morals pertinent to dating and sex set down by his religion may not coincide with those expected by his peers. Even the clothes he wants to wear, and may wear on school days, may be inappropriate for Sundays. Any new inputs may disrupt the attitude he has held toward formal religion and ideas of God and right and wrong.

As neighborhoods in the United States have been formally, in some instances, and informally, in many instances, segregated by race, religion, and ethnic group, and, as neighborhood schools were the norm, through grammar school children tended to associate with other children more like them than not. The transition to junior high school was to a larger group of neighborhoods, and associations with a more diverse group. Finally, the move to high school in many cases brought the adolescent together with the wider views and beliefs of many racial, religious, and ethnic groups. One aspect of this mixing, particularly as it has been forced and dramatic at the time for the adolescent, has been the attempt to see how others believe as they become friends. It may be that greater integration of the various groups earlier will lessen the need to learn about others' differences for the first time in adolescence. However, it may also be that factors other than the situational exert the pressure at adolescence to understand oneself, others, and the world.

First, biological development at adolescence allows a range of sexual functioning which was not present before. How far to go? Should we or not? These are questions answerable on many levels and one level is morality, the bounds of which have been traditionally set by religion. So adolescents will almost of necessity confront matters for the first time having to do with expressions of sexuality and be guided, misguided, or rebel against the teachings of their religion on the subject.

Secondly, and more importantly in the framework of this book, many adolescents will develop cognitively in adolescence, which, as we have seen, will affect or relate to their views on morality and themselves. Conger (1973) also concludes that cognitive development in adolescence affects religious beliefs in the same way cognitive development is related to moral development. As an adolescent's general cognitive framework allows abstracting, so, too, his religious beliefs are likely to become more abstract and less literal.

In many ways the outlook toward religion changes over the transition from childhood to adolescence. In the following section the variety of changes will be looked at in a broad chronological context.

ATTITUDES TOWARD GOD AND RELIGION

Some psychologists have seriously doubted that children have any true religion (Kupky, 1928), yet some of the most interesting changes in a young person's ideas about God and religion take place during the transition from childhood to adolescence. Religion for the child is of this world: the metaphysical concepts are taken literally, the concepts are accepted uncritically. Often the first religious doubt is brought on with the death of a loved one near the time of puberty (Kupky, 1928).

There are many points of view on the change in religious orientation with the onset of adolescence. Some, such as Landis (1945), feel that the question of whether or not to believe is settled by the time children reach puberty, whereas Dobson (1970) believes the issue is settled by the age of five. Kiell (1964) sees rejection of the parents' religion, particularly if God is perceived as a father figure, as part of some adolescents' rejection of all things relating to their parents. While this rebellion may result in many new forms of religion such as rationalism, opportunism, or hedonism (Allport, 1950), it does not necessarily imply a rejection of the basic conviction that the moral law or ideal is somehow associated with the existence of God (Hillard, 1959). In fact, Hurlock (1967) asserts that there is little or no agnosticism and almost a complete absence of atheism in high-school students.

Although some studies have shown that approximately two-thirds of all adolescents rebel against parental and cultural religious teaching (Allport, 1960), other studies have found that two-thirds of the high school students felt religion played an important part in their lives (Boyer, 1959). Kuhlen and Arnold (1944) took a position that fits very well the notion of increasing cognitive development in relation to thinking about religion in adolescence. They said that the changes that take place are not necessarily from belief to disbelief, but from belief to "wonder about."

It is important to note that the only conclusion reported with any degree of consistency across the literature in this field is that females, at all ages, using all types of measuring devices, were more religious than males, were more active in the church, and more conservative in doctrine (Bell, 1938; Boyer, 1959; DeBord, 1969; Franzblau, 1934; Havighurst et al., 1962; Wingo, 1932).

The general changes in attitudes toward religion in adolescence may be looked at as falling around the ages of 12, 15, and 18. To changes around the 12th year, Gesell (1956) describes the Ten, the 10-year-old, as believing in God but unconcerned. God is an invisible man, and the influence of the family on religious thinking is still very strong. The Eleven is more concerned about the problem of death than the Ten. Eleven would be deeply affected by the death of a loved one or pet. Eleven, according to Gesell, sees God as a spirit, while Kupky (1928) considered Eleven's ideas to be graphically anthropomorphic. Gesell says that the Eleven senses the relationship between behavior and what happens to you; consequently, Eleven prays when he wants something.

Gesell sees the Twelve as interested in religion but skeptical. Outright disbelievers appear, which some may find shocking. For most Twelves, religion provides a good feeling. Twelves are more concerned than younger children with death and an afterlife, but their feelings are mixed between awe and wonder, fear and love.

Kuhlen and Arnold (1944) found that 94 percent of the 12-year-olds in their sample believed there is a God, and 70 percent thought God watches, punishes, and rewards. Over 70 percent of the 12-year-olds believed that only good people go to Heaven, accepted Hell as a place of punishment, believed that their prayers were answered, and that every word of the Bible was true.

Goldman (1964) suggests that for Twelves and Thirteens, there is still some anthropomorphic thinking, but that most see God as an invisible spirit. Gesell (1956) says Twelve sees God as half-man, half-spirit. Goldman goes on to say that for Twelves and Thirteens the communication of God to man is understood to be internal and subjective. They do have a conflict in separating the natural and supernatural worlds and this brings doubt about miracles.

From around 12 to 15, these views change. Kuhlen and Arnold (1944) reported a drop from 70 to 49 percent in belief in a watching, punishing, rewarding God. The disbelief in God only rose from 3 to 5 percent over the years 13 to 15, while the "wonder about" God's existence rose from 2 to 14 percent. There were also large drops in the acceptance of such statements as "Only good people go to Heaven"; most of the changes were from belief to wonder, rather than from belief to flat denial.

Gesell creates some differences between 14, 15, and 16-year-olds which can best be summarized as increasing skepticism about death. The "differences" he presents, however, seem to be very questionable standards from which to generalize.

Goldman (1964) suggests that from 13 to 17 the adolescent's prayers become increasingly altruistic. God is felt to be present in prayer. The resulting peace, calm, joy, faith, and logic are seen as evidence of His power.

The liberal trend as seen by Gesell is not substantiated by Wingo (1932) or Goldman (1964). Kuhlen and Arnold (1944) report a liberalizing of attitudes over the years 12 to 15, but this is seen as questioning rather than disbelief.

Kuhlen and Arnold report a regular increase in disbelief in a watching, punishing, rewarding God from 18 percent at 12 to 48 percent at 18. Catholics, Jews, and Protestants are increasingly seen as equally good from 67 percent at age 12 to 86 percent at age 18. By age 18, 32 percent disagree with the statement, "only good people go to Heaven," and 23 percent accepted that there were errors in the Bible.

Havighurst et al. (1962) and Boyer (1959) both reported general increases in interest in religion with increasing age. Doing a study with British students, W. P. Johnson (1967) found a significantly less favorable attitude toward religion in older students when compared with younger students. Hillard (1959), also using British subjects, supports this idea, reporting that young people engage in the most intense questioning of their younger ideas during middle and late adolescence.

Attempts have been made to understand the diverse data within a single developmental set of stages. Harms (1944) identified three stages in the religious development of children, with the last stage occurring in early adolescence. They are: (1) the fairy tale stage, with all types of fanciful ideas; (2) the realistic stage, when earlier imaginings are rejected and explanations are given in terms of natural phenomena; and (3) the individualistic stage, in which a person selects from religion that which satisfies his own needs and drives. This last stage has an interesting dimension to it, in that it is supposed that a person's concept of God may be directly influenced by the type of relation he has had with his father, upon whom the original idea of God may be based.

It must be pointed out that this whole area is fraught with contrary research, disputed research, no research, and research conclusions which are counter to and countered by religious dogma and religious dogmatists. As the Elkinds (1962) concluded in their research on religious beliefs, "none of the explanations put forward in this paper were intended as final pronouncements on the subject, but rather as guides for future research" (p. 111).

A summary of the conclusions of Goldman, who built on Piaget and all of the early researchers in the area, probably best characterizes the central cognitive view of religion in adolescence. However, so you do not get the idea that even these conclusions stand uncriticized, following is a quote from Howkins' (1966) "critique of the research and conclusions of Dr. R. Goldman":

Dr. Goldman: "I have characterized, from research evidence available, three stages of development, named prereligious, subreligious and religious. . . . The adolescent is . . . in what I would call his religious stage of development."
    Christ (Mark 10:14 and Matt. 18:2,3): "Suffer the little children to come unto me, and forbid them not: for of such is the kingdom of God." "And Jesus called a little child unto him, and set him in the midst of them, and he said, Verily I say

unto you, Except ye be converted and become as little children, ye shall not enter into the kingdom of heaven" (p. 42).[1]

Goldman (1964) says:

About the age of thirteen represents a marked watershed in religious thinking. Although fully formal operational thinking does not obviously occur until a little later most pupils have attained an intermediate stage enough to begin to think in terms of propositions and to break with concrete modes of thought. This coincides, not surprisingly, with the ability to conceive of God in symbolic, abstract and spiritualized ideas. There are still some anthropomorphic traces evident in adolescent thinking, especially with the less able pupils, but God is essentially thought of as a spirit, unseen and unseeable. . . .

As Loukes (1961) has shown, there is a later tendency to see much of previous teaching as "childish" and to reject it. . . .

Higher concepts are also expressed in thinking of the holiness of God, and the deity's relationship with man, in a more spiritual manner. . . .

During adolescence, prayers conceptually take on a different texture and from thirteen to seventeen attain a greater degree of altruism. . . .

The church is now apprehended as a fellowship of believers. . . .

The greater number of criticisms of the church are indications of more negative attitudes to religion which Hyde (1963) reveals as increasing during this time. Wright (1962) and Daines (1962) both support this in relation to brighter pupils. . . . They reveal also that although these later adolescents are very critical and often disillusioned about religion there is an expressed hunger for spiritual truth (pp. 239–241).[2]

In this section we have moved from specifics about the attitudes of adolescents toward religion back to the cognitive-developmental aspects of their attitudes toward religion. What we see in Goldman is the tight relationship between attitudes, and the confusion about the area of God and religion, for certain adolescents. The impression is that his description holds for the vast majority of adolescents. However, in speaking about adolescents in school in the United Kingdom in the early 1960's, and then qualifying his remarks to pertain solely to "brighter pupils," we can see again the degree to which many ideas about adolescents have been heavily weighted toward describing brighter adolescents who more probably will move through formal operations.

A very tentative conclusion may be that those adolescents who are able to question and wonder about God and religion at a more abstract level will do so, whereas

1. R. Goldman, *Religious Thinking from Childhood to Adolescence.* London: Routledge & Kagan Paul, 1964.
2. *Op. cit.,* pp. 239–241.

those who cannot will accept or reject the religion they are offered on the basis of personal experience and the emphasis of the times.

Changes Over Time

The question must be raised, "Are adolescents more or less religious today than in the recent past?" And although it must be raised, it really cannot be answered. Rather, the answer must be inferred.

From the conclusion of the last section what might we expect? We expect that changes in concern about religious questions and activity in religious affairs would be related to changes over time in cognitive development, i.e., a more intellectual orientation of adolescents, or a percentage of adolescents. We might expect that changes in emphasis in the greater secular world might affect adolescents' interests in this area. And as we anticipate that these changes might have lessened commitment to organized religion, we might correspondingly expect that the various churches will have made efforts to impede this trend.

Jones (1960) reported a markedly significant increase in the religious interest of girls over the years 1935–1959. Hurlock (1967) states that adolescents today talk more about religion than they did in 1935. Allport (1950) indicated that there had been a decrease in the number of direct conversions in the last 50 years and a decrease in average age of conversion. Landis (1945) suggested that as life has become increasingly secularized, religion has dissipated as a major factor in the mental conflict of the adolescent. This introductory paragraph on the subject begins to show the degree to which one's approach to the questions can influence one's conclusions.

Unfortunately most studies of high school students on this task are limited to questions about church attendance, which is a better indicator of attitudes toward formal religious organizations, and the social life of a community, than to belief in God. Before looking at attitudes toward formal religions we will look at the issue of the individual adolescent and his belief in God, and will have to rely primarily on studies of college students.

In keeping with the position taken earlier, we would expect that college students would be more advanced in cognitive development than noncollege students, probably more questioning, and therefore probably take a less traditional, less accepting view of God and organized religion. The college studies that will be referred to were carried out at Clark, Harvard, Radcliffe, Williams, and Texas universities, all highly selective colleges. The findings, therefore, should be as fully in keeping with the position taken above as from any less-selective college sample. However, the changes over time are probably in the same direction for all groups, only more dramatic and earlier for these samples.

Vernon Jones (1970) studied freshmen and seniors at Clark University from 1930–1933 to 1967–1968 using the Thurstone Chase Attitude Scales. Results are also available for Harvard and Radcliffe students for 1967.

Results of the attitude toward the deity scale show a significant decline in the attitudes of Clark freshmen toward God over these years.

The extent of this change can be gauged by comparing items evaluated as being close to the mean. ·In the 1930–33 group the mean item would be "I have a strong desire to believe in God." For the 1967 freshmen, the average item would be between "I don't know whether I ought to believe in God or not" and "I think I believe in God but really I haven't thought about it."

Interestingly, the item "I trust in God to support the right and condemn the wrong," which dropped among freshman men from 53 percent in the 1930's to 41 percent acceptance in 1967, rose to 60 percent acceptance in the late 1940's and 1950's. The item which rose the most in acceptance over those years, "God has no place in my thinking," went from 5 percent in the 1930's to 3 percent in the 1940's, 1 percent in the 1950's, to 16 percent for freshman men in the 1960's. The line of change in attitude toward God has by no means been straight over these years, but a general decline in attitude toward a belief in God is evident from the early 1930's to the late 1960's.

By looking at these groups' responses as falling into one of four categories (1—belief in a deity, 2—atheistic, 3—a middle group who neither believed nor disbelieved or would admit only to the existence of some powerful force, and 4—a group who stated that none of the alternatives sufficiently resembled their views to justify a choice between them), Jones found a decrease in belief and an increase in disbelief for men and women at Harvard and Radcliffe, as did Hastings and Hoge (1970) at Williams. The group of "none of the alternatives" grew from about 11 percent in 1948 to 19 percent at Harvard and Radcliffe and 28 percent at Williams by 1967.

Although Jones suggested that the increase in the number who chose none of the alternatives was in line with the increase of possibilities due to expansion of wealth and education to the middle classes, Hastings and Hoge asked respondents why they had chosen this response and found that in most cases they lacked a thought-out view and did not want to commit themselves to any alternative. Hastings and Hoge found no support for background and economic explanations for these changes. However, they do link these changes to the protest and political movements which began in the early 1960's, implying that political alternatives may have substituted for religious belief. Jones offers the correlate to this hypothesis in that decline in religion was steeper than the decline in theological belief. He interprets this as a discontent with the established churches' responses to the social causes of the 1960's.

A scale of religious attitudes given to University of Texas undergraduates from 1955 to 1964 by Young, Dustin, and Holtzman (1966) showed significant change in religious attitudes, toward a less favorable attitude toward organized religion, from

1958 to 1964. They report that on one item, "There is no God," there was a significant change, with 78 percent saying they strongly disagreed in 1958, while 65 percent said they disagreed strongly in 1964.

A review of the literature on high-school students shows that a healthy majority believe in God. This estimate is not supported by good replicative studies (so that change over the years may be established), but it is a constant finding. Certainly there are differences by religious affiliation but by and large high-school students believe. How can we understand this? We have shown that with increasing age students' belief diminishes. Hites (1965), investigating college students, showed for almost every student some change away from literal interpretation of religion and acceptance of its functions, in the direction of more liberalism. Havens (1964), in a study of a small college, found that at any one time about 12 percent of the students had religious conflicts and over the course of their college career about half of them had religious conflict.

Let us not forget a problem that exists in social science today. The bulk of studies of young people are on young people in school. The expectations we have for conflict and change in the existential task area, in attitudes toward God and religion, differ somewhat by status and intellectual ability. We expect, and the studies presented seem to show, that as people grow through their teens they become increasingly questioning and critical of religion and the literal acceptance of a God. Although seniors in high school are somewhat more questioning and negative than freshmen in high school, and this trend continues even more markedly in college, there is not sufficient data to allow conclusions about noncollege youth. Do their attitudes change as markedly as those of college students? We would doubt so. Both their intellectual differences from the college group and their environmental differences, i.e., the effect of college, would point to a less marked shift toward liberalism in religious attitudes.

The more positive attitudes of high-school students toward religion, then, should not be thought of as merely a developmental "phase." Rather, differences will be occurring in cognitive development within a comprehensive student body, which will eventuate, because of their future life experiences, in vastly different attitudes toward God and religion overall between the more cognitively able and the less cognitively able.

These points come out of a review of the literature on belief. Are they substantiated by the literature on participation in religious activities and church going? The various college studies reported above all report similar findings—a general decline in attitude toward organized religion by college students. The curve of decline reported by Jones (1970) is even steeper for attitude toward organized religion than for belief in the deity. Hurlock (1967) summed up the church-attendance data, noting the decrease in attendance through adolescence, with boys attending less regularly and stopping earlier than girls. The high point in liking church occurs in the eleventh grade after which attendance is more irregular for more adolescents.

Although this evidence of decline in church attendance is well documented it would be incorrect to give the impression that high-school students do not go to church in great numbers, or at least great percentages. A 1965 Purdue Opinion Panel survey of over 4,000 high-school students showed that 68 percent attended church at least once a week and an additional 10 percent went once or twice a month. This certainly does not look like an irreligious group. In fact, I doubt whether any older age group could make that statement.

Nonetheless we are faced with the fact that studies covering the postwar period, and across socioeconomic groups, persistently show a decline in high school students' interest in the church as measured by church attendance. There are differences for various religious groups with the stricter and more prestigious churches sustaining higher church attendance. But the overall trend is clear. This may be construed to show that the college students involved in these studies are just extensions of the same phenomenon. Comparing the two groups—high school and college—overall, the data seems to show a much more negative attitude on the part of college students. A Gallup poll (*New York Times*, June 1, 1969) found that, in 1965, 62 percent of American college students thought that religion was losing its influence on American life, whereas in 1969, 78 percent thought so.

From a developmental point of view, we have to consider whether this decline with age and over time is a developmental phenomenon or whether it represents a cultural phenomenon. It seems to represent both. It represents a long-term growing secularity in the society and it represents a conflict produced by greater cognitive development and intellectual experience in the population at large. Higher education and religious belief and participation are not incompatible by any means. Nonetheless higher education and higher cognitive development are related to each other and related to doubting in many areas of life including religion. Science and belief are not incompatible in and of themselves but greater involvement and education in science has been shown to affect degree of religiosity. Hastings and Hoge (1970) reported that almost 50 percent of the students at Williams in 1967 felt that there is considerable conflict between science and religion. It seems logical that religion might take some setbacks in the attitudes of high-school students in the post-Sputnik world.

Influences on Religious Belief and Participation

From the point of view of the hierarchical structure of social influence, the last paragraph dealt with the most personal aspect, individual attributes, and the least personal system, social conditions. In the following quotation, Bealer and Willets (1967) describe the average high-school student in relation to his religious interests and place this in the context of adult and parental values:

We have suggested that typically the adolescent embraces both a traditional belief system and a not immodest degree of participation in the ritualistic aspects of religion. His level of knowledge has not been systematically assessed but probably is low. In terms of the experiential dimension, his concern and interest in religion, while not clearly measured, appear to be quite high. The development of concern into deep, orthodox faith is not, however, apparently typical. The American adolescent seems reluctant to deny the idea of a supernatural, but, at the same time, is unwilling or unable to yield himself with firm conviction to the hands of the Divine. Perhaps the best label we can apply to the teenager's religious orientation is "hedging."

The characterization of the average American teenager may be equally applicable to the average American adult. Adults, too, may exhibit the same "hedging stance" as the youth. . . . We do know . . . that . . . the adolescent tends strongly to accept rather than reject parental values. What is true in other areas is probably equally true for religion. Thus, for example, in the Purdue studies, 78 percent of the youth felt their beliefs agreed with the orientation of both parents. This supposition of generational agreement has been confirmed in other studies. Thus, whether one takes the religious orientations of American adolescents to be "good" or "bad," it is vital to recognize that the dispositions do not exist in a vacuum, but in a socially supporting milieu (pp. 441–442).[3]

The theme of ambivalence toward God and church may be part of the wondering and "hedging" attitude of many adolescents, just as ambivalence in thought and deed toward parents is usual. Poor Josh, the 15-year-old hero of *There Must Be a Pony,* really feels it. He says:

. . . the most demented thing happens to me sometimes when I go to church. I'll go there feeling almost like a saint, ready to confess my sins, take Communion, and all set to ask God to please help me straighten out my life and show me what to do. Then when I actually get in church and kneel down to pray, every dirty word I've ever heard comes sailing through my mind. Isn't that the most warped thing you ever heard of? It doesn't always happen, of course, but sometimes it does (Kirkwood, 1960, p. 43).

The adolescent is influenced in this life task, as in the others, by factors at all levels, from the individual, personal, to the most global, social. As social classes differ in activity in religious areas, and as subcultural groups do, so the adolescents of these groups follow and differ. The adolescents' developmental pressures cause

3. R. C. Bealer and F. K. Willets, "The Religious Interests of American High School Youth," *Religious Education,* 1967, 62. Quoted from the September-October 1967 issue of *Religious Education* by. permission of the publisher, The Religious Education Association, 409 Prospect St., New Haven, Conn. 06510. Membership and subscription available for $15/year.

conflicts with their groups. That is, for social and personal reasons adolescents have to figure out how they stand in relation to their group norms in the existential task area as well as the other life-task areas. However, in the existential task naturally the religious background of the teenager shows inordinate influence. The following discussion of the phenomenon of religious conversion developed by Ernsberger (1974) illustrates this influence.

Religious Background Influences: Conversion Example

The bulk of the research on religious conversion is over 50 years old and may be summarized to show conversion as occurring primarily in middle to late adolescence. Clark (1929) differentiated between "definite crisis" conversion, which is more typical of conversion in later adolescence and "gradual growth" conversion, which is the culmination of a gradual process, and is more likely less intense, and likelier to occur earlier in adolescence. But overall there is no agreement in the literature on the progress or timing of conversion. However, there appears to be a consensus that in religious conversion an identifiable moment, a moment of decision, occurs. Ernsberger (1974) defines fully this moment of conversion as

> . . . the ability to recall the occasion when one became more vitally committed to previously held religious beliefs or the ability to attribute one's religious commitment to a distinct point in one's life at which one made a definite decision in favor of some religion (p. 2).

Goldman (1964) sees, from the framework of his research and theorizing, adolescence as a time for decision regarding religion. A time, not necessarily for an increase or decrease in religious activity, but as a pivotal time at which one decides to move toward or away from religious commitments. This may be seen as the "hedging" that Bealer and Willets spoke of, and the end result of this hedging or uncertainty may logically be conversion. Goldman characterized adolescents as ready for conversion.

The various religions, organized as churches or sects, differ both in their views and approaches to conversion. More usually, sects demand a conversion experience for full adult membership. Churches are less likely to ask for, expect, and maybe appreciate a conversion-type experience. In these cases adolescents are received into membership after an educational experience, and their membership is seen as a result of a cognitive, not necessarily affective, experience relating to the church.

Three large-scale surveys have been carried out fairly recently which will be compared to throw light on the influence of sect or church on religious experiences and activity in adolescence. Influences may mean that people act in a certain way or say certain things so that others will accept them. But influence may also mean, in its most potent sense, that people act and speak in these ways because they do believe, feel right, seem true to themselves, while acting in the way that the influencing individual or group directly or indirectly signifies. Clark (1958) said, "People will report conversion if it is the requirement of group membership." It may be that the influence is more significant, i.e., people will feel and notice the conversion moment, if it is required.

The three surveys include one by the strongly conversion-oriented, fundamentalist-evangelical National Sunday School Association, a confederation of sect-type churches (Zuck and Getz, 1968), another done by the three largest Lutheran denominations working jointly (Strommen, 1972), and the third by the United Presbyterian Church (Klever, Woods, and Chapman, 1971). Although these studies were not intended to be directly comparable, they present the opportunity for comparison because they were carried out at around the same time. Fairly good sampling techniques were used to obtain representative samples from within each of their denominational groups, and they have sufficient similarity in research questions, and detailed data presented for the 15 to 18-year-old group to allow comparisons.

The National Sunday School Association (Zuck and Getz, 1968) survey youth had almost all experienced conversion prior to age 17. Of their sample, 91.7 percent had converted and could specify the age at which they had converted. Interestingly, about 62 percent had converted before they were 12 years old, 21.2 percent converted between 12 and 14, and 8.1 percent between 15 and 17. These figures reflect the intensity of the influence of the parents' religious experience on the age of conversion. For those subjects whose two parents had converted, 76 percent of the adolescents converted before the age of 12 and 24 percent after the age of 12. If only the father or only the mother had converted, about 56 percent of the youth converted before the age of 12 and 44 percent after the age of 12. In families where neither the mother nor father had converted, 34 percent of the adolescents who eventually converted did so before they were 12, whereas 66 percent converted after the age of 12. The data indicates that in these sects, where there is strong pressure to have a conversion experience from the total religious community as well as, presumably, the parents, the age of conversion is strongly related to the religious experience of the parents.

How does this group compare to the others in terms of the longer-term adherence to the tenets of their religion? That is to say, do adolescents in each of these three religious groups become less interested in and active in their organized church, or do they follow the ethical-behavioral rules established by the church?

The Lutheran adolescents gave evidence of "backsliding," showed a tendency to move away from the peak of religious commitment, at the end of their formal religious education, which occurs around the beginning of 9th grade. Strommen (1972) showed that a factor on the questionnaire called "The Heart of Lutheran Piety" began to decline in importance at age 15 to a low at age 21 to 22. The

Presbyterian study (Klever, Woods, and Chapman, 1971) found no decline in religious commitment with age or year in high school, and conversely no rise in religious commitment during this time, either.

Contrary to this evidence on youth who had gone through the ordinary church confirmation process, the National Sunday School Association youth who had gone through a conversion showed steady growth through the high school years in commitment to the conservative, evangelical doctrines of their sect. In response to the question, "To what extent have you questioned the following (16) doctrines in the last six months?" about 25 percent of the 9th graders said they had questioned much and 52.7 percent said they did not question, whereas only 11.5 percent of the 12th graders said they had questioned much and 68.4 percent of the 12th graders said they had not questioned these doctrines.

It would appear that the sects which demand an unquestioning faith get a less questioning faithful. Many studies of Jewish youth show more questioning, more doubting, less attendance at religious services, a greater effect of higher education and experience with science on their faith, than is the case with youth of other, more demanding, or more authoritarian religions. For the three groups studied in these surveys the decline in religious commitment generally found for adolescents does not show itself to any degree in one group, and is the opposite of expected in another. So influence of religious background and affiliation is great in adolescence as the adolescent relates to religion, and may be a more important factor than others on this task. However, the personality, the personal factor, accounts for much of the individual's questioning in the unquestioning group, and the blind adherence of some in the less authoritarian group.

If, as we have seen, the NSSA youth adhere to the tenets of the faith within the church more than the other youth, do they also do so when away from the church, when the moral authority of the church should apply to social behaviors? Premarital sexual intercourse is as negatively sanctioned by the Luthern church as it is in the evangelical tradition, yet 48 percent of the Luthern youth showed permissive attitudes on this issue, whereas only 10 percent of the evangelical youth did. Neither Presbyterian nor NSSA churches condone smoking or drinking. Of the Presbyterian youth, 41 percent admitted having smoked; and 22 percent of the NSSA youth admitted to it. Fifty-five percent of the Presbyterian youth had drunk wine, whereas 22 percent of the NSSA youth had consumed alcoholic beverages. Although these are by no means perfect measures of adherence to the tenets of the religion and are compounded by many social and familial factors, it would appear that those adolescents from these samples who say they believe more also act as if they do.

It is intriguing to consider the influence of and reason for the seeming upsurge in recent years of extreme religious youth movements. Some of these movements have been organized within the existing bureaucracies of the churches as active efforts to "hold" and "gather in" youth. These movements may be extensions of historical efforts with youth, but are also reactions to the perceived decrease in religious interest and activity in America today.

Some of these movements, such as the "Jesus Freaks," are not affiliated in many instances with the organized church. The central theme in these movements is "total commitment" and "community." It appears that adolescents who "belong" to these groups feel satisfied (for some period of time) for two reasons—one concrete and one abstract—one extreme conventional and one extreme ideal or Utopian.

On one hand, groups such as the "Children of God" and the "Hare Krishnas" are simple and basic in lifestyle and definite, clear, and concrete in proscribing right and wrong, moral values. On the other hand these groups are seen as Utopian—an extreme, complete ideal—an "answer," the "answer." For the adolescent at the concrete-operational stage, confronting the confused adolescent and adult worlds, these groups have appeal. For the precocious formal-operational adolescent these groups provide a "possibility" in which they can participate. For the adolescent developing and in transition from "pure" concrete to "pure" formal thought—and as we have seen few adolescents are "purely" one or the other—there is potential for satisfaction in both extremes. One can feel that he or she is "part of the solution" while still having absolute guidelines.

We remain with these "extreme" alternatives in the religious life-task area, and "extreme" alternatives in other life-task areas—political-community, sex-love, intellectual-nonintellectual, etc. Extreme lifestyles and goals have and will always be attractive to individuals for personal, personality, reasons. The influence hierarchy will be differentially effective at each level for cultural and societal reasons at different historical times. And in the existential-religious life task, as in the other life-task areas, the extreme, new, and/or different, as well as the conventional and traditional, will appear and attract some adolescents some of the time.

Adolescence is the time during which overt expressions of disbelief in God are more frequent than at any subsequent age. Paradoxically, adolescence is also seen as "the most religious period of all. The fact is that these extremes may be encountered at different times in the same youngsters" (Linn and Schwartz, 1958, p. 49).

It is probably fitting to conclude this book with the above quote, which reminds us that even if we have begun to understand the extremes and paradoxes of adolescence, through adult eyes it still *remains* a paradox. But on a more hopeful note, I will close the chapter on the existential life task with Albert Einstein's view of religion:

My religion consists of a humble admiration of the illimitable superior spirit who reveals himself in the slight details we are able to perceive with our frail and feeble minds. That deeply emotional conviction of the presence of a superior power, which is revealed in the incomprehensible universe, forms my idea of God (*New York Times* Obituary, April 19, 1955).

References

Achenbach, T., and Zigler, E. Social competence and self-image disparity in psychiatric and nonpsychiatric patients. *Journal of Abnormal and Social Psychology*, 1963, 67, 197–205.

Adams, J. F. Adolescents' identification of personal and national problems. *Adolescence*, 1966, 1, 240–250.

Adler, A. *What life should mean to you.* London: Allen and Unwin, 1932.

Adult functional competency: A summary. University of Texas at Austin, Division of Extension, Adult Performance Level Project, March 1975.

Allen, G., and Martin, C. G. *Intimacy.* Chicago: Cowles Book Co., 1971.

Allport, G. W. *Personality: A psychological interpretation.* New York: Holt, 1937.

Allport, G. W. *The individual and his religion.* New York: Macmillan, 1950.

Allport, G. W. *Becoming.* New Haven: Yale University Press, 1955.

Allport, G. W. *Pattern and growth in personality.* New York: Holt, 1961.

Allport, G. W. Crises in normal personality development. *Teachers College Record*, 1964, 66, 235–241.

Almquist, E. M., and Angrist, S. S. Career salience and atypicality of occupational choice among college women. *Journal of Marriage and the Family*, 1970, 32(2), 242–248.

Ambron, S. R. *Child development.* San Francisco: Rinehart Press, 1975.

Anderson, J. *The psychology of development and personal adjustment.* New York: Holt, 1949.

Anderson, J. E. Prediction of adjustment over time. In I. Iscoe and H. A. Stevenson (eds.) *Personality development in children.* Austin: University of Texas Press, 1960.

Ansbacher, H. L., and Ansbacher, R. R. (eds.) *The individual psychology of Alfred Adler: A systematic presentation in selections from his writings.* New York: Basic Books, © 1956.

Ansbacher, H. L., and Ansbacher, R. R. *Superiority and social interest: Alfred Adler.* Evanston, Ill.: Northwestern University Press, 1964.

Arbus, D. *Diane Arbus.* Millerstown, N.Y.: Aperture Books, 1972.

Arlin, P. K. Cognitive development in adulthood: A fifth stage? *Developmental Psychology*, 1975, 11(5), 602–606.

Armour, R. *A diabolical dictionary of education*. New York: McGraw-Hill, 1969.

Arnold, R. A. The achievement of boys and girls taught by men and women teachers. *Elementary School Journal*, 1968, *68*, 367–371.

Auden, W. H. *Epistle to a godson and other poems*. New York: Random House, 1972.

Ausubel, D. P. *Theory and problems of adolescent development*. New York: Grune and Stratton, 1954.

Ausubel, D. P. *Educational psychology: A cognitive view*. New York: Holt, 1968.

Ausubel, D., and Ausubel, P. Cognitive development in adolescence. *Review of Educational Research*, 1966, *36*(4), 403–413. Copyright 1966, American Educational Research Association, Washington, D.C.

Baltes, P. B., and Nesselroade, J. R. Cultural change and adolescent personality development: An application of longitudinal sequences. *Developmental Psychology*, 1972, *7*(3), 244–256.

Bamber, J. H. Adolescent marginality—A further study. *Genetic Psychology Monographs*, 1973, *33*, 3–21.

Bandura, A., and Walters, R. H. *Social learning and personality development*. New York: Holt, 1963.

Bardwick, J. M. *Psychology of women*. New York: Harper and Row, 1971.

Barker, R. G. Ecology and motivation. *Nebraska Symposium on Motivation*, 1960, *8*, 1–50.

Barker, R. G. *The definition of ecology and psychology: Concepts and method for an ecobehavioral science*. Stanford, Cal.: Stanford University Press, 1968.

Barker, R. G., and Gump, P. V. (eds.) *Big school, small school: High school size and student behavior*. Stanford, Cal.: Stanford University Press, 1964.

Barker, R. G., and Wright, H. F. *Midwest and its children: The psychological ecology of an American town*. New York: Row, Peterson, 1954.

Baron, R. A., Byrne, D., and Griffit, W. *Social psychology: Understanding human interaction*. Boston: Allyn and Bacon, 1974.

Baruch, G. K. Maternal influence upon college women's attitude toward women and work. *Developmental Psychology*, 1972, *6*, 32–37.

Baum, M., et al. Unified effort of a junior high school faculty to "encourage success" for seventh graders. *Reporting Research*. Oregon Board of Education, October 1968.

Bealer, R. C., and Willets, F. K. The religious interests of American high school youth. *Religious Education*, September–October 1967, *62*, 435–444.

Bell, A. P. Role modeling of fathers in adolescence and young adulthood. *Journal of Counseling Psychology*, 1969, *16*, 30–35.

Bell, H. M. *Youth tell their story*. Washington, D.C.: American Council on Education, 1938.

Bell, R. R., and Chaskes, J. B. Premarital sexual experience among coeds, 1958 and 1968. *Journal of Marriage and the Family*, 1970, *32*, 81–84.

Bem, D. J., and Allen, A. On predicting some of the people some of the time: The search for cross-situational consistencies in behavior. *Psychological Review*, 1974, *81*, 506–520.

Bem, S. L. Sex role adaptability: One consequence of psychological androgeny. *Journal of Personality and Social Psychology*, 1975, *31*(4), 634–643.

Bender, L. Childhood schizophrenia. *Psychiatric Quarterly*, 1953, *27*, 663–679.

Benedict, R. *Patterns of culture.* New York: New American Library, 1934.

Berger, B. M. On the youthfulness of youth culture. *Social Research*, 1963, *30*, 319–342.

Berry, W. T. C., and Cowin, P. J. Conditions associated with the growth of boys, 1950–1951. *British Medical Journal*, 1954, *1*, 847–851.

Bhatnagar, K. P. Academic achievement as a function of one's self-concepts and ego functions. *Education and Psychology Review*, 1966, *6*(4), 178–182.

Bidwell, C. E., and Kasarda, J. D. School district organization and student achievement. *American Sociological Review*, 1975, *40*, 55–70.

Bieliauskas, V. J. A new look at "masculine protest." *Journal of Individual Psychology*, 1974, *30*, 92–97.

Blau, P. M., et al. Occupational choice: A conceptual framework. *Industrial Labor Relations Review*, 1956, *9*, 531–543.

Bledsoe, J. Self-concept of children and their intelligence, achievement, interests, and anxiety. *Childhood Education*, 1967, *43*, 436–438.

Bloch, H. A., and Niederhoffer, A. *The gang: A study in adolescent behavior.* New York: Philosophical Library, 1958.

Blocher, D. H., and Schutz, R. A. Relationships among self-description, occupational stereotypes, and vocational preferences. *Journal of Counseling Psychology*, 1961, *8*, 314–317.

Block, J. H. Conceptions of sex role: Cross-cultural and longitudinal perspectives. *American Psychologist*, 1973, *28*, 512–526.

Block, J. H., Haan, N., and Smith, M. B. Activism and apathy in contemporary adolescents. In J. F. Adams (ed.) *Understanding adolescence.* Boston: Allyn and Bacon, 1973.

Blos, P. *On adolescence: A psychoanalytic interpretation.* New York: Free Press, 1962.

Borow, H. Career development in adolescence. In J. F. Adams (ed.) *Understanding adolescence.* Boston: Allyn and Bacon, 1973.

Boyer, W. H. A survey of youth attitudes, opinion, and objectives of high school students in the Milwaukee area. *Journal of Educational Sociology*, 1959, *32*(5), 344–348.

Bradway, K. P., and Thompson, C. W. Intelligence at adulthood: A twenty-five year follow-up. *Journal of Educational Psychology*, 1962, *53*, 1–14.

Bralver, E., and Jacobs, L., Jr. *Teen-agers inside out.* New York: Washington Square Press, 1974.

Brim, O. G. *Sociology and the field of education.* New York: Russell Sage Foundation, 1958.

Brittain, C. V. Adolescent choices and parent-peer cross-pressures. *American Sociological Review*, 1967, *28*(3), 385–391.

Brittain, C. V. A comparison of rural and urban adolescents with respect to peer vs. parent compliance. *Adolescence*, 1969, *4*(13), 57–68.

Broderick, C. Social heterosexual development among urban Negroes and whites. *Journal of Marriage and the Family*, 1965, *27*, 200–203.

Brookover, W. B., Erikson, E. L., and Joiner, L. M. Self concept of ability and school achievement. III: Relationship of self-concept to achievement in high school. U.S. Office of Education, Cooperative Research Project No. 2831. East Lansing: Office of Research and Publications, Michigan State University, 1967.

Brown, D. G. Sex role development in a changing culture. *Psychological Bulletin*, 1958, *55*, 232–242.

Buxton, C. E. *Adolescents in school*. New Haven: Yale University Press, 1973.

Byrne, D., and Griffith, W. A developmental investigation of the law of attraction. *Journal of Personality and Social Psychology*, 1966, *4*, 699–703.

Cameron, P. The generation gap: Beliefs about sexuality and self-reported sexuality. *Developmental Psychology*, 1970, *3*, 272. (a)

Cameron, P. The generation gap: Which generation is believed powerful versus generational members' self-appraisals of power. *Developmental Psychology*, 1970, *3*, 403–404. (b)

Campbell, P. B. Self-concept and academic achievement in middle grade public school dissertation. Unpublished doctoral dissertation, Wayne State University, 1965.

Cannon, K. L., and Long, R. Premarital sexual behavior in the sixties. *Journal of Marriage and the Family*, February 1971, 36–49.

Carlin, L. O. Vocational decisions and high school experiences. *Vocational Guidance Quarterly*, 1960, *8*, 168–170.

Carter, T. P. The negative self-concepts of Mexican-American students. *School and Society*, 1968, *96*, 217–219.

Cartwright, D. Lewinian theory as a contemporary systematic framework. In S. Koch (ed.) *Psychology: A study of a science* (Vol. 2). New York: McGraw-Hill, 1959.

Case, D., and Collinson, J. M. The development of formal thinking in verbal comprehension. *British Journal of Educational Psychology*, 1962, *32*, 103–111.

Chabassol, D. J., and Thomas, D. C. Sex and age differences in problems and interests of adolescents. *Journal of Experimental Education*, 1969, *38*, 16–23.

Charters, W. W., Jr. The social background of teaching. In N. L. Gage (ed.) *Handbook of research on teaching*. Chicago: Rand McNally, 1963.

Cherry, N. Components of occupational interest. *British Journal of Educational Psychology*, 1974, *44*, 22–30.

Christensen, H. T., and Gregg, C. F. Changing sex norms in America and Scandinavia. *Journal of Marriage and the Family*, 1970, *32*, 616–627.

Clark, E. T. *The psychology of religion awakening.* New York: Macmillan, 1929.

Clark, K. *Another part of the wood: A self-portrait.* New York: Harper and Row, 1974.

Clark, W. H. *The psychology of religion.* New York: Macmillan, 1958.

Coelho, G. V., Silber, E., and Hamburg, D. A. Use of the student TAT to assess coping behavior in hospitalized, normal and exceptionally competent college freshmen. *Perceptual and Motor Skills,* 1961, *14,* 355–366.

Cofer, C. N., and Appley, M. H. *Motivation: Theory and research.* New York: Wiley, 1964.

Coleman, J. S. *The adolescent society.* New York: Free Press, 1961.

Coleman, J. S. How do the young become adults? *Review of Educational Research,* 1972, *42*(4), 431–440.

Coleman, J. S., et al. *Equality of educational opportunity.* U.S. Department of Health, Education and Welfare, 1966.

Collins, J. K., and Thomas, N. T. Age and susceptibility to same sex peer pressure. *British Journal of Educational Psychology,* 1972, *42,* 83–85.

Committee on Adolescence, Group for the Advancement of Psychiatry. *Normal adolescence: Its dynamics and impact.* New York: Scribner's, 1968.

Conant, J. B. *The comprehensive high school:* A second report to interested citizens. New York: McGraw-Hill, 1967.

Conger, J. J. *Adolescence and youth: Psychological development in a changing world.* New York: Harper and Row, 1973.

Cooley, C. H. *Human nature and the social order.* New York: Scribner's, 1902.

Costanzo, P. R., and Shaw, M. E. Conformity as a function of age level. *Child Development,* 1966, *37,* 967–975.

Crane, A. R. The development of moral values in children. *British Journal of Educational Psychology,* 1958, *28,* 201–208.

Crites, J. O. Parental identification in relation to vocational interest development. *Journal of Educational Psychology,* 1962, *53,* 262–270.

Crites, J. O. *Vocational psychology.* New York: McGraw-Hill, 1969.

Curry, R. L. The effect of socioeconomic status on the scholastic achievement of sixth-grade children. *British Journal of Educational Psychology,* 1962, *32,* 46–49.

Daines, J. W. An enquiry into the methods and effects of religious education in sixth forms. University of Nottingham Institute of Education, 1962.

Damon, A., Damon, S. T., Reed, R. B., and Valadian, I. Age at menarche of mothers and daughters, with a note on accuracy of recall. *Human Biology,* 1969, *41,* 161–175.

Davis, K. E. Sex on the campus: Is there a revolution? *Medical Aspects of Human Sexuality,* Winter 1970.

DeBord, L. W. Adolescent religious participation: An example of substructure and church attendance. *Adolescence,* 1969, *4*(16), 557–570.

Derbyshire, R. L., and Brody, E. B. Marginality, identity, and behavior in the American

Negro: A functional analysis. *International Journal of Social Psychiatry*, 1964, *10*, 7–13.

Dobson, I. *Dare to discipline.* Wheaton, Ill.: Tyndale House, 1970.

Douglas, J. W. B. *The home and the school.* London: MacGibbon and Kee, 1964.

Douvan, E. Sex differences in adolescent character processes. *Merrill-Palmer Quarterly*, 1960, *6*, 203–211.

Douvan, E., and Adelson, J. *The adolescent experience.* New York: Wiley, 1966.

Douvan, E., and Gold, M. Modal patterns in American adolescence. In L. W. Hoffman and M. L. Hoffman (eds.) *Review of child development research* (Vol. 2). New York: Russell Sage Foundation, 1966.

Dreikurs, R. *Fundamentals of Adlerian psychology.* Chicago: Alfred Adler Institute, 1953.

Dreikurs, R. The scientific revolution. *Humanist*, Jan/Feb 1966, 1–6.

Dreikurs, R., and Mosak, H. H. The tasks of life I. Adler's three tasks. *The Individual Psychologist*, 1966, *4*(1), 18–22.

Dreikurs, R., and Mosak, H. H. The tasks of life II. The fourth life task. *The Individual Psychologist*, 1967, *4*(2), 51–55.

Dreyer, P. H. Sex, sex roles, and marriage among youth in the 1970s. In R. J. Havighurst and P. H. Dreyer (eds.) *Youth: The 74th yearbook of the National Society for the Study of Education.* Chicago: University of Chicago Press, 1975.

Dudek, S., Lester, E., Goldberg, J., and Dyer, G. Relationship of Piaget measures to standard intelligence and motor scales. *Perceptual and Motor Skills*, 1969, *28*, 351–362.

Dunphy, D. C. The social structure of urban adolescent peer groups. *Sociometry*, 1963, *26*(2), 230–246.

Edmiston, S. Review of *Psychology and sex differences. New York Times Book Review*, April 13, 1975, p. 3.

Ehrman, W. *Premarital dating behavior.* New York: Henry Holt & Co., 1962.

Ehrmann, W. Marital and nonmarital sexual behavior. In H. T. Christensen (ed.) *Handbook of marriage and the family.* Chicago: Rand McNally, 1964.

Eisenberg, L. The autistic child in adolescence. *American Journal of Psychiatry*, 1956, *112*, 607–612.

Eisenberg, L. A developmental approach to adolescence. In D. Rogers (ed.) *Issues in adolescent psychology.* New York: Appleton-Century-Crofts, 1969.

Eitzen, D. S. Athletics in the status system of male adolescents: A replication of Coleman's *The adolescent society. Adolescence*, 1975, *38*(10), 265–276.

Elkind, D. Quantity concepts in junior and senior high school students. In R. Grinder (ed.) *Studies in adolescence.* New York: Macmillan, 1963.

Elkind, D. Adolescent cognitive development. In J. F. Adams (ed.) *Understanding adolescents.* Boston: Allyn and Bacon, 1968.

Elkind, D. Egocentrism in adolescence. In R. E. Grinder (ed.) *Studies in adolescence.* New York: Macmillan, 1969.

Elkind, D. *A sympathetic understanding of the child six to sixteen.* Boston: Allyn and Bacon, 1971.

Elkind, D., and Elkind, S. Varieties of religious experience in young adolescents. *Journal of the Scientific Study of Religion,* 1962, 2, 102–112.

Elkin, F., and Westley, W. A. The myth of adolescent culture. *American Sociological Review,* December 1955.

Ellis, L. J., and Bentler, P. M. Traditional sex-determined role standards and sex stereotypes. *Journal of Personality and Social Psychology,* 1973, *25*(1), 28–34.

Employment of School-Age Youth, October 1973, Special Labor Force Report 170, U.S. Department of Labor, Bureau of Labor Statistics, 1974.

Englander, M. E. A psychological analysis of vocational choice: Teaching. *Journal of Counseling Psychology,* 1960, 7, 257–264.

Epstein, S. The self-concept revisited. *American Psychologist,* 1973, *28*, 404–416.

Erikson, E. H. Identity and the life cycle. *Psychological Issues,* 1959, *1*(1).

Erikson, E. H. *Childhood and society.* New York: Norton, 1963.

Erikson, E. H. *Identity, youth and crisis.* New York: Norton, 1968.

Ernsberger, D. J. Adolescent conversion and the existential task. Unpublished paper, University of Texas at Austin, 1974. (mimeo)

Ernsberger, D. J. Intrinsic-extrinsic religious identification and level of moral development. Dissertation proposal, Department of Educational Psychology, The University of Texas at Austin, July 1975.

Falk, J. M., Leifer, M., Manaster, G. J., Rosner, T. T., Schedler, P., and Turner, B. F. The secular trend. Working paper, 1965. (mimeo)

Faust, M. S. Developmental maturity as a determinant in prestige of adolescent girls. *Child Development,* 1960, *31*, 173–184.

Feldman, D., and Markwalder, W. Systematic scoring of ranked distractions for the assessment of Piagetian reasoning levels. *Educational and Psychological Measurement,* 1971, *31*, 346–362.

Fenichel, O. *The psychoanalytic theory of neurosis.* New York: Norton, 1945.

Fink, M. B. Self-concept as it relates to academic achievement. *California Journal of Educational Research,* 1962, *13*, 57–62.

Fleege, U. H. *Self-revelation of the adolescent boy.* Milwaukee: Bruce, 1945.

Fodor, E. M. Resistance to social influence among adolescents as a function of level of moral development. *Journal of Social Psychology,* 1971, *85*, 121–126.

Franzblau, A. N. *Religious belief and character among Jewish adolescents.* New York: Columbia University Press, 1934.

Frazier, A., and Lisonbee, L. K. Adolescent concerns with physique. *School Review,* 1950, *58*, 397–405.

Freud, A. Adolescence as a developmental disturbance. In G. Caplan and S. Lebovici (eds.) *Adolescence: Psychosocial perspectives.* New York: Basic Books, 1969.

Freud, S. *New introductory lectures on psychoanalysis.* Translated by W. J. H. Sprott. New York: Norton, 1933.

Freud, S. *A general introduction to psychoanalysis* (Joan Riviere, trans.). New York: Permabooks, 1953.

Freundlich, D., and Kohlberg, L. Moral judgment in youthful offenders. Howard University, 1971. (mimeo)

Frisk, M., et al. Psychological problems in adolescents showing advanced or delayed physical maturation. *Adolescence*, 1966, *1*(2), 126–140.

Gallagher, J. McC. Cognitive development and learning in the adolescent. In J. F. Adams (ed.) *Understanding adolescence.* Boston: Allyn and Bacon, 1973.

Gardner, R., and Moriarty, A. *Personality development at preadolescence.* Seattle: University of Washington Press, 1968.

Gawronski, D. A., and Mathis, C. Differences between over-achieving, normal-achieving, and under-achieving high school students. *Psychology in Schools*, 1965, 2, 152–155.

Gesell, A. L., Ilg, F. L., and Ames, L. B. *Youth: The years from ten to sixteen.* New York: Harper and Row, 1956.

Getzels, J. W., and Jackson, P. W. The teacher's personality and characteristics. In N. L. Gage (ed.) *Handbook of research on teaching.* Chicago: Rand McNally, 1963.

Gillespie, J. W., and Allport, G. *Youth's outlook on the future.* Garden City, N.Y.: Doubleday, 1955.

Ginsburg, H. *The myth of the deprived child: Poor children's intellect and education.* Englewood Cliffs, N.J.: Prentice-Hall, 1972.

Ginsburg, H., and Opper, S. *Piaget's theory of intellectual development.* Englewood Cliffs, N.J.: Prentice-Hall, 1969.

Ginzberg, E. Toward a theory of occupational choice: A restatement. *Vocational Guidance Quarterly*, 1972, *20*, 169–176.

Ginzberg, E., Ginsburg, S. W., Axelrad, S., and Herma, J. L. *Occupational choice: An approach to a general theory.* New York: Columbia University Press, 1951.

Glass, D. C. Theories of consistency and the study of personality. In E. F. Borgatta and W. W. Lambert (eds.) *Handbook of personality theory and research.* Chicago: Rand McNally, 1968.

Gleuck, J., and Gleuck, E. *Unraveling juvenile delinquency.* Cambridge: Harvard University Press, 1950.

Goethals, G. W., and Klos, D. S. *Experiencing youth: First-person accounts.* Boston: Little, Brown, 1970.

Goldburgh, S. J. *The experience of adolescence.* Cambridge, Mass.: Schenkman, 1965.

Goldman, R. *Religious thinking from childhood to adolescence.* London: Routledge and Kegan Paul, 1964.

Goodman, N. The adolescent's reference set. Paper presented at the annual meeting of the American Sociological Association, 1965.

Goodman, N. Adolescent norms and behavior: Organization and conformity. *Merrill-Palmer Quarterly*, 1969, *15*, 199–211.

Goodnow, J. A test of milieu effects with some of Piaget's tasks. *Psychological Monographs*, 1962, *72*(36, Whole No. 555).

Gottlieb, D., and Ramsey, C. *The American adolescent*. Homewood, Ill.: Dorsey Press, 1964.

Grannis, J. C. Going beyond labels: The significance of social class and ethnicity for education. *Equal Opportunity Review*, Teachers College, Columbia University, July 1975.

Gray, D. F., and Gair, E. L. The congruency of adolescent self-perceptions with those of parents and best friends. *Adolescence*, 1974, *9*, 299–303.

Gray, S. W. Masculinity-femininity in relation to anxiety and social acceptance. *Child Development*, 1957, *28*, 203–214.

Greenfield, P. Oral and written language: The consequences for cognitive development in Africa and the United States. Paper presented at the annual meeting of the American Educational Research Association, Chicago, February 1968.

Gump, P. V. *Big schools, small schools*. Moravia, N.Y.: Chronicle Guidance Publications, 1966.

Haan, N., Smith, M., and Block, J. Moral reasoning and young adults: Political-social behavior, family background, and personality correlates. *Journal of Personality and Social Psychology*, 1968, *10*(3), 183–201.

Hall, C. S., and Lindzey, G. Theories of personality. New York: Wiley, 1957.

Hall, G. S. *Adolescence*. 2 vols. New York: Appleton-Century-Crofts, 1916.

Haller, A. O., and Miller, I. W. The occupational aspiration scale: Theory, structure and correlates. East Lansing: Tech. Bulletin 288, Agricultural Experimentation Station, Michigan State University, 1963.

Hamachek, D. E. Toward more effective teaching. In D. E. Hamachek (ed.) *Human dynamics in psychology and education*. Boston: Allyn and Bacon, 1972.

Harmon, L. W. The childhood and adolescent career plans of college women. *Journal of Vocational Behavior*, 1971, *1*(1), 45–56.

Harms, E. The development of religious experience in children. *American Journal of Sociology*, 1944, *50*, 112–122.

Harrison, D. E., Bennett, W. H., and Globe, G. H. Sexual permissiveness: White and black high school students. *Journal of Marriage and the Family*, 1969, *31*, 783–787.

Harrison, F. I. Relationship between home background, school success, and adolescent attitudes. *Merrill-Palmer Quarterly*, 1968, *14*, 331–344.

Hastings, P. K., and Hoge, D. R. Religious change among college students over two decades. *Social Forces*, 1970, *49*, 16–28.

Havens, J. Studies in religious conflicts in college students. *Journal of Social Psychology*, 1964, *64*, 77–87.

Havighurst, R. J. *The public schools of Chicago*. Chicago: The Board of Education of the City of Chicago, 1964.

Havighurst, R. J. Unrealized potentials of adolescents. *National Association of Secondary School Principals Bulletin*, 1966, *50*, 75–96.

Havighurst, R. J. *Developmental tasks and education*. New York: McKay, 1972.

Havighurst, R. J., et al. *Growing up in River City*. New York: Wiley, 1962.

Havighurst, R. J., and Dreyer, P. H. *The national study of American Indian education*. Minneapolis: Center for Urban and Regional Affairs, University of Minnesota, 1971.

Havighurst, R. J., and Dreyer, P. H. Youth and cultural pluralism. In R. J. Havighurst and P. H. Dreyer (eds.) *Youth*. 74th Yearbook NSSE. Chicago: University of Chicago Press, 1975.

Havighurst, R. L., and Neugarten, B. L. *Society and education* (3rd ed.). Boston: Allyn and Bacon, 1967.

Hawley, P. What women think men think: Does it affect their career choice? *Journal of Counseling Psychology*, 1971, *18*(3), 193–199.

Hayakawa, S. I. *Language and thought in action*. New York: Harcourt, 1964.

Heath, R. W., and Nielson, M. A. The research basis for performance-based teacher education. *Review of Educational Research*, 1974, *44*(4), 463–484.

Heilbrun, A. B., Jr. Sex role identity in adolescent females: A theoretical paradox. *Adolescence*, 1968, *3*(9), 79–88.

Herrnstein, R. IQ. *Atlantic*, 1971, 43–64.

Higgens-Trenk, A., and Gaite, A. Elusiveness of formal operational thought in adolescents. *Proceedings of the 79th Annual Convention of the American Psychological Association*, 1971.

Hillard, F. H. The influence of religious education upon the development of children's moral ideas. *The British Journal of Educational Psychology*, 1959, *39*(1), 50–59.

Hites, R. W. Changes in religious attitudes during the four years of college. *Journal of Social Psychology*, 1965, *66*, 51–63.

Hoebel, E. A. *The Cheyennes: Indians of the Great Plains*. New York: Holt, 1960.

Holden, G. S. Scholastic aptitude and the relative persistence of vocational choice. *Personnel and Guidance Journal*, 1961, *40*, 36–41.

Holland, J. L. A personality inventory employing occupational titles. *Journal of Applied Psychology*, 1958, *42*, 336–342.

Holland, J. L. Major programs of research on vocation behavior. In H. Borow (ed.) *Man in a world at work*. Boston: Houghton Mifflin, 1964.

Holland, J. L. *The psychology of vocational choice*. Waltham, Mass.: Blaisdell, 1966.

Hollingshead, A. B. *Elmstown's youth*. New York: Wiley, 1949.

Holtzman, W. H., Diaz-Guerrero, R., Swartz, J. D., and Lara Tapia, L. Cross-cultural longitudinal research in child development. In J. P. Hill (ed.) *Minnesota symposia on child psychology* (Vol. 2). Minneapolis: University of Minnesota Press, 1968.

Homosexuality: A symposium of the causes and consequences—social and psychological—of sexual inversion. *Playboy*, April 1971, 61ff.

Howkins, K. G. *Religious thinking and religious education.* London: Tyndale Press, 1966.

Hunt, J. McV. *Intelligence and experience.* New York: The Ronald Press, 1961.

Hurlock, E. B. *Child development.* New York: McGraw-Hill, 1964.

Hurlock, E. B. *Adolescent development.* New York: McGraw-Hill, 1967.

Hurlock, E. B. *Developmental psychology.* New York: McGraw-Hill, 1975.

Husbands, C. T. Some social and psychological consequences of the American dating system. *Adolescence*, 1970, V, 20, 451–462.

Huttenlocher, J. Development of formal reasoning on concept formation problems. *Child Development*, 1964, *35*, 1233–1242.

Hyde, K. E. Religious concepts and religious attitudes. *Educational Review*, Feb/June 1963.

Illich, I. *Deschooling society.* New York: Harper and Row, 1971.

Individual Psychology News Letter, May/June, 1973, *22*(3), 55.

Inhelder, B., and Piaget, J. *The growth of logical thinking from childhood to adolescence.* New York: Basic Books, 1958.

Jackson, P. W., and Getzels, J. W. Psychological health and classroom functioning: A study of dissatisfaction with school among adolescents. *Journal of Educational Psychology*, 1959, *50*, 295–300.

Jackson, P. W., and Lahaderne, H. M. Scholastic success and attitude toward school in a population of sixth graders. *Journal of Educational Psychology*, 1967, *58*, 15–18.

Jackson, S. The growth of logical thinking in normal and subnormal children. *British Journal of Educational Psychology*, 1965, *35*, 255–258.

James, W. *Psychology: The briefer course.* New York: Holt, 1910.

Jennings, J. Children, sugar and premature sexuality. *Prevention*, October 1975, 178–184.

Jessor, S. L., and Jessor, R. Maternal ideology and adolescent problem behavior. *Developmental Psychology*, 1974, *10*, 246–254.

Jessor, S. L., and Jessor, R. Transition from virginity to nonvirginity among youth: A social-psychological study over time. *Developmental Psychology*, 1975, *11*(4), 473–484.

Johnson, E. G. The impact of high school teachers on the educational plans of college freshmen. Testing and Counseling Service Report No. 32. Orono: University of Maine, 1967. (mimeo)

Johnson, W. P. The religious attitude of secondary modern country school pupils. *The British Journal of Educational Psychology*, 1967, *37*(1), 132–133.

Johnston, L. D., and Bachman, J. G. The functions of educational institutions in adolescent development. In J. F. Adams (ed.) *Understanding adolescents.* Boston: Allyn and Bacon, 1973.

Jones, M. C. The later careers of boys who were early- or late-maturing. *Child Development,* 1957, *28,* 113–128.

Jones, M. C. A comparison of the attitudes and interests of ninth-grade students over two decades. *The Journal of Educational Psychology,* 1960, *51*(4), 175–186.

Jones, M. C. Psychological correlates of somatic development. *Child Development,* 1965, *36,* 899–911.

Jones, M. C., and Bayley, N. Physical maturing among boys as related to behavior. *Journal of Educational Psychology,* 1950, *41,* 129–148.

Jones, M. C., and Mussen, P. H. Self-conceptions, motivations and interpersonal attitudes of early- and late-maturing girls. *Child Development,* 1958, *29,* 491–501.

Jones, V. Attitudes of college students and their change. *Genetic Psychological Monographs,* 1970, *81,* 3–80.

Jurich, A. P., and Jurich, J. A. The effect of cognitive moral development upon the selection of premarital sexual standards. *Journal of Marriage and the Family,* November 1974, 736–741.

Kaats, G. R., and Davis, K. E. The dynamics of sexual behavior of college students. *Journal of Marriage and the Family,* 1970, *32,* 390–399.

Kagan, J., and Moss, H. *Birth to maturity.* New York: Wiley, 1962.

Kahl, J. A. *The American class structure.* New York: Holt, 1957.

Kanter, J. F., and Zelnik, M. Sexual experience of young unmarried women in the United States. *Family Planning Perspectives,* 1972, *4,* 9–18.

Katz, P., and Zigler, E. Self-image disparity: A developmental approach. *Journal of Personality and Social Psychology,* 1967, *5,* 186–195.

Keasey, C. B. Implicators of cognitive development for moral reasoning. In D. J. DePalma and J. M. Foley (eds.) *Moral development: Current theory and research.* Hillsdale, N.J.: Lawrence Erlbaum Associates, 1975, 39–56.

Keniston, K. Student activism, moral development, and morality. *American Journal of Orthopsychiatry,* 1970, *40,* 577–592.

Keniston, K. Prologue: Youth as a stage of life. In R. J. Havighurst and P. H. Dreyer (eds.) *Youth.* 74th Yearbook NSSE. Chicago: University of Chicago Press, 1975.

Kennedy, W. A. *Child psychology.* Englewood Cliffs, N.J.: Prentice-Hall, 1975.

Kerpelman, L. C. Student activism and ideology in higher education institutions. Final Report, Project No. 8A-028, Bureau of Research, Office of Education, March 1970.

Kiell, N. *The universal experience of adolescence.* New York: International Universities Press, 1964.

Kinsey, A. C., Pomeroy, W. B., and Martin, C. E. *Sexual behavior in the human male.* Philadelphia: W. B. Saunders, 1948.

Kinsey, A. C., Pomeroy, W. B., and Martin, C. E. *Sexual behavior in the human female.* Philadelphia: Saunders, 1953.

Kirkwood, J. *There must be a pony.* New York: Avon Books, 1960.

Klausmeier, H. J., and Goodwin, W. *Learning and human abilities.* New York: Harper and Row, 1966.

Kleiber, D. A., and Manaster, G. J. Youth's outlook on the future: A past-present comparison. *Journal of Youth and Adolescence*, 1972, *1*(3).

Kleinfeld, J. The relative importance of teachers and parents in the formation of Negro and white students' academic self-concept. *Journal of Educational Research*, 1972, *65*(5), 211–212.

Klever, G. L., Woods, R. T., and Chapman, W. T. *The world of church youth.* Philadelphia: Board of Christian Education, United Presbyterian Church U.S.A., 1971.

Knight, J. A. Adolescent development and religious values. *Pastoral Psychology*, 1969, *20*, 39–43.

Kohlberg, L. The development of modes of moral thinking and choice in the years ten to sixteen. Unpublished doctoral dissertation, University of Chicago, 1958.

Kohlberg, L. The development of children's orientations toward a moral order: Sequence in the development of moral thought. *Vita Humana*, 1963, *6*, 11–33. (a)

Kohlberg, L. Moral development and identification. In H. W. Stevenson (ed.) *Child psychology.* Chicago: National Society for the Study of Education, 1963. (b)

Kohlberg, L. Development of moral character and ideology. In M. L. Hoffman (ed.) *Review of child development research* (Vol. 1). New York: Russell Sage Foundation, 1964.

Kohlberg, L. A cognitive-developmental analysis of children's sex-role concepts and attitudes. In E. E. Maccoby (ed.) *The development of sex differences.* Stanford, Cal.: Stanford University Press, 1966.

Kohlberg, L. Moral and religious education and the public schools: A developmental view. In T. Sizer (ed.) *Religion and public education.* Boston: Houghton-Mifflin, 1967.

Kohlberg, L. Moral development. In *International Encyclopedia of the Social Sciences.* New York: Crowell, Collier, and Macmillan, 1968.

Kohlberg, L. Stage and sequence: The cognitive-developmental approach to socialization. In D. A. Goslin (ed.) *Handbook of socialization theory and practice.* Chicago: Rand McNally, 1969. © 1969 Rand McNally College Publishing Company, Chicago.

Kohlberg, L. Continuities and discontinuities in childhood and adult moral development revisited. In *Collected papers on moral development and moral education.* Mimeo, 1973.

Kohlberg, L., and Gilligan, C. The adolescent as a philosopher: The discovery of the self in a postconventional world. *Daedalus*, Fall 1971, 1051–1086.

Kohlberg, L., and Kramer, R. Continuities and discontinuities in childhood and adult moral development. *Human Development*, 1969, *12*, 93–120.

Kohlberg, L., and Turiel, E. *Recent research in moral development.* New York: 1971.

Konopka, G. Adolescent girls: A two year study. Center for Youth Development and Research Quarterly Focus. University of Minnesota, Fall 1975.

Kramer, R. Moral development in young adulthood. Unpublished doctoral dissertation, University of Chicago, 1968.

Krebs, R. L. Moral judgment and ego controls as determinants of resistance to cheating. Unpublished manuscript, 1971.

Krogman, W. M. A handbook of the measurement and interpretation of height and weight in the growing child. *Monograph for Social Research on Child Development,* 1943, *13*(3), (Whole No. 48).

Kuhlen, R. G. *The psychology of adolescent development.* New York: Harper and Row, 1952.

Kuhlen, R. G., and Arnold, M. Age differences in religious beliefs and problems during adolescence. *The Journal of Genetic Psychology,* 1944, *50,* 291–300.

Kuhn, D., Langer, J., Kohlberg, L., and Haan, N. The development of formal operations in logical and moral judgment. Unpublished manuscript, 1971.

Kupky, O. *The religious development of adolescents.* New York: Macmillan, 1928.

Lahaderne, H. M. Attitudinal and intellectual correlates of attention: A study of four sixth grade classrooms. *Journal of Educational Psychology,* 1968, *59,* 320–324.

Landis, P. H. *Adolescence and youth.* New York: McGraw-Hill, 1945.

Landsbaum, J. B., and Willis, R. H. Conformity in early and late adolescence. *Developmental Psychology,* 1971, *4*(3), 334–337.

Larson, L. E. An examination of the salience hierarchy during adolescence: The influence of the family. *Adolescence,* 1974, *9*(35), 317–332.

Lavin, D. E. *The prediction of academic performance.* New York: Russell Sage Foundation, 1965.

Learning less. *Time,* March 31, 1975.

Lecky, P. *Self-consistency: A theory of personality.* New York: Island Press, 1945.

Lecky, P. *Self-consistency.* New York: Island Press, 1951.

Leidy, T. R., and Starry, A. R. The American adolescent—A bewildering amalgam. *National Education Association Journal,* 1967, *56,* 8–12.

Leming, J. S. Moral reasoning, sense of control, and social-political activism among adolescents. *Adolescence,* 1974, *9,* 507–528.

Lerner, R. M., and Knapp, J. R. Actual and perceived intrafamilial attitudes of late adolescents and their parents. *Journal of Youth and Adolescence,* 1975, *4,* 17–36.

Lewin, K. *Principles of topological psychology.* New York: McGraw-Hill, 1936.

Lewin, K. Field theory and experiment in social psychology: Concepts and methods. *American Journal of Sociology,* 1939, *44,* 868–897.

Lewin, K. *Field Theory in social science.* New York: Harper and Row, 1951.

Lidz, T. The adolescent and his family. In G. Caplan and S. Lebovici (eds.) *Adolescence: Psychosocial perspectives.* New York: Basic Books, 1969.

Linn, L., and Schwartz, L. W. *Psychiatry and religious experience.* New York: Random House, 1958.

Loukes, H. *Teenage religion.* London: SCM Press, 1961.

Lovell, K. A follow-up study of Inhelder and Piaget's *The growth of logical thinking.* *British Journal of Psychology,* 1961, *52,* 143–153.

Lovell, K. Developmental processes in thought. *Journal of Experimental Education,* 1968, *37,* 14–21.

Lovell, K. Some problems associated with formal thought and its assessment. In D. R. Green et al. (eds.) *Measurement and Piaget.* New York: McGraw-Hill, 1971.

Lovell, K., and Butterworth, I. Abilities underlying the understanding of proportionality. *Mathematics Teaching,* 1966, *37,* 5–9.

Lovell, K., and Shields, J. Some aspects of the study of the gifted child. *British Journal of Educational Psychology,* 1967, *37,* 201–208.

Lowrie, S. H. Dating theories and student responses. *American Sociological Review,* 1951, 334–340.

Luckey, E., and Nass, G. A. A comparison of sexual attitudes and behavior in an international sample. *Journal of Marriage and the Family,* May 1969, 364–379.

Lynn, D. B. A note on sex differences in the development of masculine and feminine identification. *Psychology Review,* 1959, *66,* 126–135.

Lynn, D. B. Sex role and parental identification. *Child Development,* 1962, *33,* 555–564.

McCandless, B. R. *Adolescents: Behavior and development.* Hinsdale, Ill.: Dryden Press. 1970.

Maccoby, E. E., and Jacklin, C. N. *The psychology of sex differences.* Stanford, Cal.: Stanford University Press, 1974.

McCord, W., McCord, J., and Zola, I. *Origins of crime: A new evaluation of the Cambridge-Somerville youth study.* New York: Columbia University Press, 1959.

MacFarlane, J., Allen, L., and Honzik, M. *A developmental study of the behavior problems of normal children between 21 months and 14 years.* Berkeley: University of California Press, 1954.

Maddi, S. *Personality theories: A comparative analysis.* Homewood, Ill.: Dorsey Press, 1968.

Malina, R. M. Adolescent changes in size, build, composition and performance. *Human Biology,* 1974, *46,* 117–131.

Mallet-Joris, F. *The paper house.* New York: Farrar, Straus, and Giroux, 1971.

Manaster, G. J. Coping styles, sense of competence, and achievement. Unpublished doctoral dissertation, University of Chicago, 1969.

Manaster, G. J. Coping style, sense of competence, and achievement. Paper presented at the annual meeting of the American Educational Research Association Meeting, 1972.

Manaster, G. J., Ahuja, S. J., and Pannu, P. S. Occupational aspirations and expectations of adolescents in India. *Journal of Psychological Research,* 1976, *20,* in press.

Manaster, G. J., and Ahumada, R. Adolescent occupational aspirations and expectations in Puerto Rico and Mexico. *Revista Internamericana de Psicologia,* 1970, *4,* 81–94.

Manaster, G. F., and Friedman, S. T. Premed students' survivability and specialization. *Psychological Reports*, in press.

Manaster, G. J., and Havighurst, R. J. *Cross-national research: Social-psychological methods and problems*. Boston: Houghton Mifflin, 1972.

Manaster, G. J., and King, M. R. Mexican-American group cohesiveness and academic achievement. *Urban Education*, October 1972, 235–240.

Manaster, G. J., and King, M. Early recollections of male homosexuals. *Journal of Individual Psychology*, 1973, *29*, 26–33.

Manaster, G. J., and Perryman, T. B. Early recollection and occupational choice. *Journal of Individual Psychology*, 1974, *30*, 232–237.

Manaster, G. J., Saddler, C. D., and Williamson, L. The ideal self and cognitive development in adolescence. University of Texas at Austin, 1976. (mimeo)

Markwell, M. Life in our village. In L. Hughes (ed.) *An African treasury*. New York: Pyramid Publications, 1961.

Martineau, P. Adulthood in the adolescent perspective. *Adolescence*, 1966, I, *3*, 272–280.

Maslow, A. H. *Motivation and personality*. New York: Harper and Row, 1954.

Mayle, P. *What's happening to me?* Secacus, N.J.: Lyle Stuart, Inc., 1975.

Mead, M. Growing up in New Guinea. New York: New American Library, 1935.

Meisels, M., and Canter, F. M. A note on the generation gap. *Adolescence*, 1971, *6*, 523–530.

Meissner, W. W. Some indications of sources of anxiety in adolescent boys. *Journal of Genetic Psychology*, 1961, *99*, 65–73.

Miller, D. C., and Form, W. *Industrial sociology*. New York: Harper and Row, 1951.

Miller, G. W. Factors in school achievement and social class. *Journal of Educational Psychology*, 1970, *61*, 260–269.

Mirande, A. M. Reference group theory and adolescent sexual behavior. *Journal of Marriage and the Family*, 1968, *30*, 572–577.

Mischel, W. *Personality and assessment*. New York: Wiley, 1968.

Mischel, W. Continuity and change in personality. *American Psychologist*, 1969, *24*, 1012–1018.

Mischel, W. Sex-typing and socialization. In P. H. Mussen (ed.) *Carmichael's manual of child psychology*. New York: Wiley, 1970.

Mischel, W. On the empirical dilemmas of psychodynamic approaches: Issues and alternatives. *Journal of Abnormal Psychology*, 1973, *82*, 335–344.

Money, J., and Clopper, R. R., Jr. Psychosocial and psychosexual aspects of errors of pubertal onset and development. *Human Biology*, 1974, *46*, 173–181.

Monge, R. H. Developmental trends in factors of adolescent self-concept. *Developmental Psychology*, 1973, *8*(3), 382–393.

Mood, A. Do teachers make a difference? In *Do teachers make a difference? A report on recent research on pupil achievement*. Washington, D.C.: Bureau of Educational Personnel Development, Office of Education, 1970.

Morgan, J. C. Adolescent problems and the mooney problem check list. *Adolescence*, 1969, *4*, 111–126.

Morris, H. Aggressive behavior disorders of childhood. *American Journal of Psychiatry*, 1956, *112*, 991–996.

Morrison, R. L. Self-concept implementation in occupational choices. *Journal of Counseling Psychology*, 1962, *9*, 255–260.

Mosak, H. H., and Dreikurs, R. The life tasks III. The fifth life task. *The Individual Psychologist*, 1967, *5*(1), 16–22.

Moss, J. J., Apolonio, F., and Jensen, M. The premarital dyad during the sixties. *Journal of Marriage and the Family*, 1971, *33*, 1–10.

Mullener, N., and Laird, J. D. Some developmental changes in the organization of self-evaluations. *Developmental Physchology*, 1971, *5*(2), 233–236.

Munns, M. Is there really a generation gap? *Adolescence*, 1971, *6*, 197–206.

Munns, M. The values of adolescents compared with parents and peers. *Adolescence*, 1972, *7*, 519–524.

Murphy, L. B. *The widening world of childhood: Paths toward mastery.* New York: Basic Books, 1962.

Mussen, P. H., and Bouterline-Young, H. Relationship between rate of physical maturing and personality among boys of Italian descent. *Vita Humana*, 1964, *7*, 186–200.

Mussen, P. H., Conger, J. J., and Kagan, J. *Child development and personality.* New York: Harper and Row, 1969.

Mussen, P. H., and Jones, M. C. Self-conceptions, motivations and interpersonal attitudes of late- and early-maturing boys. *Child Development*, 1957, *28*, 243–256.

Mussen, P. H., and Jones, M. C. The behavior-inferred motivations of late- and early-maturing boys. *Child Development*, 1958, *29*, 61–67.

Muuss, R. E. *Theories of adolescence.* New York: Random House, 1968.

Neilson, P. Shirley's babies after fifteen years. *Journal of Genetic Psychology*, 1948, *73*, 175–186.

Neimark, E. D. Intellectual development during adolescence. In F. D. Horowitz (ed.) *Review of child development research.* Vol. 4, Chicago: University of Chicago Press, 1975.

Nesselroade, J. R., and Baltes, P. B. Adolescent personality development and historical change: 1970–1972. *Monographs of the Society for Research in Child Development*, 1974, *39*, 1.

Neufield, I. Application of individual psychological concepts in psychosomatic medicine. *Journal of Individual Psychology*, 1955, *11*, 104–117.

Nichols, R. C. Nature and nurture in adolescence. In J. F. Adams (ed.) *Understanding adolescents.* Boston: Allyn and Bacon, 1973.

Noblitt, G. L., and Asher, W. Characteristics of senior high school students who work for pay. *Vocational Guidance Quarterly*, 1971, *19*, 254–257.

Nowicki, S., and Segal, W. Perceived parental charactristics, locus of control orientation, and behavioral correlates of locus of control. *Developmental Psychology*, 1974, *10*, 33–37.

Offer, D. Studies of normal adolescents. *Adolescence*, 1966/1967, *1*(4), 305–320.

Offer, D. *The psychological world of the teen-ager.* New York: Basic Books, 1969.

Offer, D., and Offer, J. A longitudinal study of normal adolescent boys. *American Journal of Psychiatry*, 1970, *126*, 917–924.

Oppenheimer, E. A. The relationship between certain self-constructs and occupational preferences. *Journal of Counseling Psychology*, 1966, *13*, 191–197.

Oshman, H., and Manosevitz, M. The impact of the identity crisis on the adjustment of late adolescent males. *Journal of Youth and Adolescence*, 1974, *3*(3), 207–216.

Osipow, S. H. *Theories of career development.* New York: Appleton-Century-Crofts, 1968.

Osipow, S. H., Ashby, J. D., and Wall, H. W. Personality types and vocational choice: A test of Holland's theory. *Personnel and Guidance Journal*, 1966, *45*, 37–42.

Osterrieth, P. A. Adolescence: Some psychological aspects. In G. Caplan and S. Lebovici (eds.) *Adolesence: Psychology perspectives.* New York: Basic Books, 1969.

Packard, V. *The sexual wilderness.* New York: Pocket Books, 1970.

Parson, T., and Bales, R. F. *Family, socialization, and interaction process.* Glencoe, Ill.: The Free Press, 1955.

Parsons, F. *Choosing a vocation.* Boston: Houghton Mifflin, 1909.

Patterson, F. The purpose and trend of the conference. In W. C. Kvaraceus et al. (eds.) *Negro self-concept: Implications for school and citizenship.* New York: McGraw-Hill, 1965.

Pearson, H. *G.B.S.: A full length portrait.* New York: Harper and Row, 1942.

Peck, R. F. et al. *Coping styles and achievement: A cross-national study of school children.* Vol. 5, Final Report, HEW, Contract OE-85-063, 1973.

Peck, R. F., and Galliani, C. Intelligence, ethnicity, and social roles in adolescent society. *Sociometry*, 1962, *25*(1), 64–72.

Peck, R. F., and Havighurst, R. J. *The psychology of character development.* New York: Wiley, 1960.

Peel, E. A. *The pupil's thinking.* London: Oldbourne, 1960.

Peel, E. A. Intellectual growth during adolescence. In R. E. Grinder (ed.) *Studies in adolescence.* New York: Macmillan, 1963.

Peel, E. A. Generalising and abstracting. *Nature*, 1971, *230*, 5296, 600.

Peel, E. A. Predilection for generalising and abstracting. *British Journal of Educational Psychology*, 1975, *45*, 177–188.

Perrone, P. A. Factors influencing high school seniors' occupational preferences. *Personnel and Guidance Journal*, 1964, *42*, 976–980.

Petroni, F. A. Adolescent liberalism. The myth of a generation gap. *Adolescence*, 1972, *26*, 221–232.

Phelps, H. R., and Horrocks, J. E. Factors influencing informal groups of adolescents. *Child Development*, 1958, *29*, 69–86.

Piaget, J. *The psychology of intelligence.* New York: Harcourt, 1947.

Piaget, J. *The moral judgment of the child.* Glencoe, Ill.: Free Press, 1948. (Originally published, 1932)

Piaget, J. Three lectures. *Bulletin of the Menninger Clinic*, 1962, *26*, 120–145.

Piaget, J. Problems of equilibration. In C. F. Nodine, J. M. Gallagher, and R. H. Humphreys (eds.) *Piaget and Inhelder: On equilibration.* Philadelphia: The Jean Piaget Society, 1972. (a)

Piaget, J. Intellectual evaluation from adolescence to adulthood. *Human Development*, 1972, *15*, 1–12. (b)

Piaget, J., and Inhelder, B. *The psychology of the child.* New York: Basic Books, 1969.

Ponzo, Z., and Strowig, R. W. Relations among self-role identity and selected intellectual and non-intellectual factors for high school freshmen and seniors. *Journal of Educational Research*, 1973, *67*(3), 137–141.

Porter, J. K. Predicting the vocational plans of high school senior boys. *Personnel and Guidance Journal*, 1954, *33*, 215–218.

Powell, G. J., and Fuller, M. Self-concept and school desegregation. *American Journal of Orthopsychiatry*, 1970, *40*, 303–304.

Prather, H. *Notes to myself.* Moab, Utah: © Real People Press, 1970.

Purkey, W. W. *Self-concept and school achievement.* Englewood Cliffs, N.J.: Prentice-Hall, 1970.

Ramsey, C. V. Sex information of younger boys. *American Journal of Orthopsychiatry*, 1943, *13*, 347–352.

Reiss, I. L. *Premarital sexual standards in America.* New York: Free Press, 1960.

Reiss, I. L. The sexual renaissance: A summary and analysis. *Journal of Social Issues*, 1966, *22*, 123–137.

Reiss, I. L. *The social context of premarital sexual permissiveness.* New York: Holt, 1967.

Reiss, I. L. America's sex standards—How and why they're changing. *Transaction*, 1968, *5*, 26–32.

Reiss, I. L. Premarital sexual standards. In C. B. Broderick and J. Bernard (eds.) *The individual, sex, and society.* Baltimore: Johns Hopkins Press, 1969.

Reister, A. E., and Zucker, R. A. Adolescent social structure and drinking behavior. *Personnel and Guidance Journal*, 1968, *46*, 304–312.

Rest, J. Developmental hierarchy in preference and comprehension of moral judgment. Unpublished doctoral dissertation, University of Chicago, 1968.

Rest, J., Turiel, E., and Kohlberg, L. Relations between level of moral judgment and preference and comprehension of the moral judgment of others. *Journal of Personality*, 1969, *37*, 225–252.

Rice, F. P. *The adolescent: Development, relationships and culture.* Boston: Allyn and Bacon, 1975.

Roe, A. *The psychology of occupations.* New York: Wiley, 1956.

Roe, A. Early determinants of vocational choice. *Journal of Counseling Psychology*, 1957, *4*, 212–217.

Roe, A., and Siegelman, M. The origins of interest. *APGA Inquiry Studies, No. 1.* Washington, D.C.: American Personnel and Guidance Association, 1964.

Roff, M., and Sells, S. B. Relations between intelligence and sociometric status in groups differing in sex and socio-economic background. *Psychological Reports*, April 1965, 511–516.

Rogers, C. R. *Client-centered therapy.* New York: Houghton Mifflin, 1951.

Rogers, D. *Adolescence: A psychological perspective.* Monterey, Cal.: Brooks/Cole, 1972. (a)

Rogers, D. *The psychology of adolescence.* New York: Appleton-Century-Crofts, 1972. (b)

Rosen, B. C. *Adolescent religion: The Jewish teen-ager in American society.* Cambridge, Mass.: Schenkman, 1965.

Rosenberg, M. *Society and the adolescent self-image.* Princeton, N.J.: Princeton University Press, 1965.

Rosenkrantz, P., et al. Sex-role stereotypes and self-concepts in college students. *Journal of Consulting and Clinical Psychology*, 1968, *32*(3), 287–295.

Rosenshine, B., and Furst, N. Research on teacher performance criteria. In B. O. Smith (ed.) *Research in teacher education: A symposium.* Englewood Cliffs, N.J.: Prentice-Hall, 1971.

Royce, J. E. Does person or self imply dualism? *American Psychologist*, October 1973, 883–886.

Rudy, A. J. Sex role perceptions in early adolescence. *Adolescence*, 1968, *3*(12), 453–470.

Saltzstein, L., Diamond, R. M., and Belenky, M. Moral judgment level and conformity behavior. *Developmental Psychology*, 1972, *7*, 327–336.

Salzman, L. Adolescence: Epoch or disease. *Adolescence*, 1973, *8*, 247–256.

Schaie, K. W. A general model for the study of developmental problems. Psychological Bulletin, 1965, *64*, 92–107.

Schoeppe, A., and Havighurst, R. J. A validation of development and adjustment hypotheses of adolescence. *Journal of Educational Psychology*, 1952, *43*, 339–353.

Schulz, D. D. *The changing family.* Englewood Cliffs, N.J.: Prentice-Hall, 1972.

Schutz, R. A., and Blocher, D. H. Self-satisfaction and level of occupational choice. *Personnel and Guidance Journal*, 1961, *39*, 595–598.

Schwarzweller, H. K., and Lyson, T. A. Social class, parental interest and the educational plans of American and Norwegian rural youth. *Sociology of Education*, 1974, *47*, 443–465.

Scottish Council for Research in Education. *Social implications of the 1947 Scottish mental survey.* London: University Press, 1953.

Segal, S. J. A psychoanalytic analysis of personality factors in vocational choice. *Journal of Counseling Psychology*, 1961, *8*, 202–210.

Segal, S. J., and Szabo, R. Identification in two vocations: Accountants and creative writers. *Personnel and Guidance Journal*, 1964, *43*, 252–255.

Seidman, J. *The adolescent.* New York: Dryden, 1953.

Seward, G. H., and Williamson, R. C. A cross-national study of adolescent professional goals. *Human Development*, 1969, *12*, 248–254.

Seward, G. H., and Williamson, R. C. (eds.) *Sex roles in changing society.* New York: Random House, 1970.

Sewell, W. H. Inequality of opportunity for higher education. *American Sociological Review*, 1971, *36*, 793–809.

Shainberg, D. It really blew my mind: A study of adolescent cognition. *Adolescence*, 1970, *5*, 17–36.

Sherif, C. W. Adolescence: Motivational, attitudinal and personality factors. *Review of Educational Research*, 1966, *36*(4), 437–449.

Sherif, M., and Sherif, C. W. *Reference groups.* New York: Harper and Row, 1964.

Sherif, M., and Sherif, C. W. (eds.) *Problems of youth.* Chicago: Aldine, 1965.

Shibutani, T. *Society and personality.* Englewood Cliffs, N.J.: Prentice-Hall, 1961.

Sieg, A. Why adolescence occurs. *Adolescence*, 1971, *23*(6), 337–348.

Silberman, C. E. *Crisis in the classroom.* New York: Random House, 1970.

Simmons, R. G., Rosenberg, F., and Rosenberg, M. Disturbance in the self-image at adolescence. *American Sociological Review*, 1973, *38*(5), 553–568.

Simon, W., and Gagnon, J. H. (eds.) *The sexual scene.* Chicago: Trans-Action Books, 1970.

Simpson, R. L. Parental influence, anticipatory socialization, and social mobility. *American Sociological Review*, 1962, *27*, 517–522.

Skipper, J. K., Jr., and Nass, G. Dating behavior: A framework for analysis and an illustration. *Journal of Marriage and the Family*, 1966, *30*, 412–420.

Smith, T. E. Some bases for parental influence upon late adolescents: An application of a social power model. *Adolescence*, 1970, *5*, 323–338.

Snygg, D., and Combs, A. W. Individual behavior. New York: Harper and Row, 1949.

Soares, A. T., and Soares, L. M. Self-perceptions of culturally disadvantaged children. *American Educational Research Journal*, 1969, *6*, 31–49.

Soares, A. T., and Soares, L. M. Critique of Soares' and Soares' "Self-perceptions of culturally disadvantaged children"—A reply. *American Educational Research Journal*, 1970, *7*, 631–635.

Soares, A. T., and Soares, L. M. Comparative differences in the self-perceptions of disadvantaged and advantaged students. *Journal of School Psychology*, 1971, *9*, 424–429.

Soares, L. M., and Soares, A. T. Self-concepts of disadvantaged and advantaged students. *Child Study Journal*, 1970/1971, *1*, 69–73.

Solomon, J. C. *Family identity*, 1972, 7, 511–518.

Sorensen, R. C. *Adolescent sexuality in contemporary America: Personal values and sexual behavior, ages 13–19*. New York: World Publishing Co., 1973.

Spencer, C. P. Selective secondary education, social class and the development of adolescent subcultures. *British Journal of Educational Psychology*, 1972, 42(1), 1–12.

Staton, T. F. *Dynamics of adolescent adjustment*. New York: Macmillan, 1963.

Steinmann, A. A study of the concept of the feminine role of 51 middle-class American families. *Genetic Psychology Monographs*, 1963, 67, 275–352.

Stendler, C. B. (ed.) *Readings in child behavior and development*. New York: Harcourt, 1964.

Stephens, B., and McLaughlin, J. Analysis of performance by normals and retardates on Piagetian reasoning assessments as a function of verbal ability. *Perceptual and Motor Skills*, 1971, 32, 868–870.

Stephens, W. B., Piaget, J., and Inhelder, B. Application of theory and diagnostic techniques to the area of mental retardation. *Education and Training of Mentally Retarded*, 1966, 1, 75–87.

Stephenson, R. M. Occupational aspirations and plans of 443 ninth graders. *Journal of Educational Research*, 1955, 49, 27–35.

Stockin, B. G. A test of Holland's occupational level formulation. *Personnel and Guidance Journal*, 1964, 42, 599–602.

Stone, L. J., and Church, J. *Childhood and adolescence* (2nd ed.). New York: Random House, 1968.

Strang, R. *The adolescent views himself*. New York: McGraw-Hill, 1957.

Strommen, M. P. *A study of generations*. Minneapolis: Augsburg, 1972.

Stubbins, J. The relationship between level of vocational aspiration and certain personal data: A study of some traits and influences bearing on the prestige level of vocational choice. *Genetic Psychology Monographs*, 1950, 41, 327–408.

Super, D. E. Vocational adjustment: Implementing a self-concept. *Occupations*, 1951, 30, 88–92.

Super, D. E. *The psychology of careers*. New York: Harper and Row, 1957.

Super, D. E. Computers in support of vocational development and counseling. In H. Borow (ed.) *Career guidance for a new age*. Boston: Houghton Mifflin, 1973.

Super, D. E., et al. *Vocational development: A framework for research*. New York: Bureau of Publications, Teachers College, Columbia University, 1957.

Super, D. E., et al. *Career development: Self-concept theory*. Princeton, N.J.: College Entrance Examination Board, 1963.

Super, D. E., and Bachrach, P. B. *Scientific careers and vocational development theory*. New York: Teachers College Bureau of Publications, 1957.

Super, D. E., and Crites, J. O. *Appraising vocational fitness* (Rev. ed.). New York: Harper and Row, 1962.

Swift, D. F. Family environment and 11 + success: Some basic predictors. *British Journal of Educational Psychology*, 1967, *37*, 10–21.

Tanner, J. M. *Education and physical growth*. London: University of London Press, 1961.

Tanner, J. M. *Growth at adolescence* (2nd ed.). Oxford: Blackwell Scientific Publications, Ltd., 1962.

Tanner, J. M. In G. A. Harrison, J. S. Weiner, J. M. Tanner, and N. A. Barnicot (eds.) *Human biology: An introduction to human evolution, variation and growth*. Oxford: Clarendon Press, 1964.

Tanner, J. M. The trend towards earlier physical maturation. Working paper, 1965.

Tanner, J. M. Earlier maturation in man. *Scientific American*, 1968, *218*, 21–27.

Tanner, J. M. Sequence, tempo, and individual variation in the growth and development of boys and girls aged twelve to sixteen. *Daedalus*, 1971, *100*(Fall), 907–930.

Tavormina, J. B. Current perspectives on adolescence. *Contemporary Psychology*, 1974, *19*, 403–404.

Taylor, P. H. Children's evaluations of the characteristics of the good teacher. *British Journal of Educational Psychology*, 1962, *32*, 258–266.

Terman, L. M., et al. *Genetic studies of genius I: Mental and physical traits of a thousand gifted children*. Stanford, Cal.: Stanford University Press, 1925.

Thomas, D. L., and Weigert, A. J. Socialization and adolescent conformity to significant others: A cross-national analysis. *American Sociological Review*, 1971, *36*, 835–847.

Thomas, I. E. Family correlates of student political activism. *Developmental Psychology*, 1971, *4*, 206–214.

Thomas, L. *The occupational structure and education*. Englewood Cliffs, N.J.: Prentice-Hall, 1956.

Thornburg, H. D. Adolescence: A re-interpretation. *Adolescence*, 1970, *5*, 463–484.

Thornburg, H. D. Peers: Three distinct groups. In H. D. Thornburg (ed.) *Preadolescent development*. Tucson: University of Arizona Press, 1974.

Thrasher, F. M. *The gang*. Chicago: University of Chicago Press, 1936.

Tolman, E. Kurt Lewin: 1890–1947. *Psychological Record*, 1948, *55*, 1–4.

Tomlinson-Keasey, C., and Keasey, C. B. The mediating role of cognitive development in moral judgment. *Child Development*, 1974, *45*, 291–298.

Toward a social report. U. S. Department of Health, Education and Welfare, Washington, D.C.: Government Printing Office, 1969.

Trowbridge, N. T. Self-concept of disadvantaged and advantaged children. Paper presented at the annual meeting of the American Educational Research Association, Minneapolis, March 1970. (a)

Trowbridge, N. T. Effects of socio-economic class on self-concept of children. *Psychology in the Schools*, 1970, *7*, 304–306. (b)

Tseng, M. S. Social class, occupational aspiration and other variables. *Journal of Experimental Education*, 1971, *39*, 88–92.

Tuddenham, R. The constancy of personality ratings over two decades. *Genetic Psychological Monographs*, 1959, *60*, 3–29.

Turiel, E. Developmental processes in the child's moral thinking. In P. Mussen, J. Langer, and M. Covington (eds.) *New directions in developmental psychology*. New York: Holt, 1969.

Turiel, E. Conflict and transition in adolescent moral development. *Child Development*, 1974, *45*, 14–29.

The Un-Radical Young. *Life Magazine*, January 8, 1971, 22–30.

U'Ren, R. C. A perspective on self-esteem. *Comprehensive Psychiatry*, 1971, *12*, 466–472.

Vener, A. M., and Stewart, C. S. Adolescent sexual behavior in America revisited: 1970–1973. *Journal of Marriage and the Family*, 1974, *36*, 728–735.

Vener, A. M., Stewart, C. S., and Hager, D. L. The sexual behavior of adolescents in middle America: Generational and American-British comparisons. *Journal of Marriage and the Family*, 1972, *34*, 696–705.

Vernon, P. Environmental handicaps and intellectual development: Part I. *British Journal of Educational Psychology*, 1965, *35*, 9–20.

Wallach, M. A. Research in children's thinking. In *Child Psychology, 62nd Yearbook, Part I*, NSSE, University of Chicago, 1963.

Warner, W. L., Meeker, M. L., and Eells, K. *Social class in America*. New York: Harper Torchbooks, 1960.

Waterbor, R. Experiential bases of the sense of self. *Journal of Personality*, 1972, *40*, 162–179.

Watson, E. H., and Lowrey, G. H. *Growth and development of children*. Chicago: Year Book Publishers, 1951.

Weatherley, D. Self-perceived rate of physical maturation and personality in late adolescence. *Child Development*, 1964, *35*, 1197–1210.

Webb, A. Sex role preference and adjustment in early adolescence. *Child Development*, 1963, *34*, 609–618.

Weisbroth, S. P. Moral judgment, sex, and parental identification in adults. *Developmental Psychology*, 1970, *2*, 396–402.

We the Americans: Our education. U.S. Department of Commerce, Bureau of the Census, Washington, D.C.: Government Printing Office, June 1973.

We the Youth of America. U.S. Department of Commerce, Bureau of the Census, Washington, D.C.: Government Printing Office, June 1973.

White, R. W. Sense of interpersonal competence. In R. W. White (ed.) *The study of lives*. New York: Atherton, 1964.

Wicker, A. W. Undermanning, performances, and students' subjective experiences in behavior settings of large and small high schools. *Journal of Personality and Social Psychology*, 1968, *10*, 255–261.

Williams, J. E., Bennett, S. M., and Best, D. L. Awareness and expression of sex stereotypes in young children. *Developmental Psychology*, 1975, *11*(5), 635–642.

Wilson, A. B. Residential segregation of social classes and aspirations of high school boys. *American Sociological Review*, 1959, *24*, 836–845.

Wingo, K. A study of religious attitudes of a group of high school boys and girls. Unpublished master's thesis, University of Texas at Austin, 1932.

Wohlwill, J. F. Methodology and research strategy in the study of developmental change. In L. R. Goulet and P. B. Baltes (eds.) *Life-span developmental psychology*. New York: Academic Press, 1970.

Wolf, A. J. Consciousness four. *Yale Alumni Magazine*, November 1974, 19–21.

Wright, D. S. A study of religious belief in sixth form boys. *Research and Studies*, October 1962, 24.

Wylie, R. *The self-concept: A critical review of pertinent literature*. Lincoln, Neb.: University of Nebraska Press, 1961.

Wylie, R. C. Children's estimates of the school-work ability as a function of sex, race, and socioeconomic level. *Journal of Personality*, 1963, *31*, 204–224.

Yarrow, L., and Yarrow, M. Personality continuity and change in the family context. In P. Worchel and D. Byrne (eds.) *Personality change*. New York: Wiley, 1964.

Youmans, E. G. Occupational expectations of twelfth grade Michigan boys. *Journal of Experimental Education*, 1956, *24*, 259–271.

Young, R. K., Dustin, P. S., and Holtzman, W. H. Change in attitude toward religion in a southern university. *Psychological Reports*, 1966, *18*, 39–46.

Yudin, L. Formal thought in adolescence as a function of intelligence. In E. Evans (ed.) *Adolescents: Readings in behavior and development*. Hinsdale, Ill.: Dryden Press, 1970.

Zelnik, M., and Kantner, J. F. The probability of premarital intercourse. *Social Science Research*, September 1972, 335–341.

Zirkel, P. A., and Moses, E. G. Self-concept and ethnic group membership among public school students. *American Educational Research Journal*, 1971, *8*, 253–265.

Zuck, R. B., and Getz, G. A. *Christian youth—An in-depth study*. Chicago: Moody, 1968.

Name Index

Achenbach, T., 667
Adams, J. F., 277
Adelson, J., 225, 242, 254, 255, 257, 279
Adler, A., 12–13, 75, 77, 84–86, 88, 127–128, 163, 166
Ahuja, S. J., 228
Ahumada, R., 228
Allen, A., 100
Allen, G., 161, 163
Allen, L., 89
Allport, G. W., 83–84, 86, 271, 273, 287, 291
Almquist, E. M., 229
Ambron, S. R., 4
American Society of Adlerian Psychology, 12
Anderson, J., 4, 89
Angrist, S. S., 229
Ansbacher, H. H., 12, 75, 84–86, 88, 127, 163, 166
Ansbacher, R R., 12, 75, 84–86, 88, 127, 163, 166
Apolonio, F., 149–150
Appley, M. H., 134
Arbus, D., 115
Aristotle, 74
Arlin, P. K., 44, 120
Armour, R., 225
Arnold, M., 287, 288–289
Arnold, R. A., 183
Ashby, J. D., 222
Asher, W., 210
Auden, W. H., 275
Ausubel, D. P., 6, 36, 39, 40, 193–194, 241, 244, 248
Ausubel, P., 36, 39, 40

Bachman, J. G., 187
Bachrach, P. B., 212, 215
Bales, R. F., 232
Baltes, P. B., 96–99
Bamber, J. H., 112–113
Bandura, A., 89–90

Bardwick, J. M., 255
Barker, R. G., 190
Baron, R. A., 257–258
Baruch, G. K., 236
Baum, M., 182
Bayley, M. C., 25
Bealer, R. C., 294–295, 296
Belenky, M., 240
Bell, A. P., 224
Bell, H. M., 288
Bell, R. R., 154
Bem, D. J., 100
Bem, S. L., 78–79
Bender, L., 89
Benedict, R., 6
Bennett, S. M., 74
Bennett, W. H., 158
Bentler, P. M., 77
Berger, B. M., 244–245
Best, D. L., 74
Bhatnager, K. P., 179
Bidwell, C. E., 189
Bieliauskas, V. J., 75–76
Blau, P. M., 220–221
Bledsoe, J., 180
Bloch, H. A., 6–7
Blocher, D. H., 222
Block, J., 65, 72
Block, J. H., 75, 77, 80, 274–275
Blos, P., 6
Borrow, H., 215
Bouterline-Young, H., 26
Boyer, W. H., 287–289
Bradway, K. P., 41
Bravler, E., 113, 177, 257
Brim, O. G., 191
Brittain, C. V., 236–237, 239, 258
Broderick, C., 157–158
Brody, E. B., 281

327

Subject Index